Skip·Beat!

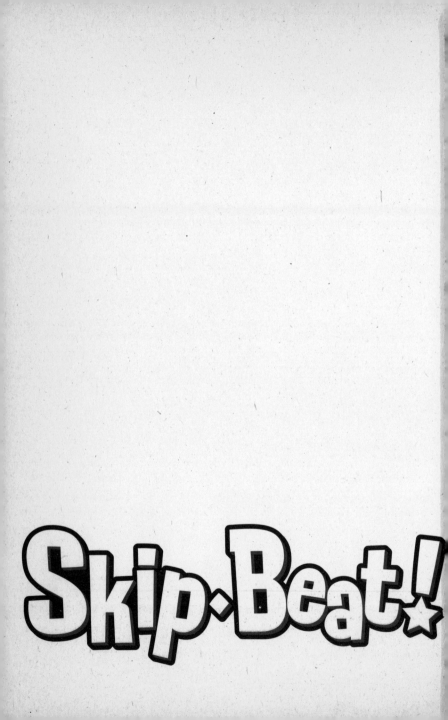

Shojo Beat

Skip·Beat!

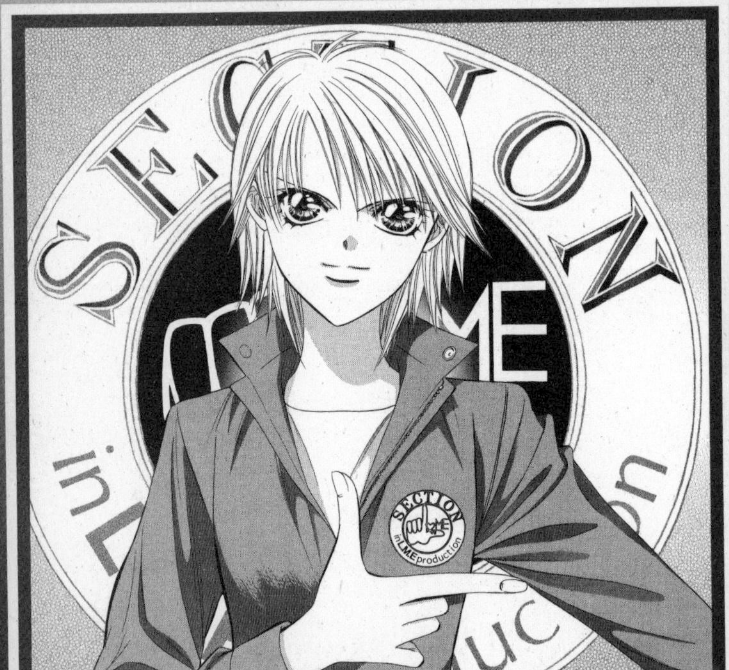
SECTION
inLMEproduction

18

Story & Art by Yoshiki Nakamura

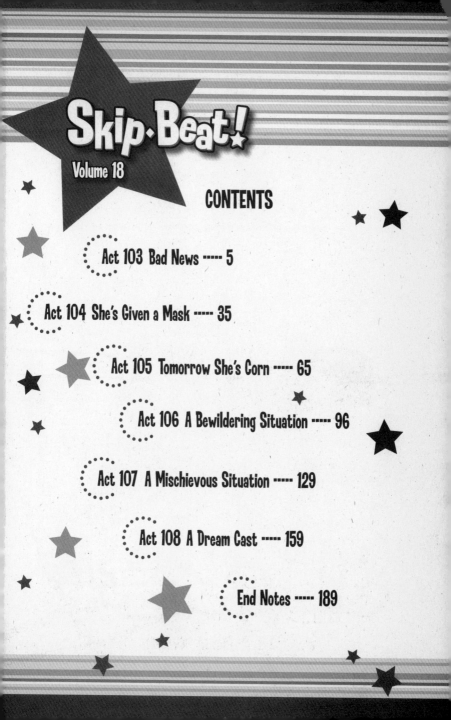

Skip·Beat!

Volume 18

CONTENTS

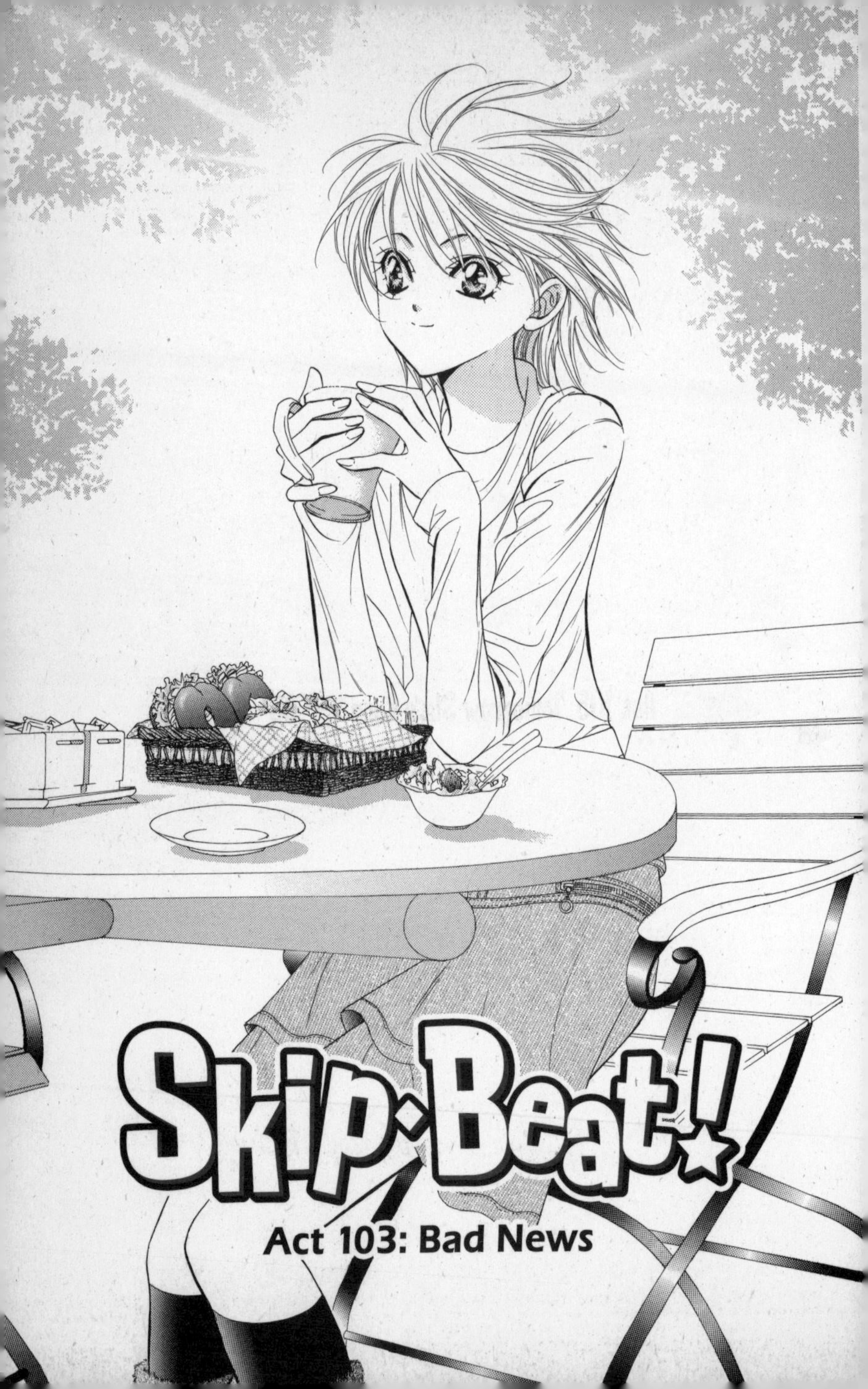

Skip·Beat!
Act 103: Bad News

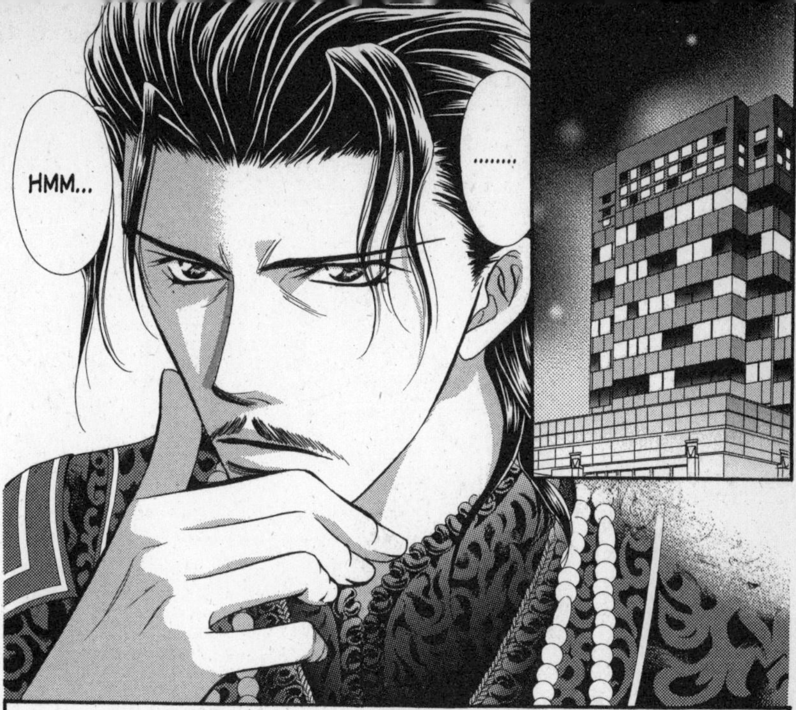
....
HMM...

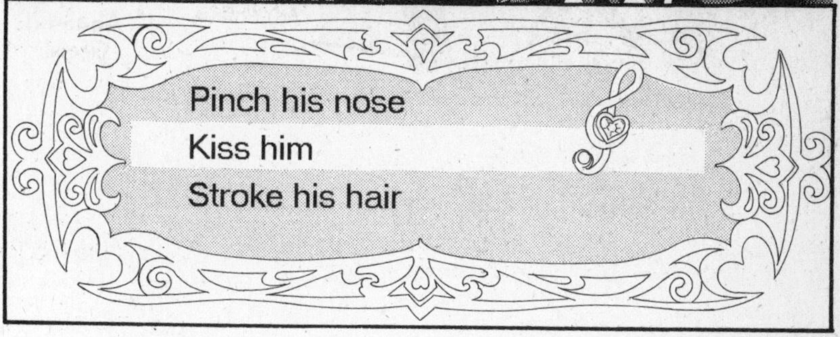
Pinch his nose
Kiss him
Stroke his hair

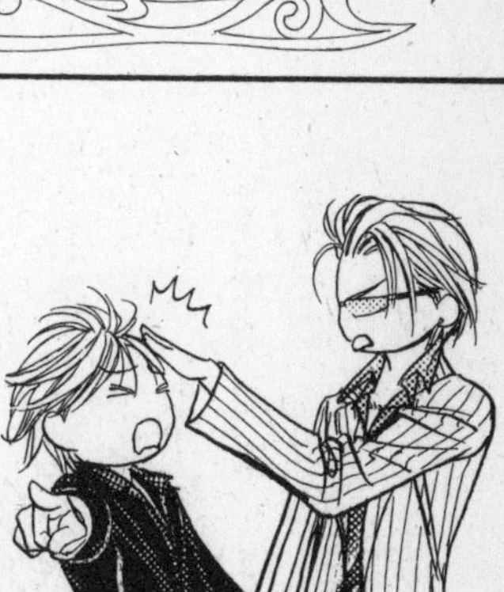

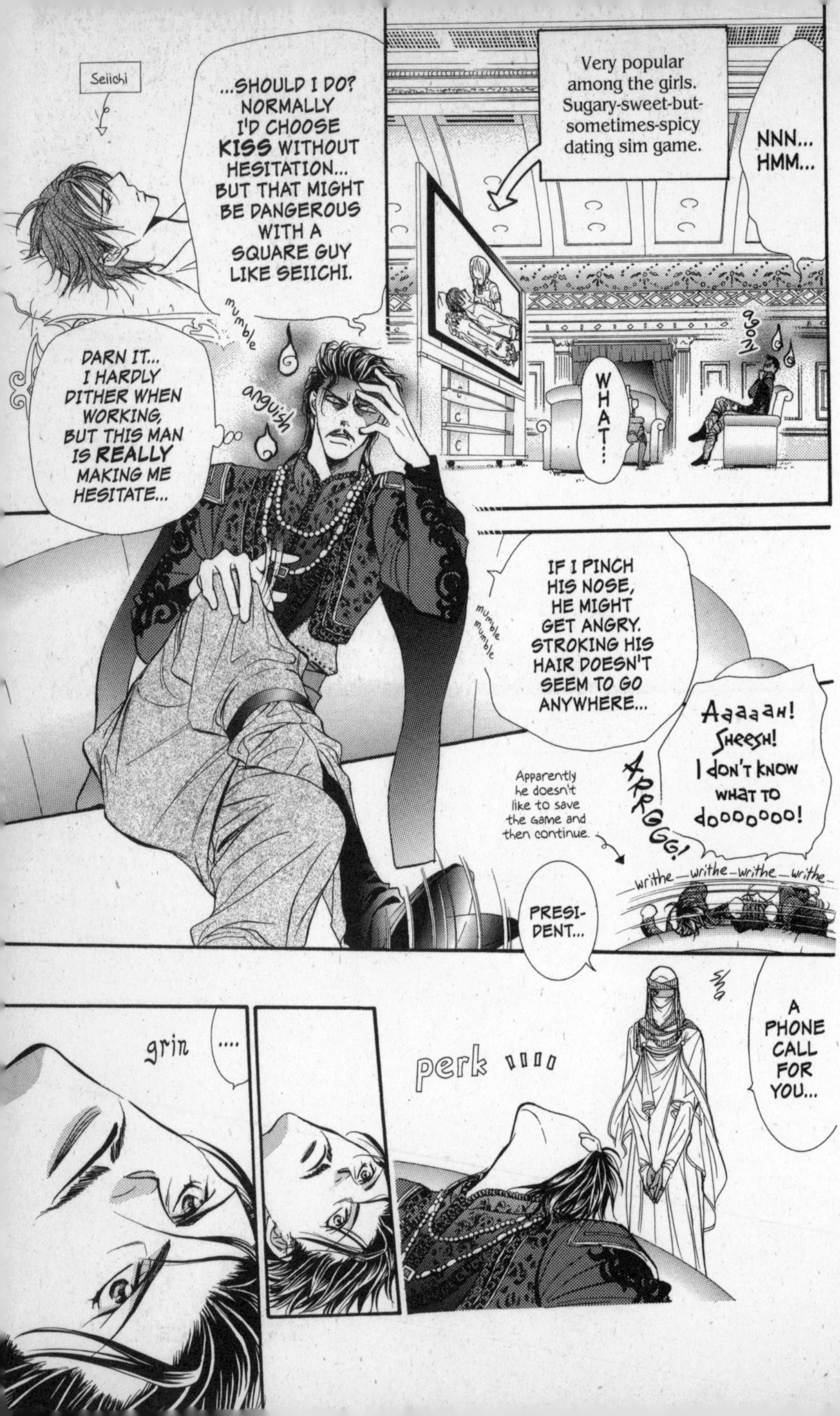
NNN... HMM...
Very popular among the girls. Sugary-sweet-but-sometimes-spicy dating sim game.
agony
WHAT...
Seiichi
...SHOULD I DO? NORMALLY I'D CHOOSE KISS WITHOUT HESITATION... BUT THAT MIGHT BE DANGEROUS WITH A SQUARE GUY LIKE SEIICHI.
mumble
anguish
DARN IT... I HARDLY DITHER WHEN WORKING, BUT THIS MAN IS REALLY MAKING ME HESITATE...
Aaaaah! Sheesh! I don't know what to doooooooo!
ARRGGG!
IF I PINCH HIS NOSE, HE MIGHT GET ANGRY. STROKING HIS HAIR DOESN'T SEEM TO GO ANYWHERE...
mumble mumble
Apparently he doesn't like to save the game and then continue.
writhe writhe writhe writhe
PRESIDENT...
A PHONE CALL FOR YOU...
sha
perk
....
grin

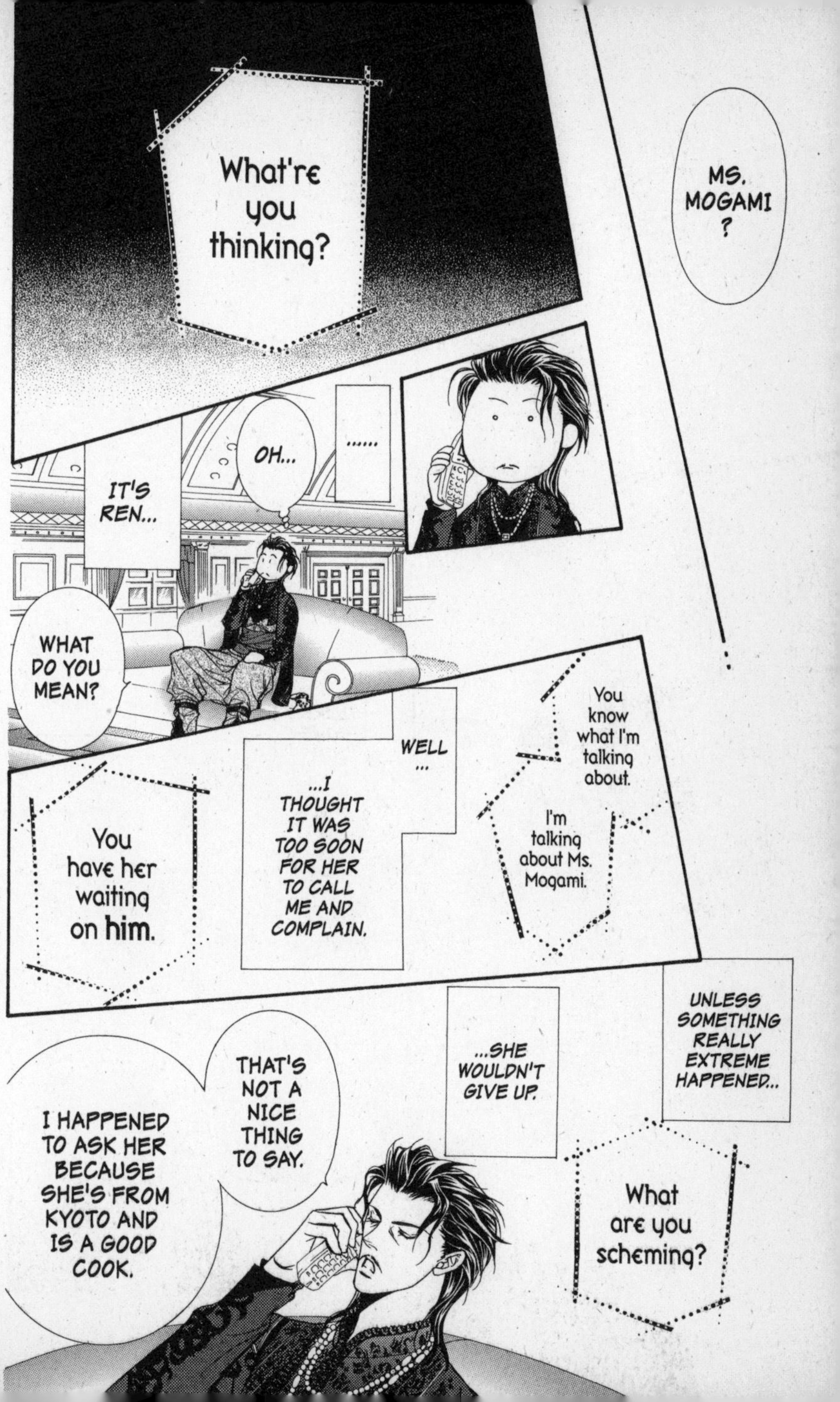
MS. MOGAMI?
What're you thinking?
......
OH...
IT'S REN...
WHAT DO YOU MEAN?
You know what I'm talking about.
I'm talking about Ms. Mogami.
WELL...
...I THOUGHT IT WAS TOO SOON FOR HER TO CALL ME AND COMPLAIN.
You have her waiting on him.
UNLESS SOMETHING REALLY EXTREME HAPPENED...
...SHE WOULDN'T GIVE UP.
What are you scheming?
THAT'S NOT A NICE THING TO SAY.
I HAPPENED TO ASK HER BECAUSE SHE'S FROM KYOTO AND IS A GOOD COOK.

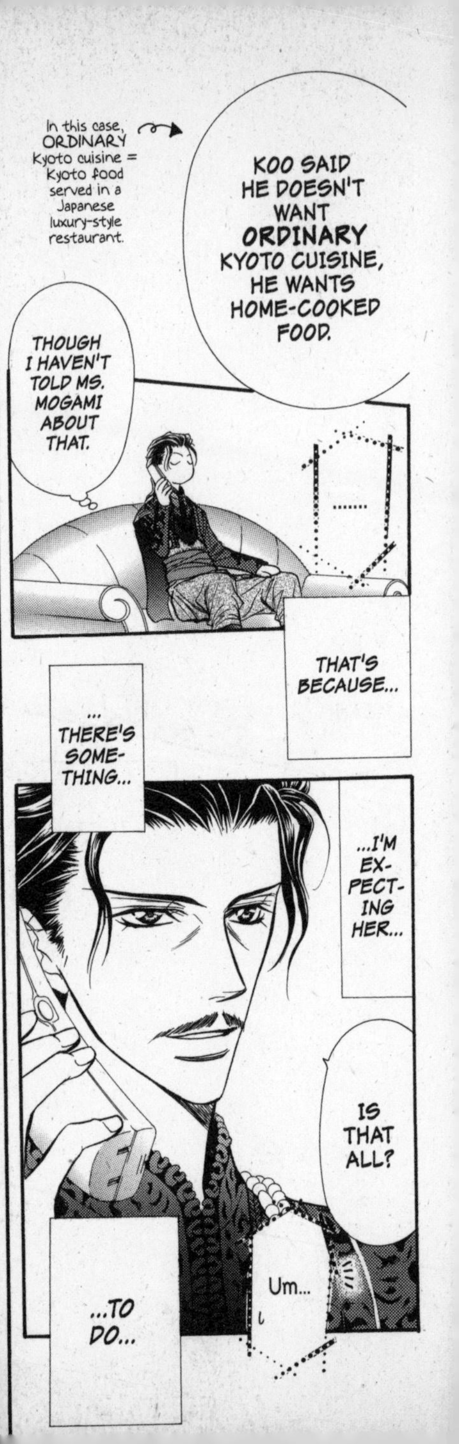
KOO SAID HE DOESN'T WANT ORDINARY KYOTO CUISINE, HE WANTS HOME-COOKED FOOD.
In this case, ORDINARY Kyoto cuisine = Kyoto food served in a Japanese luxury-style restaurant.
THOUGH I HAVEN'T TOLD MS. MOGAMI ABOUT THAT.
......
THAT'S BECAUSE...
...THERE'S SOME-THING...
...I'M EX-PECT-ING HER...
IS THAT ALL?
Um...
...TO DO...

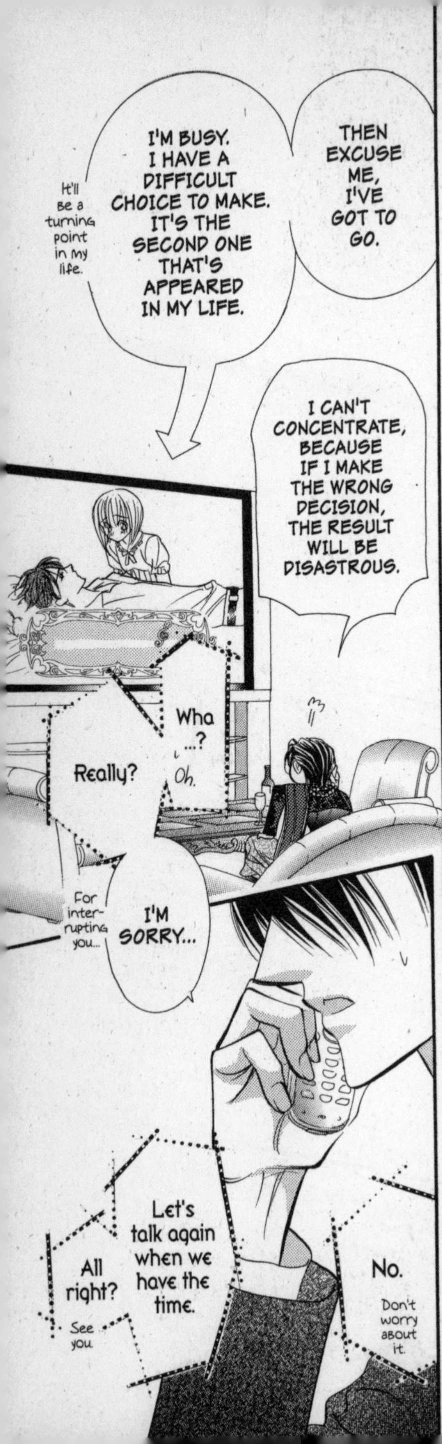
THEN EXCUSE ME, I'VE GOT TO GO.
I'M BUSY. I HAVE A DIFFICULT CHOICE TO MAKE. IT'S THE SECOND ONE THAT'S APPEARED IN MY LIFE.
It'll be a turning point in my life.
I CAN'T CONCENTRATE, BECAUSE IF I MAKE THE WRONG DECISION, THE RESULT WILL BE DISASTROUS.
Wha ...?
Oh.
Really?
I'M SORRY...
For inter-rupting you...
No.
Don't worry about it.
Let's talk again when we have the time.
All right?
See you

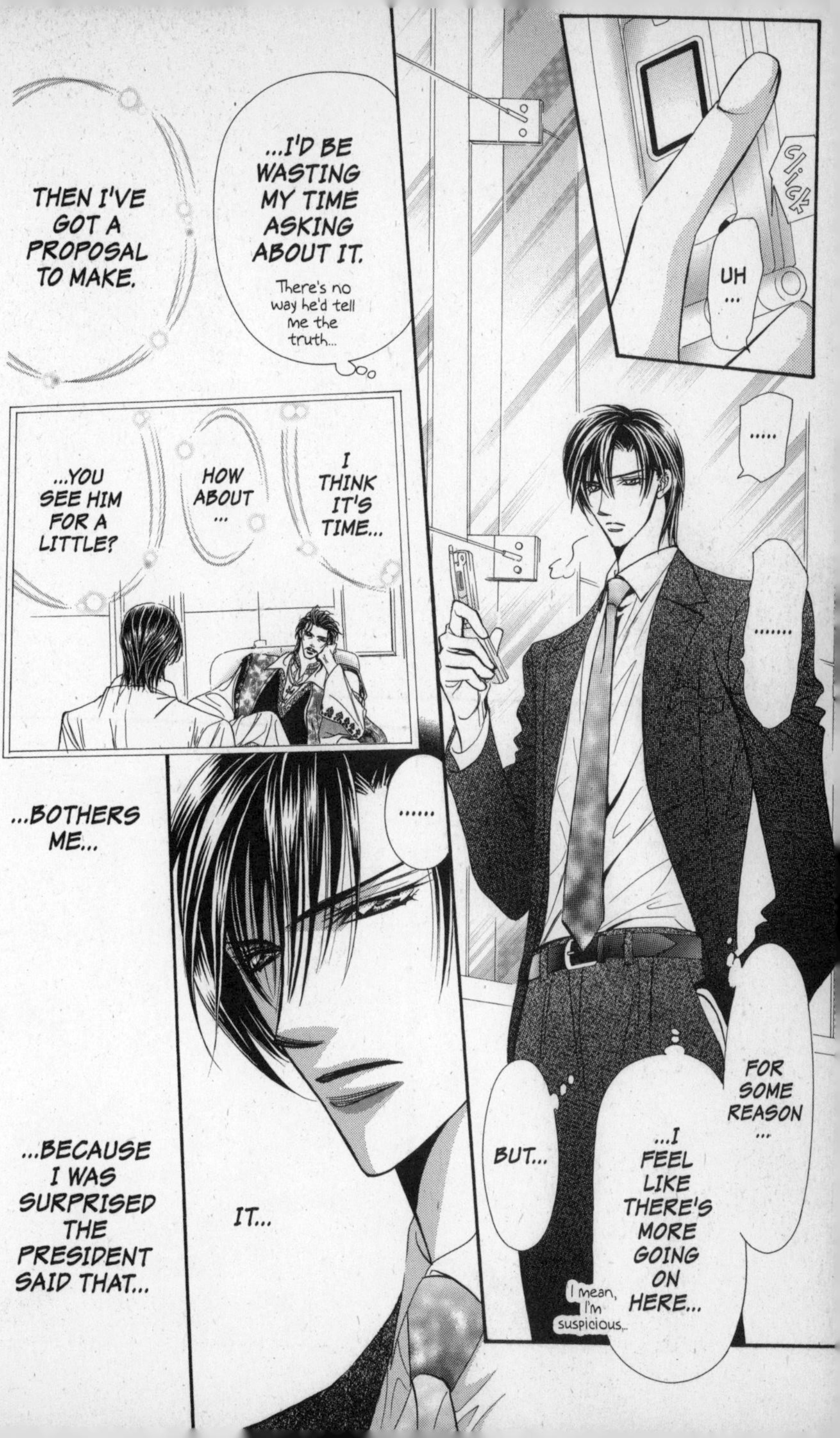

CLICK
UH...
......
......
FOR SOME REASON...
...I FEEL LIKE THERE'S MORE GOING ON HERE...
I mean, I'm suspicious..
BUT...
...I'D BE WASTING MY TIME ASKING ABOUT IT.
There's no way he'd tell me the truth...
THEN I'VE GOT A PROPOSAL TO MAKE.
I THINK IT'S TIME...
HOW ABOUT...
...YOU SEE HIM FOR A LITTLE?
......
IT...
...BOTHERS ME...
...BECAUSE I WAS SURPRISED THE PRESIDENT SAID THAT...

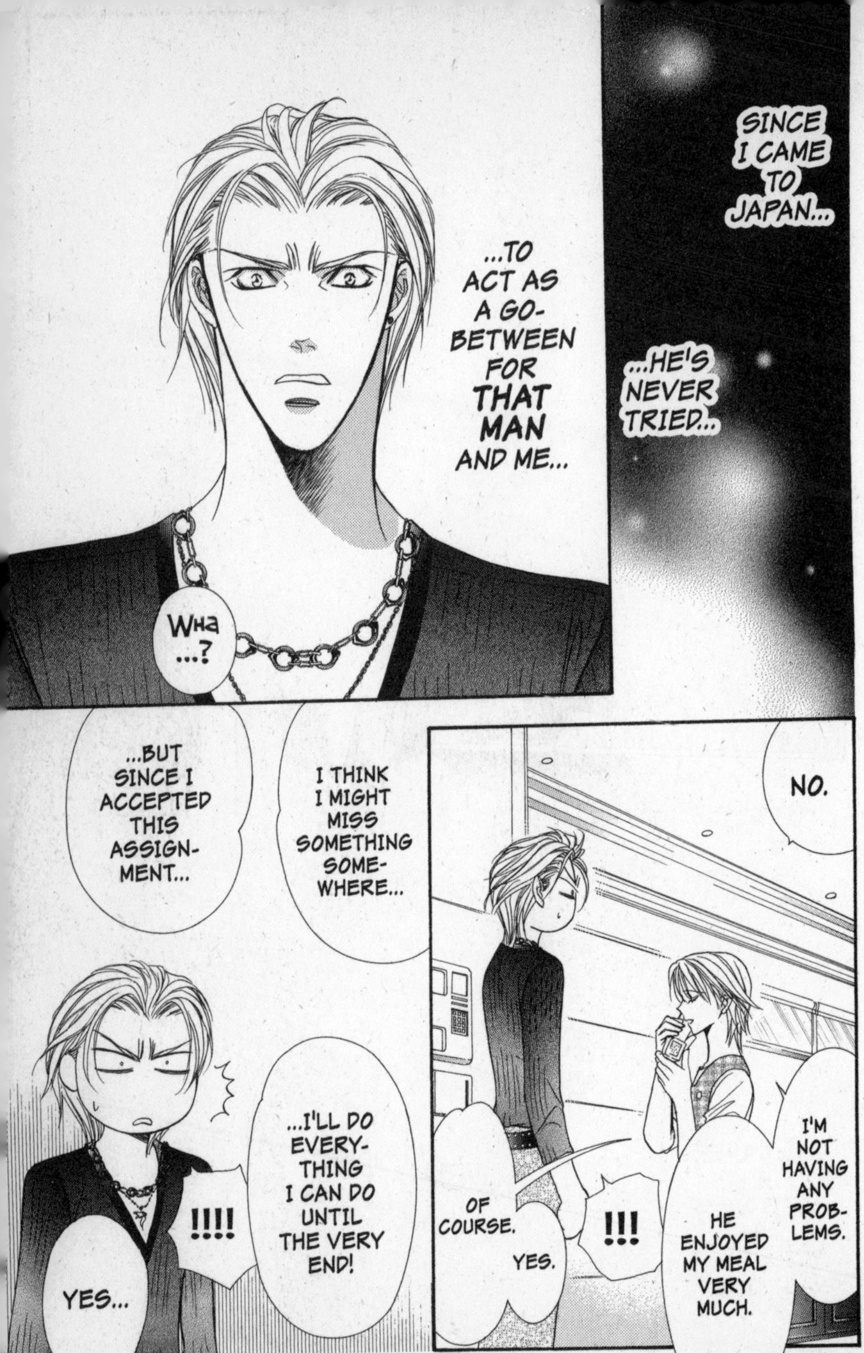
SINCE I CAME TO JAPAN...
...HE'S NEVER TRIED...
...TO ACT AS A GO-BETWEEN FOR THAT MAN AND ME...
Wha ...?
NO.
I'M NOT HAVING ANY PROBLEMS.
HE ENJOYED MY MEAL VERY MUCH.
!!!
OF COURSE.
YES.
I THINK I MIGHT MISS SOMETHING SOME-WHERE...
...BUT SINCE I ACCEPTED THIS ASSIGN-MENT...
...I'LL DO EVERY-THING I CAN DO UNTIL THE VERY END!
!!!!
YES...

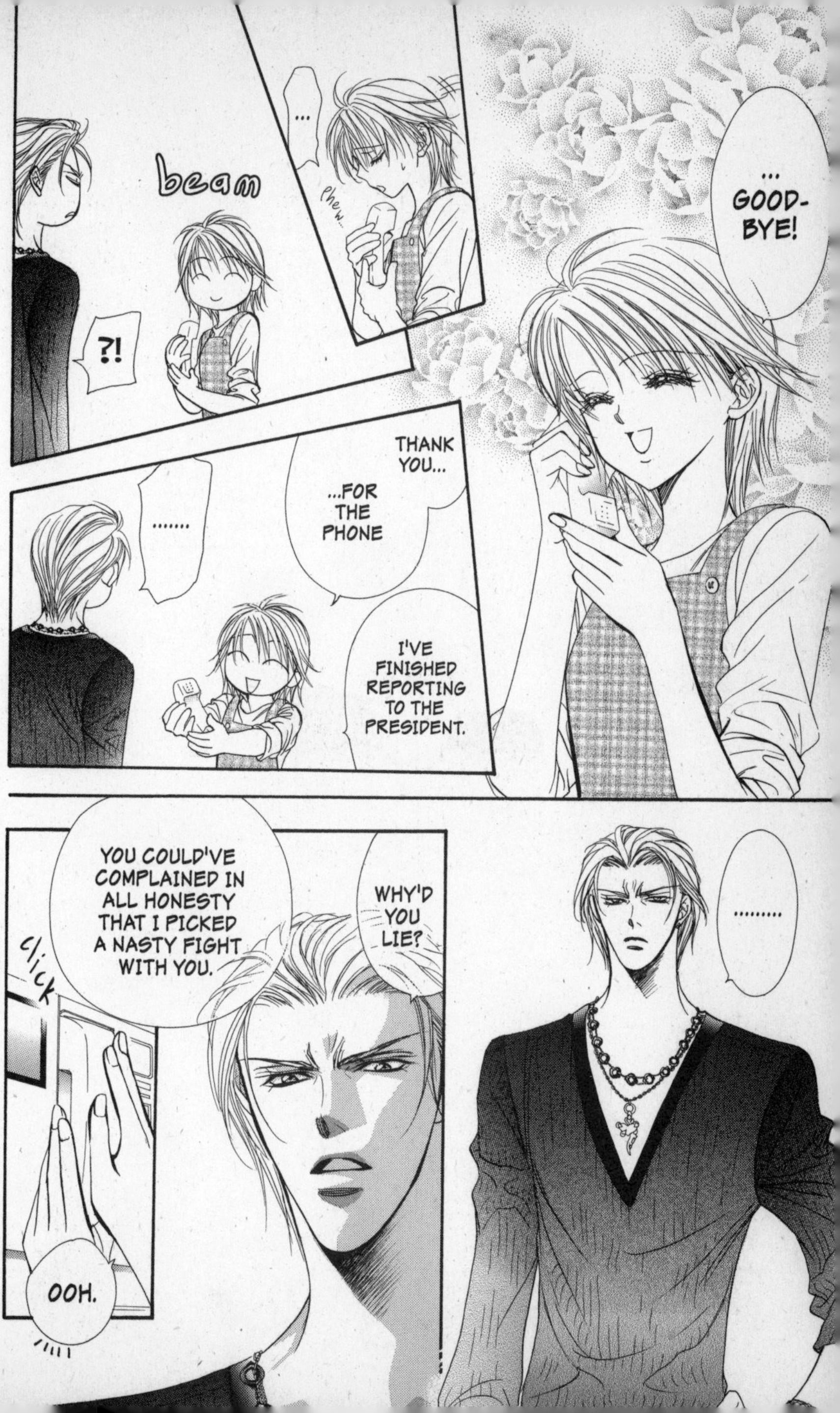
... GOOD-BYE!
...
phew...
beam
?!
THANK YOU...
...FOR THE PHONE
I'VE FINISHED REPORTING TO THE PRESIDENT.
....
....
WHY'D YOU LIE?
YOU COULD'VE COMPLAINED IN ALL HONESTY THAT I PICKED A NASTY FIGHT WITH YOU.
click
OOH.

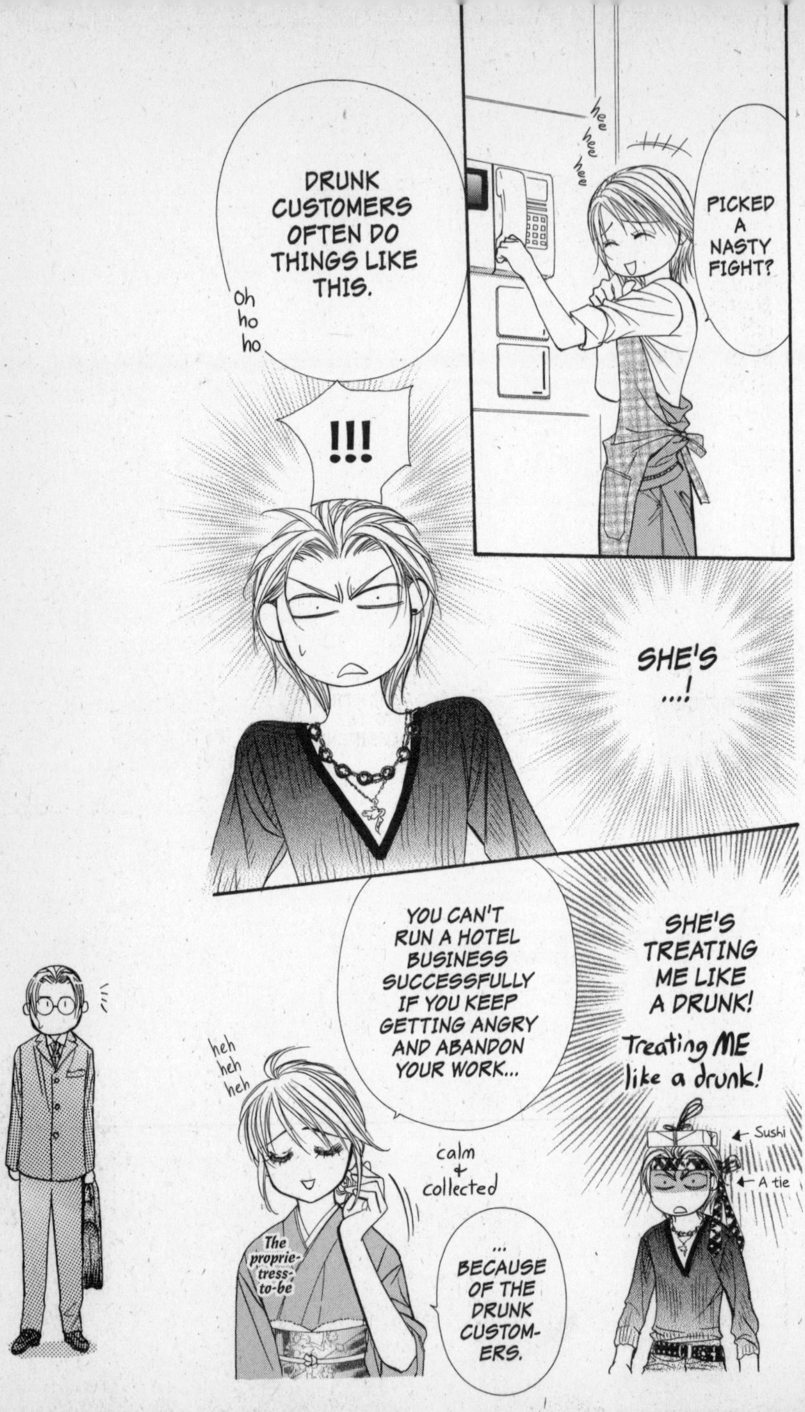
hee hee hee
PICKED A NASTY FIGHT?
DRUNK CUSTOMERS OFTEN DO THINGS LIKE THIS.
oh ho ho
!!!
SHE'S ...!
SHE'S TREATING ME LIKE A DRUNK!
Treating ME like a drunk!
Sushi
A tie
YOU CAN'T RUN A HOTEL BUSINESS SUCCESSFULLY IF YOU KEEP GETTING ANGRY AND ABANDON YOUR WORK...
heh heh heh
calm & collected
The proprie-tress-to-be
...BECAUSE OF THE DRUNK CUSTOM-ERS.

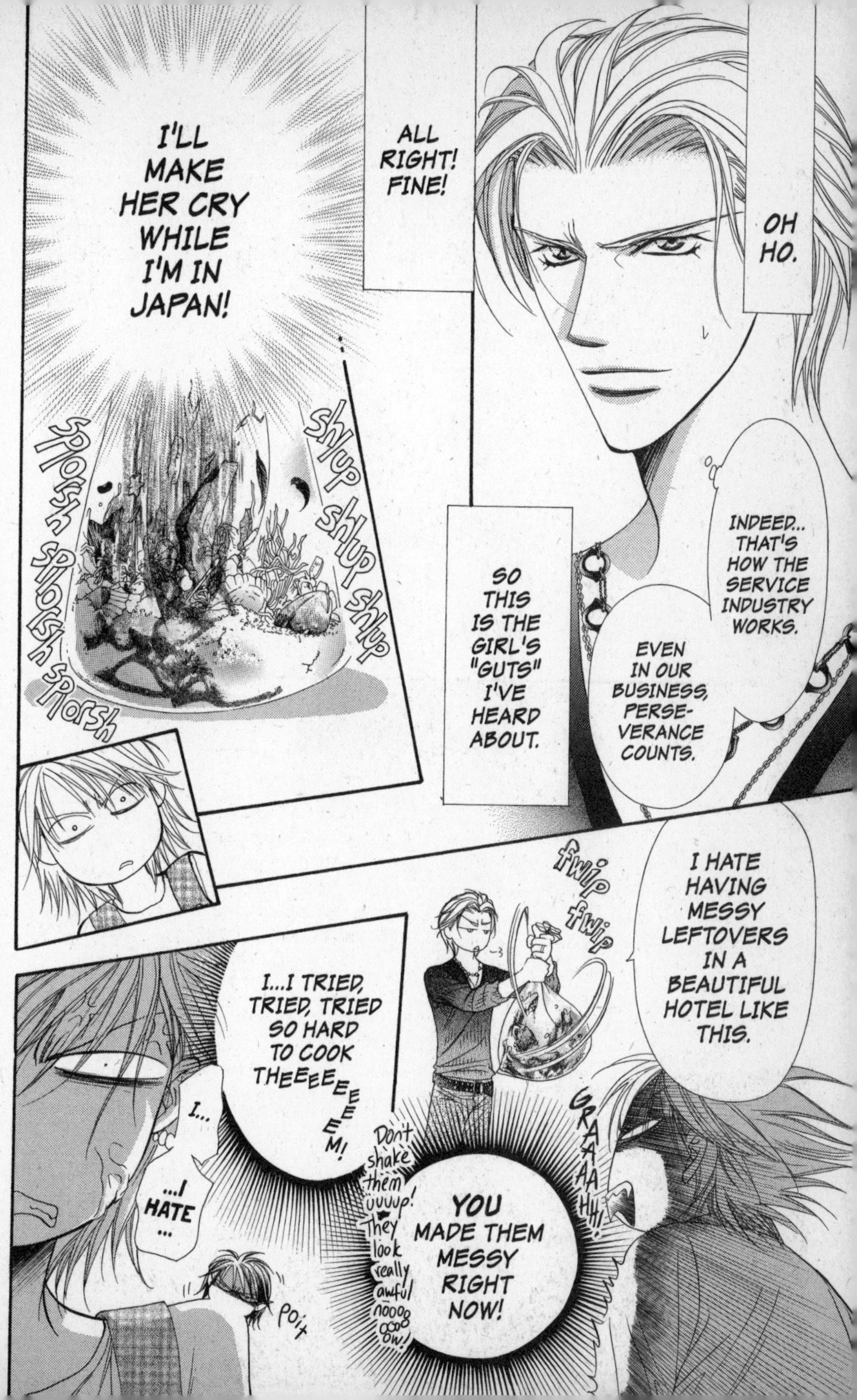
OH HO.
ALL RIGHT! FINE!
INDEED... THAT'S HOW THE SERVICE INDUSTRY WORKS.
EVEN IN OUR BUSINESS, PERSEVERANCE COUNTS.
SO THIS IS THE GIRL'S "GUTS" I'VE HEARD ABOUT.
I'LL MAKE HER CRY WHILE I'M IN JAPAN!
shlup shlup shlup
sporsh sporsh sporsh
I HATE HAVING MESSY LEFTOVERS IN A BEAUTIFUL HOTEL LIKE THIS.
fwip fwip
GRAAAAHH!
YOU MADE THEM MESSY RIGHT NOW!
Don't shake them uuuup! They look really awful noooooooow!
I...I TRIED, TRIED, TRIED SO HARD TO COOK THEEEEEEEM!
I...
...I HATE...
Poit

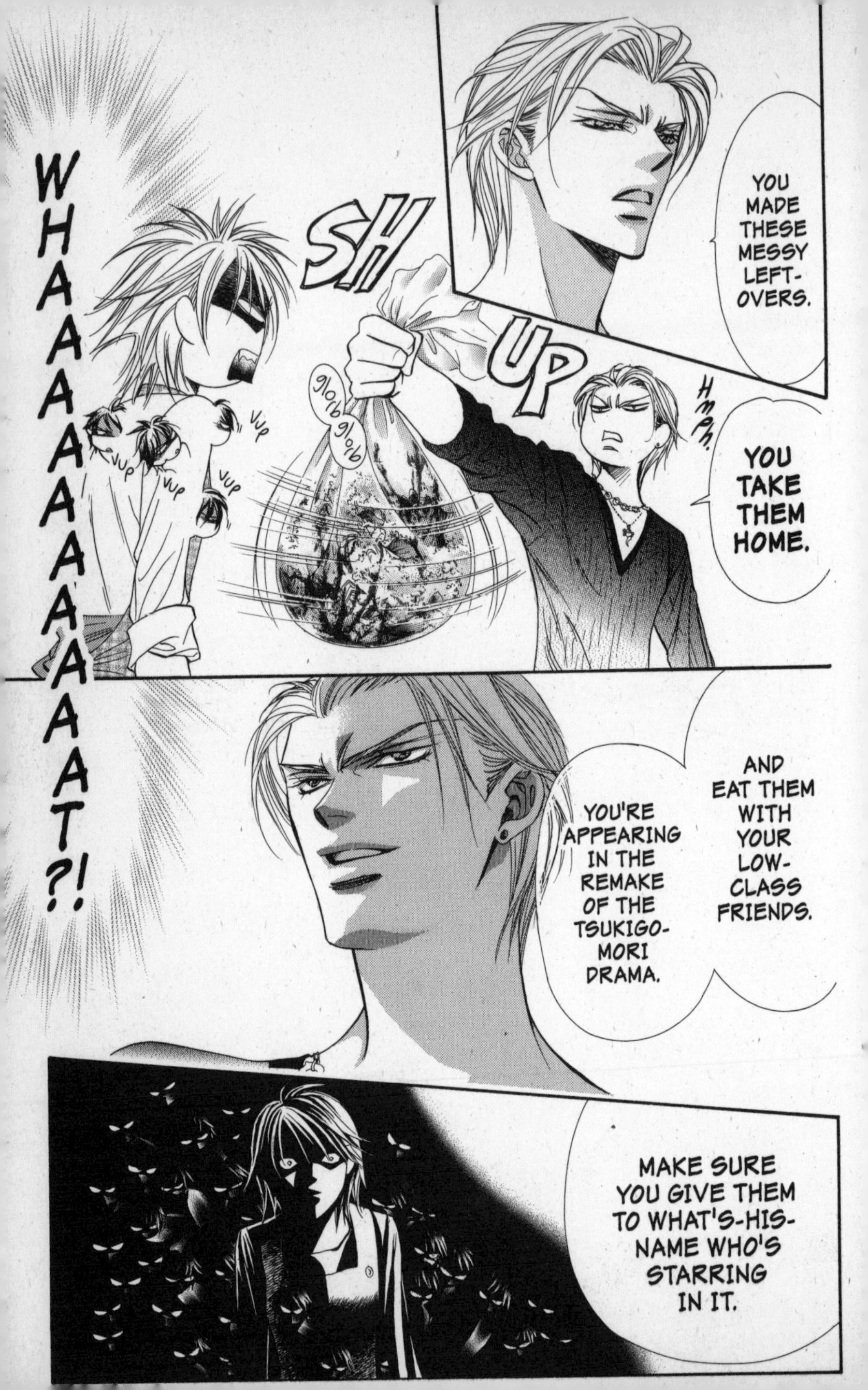

YOU MADE THESE MESSY LEFT-OVERS.
YOU TAKE THEM HOME.
HMPH.
SH UP
glob glob
VUP VUP VUP VUP
WHAAAAAAAAAAAAT?!
AND EAT THEM WITH YOUR LOW-CLASS FRIENDS.
YOU'RE APPEARING IN THE REMAKE OF THE TSUKIGO-MORI DRAMA.
MAKE SURE YOU GIVE THEM TO WHAT'S-HIS-NAME WHO'S STARRING IN IT.

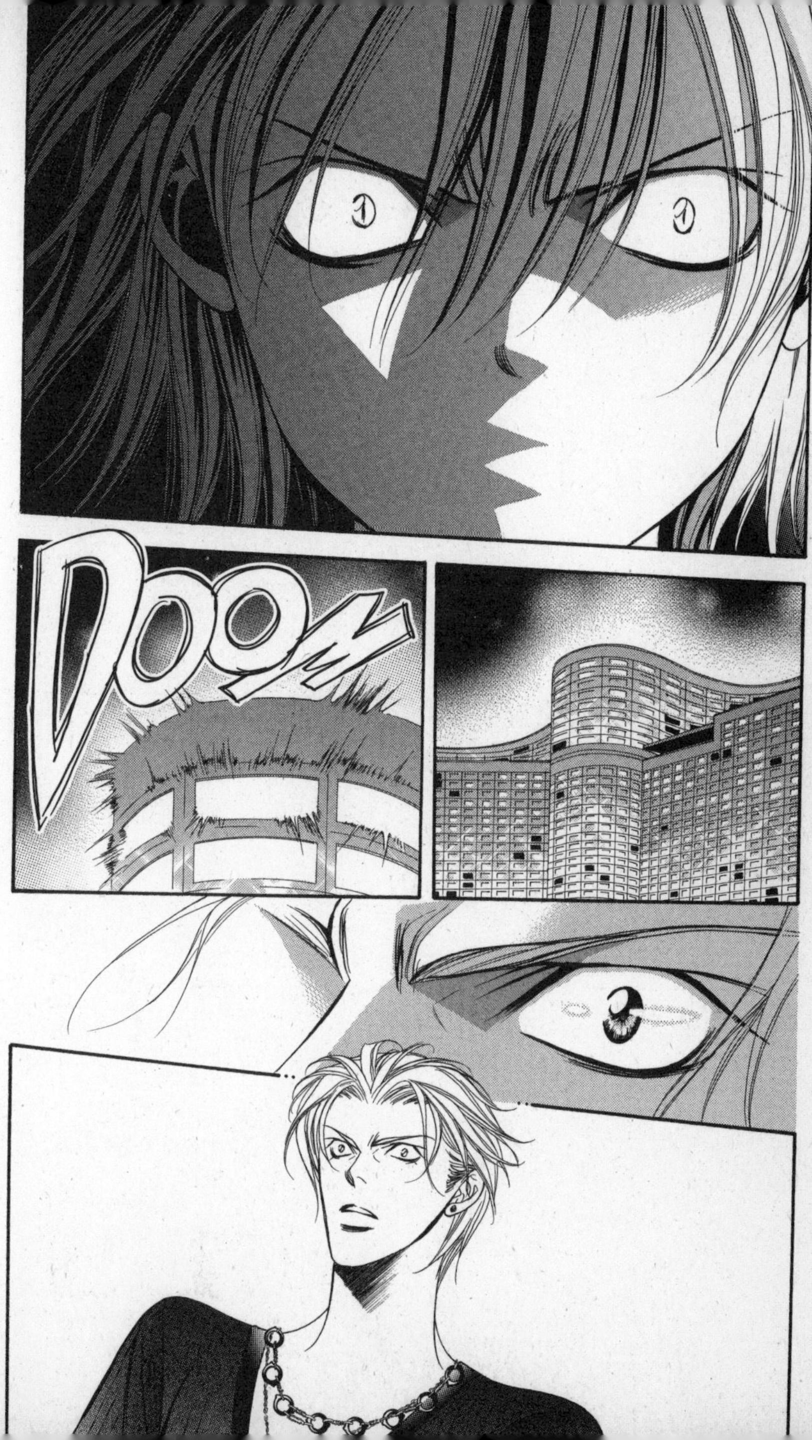
DOOM

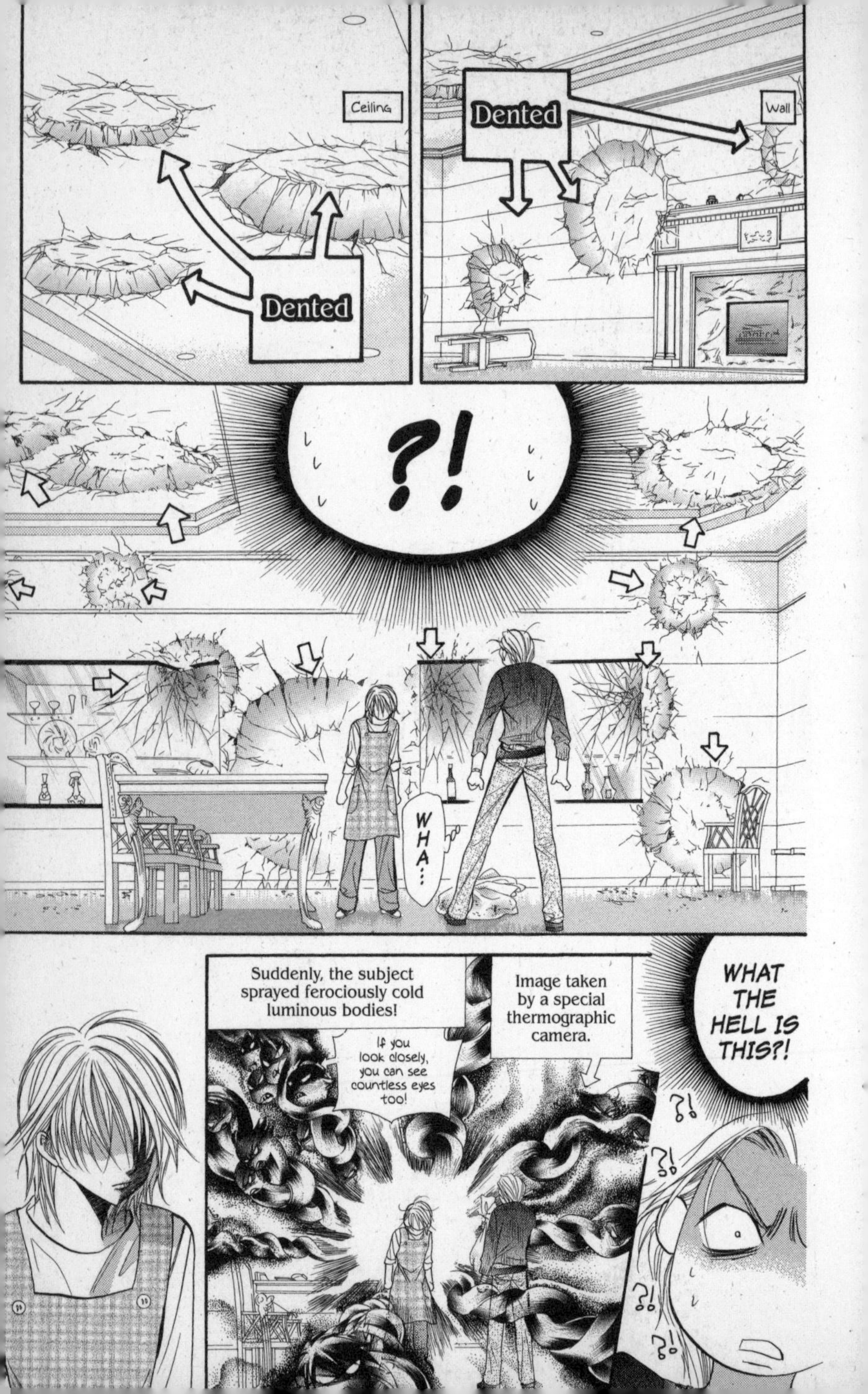
Wall
Dented
Ceiling
Dented
?!
WHA...
WHAT THE HELL IS THIS?!
?!
?!
?!
?!
Image taken by a special thermographic camera.
Suddenly, the subject sprayed ferociously cold luminous bodies!
If you look closely, you can see countless eyes too!

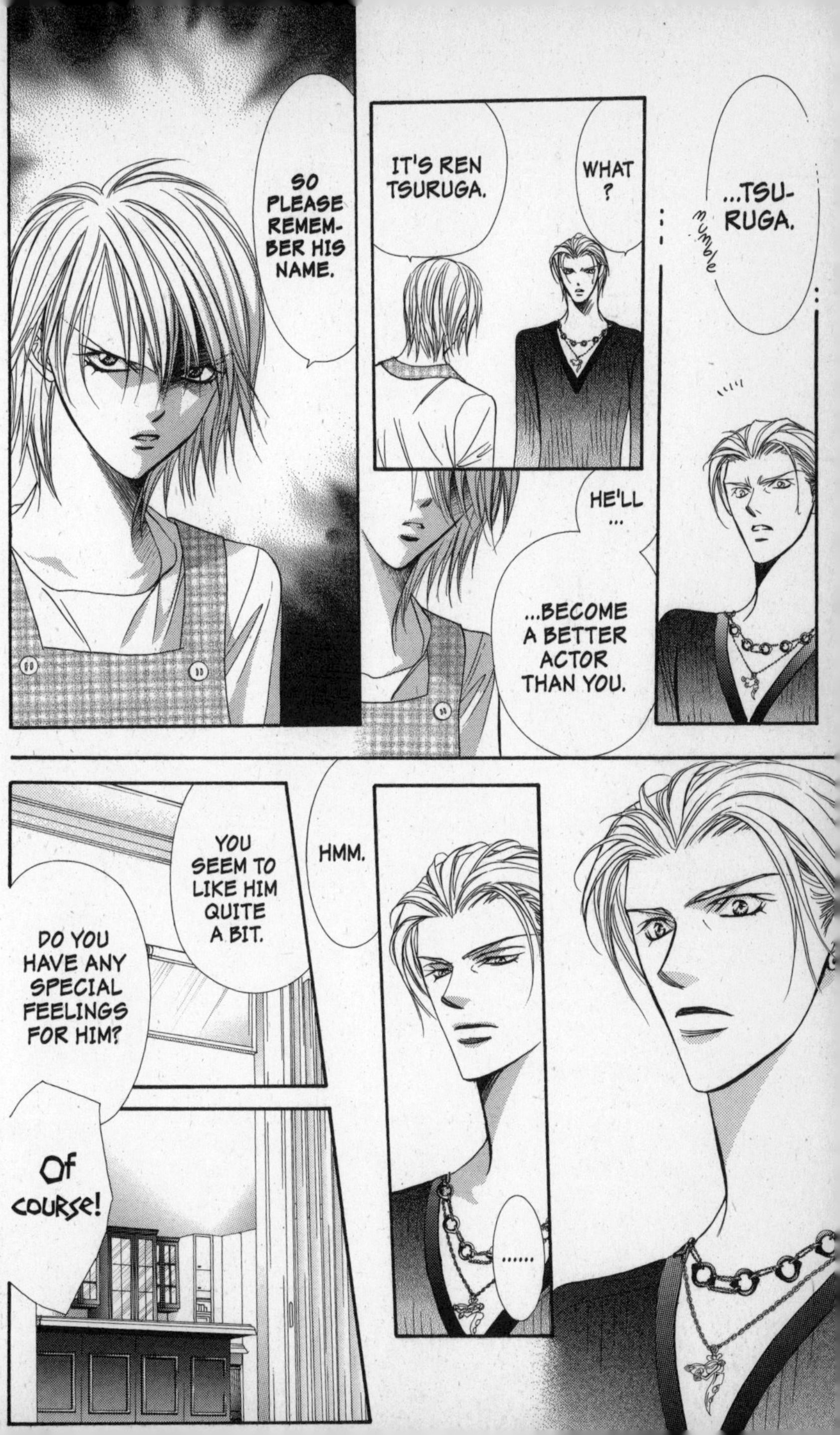
...TSU-RUGA.
mumble
WHAT?
IT'S REN TSURUGA.
SO PLEASE REMEMBER HIS NAME.
HE'LL...
...BECOME A BETTER ACTOR THAN YOU.
HMM.
......
YOU SEEM TO LIKE HIM QUITE A BIT.
DO YOU HAVE ANY SPECIAL FEELINGS FOR HIM?
Of course!

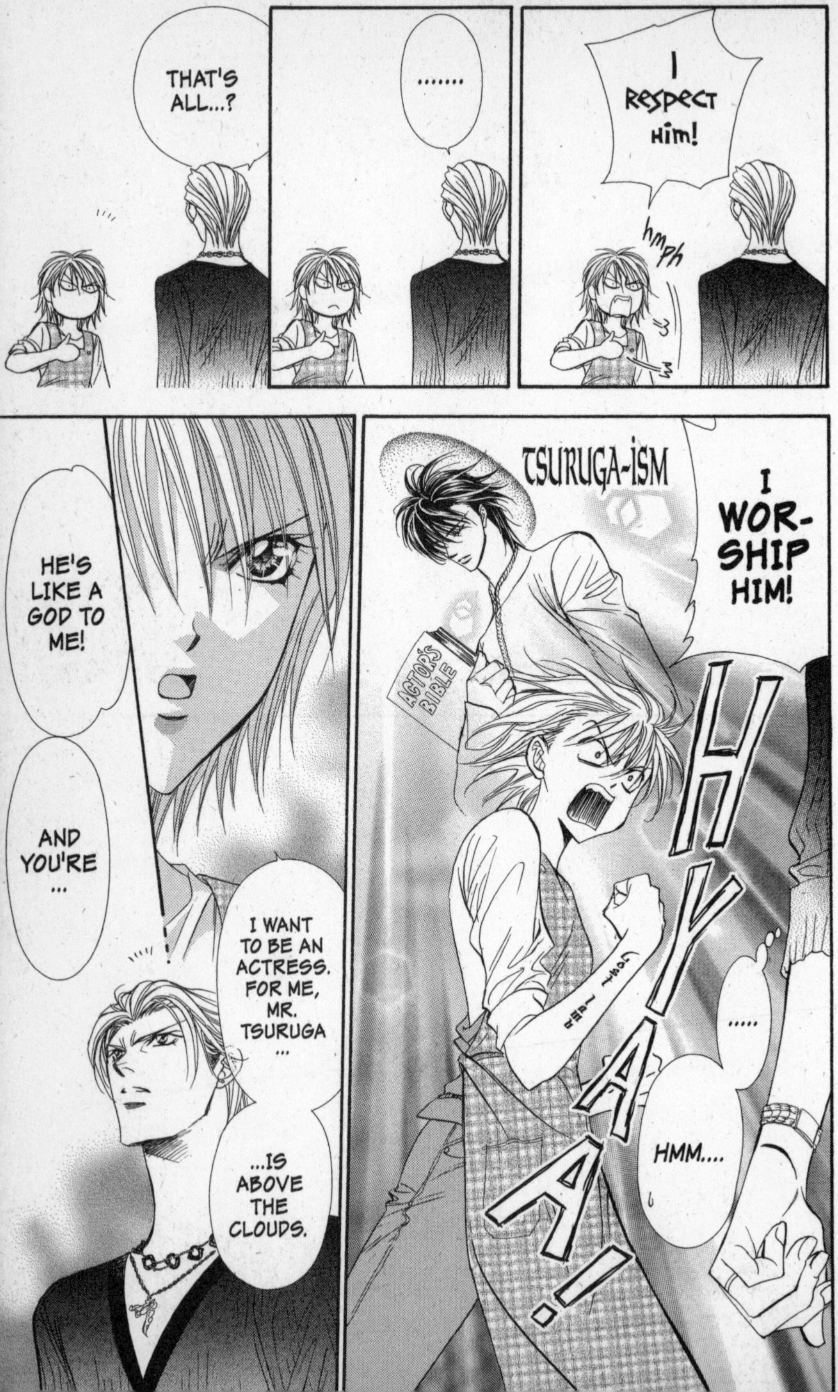
I RESPECT HIM!
hmph
....
THAT'S ALL...?
TSURUGA-ISM
I WOR-SHIP HIM!
HIYAAA!
.....
HMM....
HE'S LIKE A GOD TO ME!
I WANT TO BE AN ACTRESS. FOR ME, MR. TSURUGA ...
...IS ABOVE THE CLOUDS.
AND YOU'RE ...

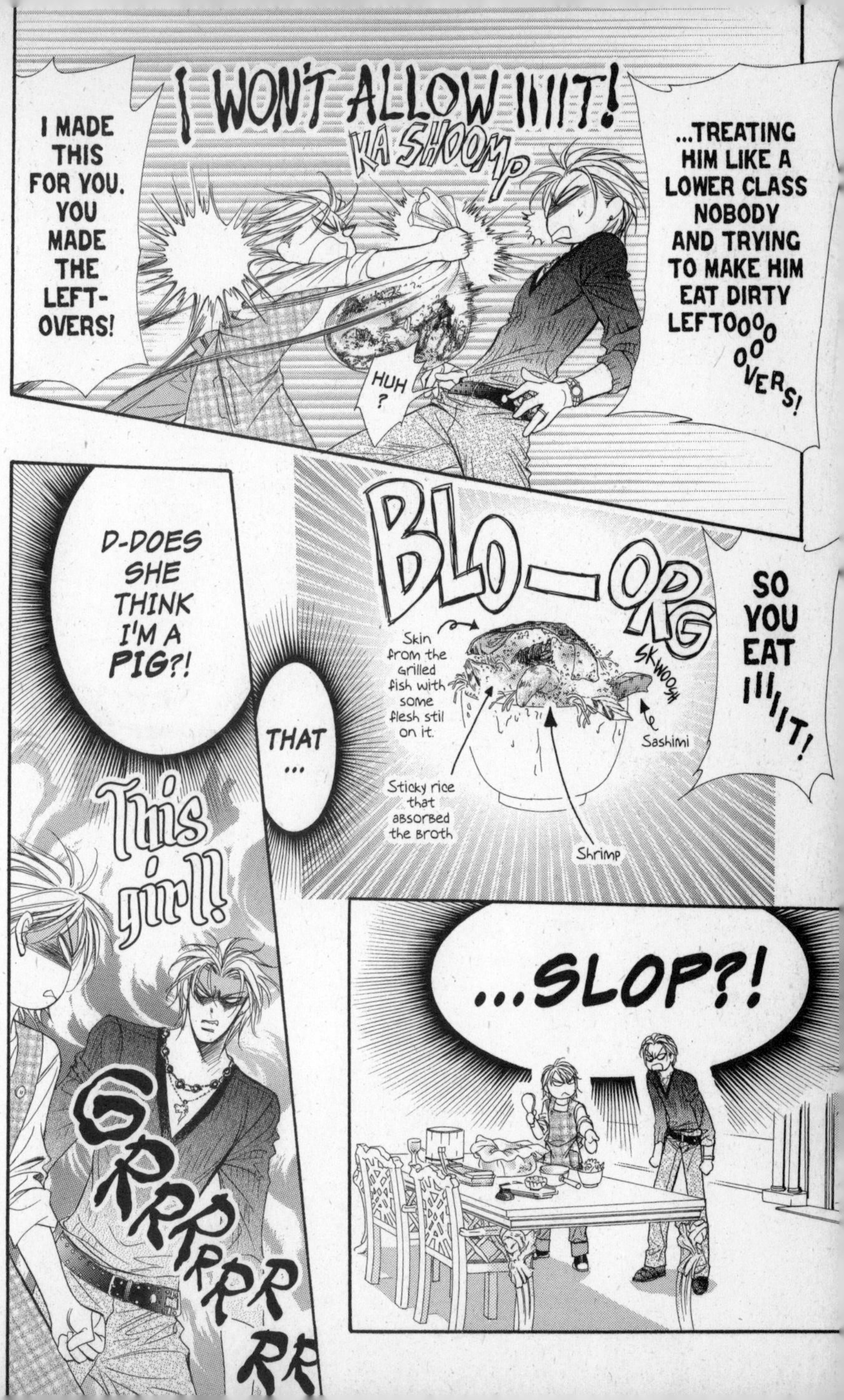
...TREATING HIM LIKE A LOWER CLASS NOBODY AND TRYING TO MAKE HIM EAT DIRTY LEFTOOOOOOVERS!
I WON'T ALLOW IIIIT!
KA SHOOMP
I MADE THIS FOR YOU. YOU MADE THE LEFT-OVERS!
HUH?
SO YOU EAT IIIIIT!
BLO—ORG
SKWOOSH
Skin from the Grilled fish with some flesh stil on it.
Sashimi
Sticky rice that absorbed the Broth
Shrimp
...SLOP?!
D-DOES SHE THINK I'M A PIG?!
THAT...
This girl!
GRRRRRRRRRR

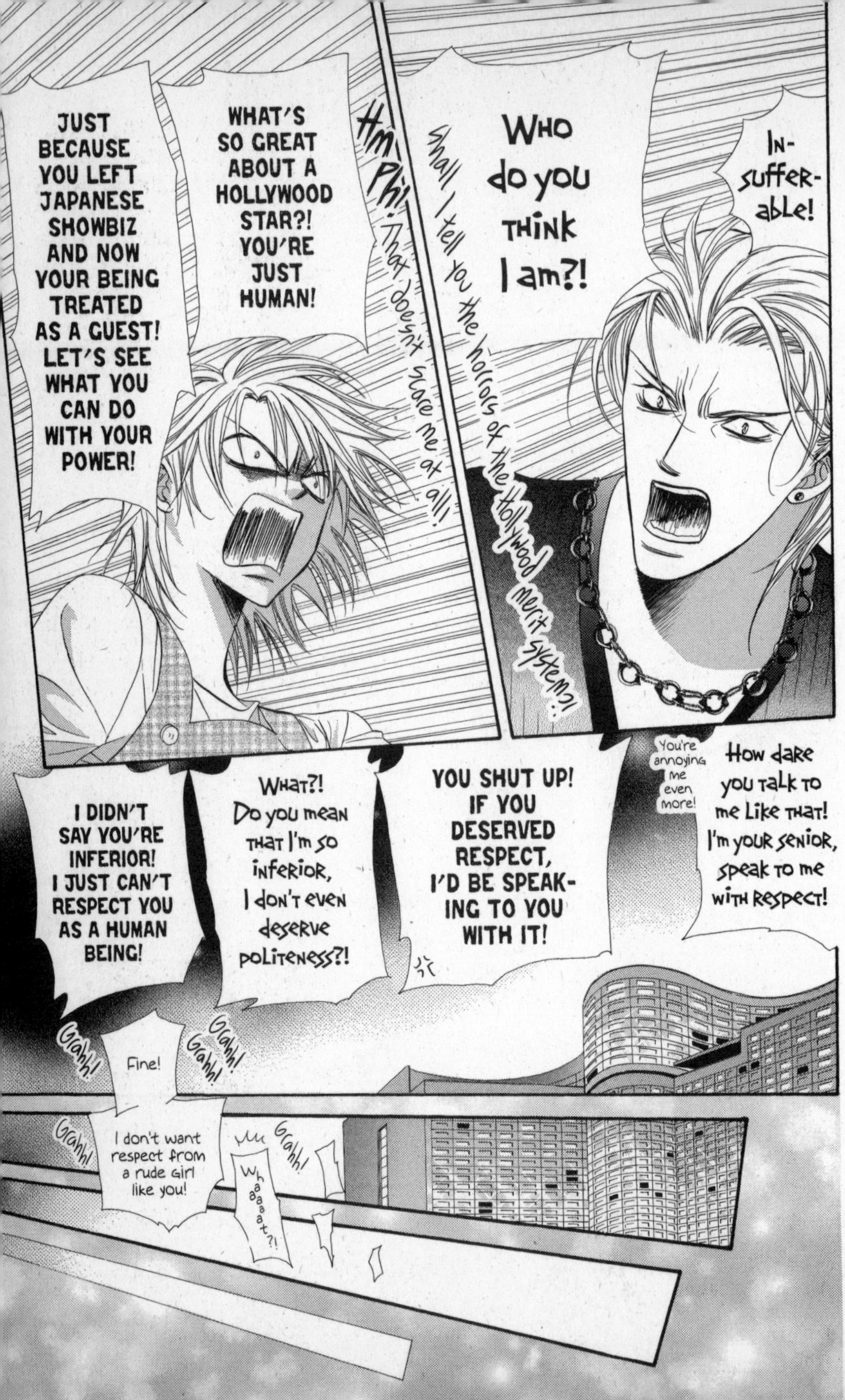
In-sufferable!
Who do you think I am?!
Shall I tell you the horrors of the Hollywood merit system?!
Hm Ph!
That doesn't scare me at all!
WHAT'S SO GREAT ABOUT A HOLLYWOOD STAR?! YOU'RE JUST HUMAN!
JUST BECAUSE YOU LEFT JAPANESE SHOWBIZ AND NOW YOUR BEING TREATED AS A GUEST! LET'S SEE WHAT YOU CAN DO WITH YOUR POWER!
How dare you talk to me like that! I'm your senior, speak to me with respect!
You're annoying me even more!
YOU SHUT UP! IF YOU DESERVED RESPECT, I'D BE SPEAK-ING TO YOU WITH IT!
What?! Do you mean that I'm so inferior, I don't even deserve politeness?!
I DIDN'T SAY YOU'RE INFERIOR! I JUST CAN'T RESPECT YOU AS A HUMAN BEING!
Grahh! Grahh!
Fine!
Grahh!
I don't want respect from a rude girl like you!
Grahh!
Grahh!
Whaaaaat?!

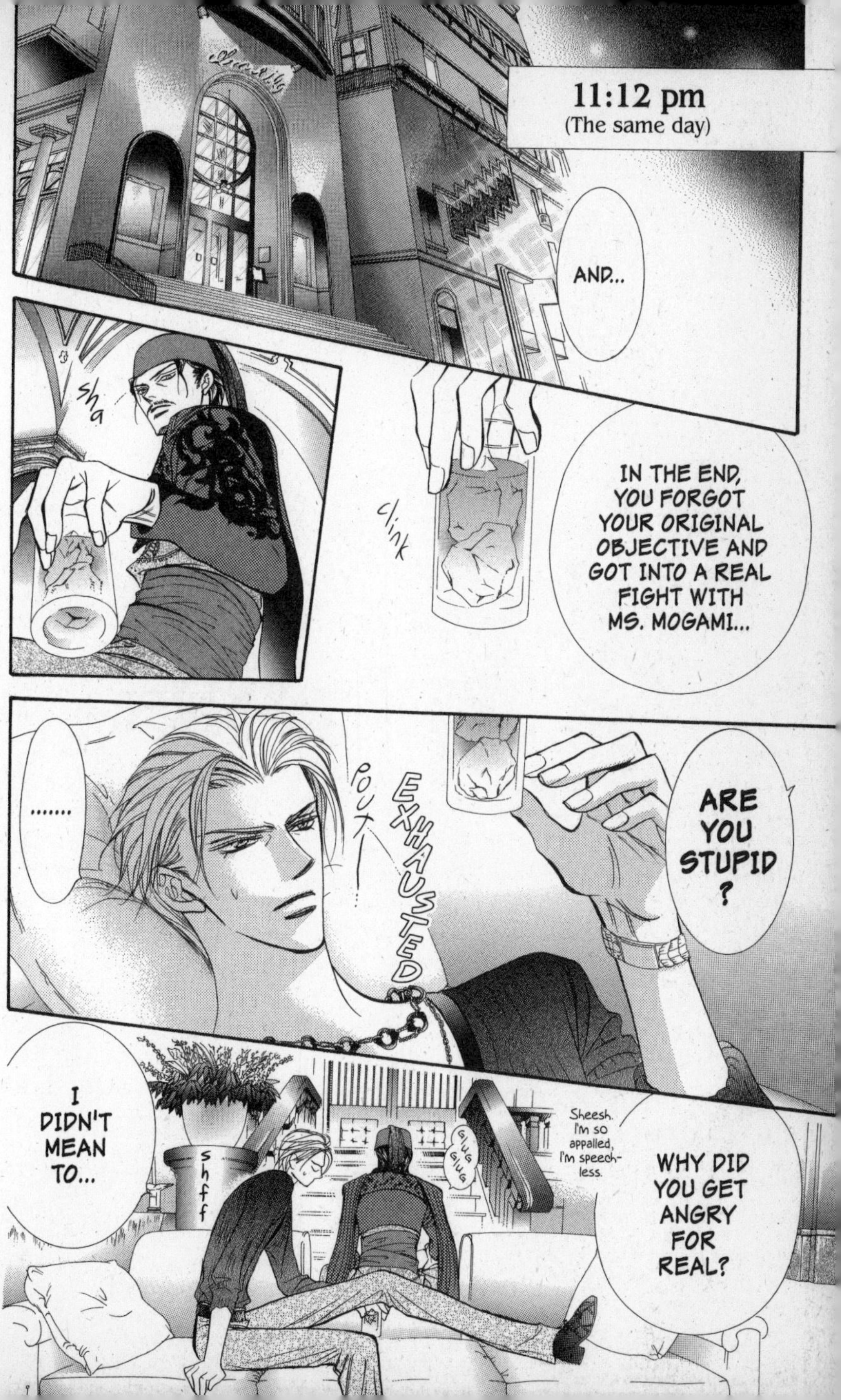
11:12 pm
(The same day)
AND...
IN THE END, YOU FORGOT YOUR ORIGINAL OBJECTIVE AND GOT INTO A REAL FIGHT WITH MS. MOGAMI...
clink
sha
ARE YOU STUPID?
EXHAUSTED
POUT
....
WHY DID YOU GET ANGRY FOR REAL?
Sheesh. I'm so appalled, I'm speechless.
glug glug
shff
I DIDN'T MEAN TO...

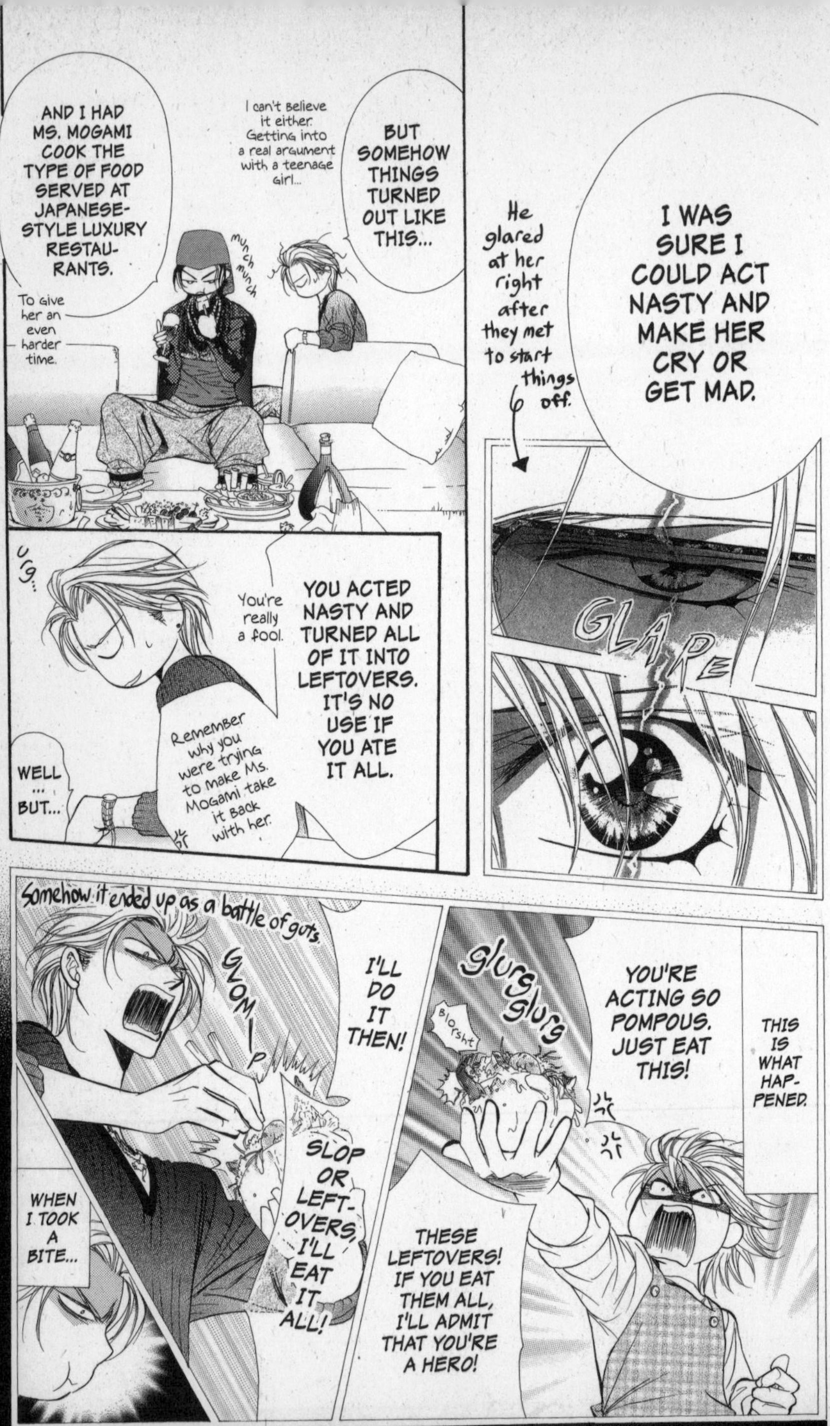
I WAS SURE I COULD ACT NASTY AND MAKE HER CRY OR GET MAD.
He glared at her right after they met to start things off.
GLARE
BUT SOMEHOW THINGS TURNED OUT LIKE THIS...
I can't believe it either. Getting into a real argument with a teenage girl...
AND I HAD MS. MOGAMI COOK THE TYPE OF FOOD SERVED AT JAPANESE-STYLE LUXURY RESTAU-RANTS.
munch munch
To give her an even harder time.
YOU ACTED NASTY AND TURNED ALL OF IT INTO LEFTOVERS. IT'S NO USE IF YOU ATE IT ALL.
You're really a fool.
Remember why you were trying to make Ms. Mogami take it back with her.
urg...
WELL... BUT...
THIS IS WHAT HAP-PENED.
YOU'RE ACTING SO POMPOUS. JUST EAT THIS!
glurg glurg
Blorsht
THESE LEFTOVERS! IF YOU EAT THEM ALL, I'LL ADMIT THAT YOU'RE A HERO!
Somehow it ended up as a battle of guts.
I'LL DO IT THEN!
GLOMP
SLOP OR LEFT-OVERS, I'LL EAT IT ALL!
WHEN I TOOK A BITE...

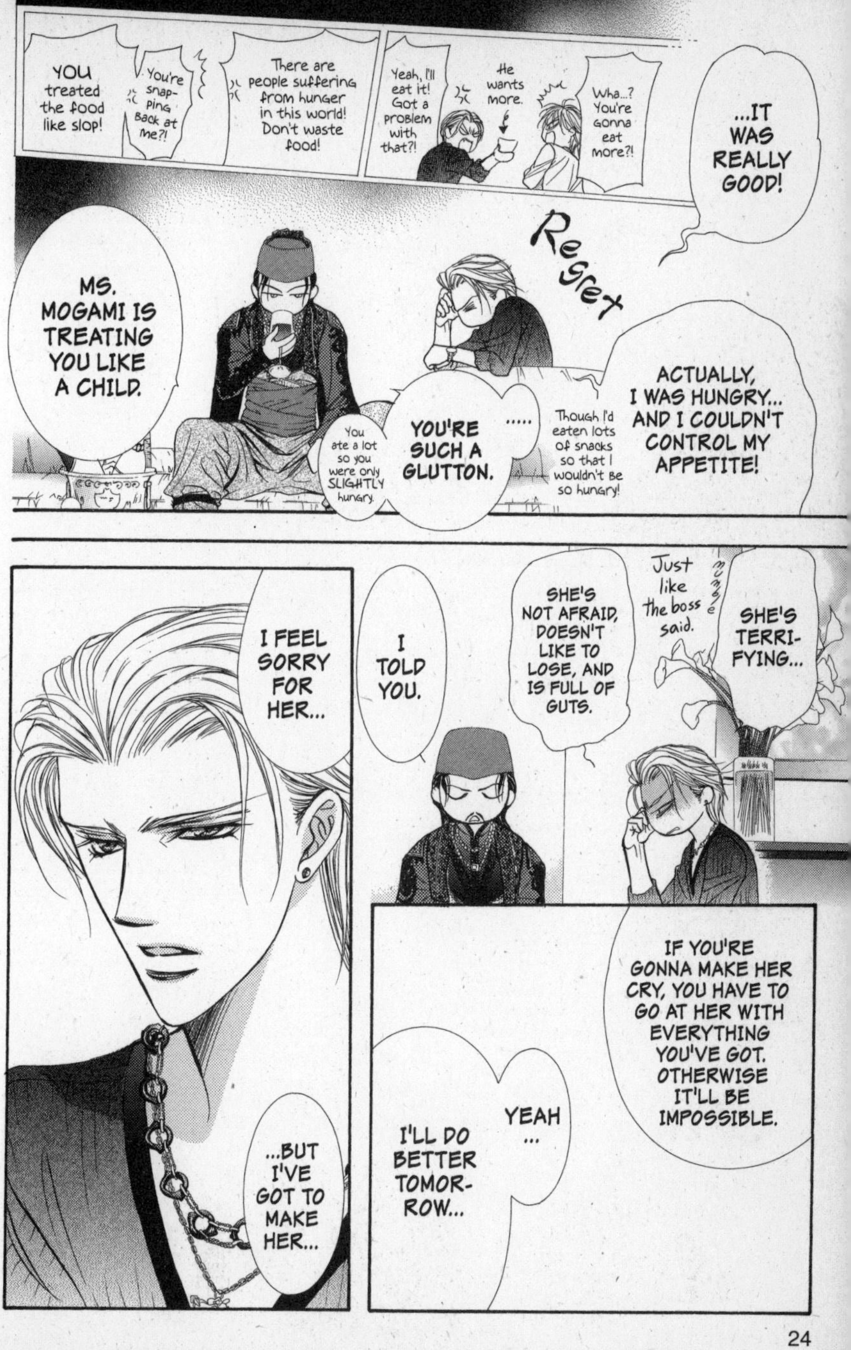
Wha...? You're gonna eat more?!
He wants more.
Yeah, I'll eat it! Got a problem with that?!
There are people suffering from hunger in this world! Don't waste food!
You're snapping back at me?!
YOU treated the food like slop!
...IT WAS REALLY GOOD!
Regret
ACTUALLY, I WAS HUNGRY... AND I COULDN'T CONTROL MY APPETITE!
Though I'd eaten lots of snacks so that I wouldn't be so hungry!
.....
YOU'RE SUCH A GLUTTON.
You ate a lot so you were only SLIGHTLY hungry.
MS. MOGAMI IS TREATING YOU LIKE A CHILD.
SHE'S TERRIFYING...
mumble
Just like the boss said.
SHE'S NOT AFRAID, DOESN'T LIKE TO LOSE, AND IS FULL OF GUTS.
I TOLD YOU.
IF YOU'RE GONNA MAKE HER CRY, YOU HAVE TO GO AT HER WITH EVERYTHING YOU'VE GOT. OTHERWISE IT'LL BE IMPOSSIBLE.
YEAH...
I'LL DO BETTER TOMORROW...
I FEEL SORRY FOR HER...
...BUT I'VE GOT TO MAKE HER...

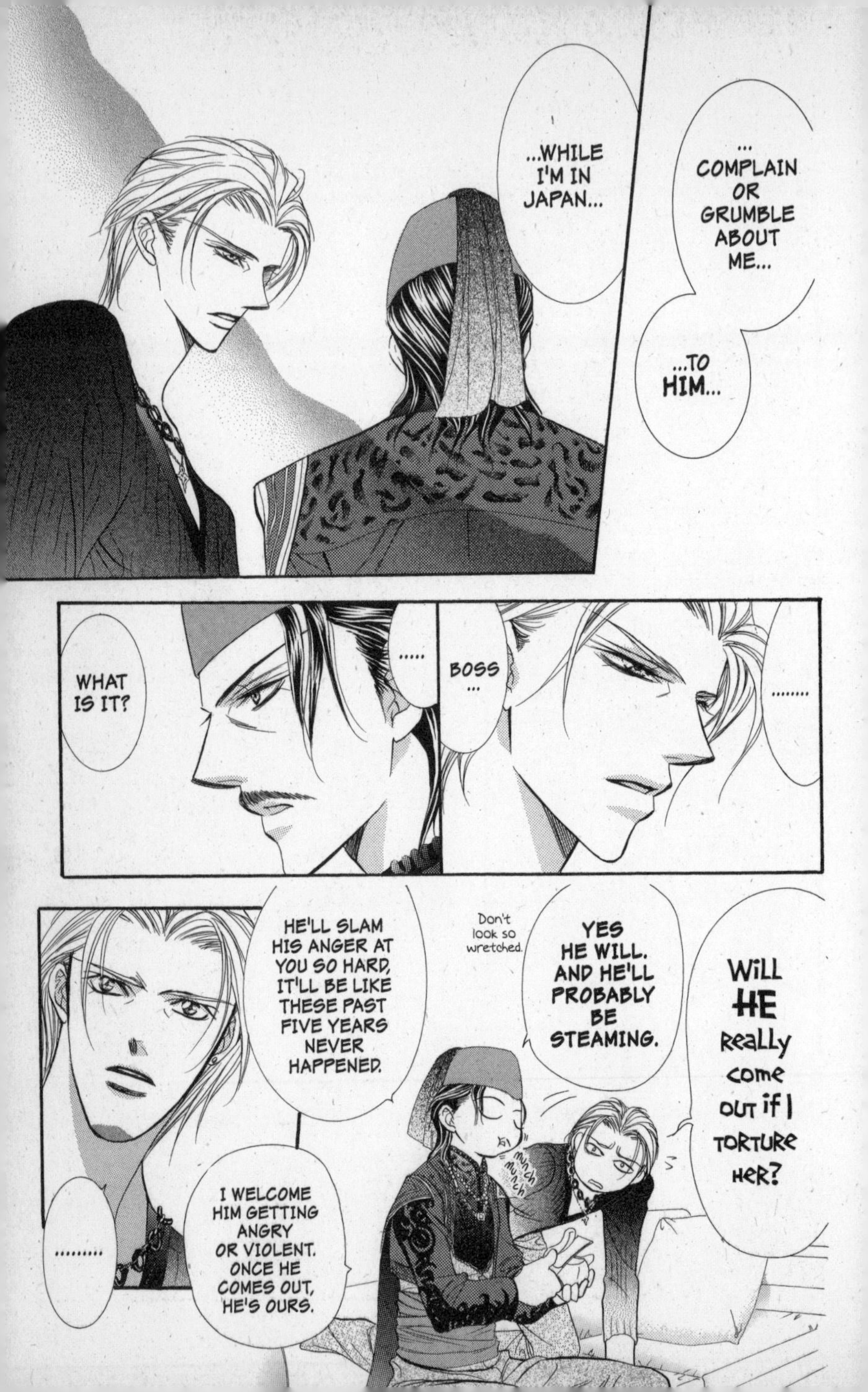
...COMPLAIN OR GRUMBLE ABOUT ME...
...TO HIM...
...WHILE I'M IN JAPAN...
....
BOSS ...
.....
WHAT IS IT?
Will HE really come out if I torture her?
YES HE WILL. AND HE'LL PROBABLY BE STEAMING.
Don't look so wretched.
munch munch munch
HE'LL SLAM HIS ANGER AT YOU SO HARD, IT'LL BE LIKE THESE PAST FIVE YEARS NEVER HAPPENED.
I WELCOME HIM GETTING ANGRY OR VIOLENT. ONCE HE COMES OUT, HE'S OURS.
....

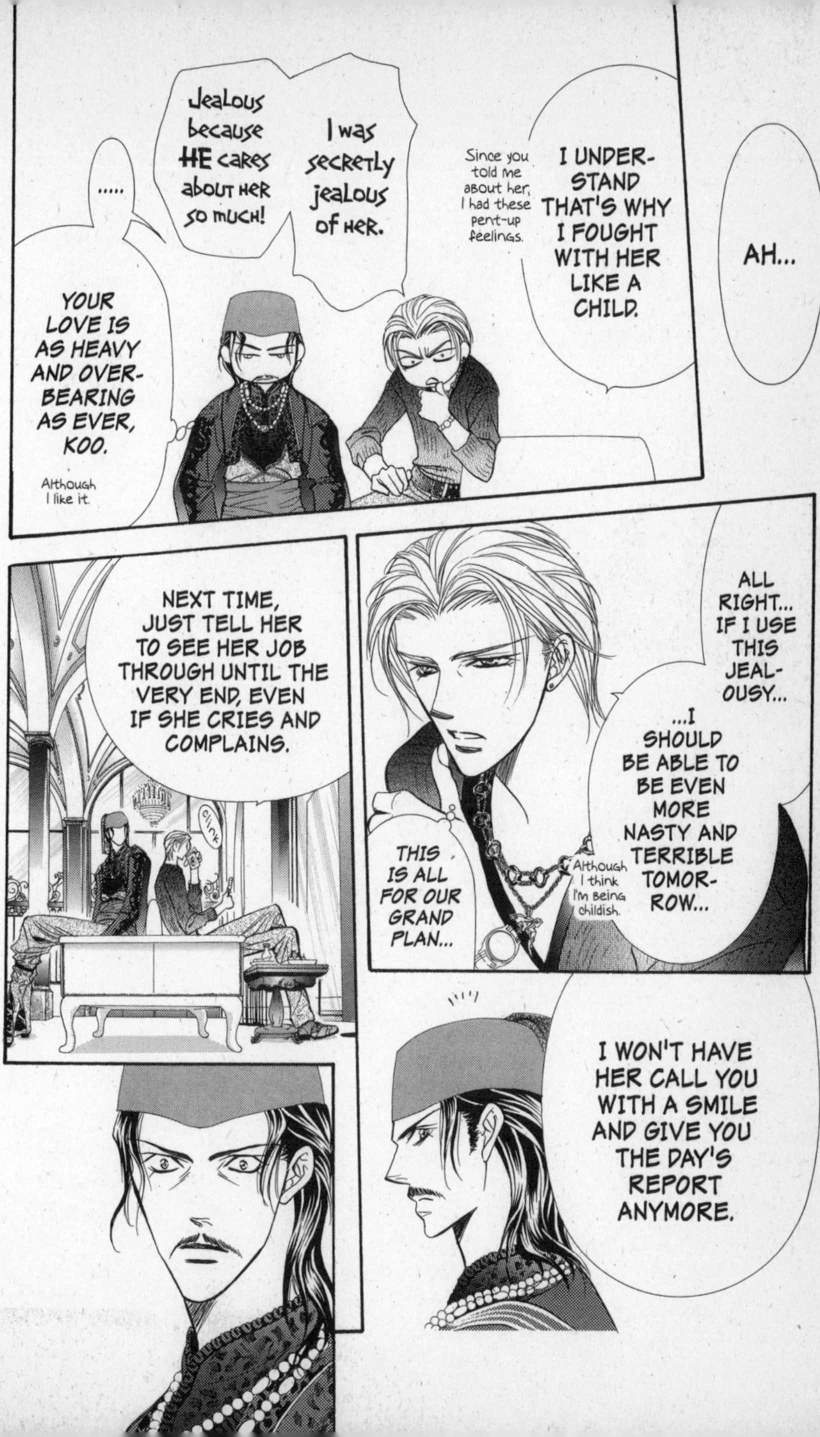
AH...
I UNDER-STAND THAT'S WHY I FOUGHT WITH HER LIKE A CHILD.
Since you told me about her, I had these pent-up feelings.
I was secretly jealous of her.
Jealous because HE cares about her so much!
.....
YOUR LOVE IS AS HEAVY AND OVER-BEARING AS EVER, KOO.
Although I like it.
ALL RIGHT... IF I USE THIS JEAL-OUSY...
...I SHOULD BE ABLE TO BE EVEN MORE NASTY AND TERRIBLE TOMOR-ROW...
Although I think I'm being childish.
THIS IS ALL FOR OUR GRAND PLAN...
NEXT TIME, JUST TELL HER TO SEE HER JOB THROUGH UNTIL THE VERY END, EVEN IF SHE CRIES AND COMPLAINS.
clink
I WON'T HAVE HER CALL YOU WITH A SMILE AND GIVE YOU THE DAY'S REPORT ANYMORE.

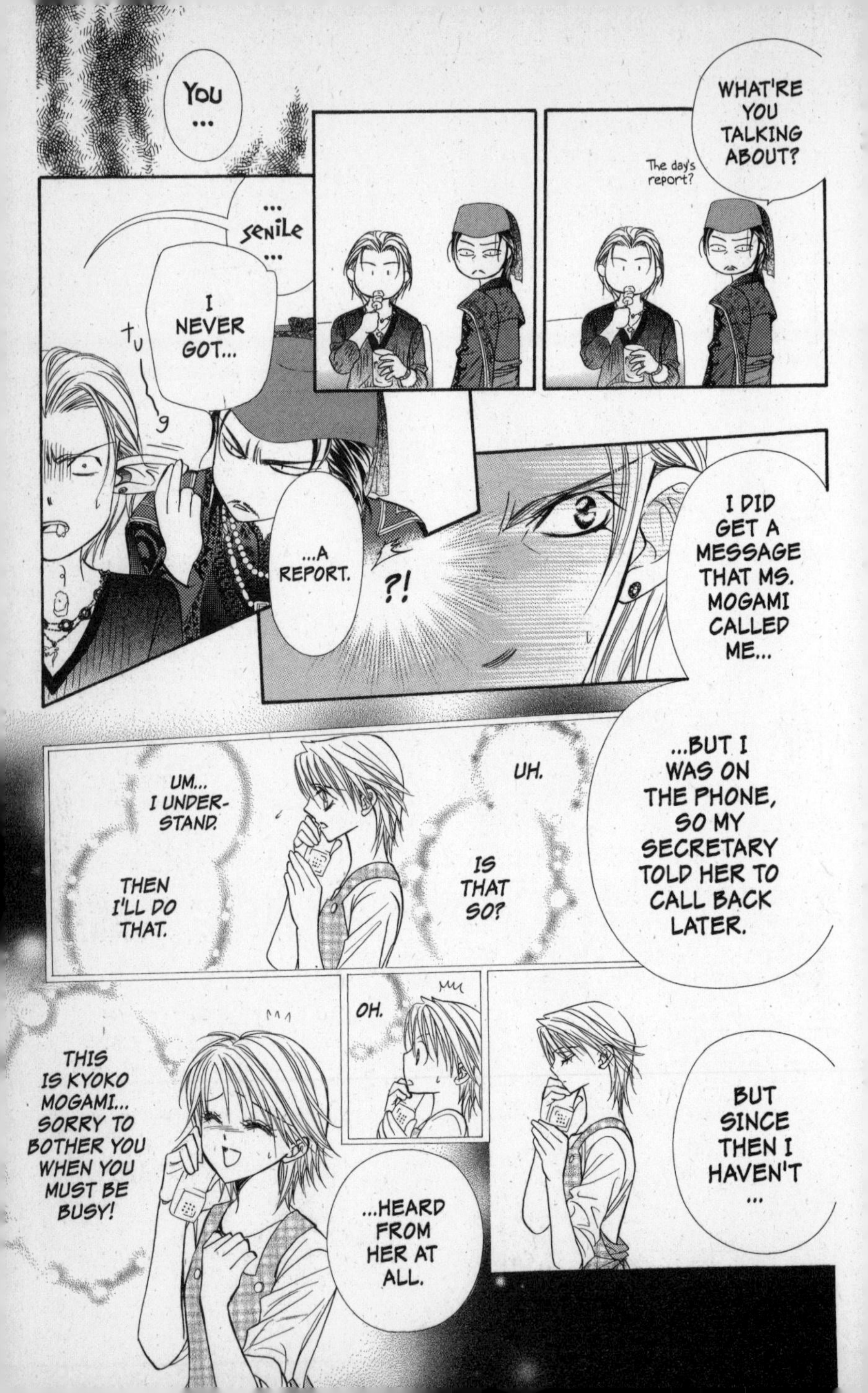
WHAT'RE YOU TALKING ABOUT?
The day's report?
YOU ...
... SENILE ...
I NEVER GOT...
...A REPORT.
?!
I DID GET A MESSAGE THAT MS. MOGAMI CALLED ME...
...BUT I WAS ON THE PHONE, SO MY SECRETARY TOLD HER TO CALL BACK LATER.
UH.
IS THAT SO?
UM... I UNDERSTAND.
THEN I'LL DO THAT.
BUT SINCE THEN I HAVEN'T ...
...HEARD FROM HER AT ALL.
OH.
THIS IS KYOKO MOGAMI... SORRY TO BOTHER YOU WHEN YOU MUST BE BUSY!

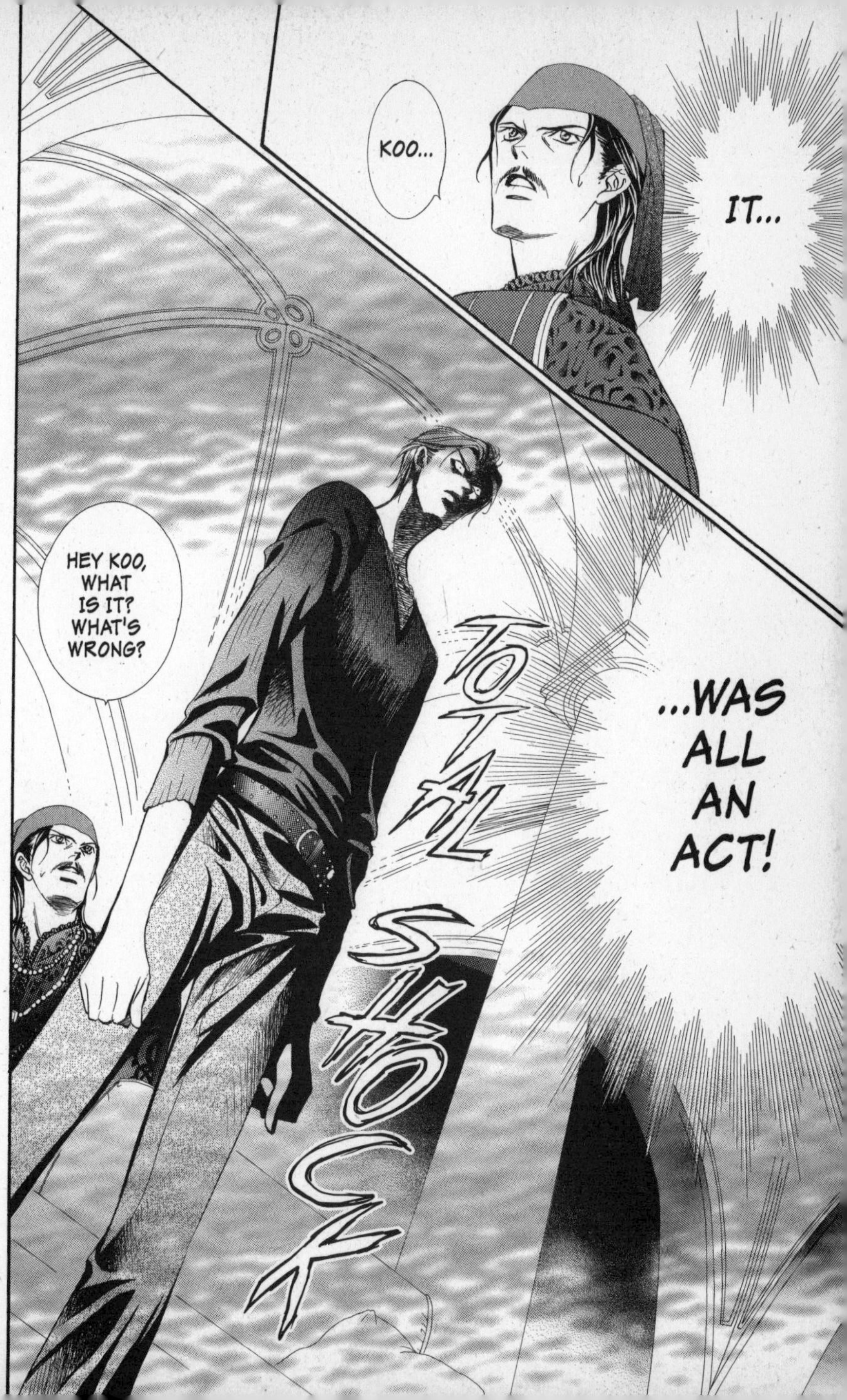
IT...
KOO...
...WAS ALL AN ACT!
TOTAL SHOCK
HEY KOO, WHAT IS IT? WHAT'S WRONG?

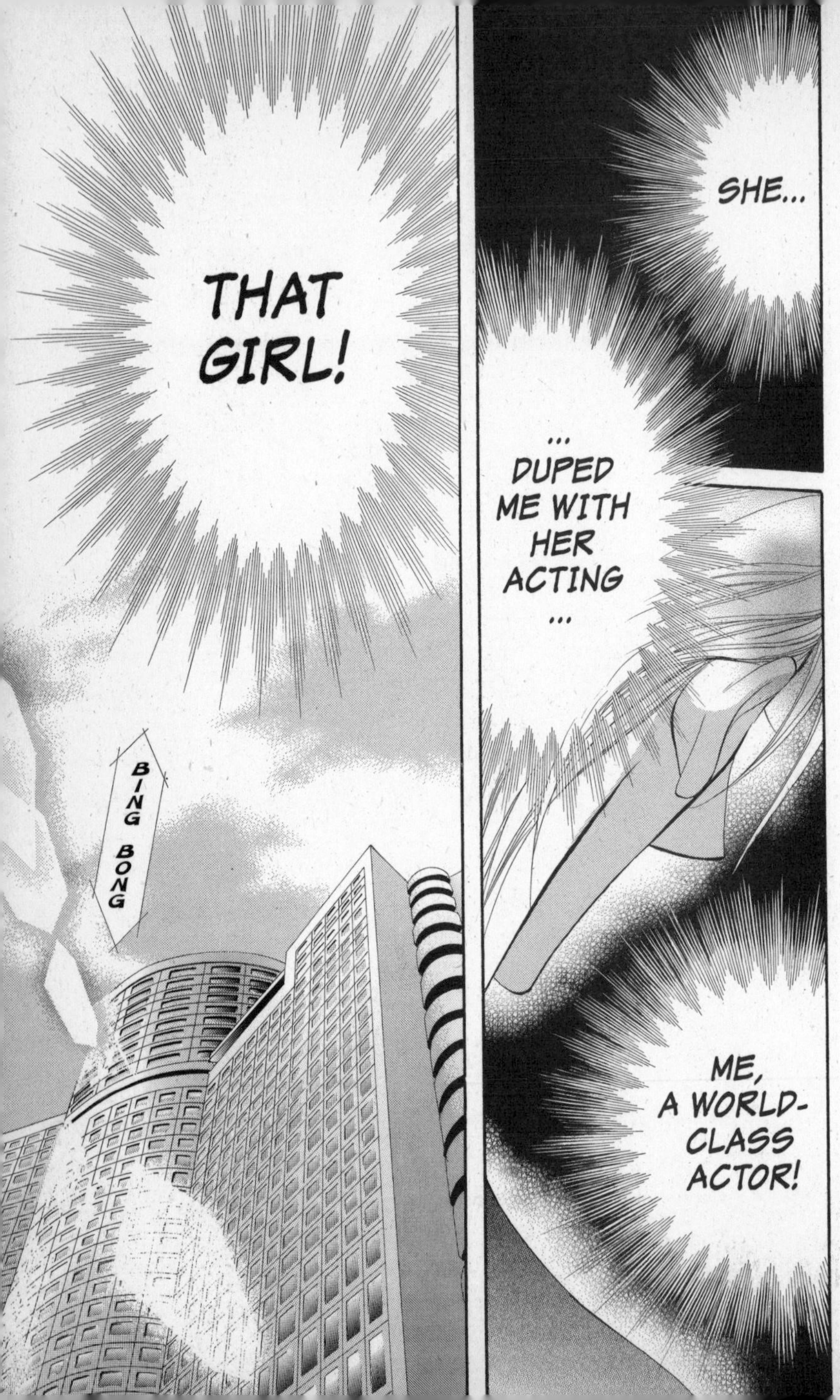
SHE...
...DUPED ME WITH HER ACTING...
ME, A WORLD-CLASS ACTOR!
THAT GIRL!
BING BONG

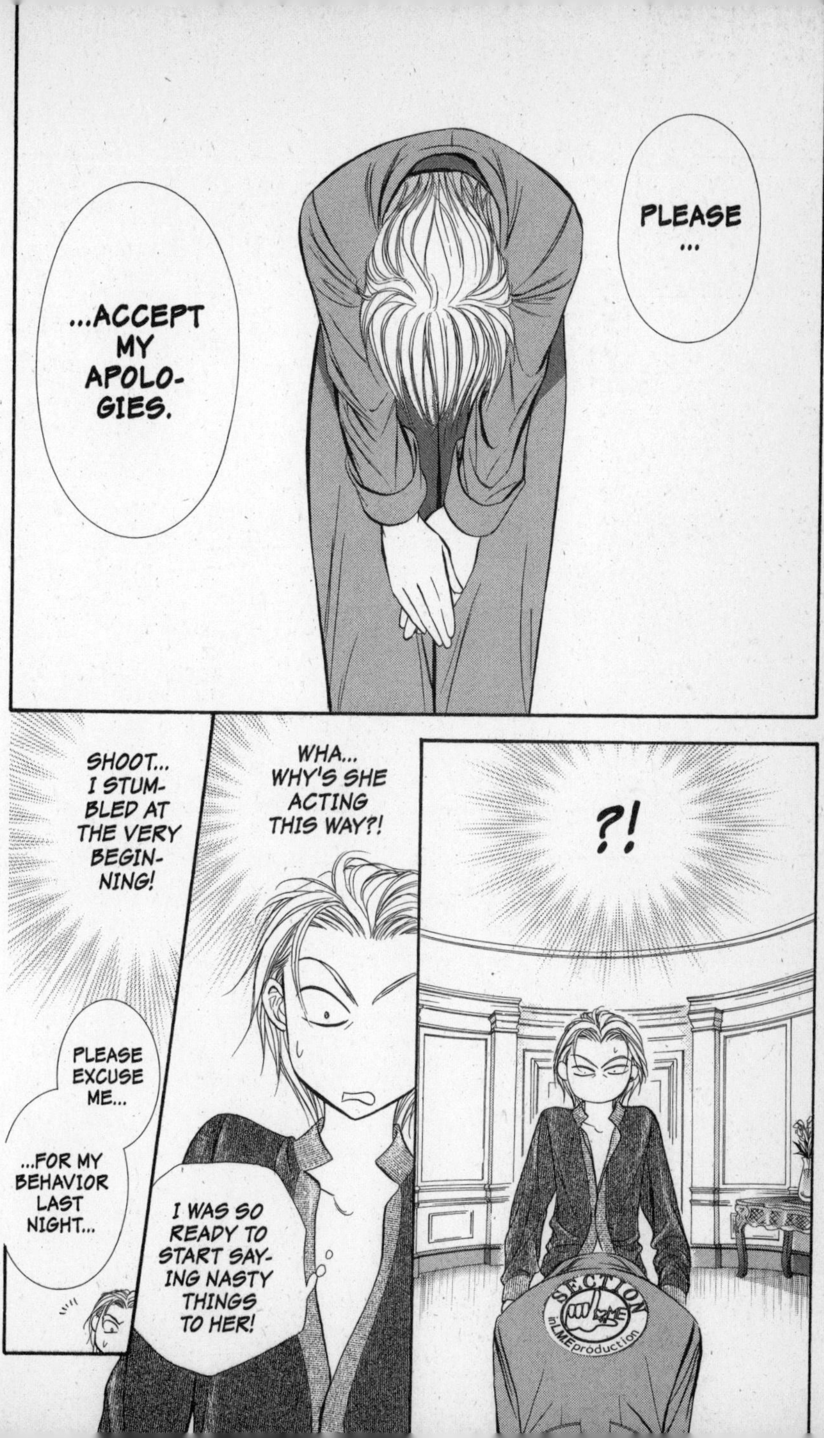
PLEASE ...
...ACCEPT MY APOLOGIES.
?!
SECTION
inLMEproduction
WHA... WHY'S SHE ACTING THIS WAY?!
SHOOT... I STUMBLED AT THE VERY BEGINNING!
I WAS SO READY TO START SAYING NASTY THINGS TO HER!
PLEASE EXCUSE ME...
...FOR MY BEHAVIOR LAST NIGHT...

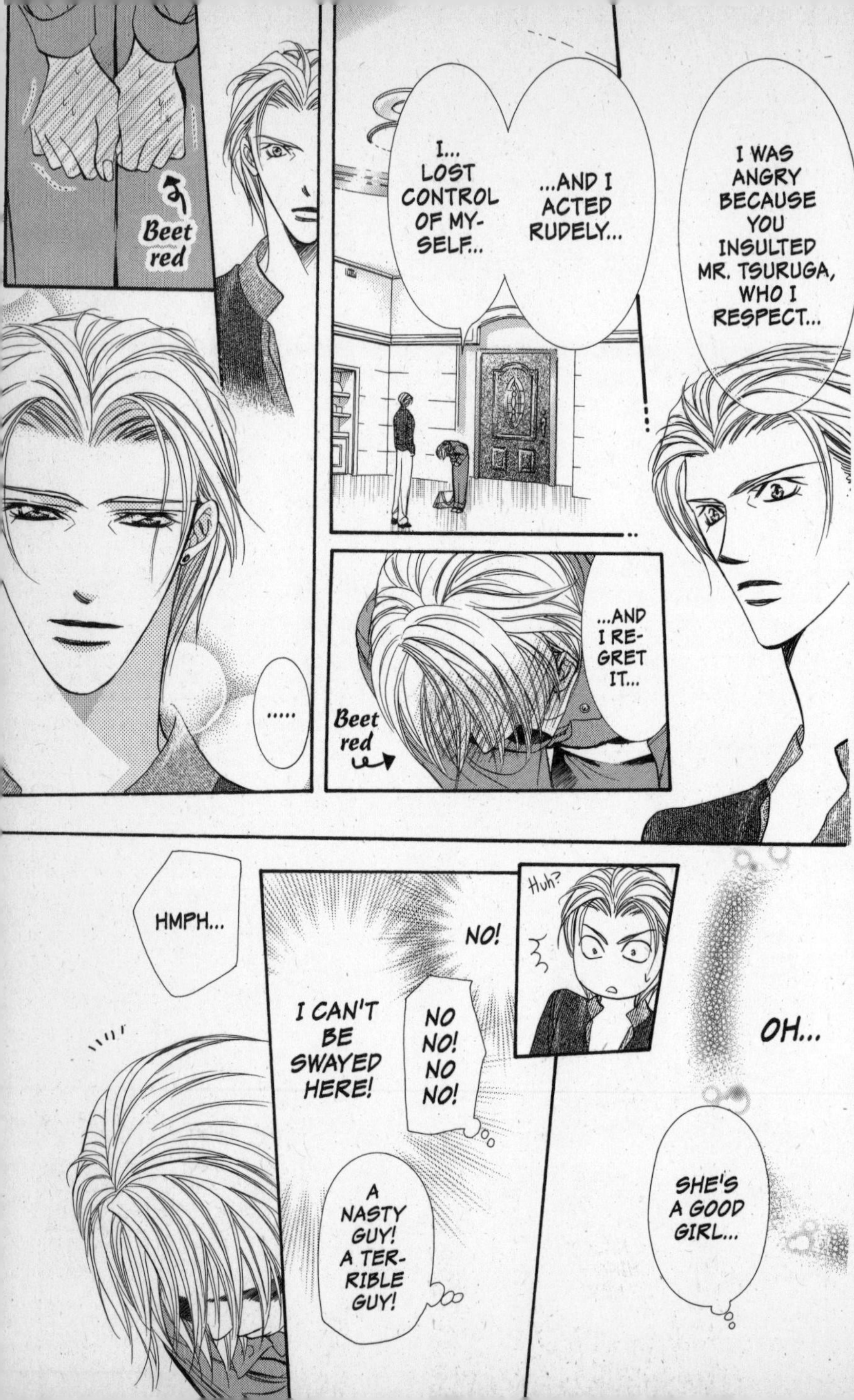
I WAS ANGRY BECAUSE YOU INSULTED MR. TSURUGA, WHO I RESPECT...
...AND I ACTED RUDELY...
I... LOST CONTROL OF MY-SELF...
...AND I RE-GRET IT...
Beet red
Beet red
.....
OH...
SHE'S A GOOD GIRL...
Huh?
NO!
NO NO! NO NO!
I CAN'T BE SWAYED HERE!
A NASTY GUY! A TER-RIBLE GUY!
HMPH...

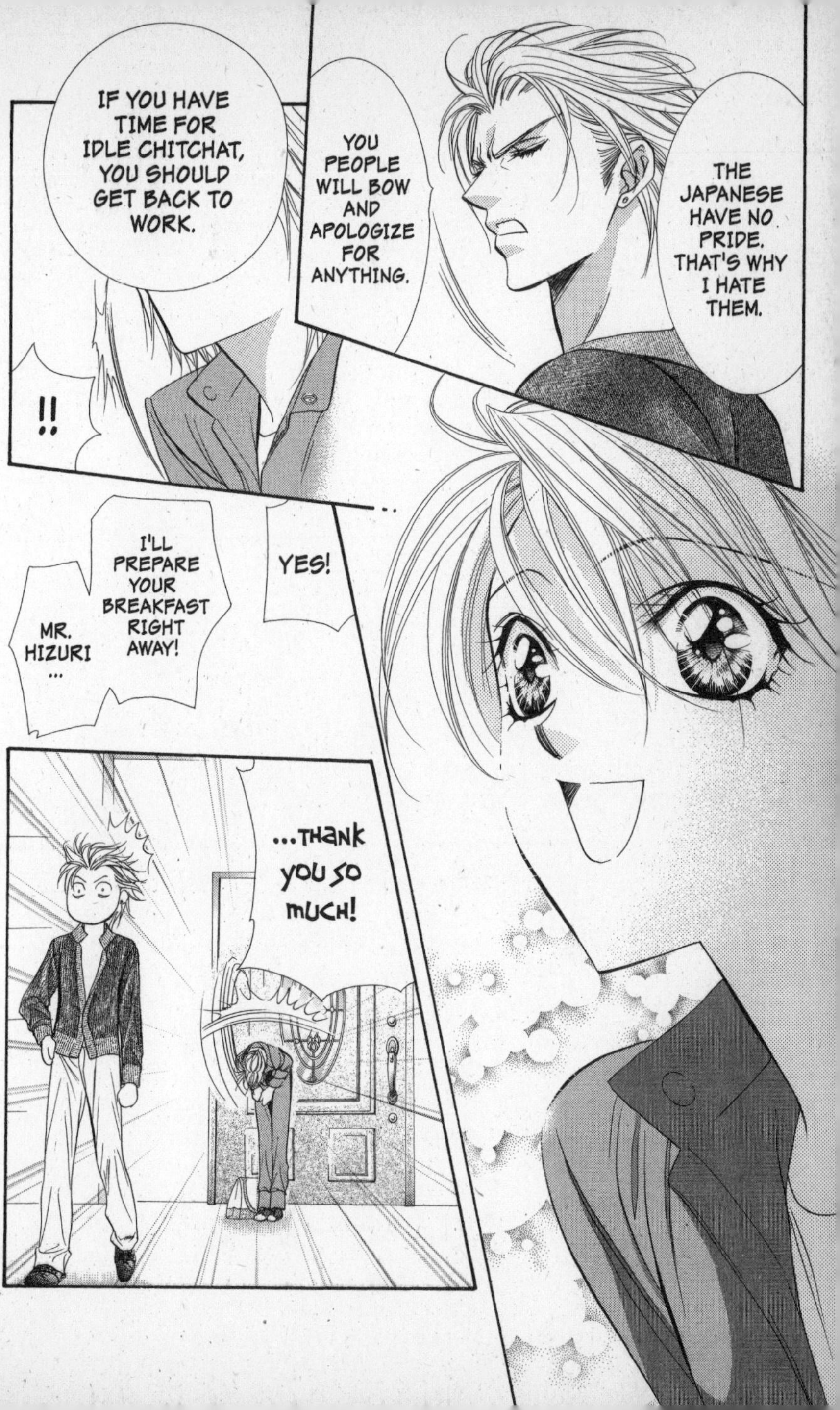
THE JAPANESE HAVE NO PRIDE. THAT'S WHY I HATE THEM.
YOU PEOPLE WILL BOW AND APOLOGIZE FOR ANYTHING.
IF YOU HAVE TIME FOR IDLE CHITCHAT, YOU SHOULD GET BACK TO WORK.
!!
...
YES!
I'LL PREPARE YOUR BREAKFAST RIGHT AWAY!
MR. HIZURI ...
...THANK YOU SO MUCH!

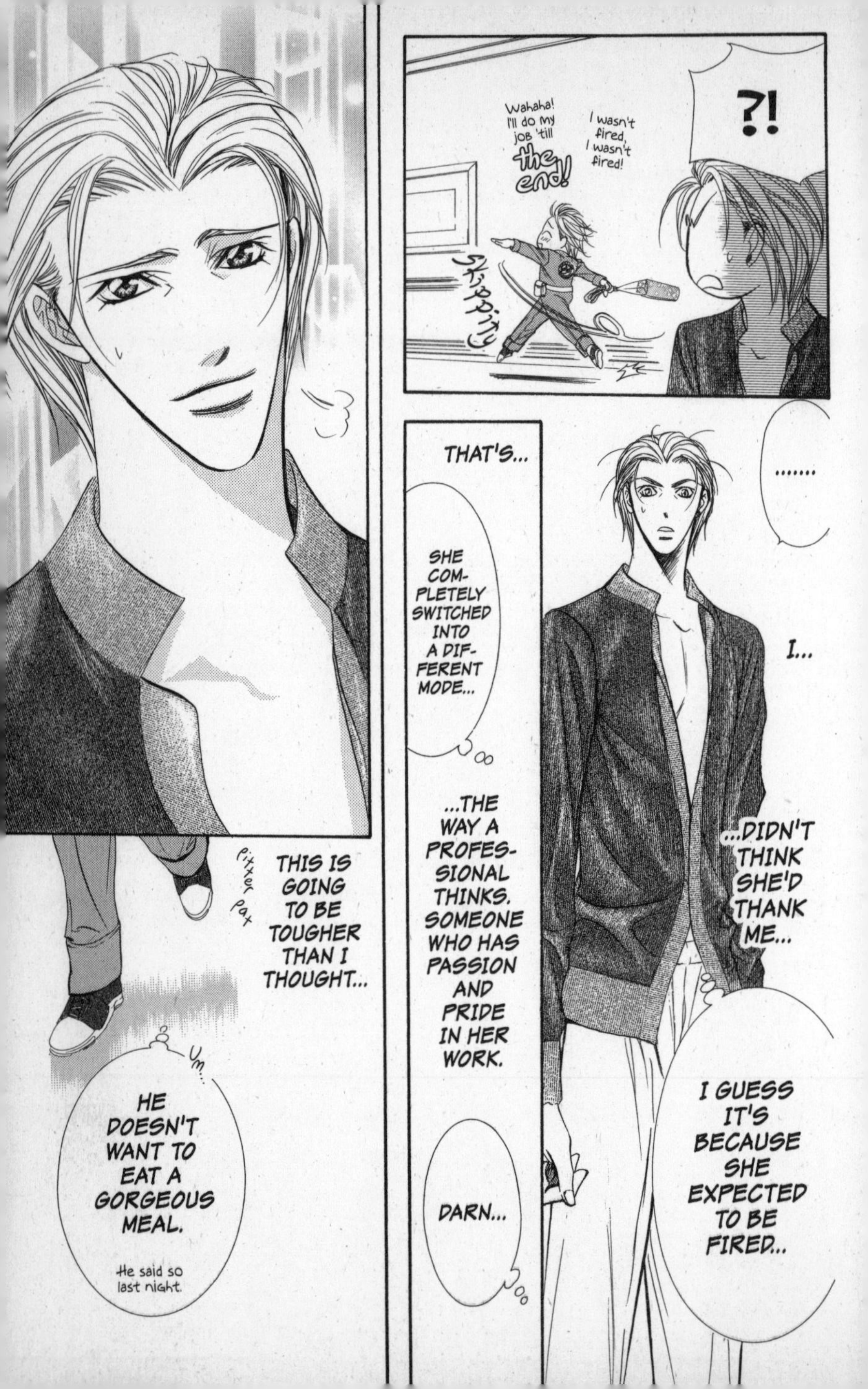
?!
I wasn't fired, I wasn't fired!
Wahaha! I'll do my job 'till the end!
Skippity
....
THAT'S...
I...
...DIDN'T THINK SHE'D THANK ME...
I GUESS IT'S BECAUSE SHE EXPECTED TO BE FIRED...
SHE COMPLETELY SWITCHED INTO A DIFFERENT MODE...
...THE WAY A PROFESSIONAL THINKS. SOMEONE WHO HAS PASSION AND PRIDE IN HER WORK.
DARN...
THIS IS GOING TO BE TOUGHER THAN I THOUGHT...
Pitter pat
Um...
HE DOESN'T WANT TO EAT A GORGEOUS MEAL.
He said so last night.

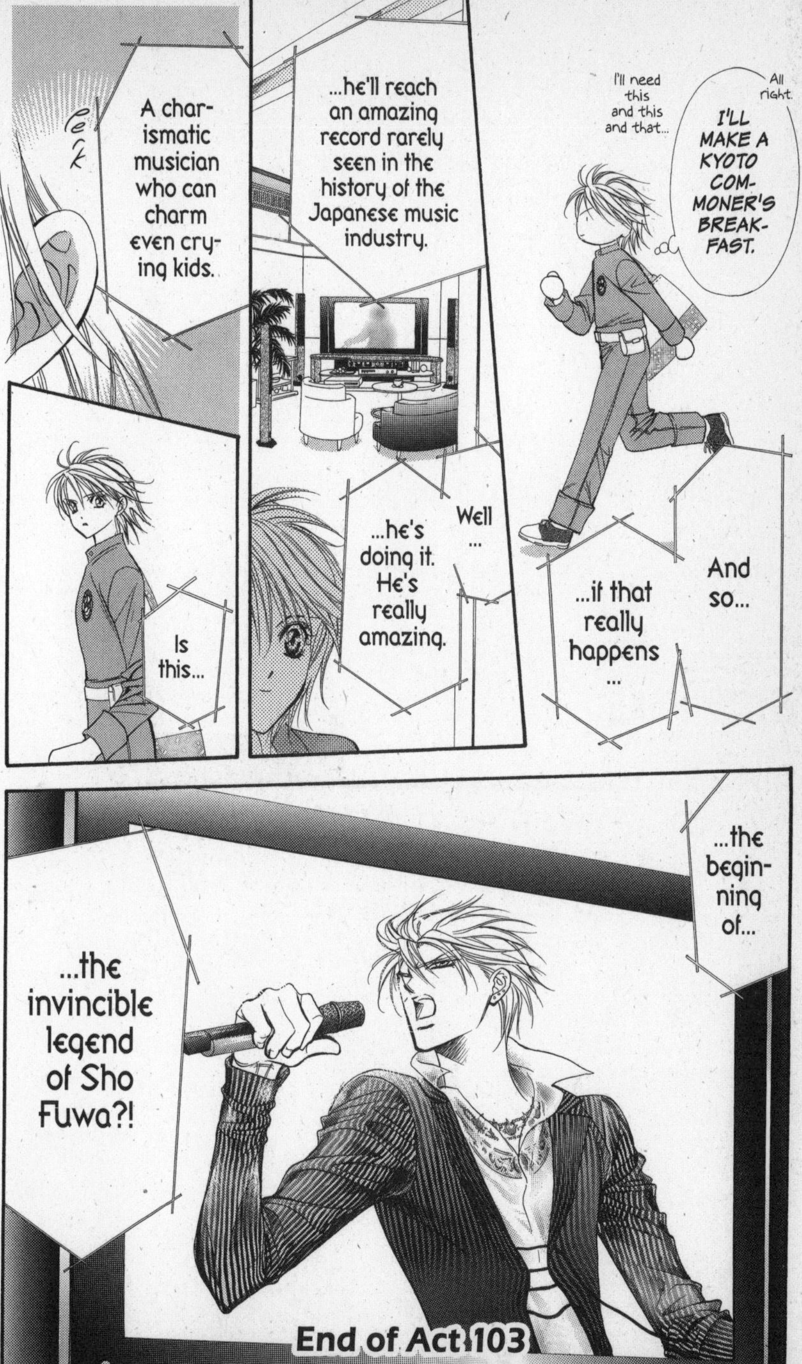
All right.
I'LL MAKE A KYOTO COMMONER'S BREAKFAST.
I'll need this and this and that...
And so...
...if that really happens...
...he'll reach an amazing record rarely seen in the history of the Japanese music industry.
Perk
A charismatic musician who can charm even crying kids.
Well...
...he's doing it. He's really amazing.
Is this...
...the beginning of...
...the invincible legend of Sho Fuwa?!
End of Act 103

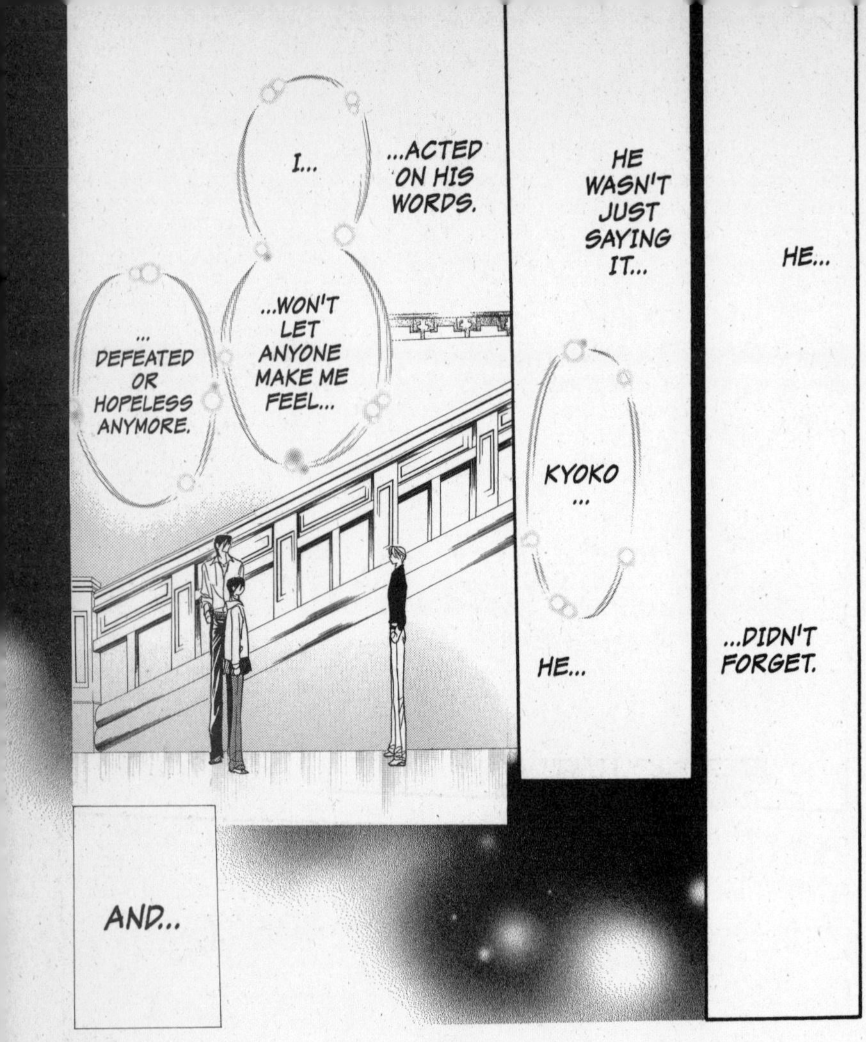
HE...
...DIDN'T FORGET.
HE WASN'T JUST SAYING IT...
KYOKO...
HE...
...ACTED ON HIS WORDS.
I...
...WON'T LET ANYONE MAKE ME FEEL...
...DEFEATED OR HOPELESS ANYMORE.
AND...

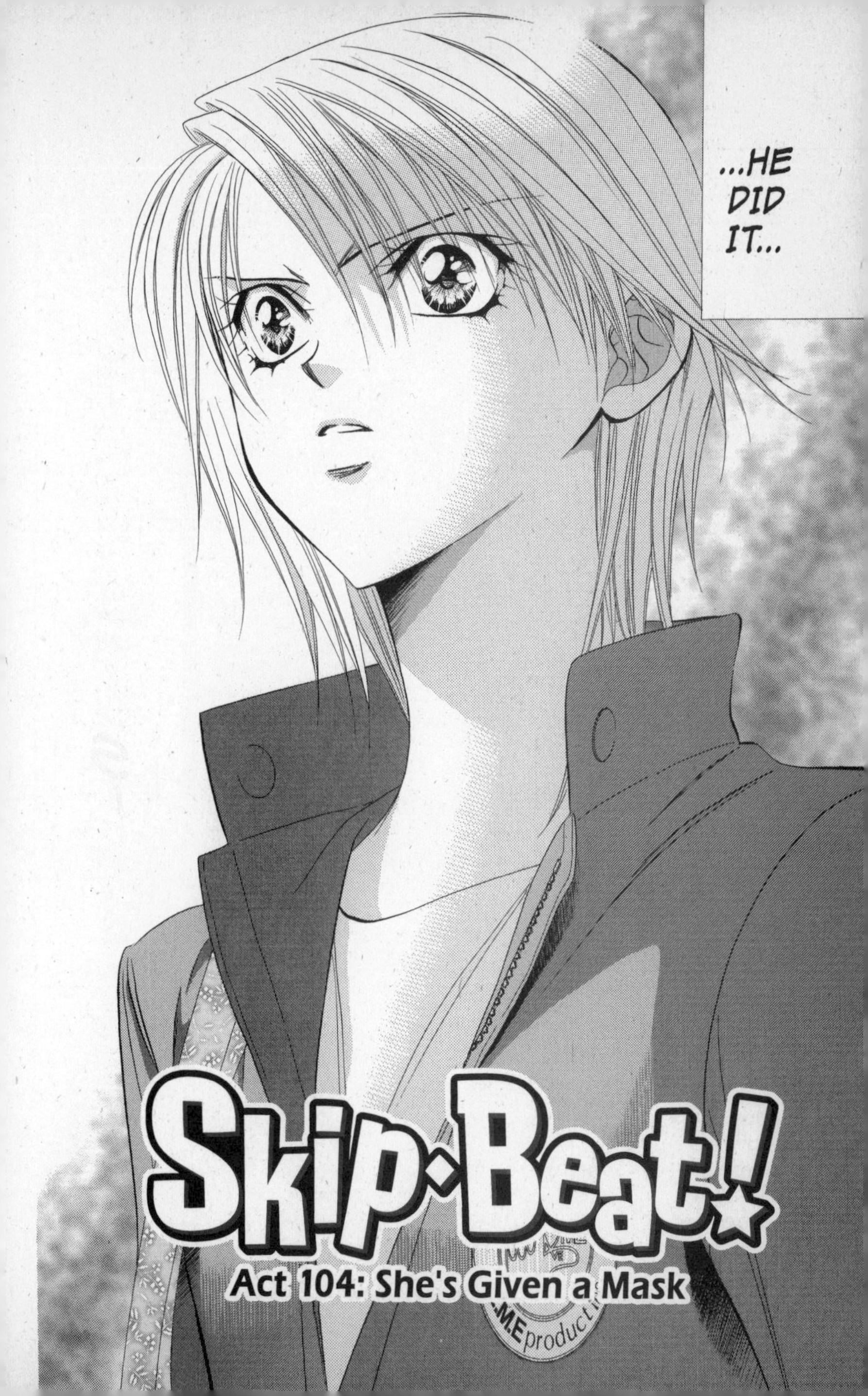
...HE DID IT...
Skip·Beat!
Act 104: She's Given a Mask
L.M.E product

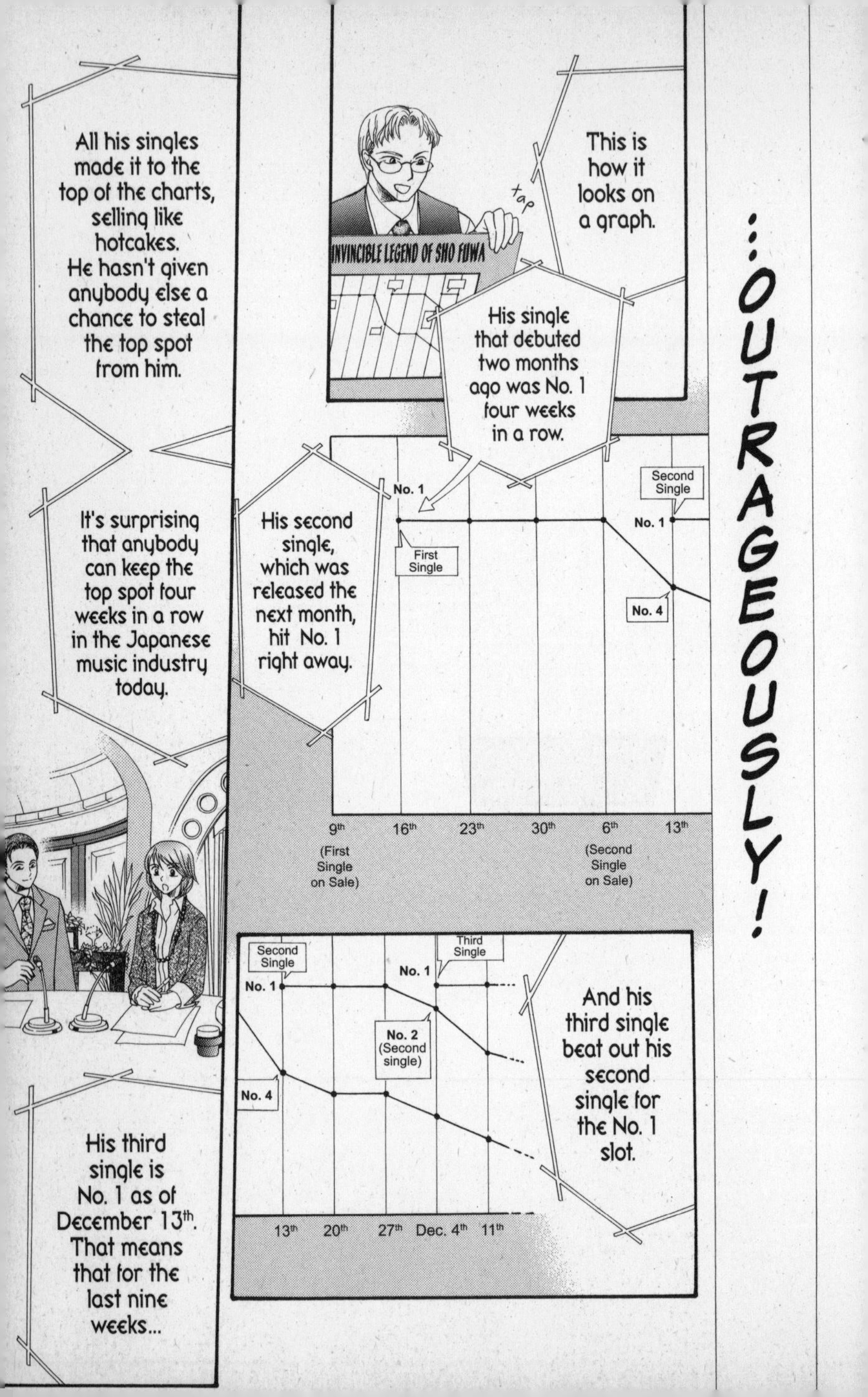
All his singles made it to the top of the charts, selling like hotcakes. He hasn't given anybody else a chance to steal the top spot from him.
xap
INVINCIBLE LEGEND OF SHO FUWA
This is how it looks on a graph.
His single that debuted two months ago was No. 1 four weeks in a row.
No. 1
First Single
Second Single
No. 1
No. 4
9th (First Single on Sale)
16th
23rd
30th
6th (Second Single on Sale)
13th
His second single, which was released the next month, hit No. 1 right away.
It's surprising that anybody can keep the top spot four weeks in a row in the Japanese music industry today.
Second Single
No. 1
Third Single
No. 1
No. 2 (Second single)
No. 4
13th
20th
27th
Dec. 4th
11th
And his third single beat out his second single for the No. 1 slot.
His third single is No. 1 as of December 13th. That means that for the last nine weeks...
...OUTRAGEOUSLY!

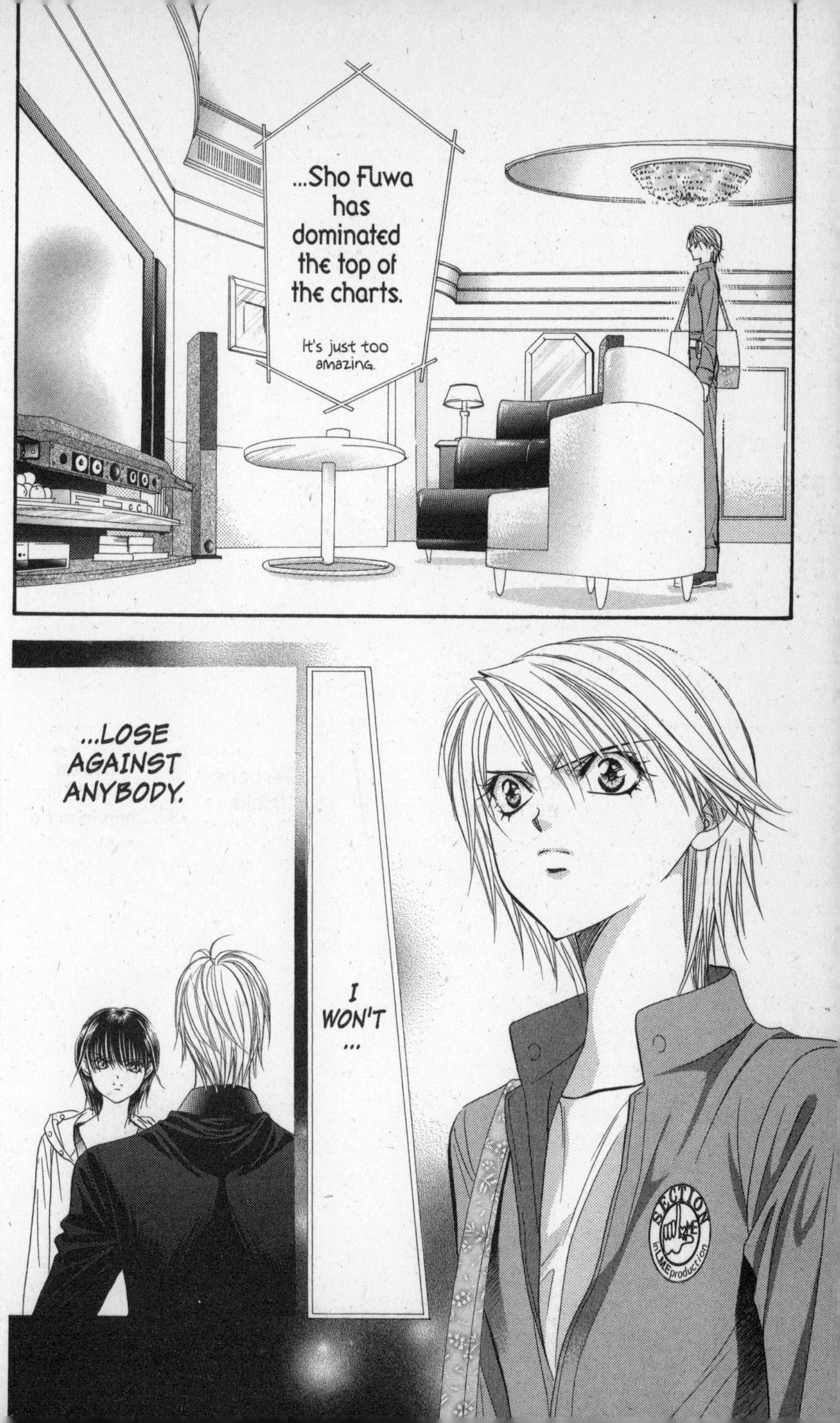
...Sho Fuwa has dominated the top of the charts.
It's just too amazing.
I WON'T ...
...LOSE AGAINST ANYBODY.
SECTION
inLMEproduction

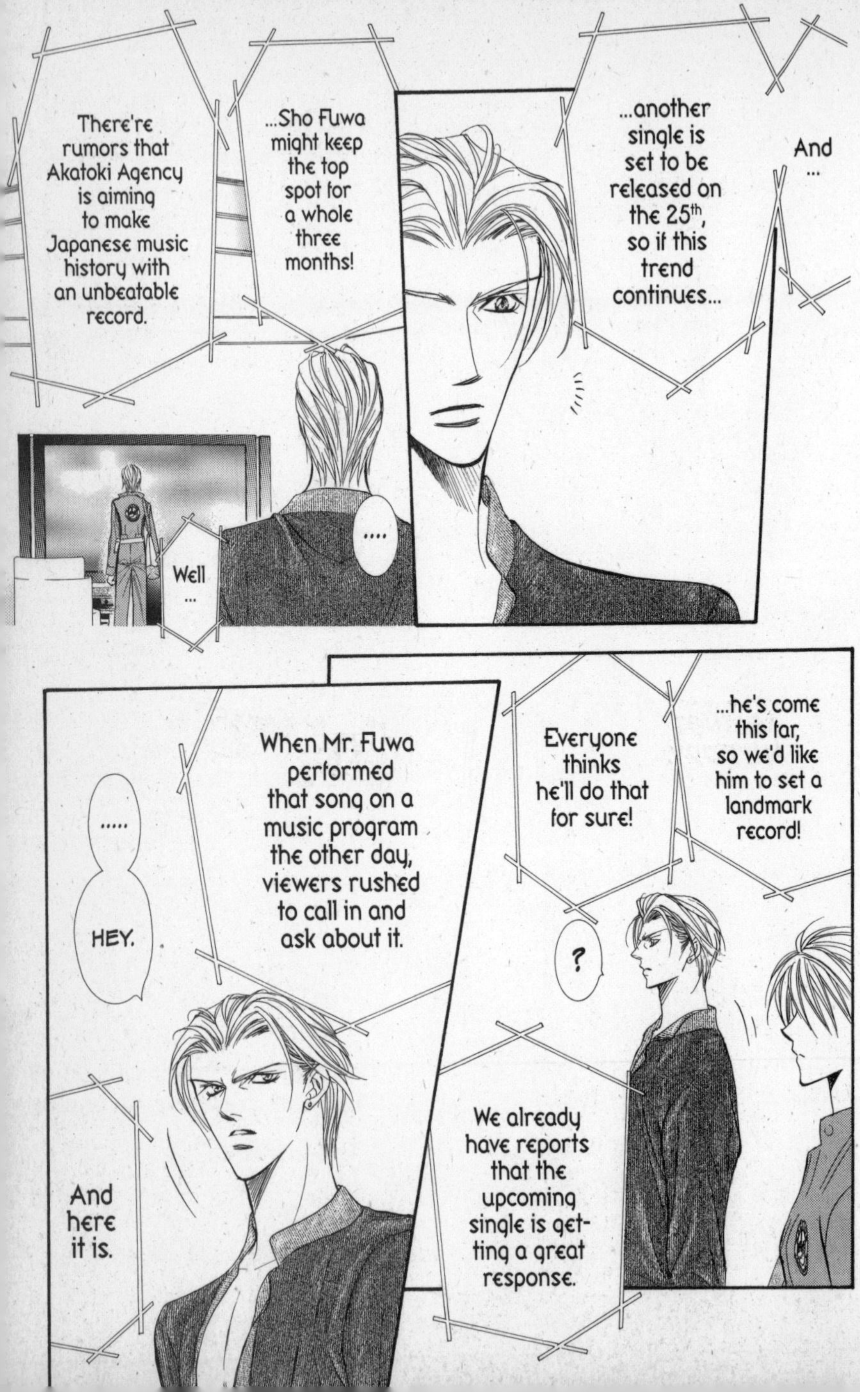

And ...
...another single is set to be released on the 25th, so if this trend continues...
...Sho Fuwa might keep the top spot for a whole three months!
There're rumors that Akatoki Agency is aiming to make Japanese music history with an unbeatable record.
....
Well ...
...he's come this far, so we'd like him to set a landmark record!
Everyone thinks he'll do that for sure!
?
We already have reports that the upcoming single is getting a great response.
When Mr. Fuwa performed that song on a music program the other day, viewers rushed to call in and ask about it.
.....
HEY.
And here it is.

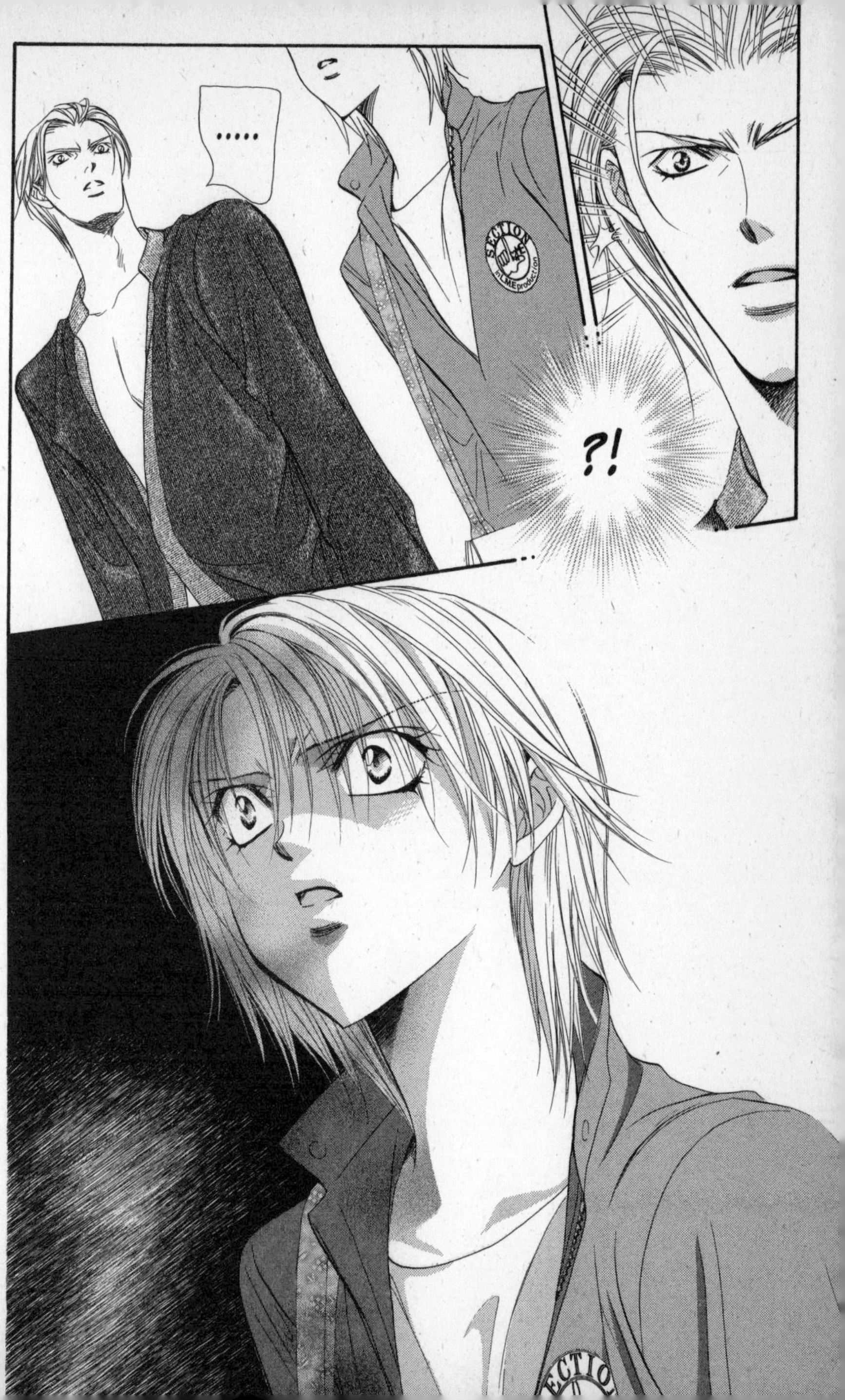
?!
.....

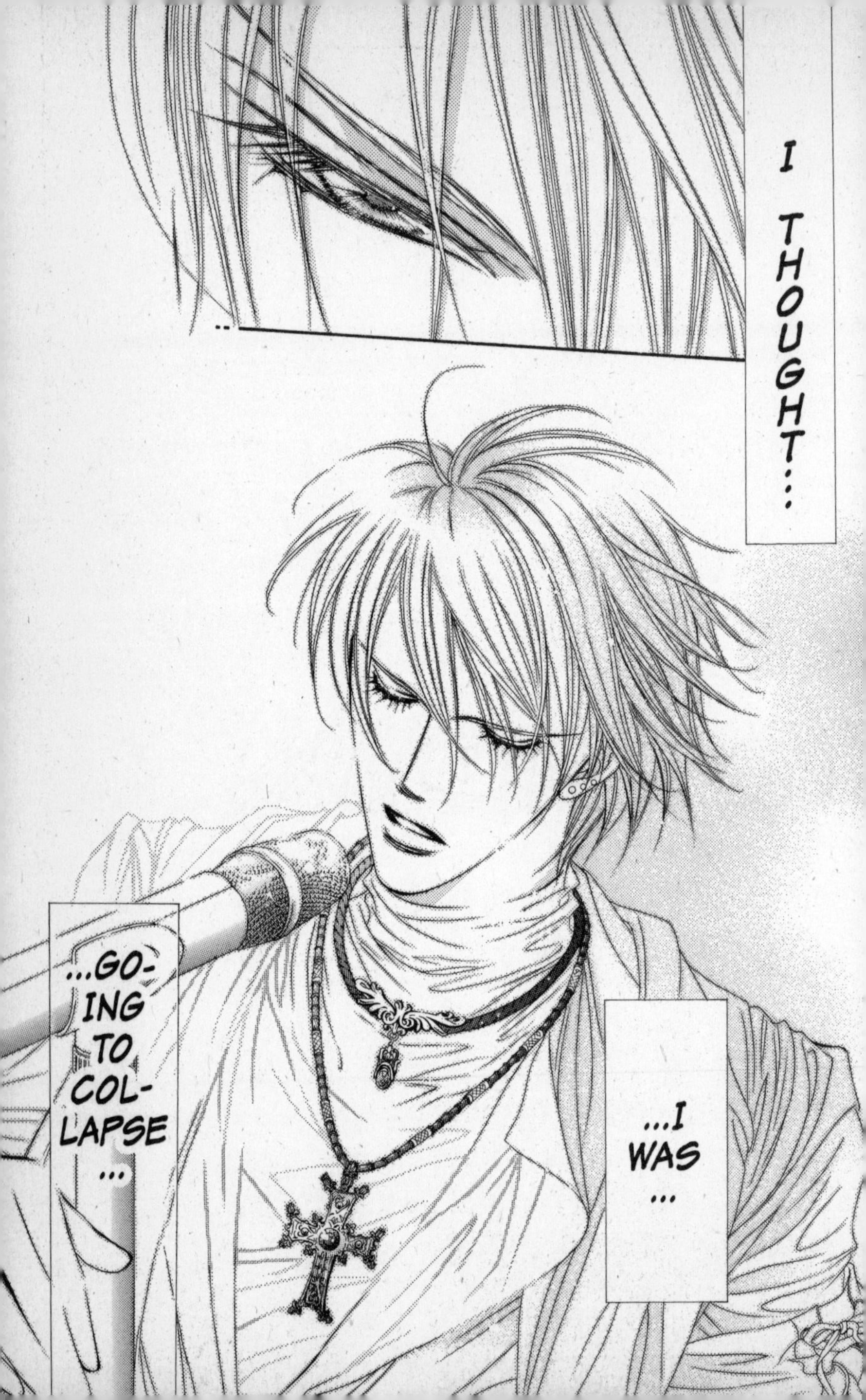
I THOUGHT...
...I WAS...
...GO-ING TO COL-LAPSE...

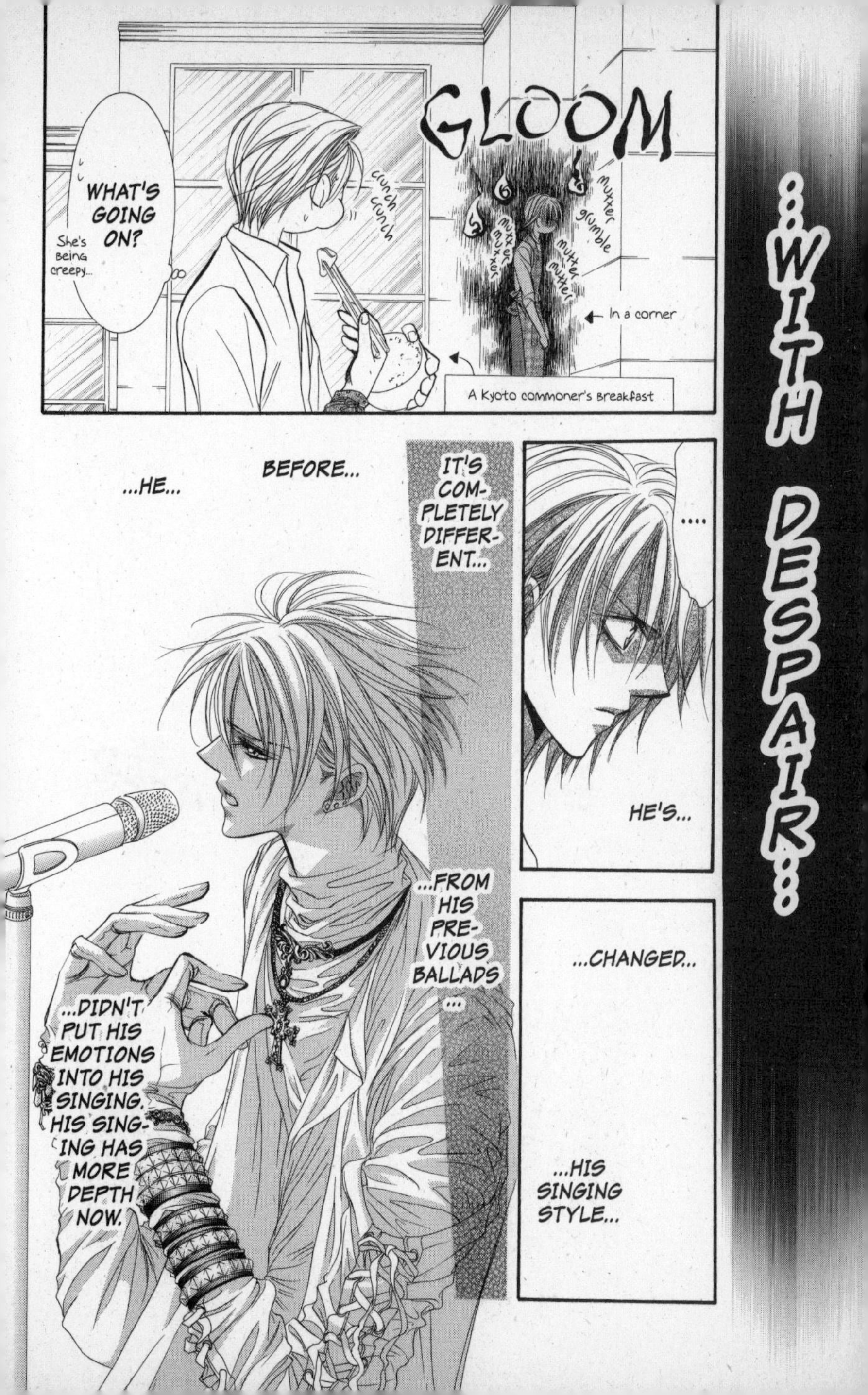
GLOOM
mutter grumble
mutter mutter
mutter mutter
In a corner
crunch crunch
WHAT'S GOING ON?
She's being creepy...
A Kyoto commoner's breakfast
....
HE'S...
...CHANGED...
...HIS SINGING STYLE...
...WITH DESPAIR...
IT'S COMPLETELY DIFFERENT...
...FROM HIS PREVIOUS BALLADS...
BEFORE...
...HE...
...DIDN'T PUT HIS EMOTIONS INTO HIS SINGING. HIS SINGING HAS MORE DEPTH NOW.

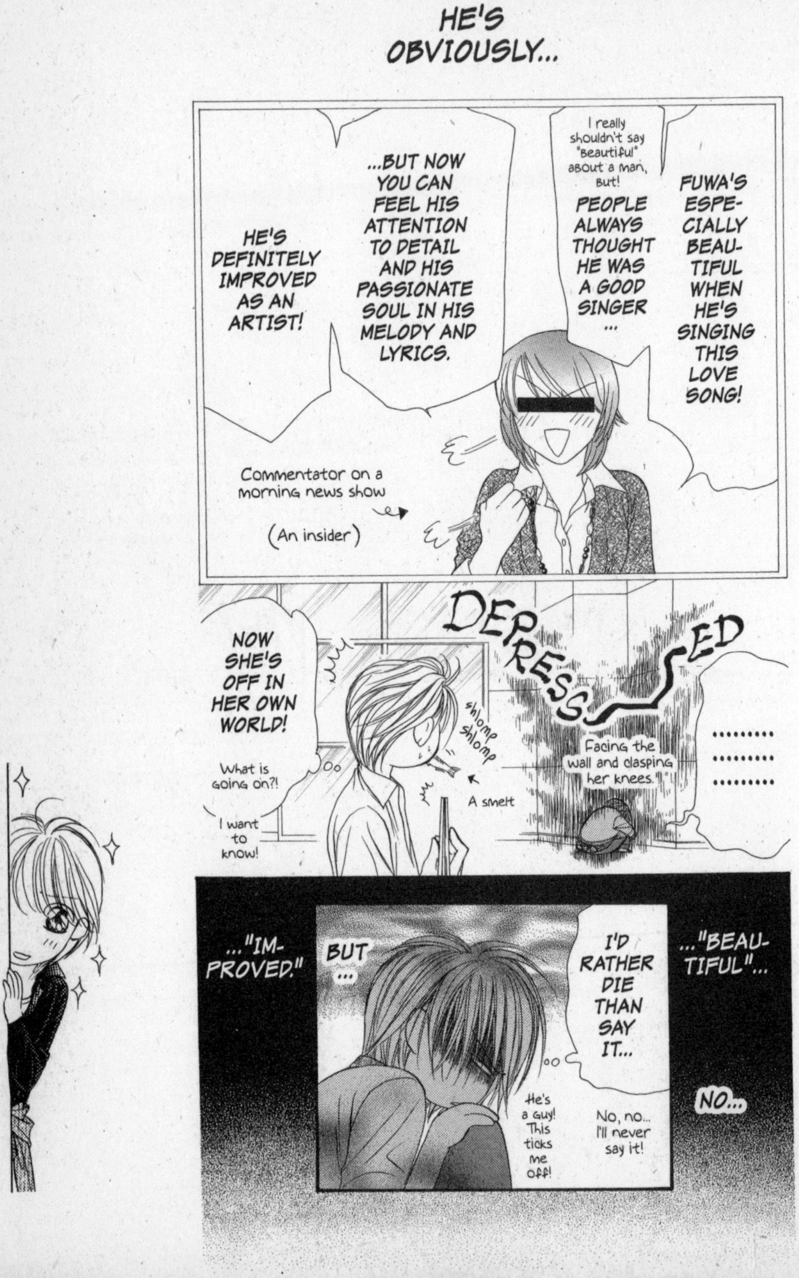
HE'S OBVIOUSLY...
FUWA'S ESPECIALLY BEAUTIFUL WHEN HE'S SINGING THIS LOVE SONG!
I really shouldn't say "Beautiful" about a man, but!
PEOPLE ALWAYS THOUGHT HE WAS A GOOD SINGER...
...BUT NOW YOU CAN FEEL HIS ATTENTION TO DETAIL AND HIS PASSIONATE SOUL IN HIS MELODY AND LYRICS.
HE'S DEFINITELY IMPROVED AS AN ARTIST!
Commentator on a morning news show
(An insider)
DEPRESSED
....
....
....
Facing the wall and clasping her knees.
A smelt
shlomp shlomp
NOW SHE'S OFF IN HER OWN WORLD!
What is going on?!
I want to know!
..."BEAUTIFUL"...
NO...
I'D RATHER DIE THAN SAY IT...
No, no... I'll never say it!
He's a guy! This ticks me off!
BUT...
..."IMPROVED."

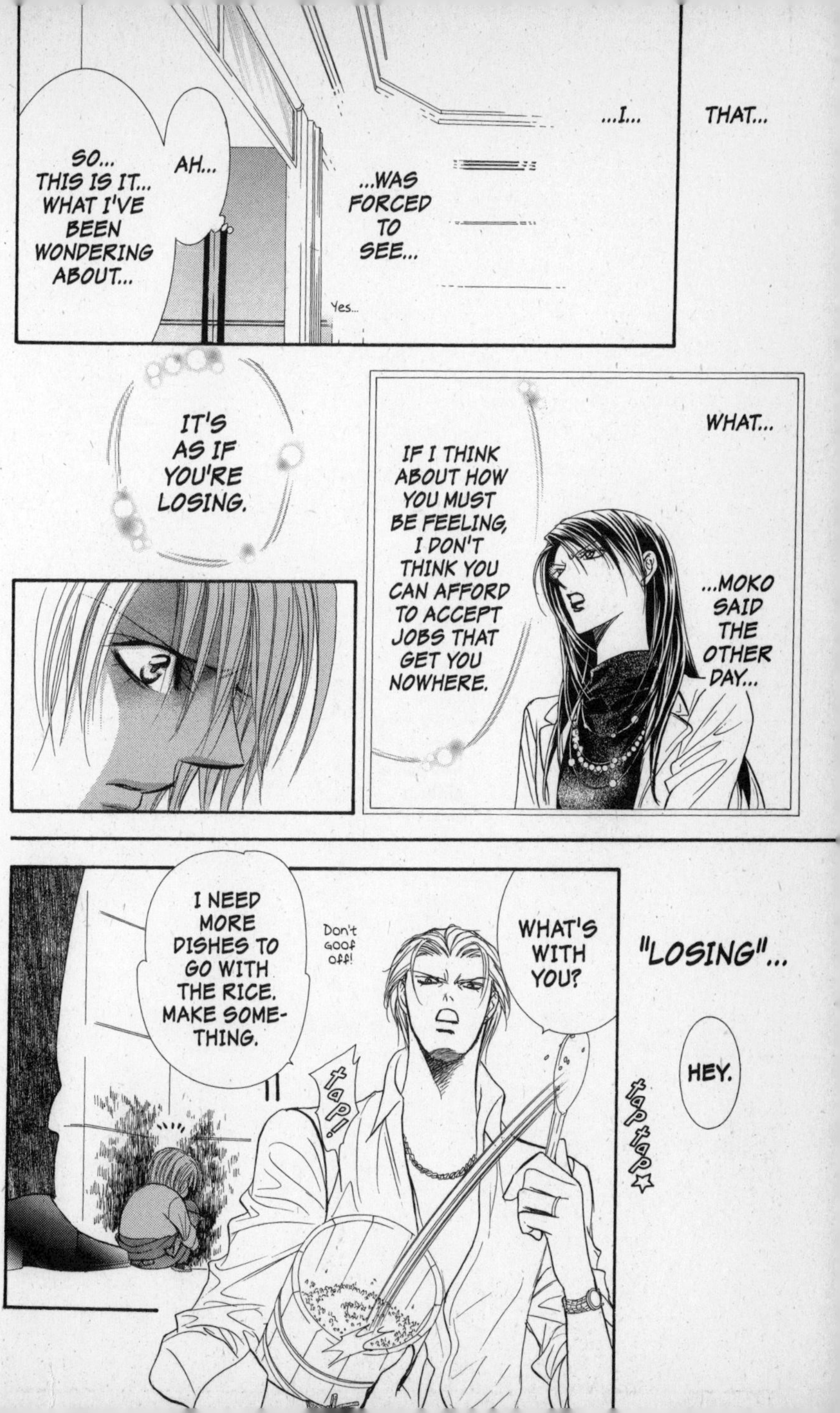
THAT...
...I...
...WAS FORCED TO SEE...
Yes...
AH...
SO... THIS IS IT... WHAT I'VE BEEN WONDERING ABOUT...
WHAT...
...MOKO SAID THE OTHER DAY...
IF I THINK ABOUT HOW YOU MUST BE FEELING, I DON'T THINK YOU CAN AFFORD TO ACCEPT JOBS THAT GET YOU NOWHERE.
IT'S AS IF YOU'RE LOSING.
"LOSING"...
HEY.
tap tap☆
WHAT'S WITH YOU?
tap!
Don't goof off!
I NEED MORE DISHES TO GO WITH THE RICE. MAKE SOME-THING.

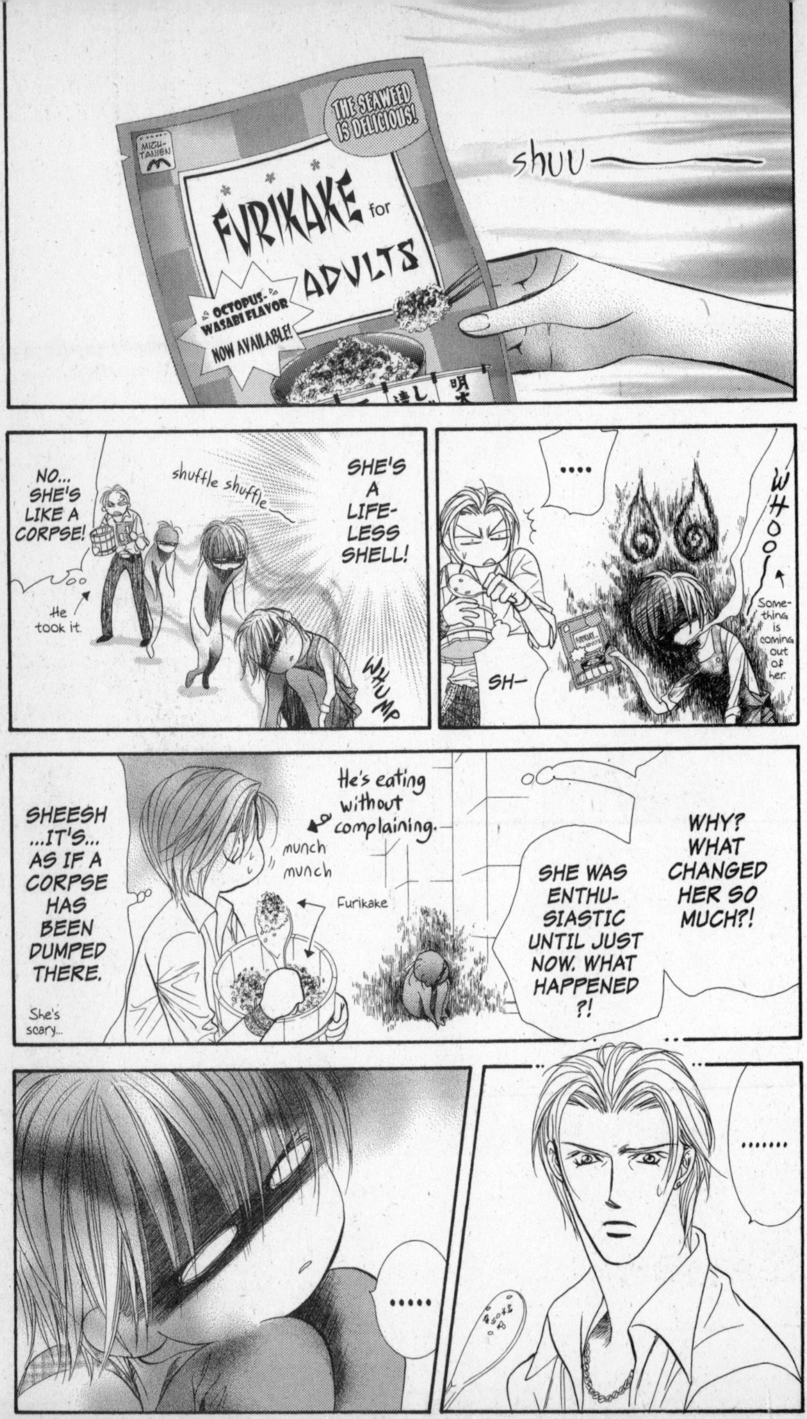
THE SEAWEED IS DELICIOUS!
MIZU-TANIEN
FURIKAKE for ADULTS
OCTOPUS-WASABI FLAVOR NOW AVAILABLE!
SHUU——————
....
WHOOO—
Something is coming out of her.
SH—
SHE'S A LIFELESS SHELL!
shuffle shuffle
NO... SHE'S LIKE A CORPSE!
He took it.
WHUMP
WHY? WHAT CHANGED HER SO MUCH?!
SHE WAS ENTHUSIASTIC UNTIL JUST NOW. WHAT HAPPENED?!
He's eating without complaining.
munch munch
Furikake
SHEESH ...IT'S... AS IF A CORPSE HAS BEEN DUMPED THERE.
She's scary...
......
.....

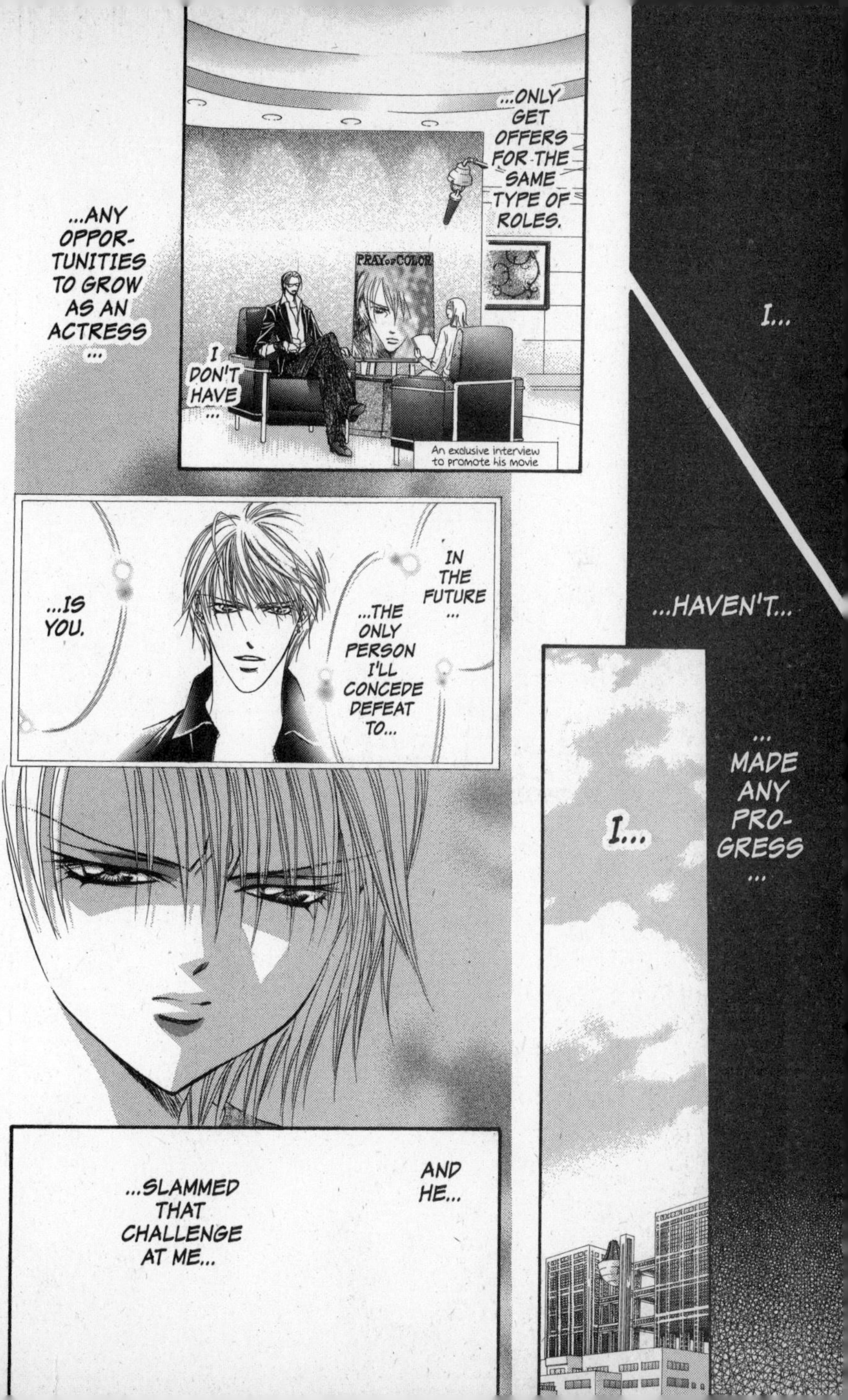
I...
...HAVEN'T...
...MADE ANY PROGRESS...
I...
...ONLY GET OFFERS FOR THE SAME TYPE OF ROLES.
PRAY OF COLOR
I DON'T HAVE...
...ANY OPPORTUNITIES TO GROW AS AN ACTRESS...
An exclusive interview to promote his movie
IN THE FUTURE...
...THE ONLY PERSON I'LL CONCEDE DEFEAT TO...
...IS YOU.
AND HE...
...SLAMMED THAT CHALLENGE AT ME...

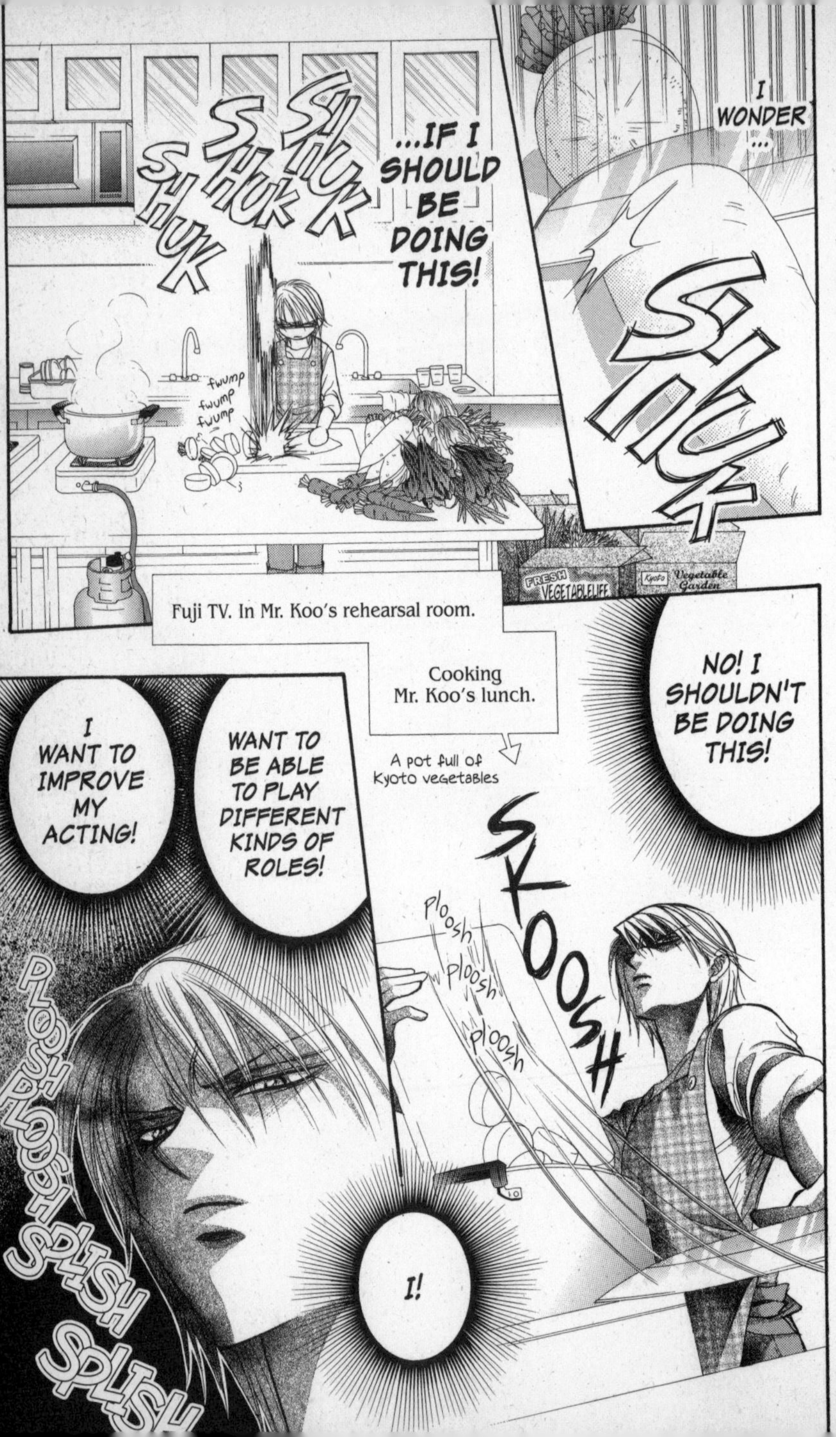
I WONDER...
SHUK
...IF I SHOULD BE DOING THIS!
SHUK SHUK SHUK SHUK
fwump fwump fwump
FRESH VEGETABLELIFE
Kyoto Vegetable Garden
Fuji TV. In Mr. Koo's rehearsal room.
Cooking Mr. Koo's lunch.
NO! I SHOULDN'T BE DOING THIS!
A pot full of Kyoto vegetables
SKOOSH
ploosh ploosh ploosh
I!
I WANT TO IMPROVE MY ACTING!
WANT TO BE ABLE TO PLAY DIFFERENT KINDS OF ROLES!
PLOSH PLOSH SPLISH SPLISH

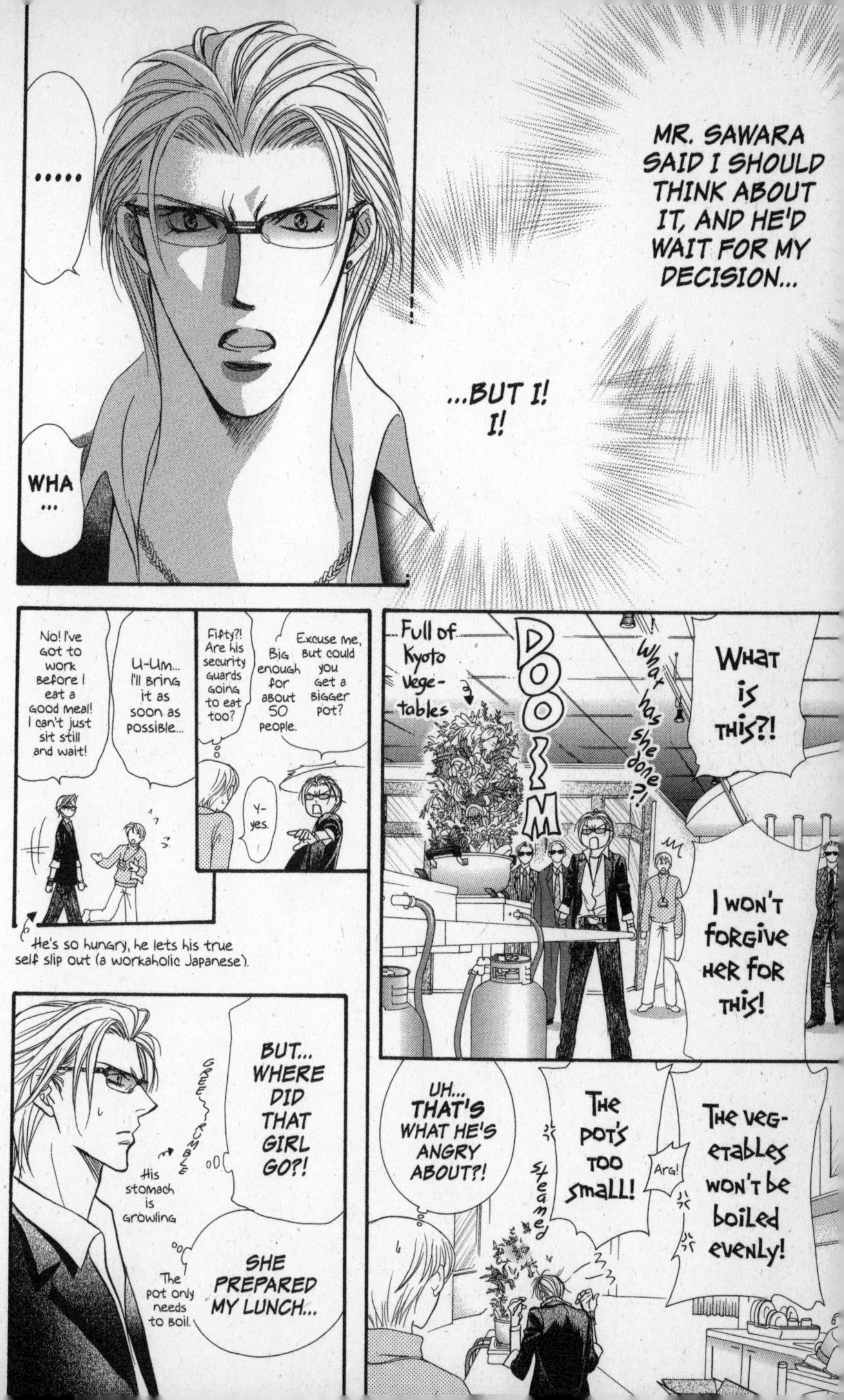
MR. SAWARA SAID I SHOULD THINK ABOUT IT, AND HE'D WAIT FOR MY DECISION...
...BUT I! I!
.....
WHA ...
WHAT is THIS?!
What has she done?!
DOOOM
Full of Kyoto vege-tables
I WON'T FORGIVE HER FOR THIS!
Excuse me, but could you get a bigger pot?
Big enough for about 50 people.
Fifty?! Are his security guards going to eat too?
Y-yes.
U-Um... I'll bring it as soon as possible...
No! I've got to work before I eat a good meal! I can't just sit still and wait!
He's so hungry, he lets his true self slip out (a workaholic Japanese).
The veg-etables won't be boiled evenly!
The pot's too small!
Arg!
Steamed
UH... THAT'S WHAT HE'S ANGRY ABOUT?!
BUT... WHERE DID THAT GIRL GO?!
GREE RUMBLE
His stomach is growling
SHE PREPARED MY LUNCH...
The pot only needs to boil.

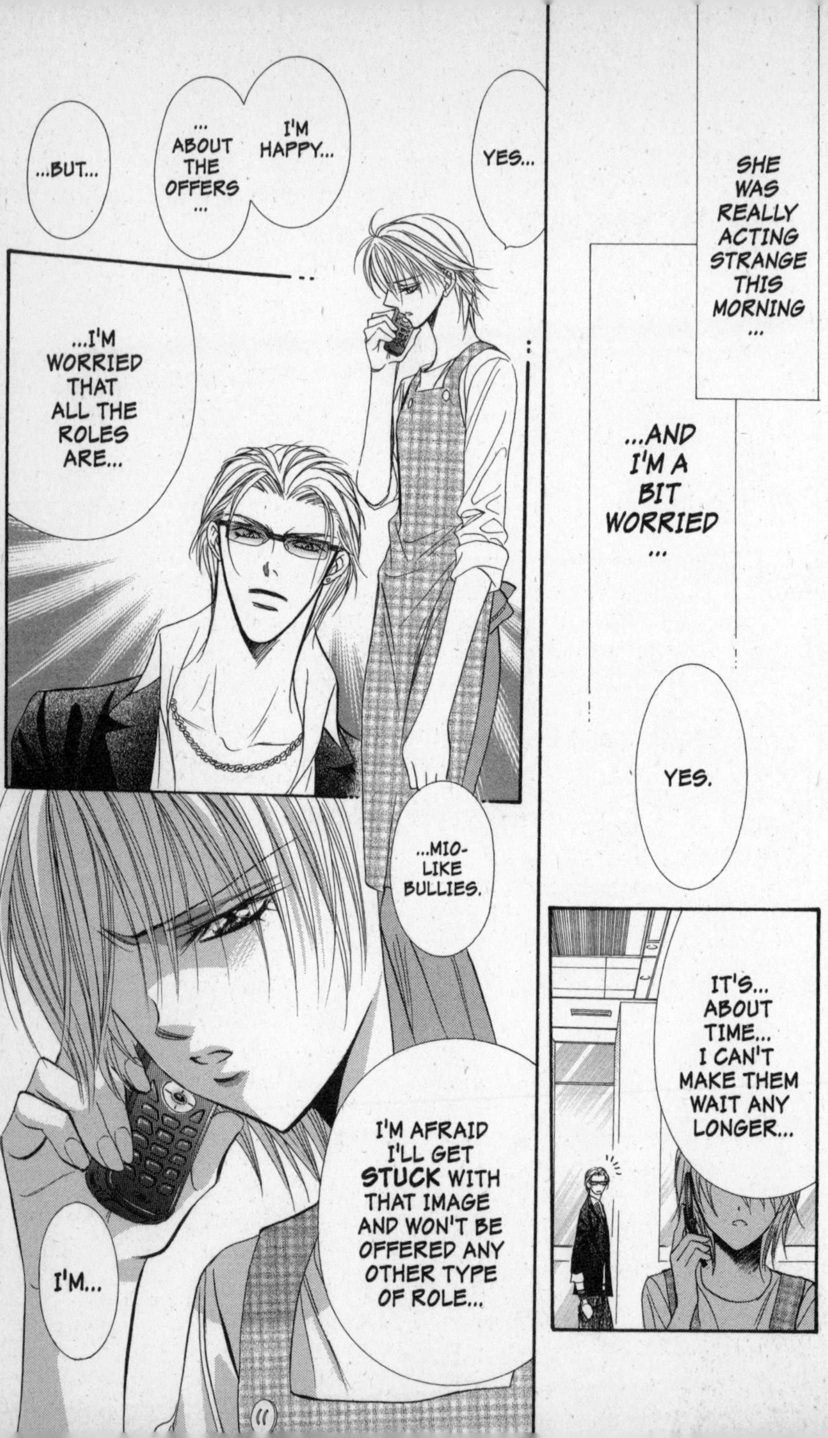
SHE WAS REALLY ACTING STRANGE THIS MORNING...
...AND I'M A BIT WORRIED...
YES.
IT'S... ABOUT TIME... I CAN'T MAKE THEM WAIT ANY LONGER...
YES...
I'M HAPPY...
...ABOUT THE OFFERS...
...BUT...
...I'M WORRIED THAT ALL THE ROLES ARE...
...MIO-LIKE BULLIES.
I'M AFRAID I'LL GET STUCK WITH THAT IMAGE AND WON'T BE OFFERED ANY OTHER TYPE OF ROLE...
I'M...

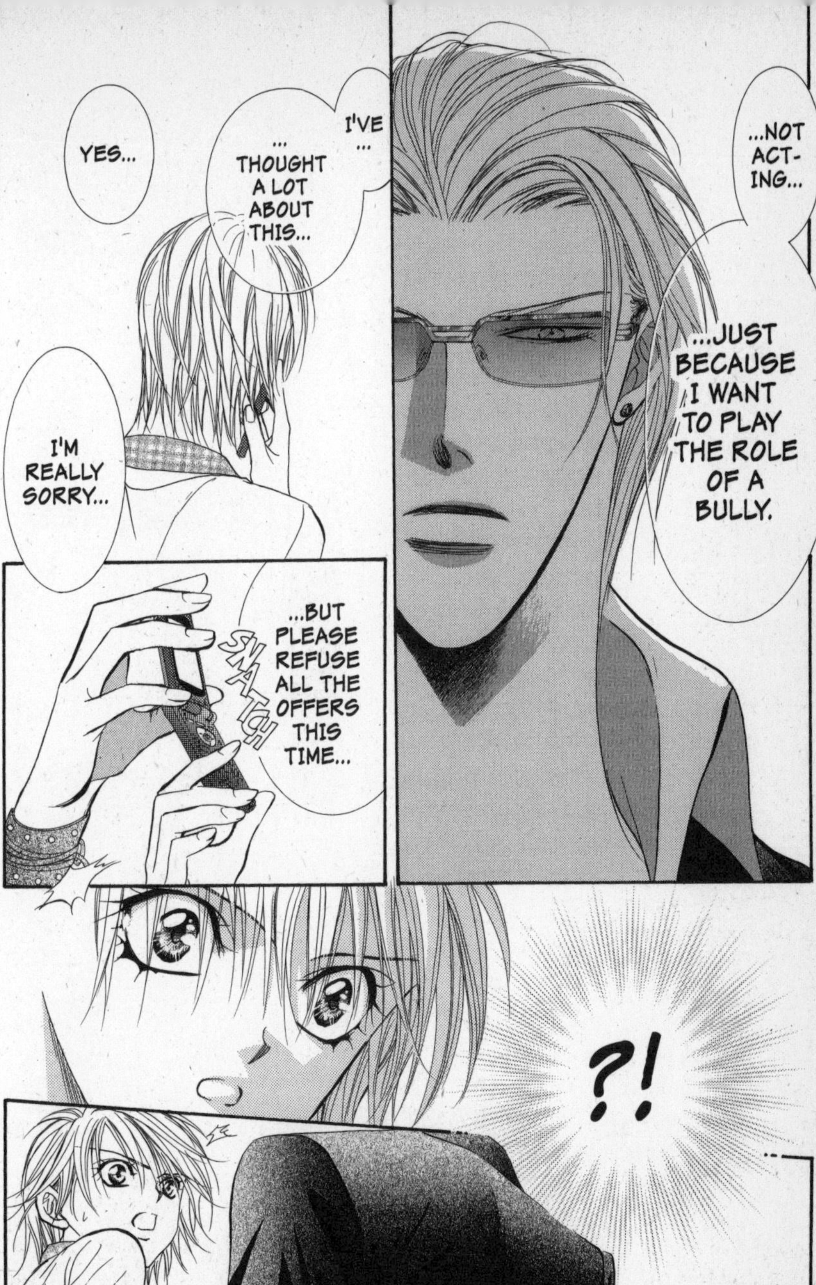
...NOT ACTING...
...JUST BECAUSE I WANT TO PLAY THE ROLE OF A BULLY.
I'VE ... ... THOUGHT A LOT ABOUT THIS...
YES...
I'M REALLY SORRY...
...BUT PLEASE REFUSE ALL THE OFFERS THIS TIME...
SNATCH
?!

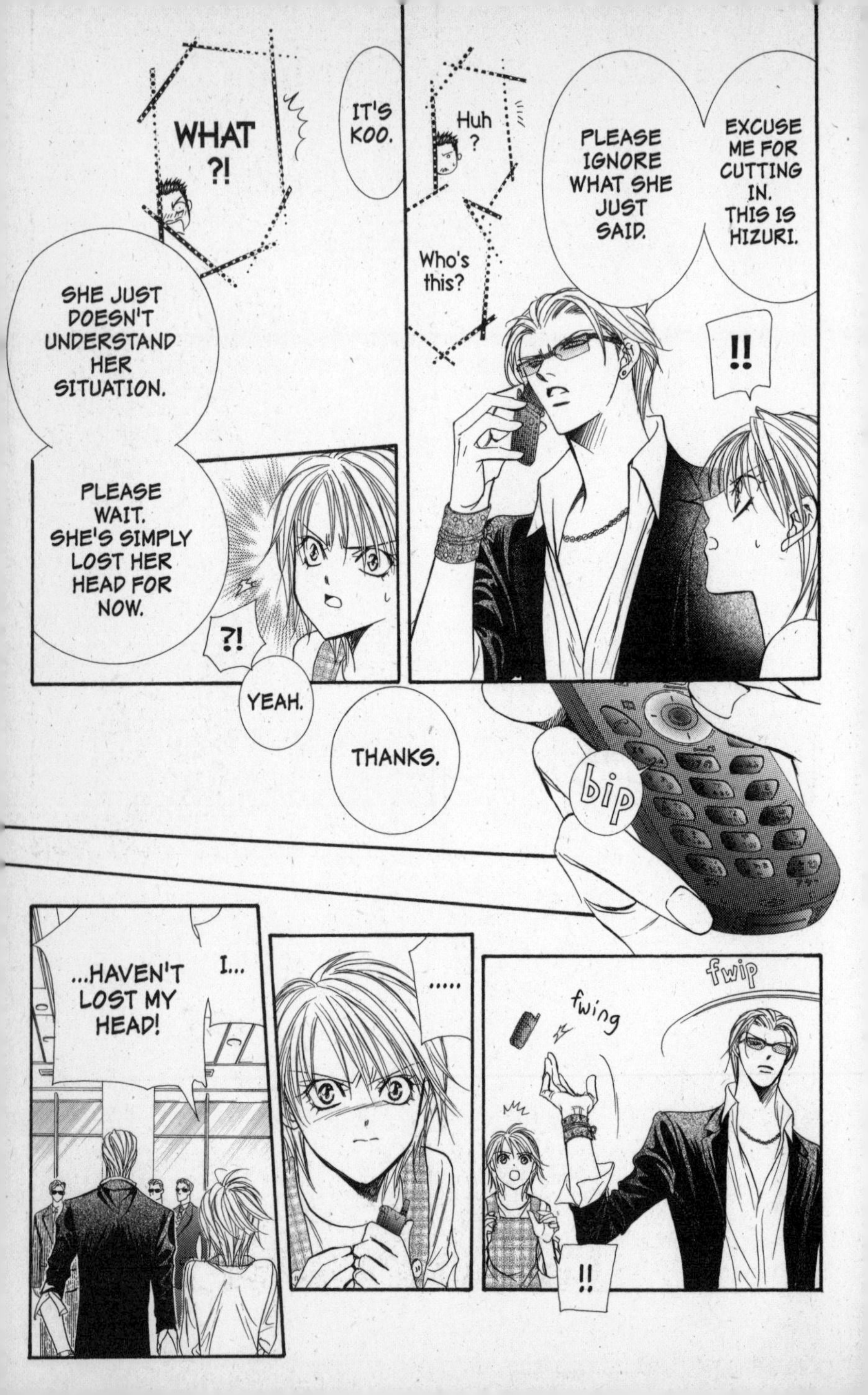
EXCUSE ME FOR CUTTING IN. THIS IS HIZURI.
PLEASE IGNORE WHAT SHE JUST SAID.
Huh ?
Who's this?
!!
IT'S KOO.
WHAT ?!
SHE JUST DOESN'T UNDERSTAND HER SITUATION.
PLEASE WAIT. SHE'S SIMPLY LOST HER HEAD FOR NOW.
?!
YEAH.
THANKS.
bip
fwip
fwing
!!
.....
I...
...HAVEN'T LOST MY HEAD!

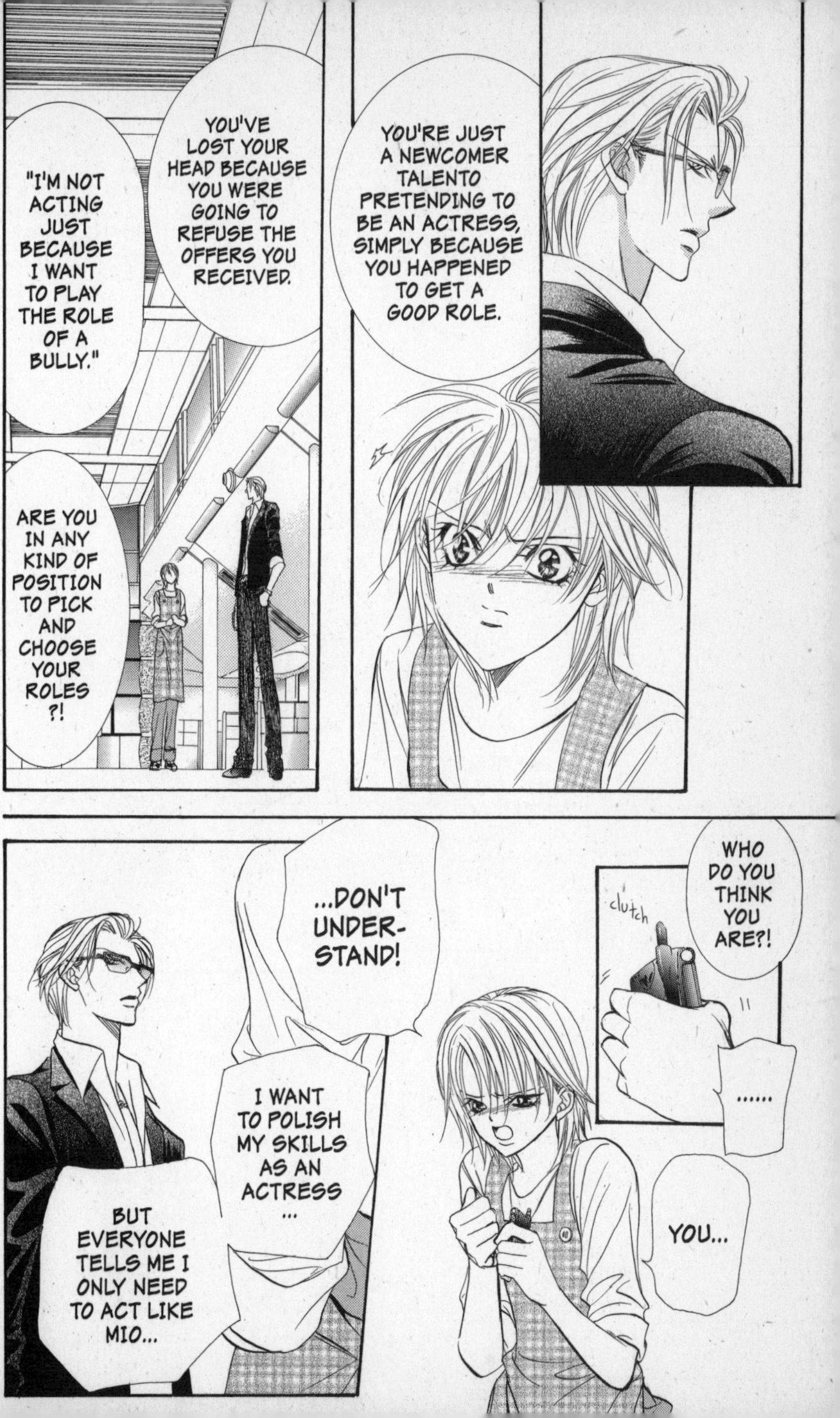
YOU'RE JUST A NEWCOMER TALENTO PRETENDING TO BE AN ACTRESS, SIMPLY BECAUSE YOU HAPPENED TO GET A GOOD ROLE.
YOU'VE LOST YOUR HEAD BECAUSE YOU WERE GOING TO REFUSE THE OFFERS YOU RECEIVED.
"I'M NOT ACTING JUST BECAUSE I WANT TO PLAY THE ROLE OF A BULLY."
ARE YOU IN ANY KIND OF POSITION TO PICK AND CHOOSE YOUR ROLES ?!
WHO DO YOU THINK YOU ARE?!
clutch
......
YOU...
...DON'T UNDER-STAND!
I WANT TO POLISH MY SKILLS AS AN ACTRESS ...
BUT EVERYONE TELLS ME I ONLY NEED TO ACT LIKE MIO...

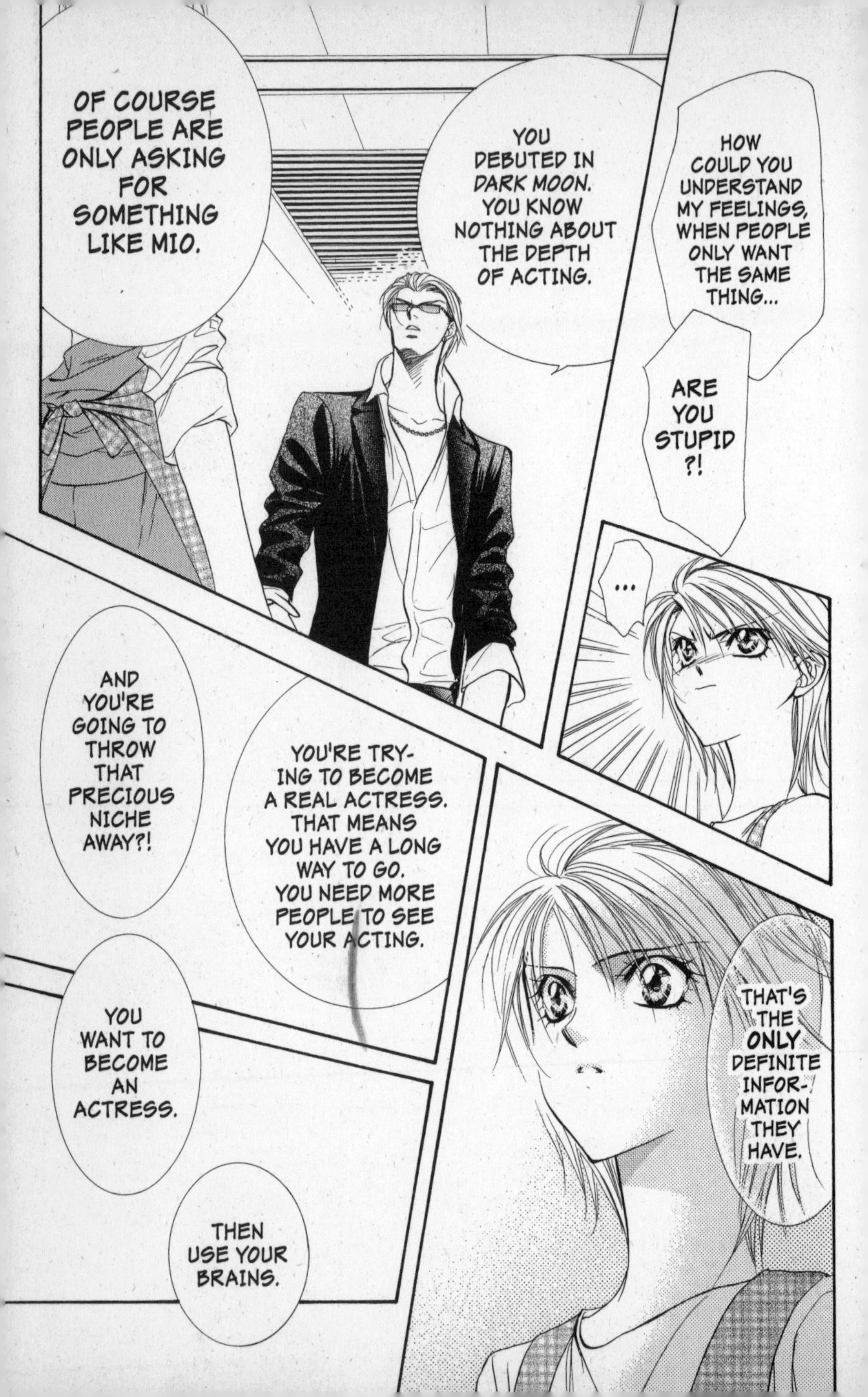
HOW COULD YOU UNDERSTAND MY FEELINGS, WHEN PEOPLE ONLY WANT THE SAME THING...
ARE YOU STUPID ?!
YOU DEBUTED IN DARK MOON. YOU KNOW NOTHING ABOUT THE DEPTH OF ACTING.
OF COURSE PEOPLE ARE ONLY ASKING FOR SOMETHING LIKE MIO.
...
THAT'S THE ONLY DEFINITE INFOR- MATION THEY HAVE.
YOU'RE TRY- ING TO BECOME A REAL ACTRESS. THAT MEANS YOU HAVE A LONG WAY TO GO. YOU NEED MORE PEOPLE TO SEE YOUR ACTING.
AND YOU'RE GOING TO THROW THAT PRECIOUS NICHE AWAY?!
YOU WANT TO BECOME AN ACTRESS.
THEN USE YOUR BRAINS.

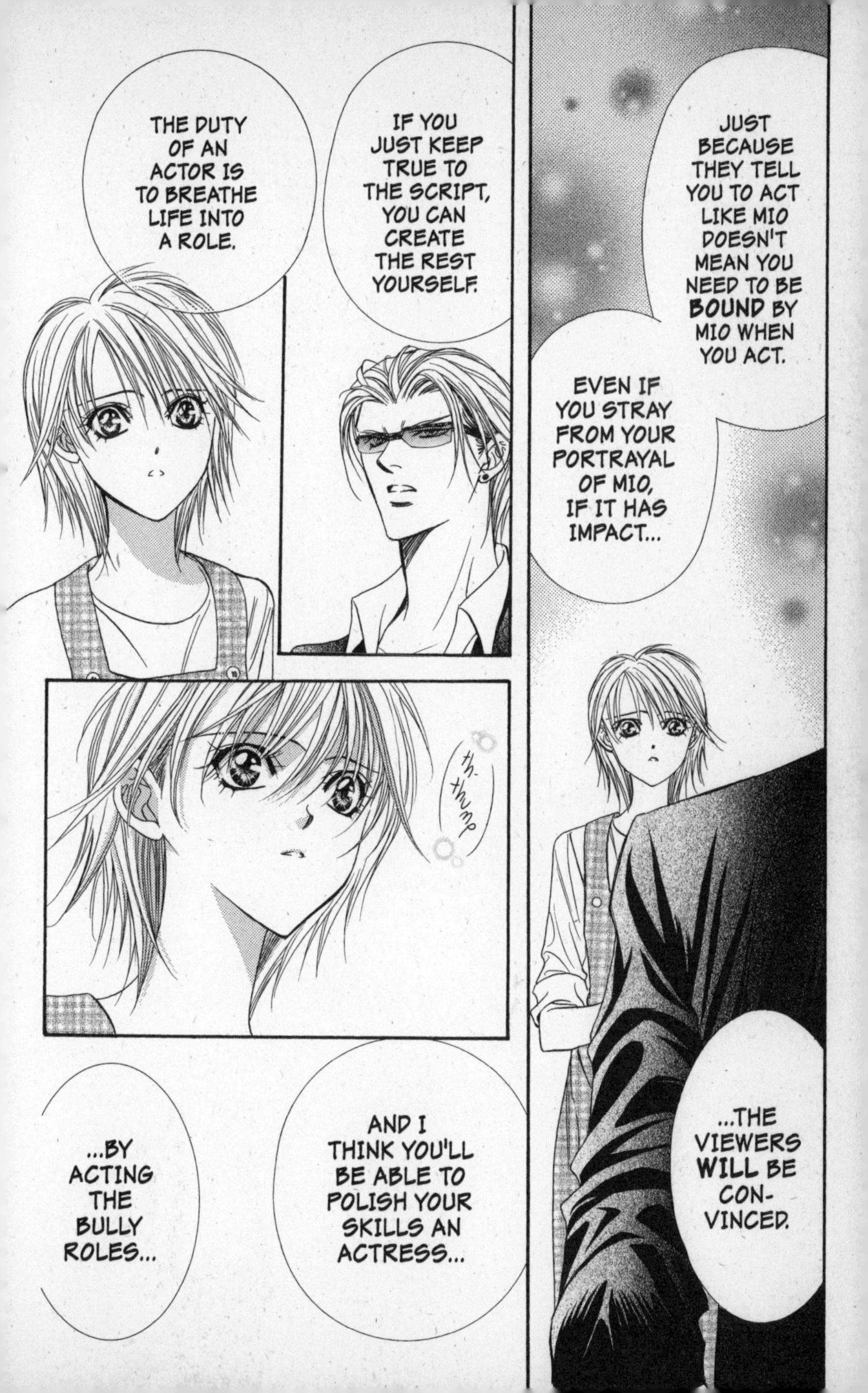
JUST BECAUSE THEY TELL YOU TO ACT LIKE MIO DOESN'T MEAN YOU NEED TO BE BOUND BY MIO WHEN YOU ACT.
EVEN IF YOU STRAY FROM YOUR PORTRAYAL OF MIO, IF IT HAS IMPACT...
...THE VIEWERS WILL BE CON-VINCED.
IF YOU JUST KEEP TRUE TO THE SCRIPT, YOU CAN CREATE THE REST YOURSELF.
THE DUTY OF AN ACTOR IS TO BREATHE LIFE INTO A ROLE.
th-thump
AND I THINK YOU'LL BE ABLE TO POLISH YOUR SKILLS AN ACTRESS...
...BY ACTING THE BULLY ROLES...

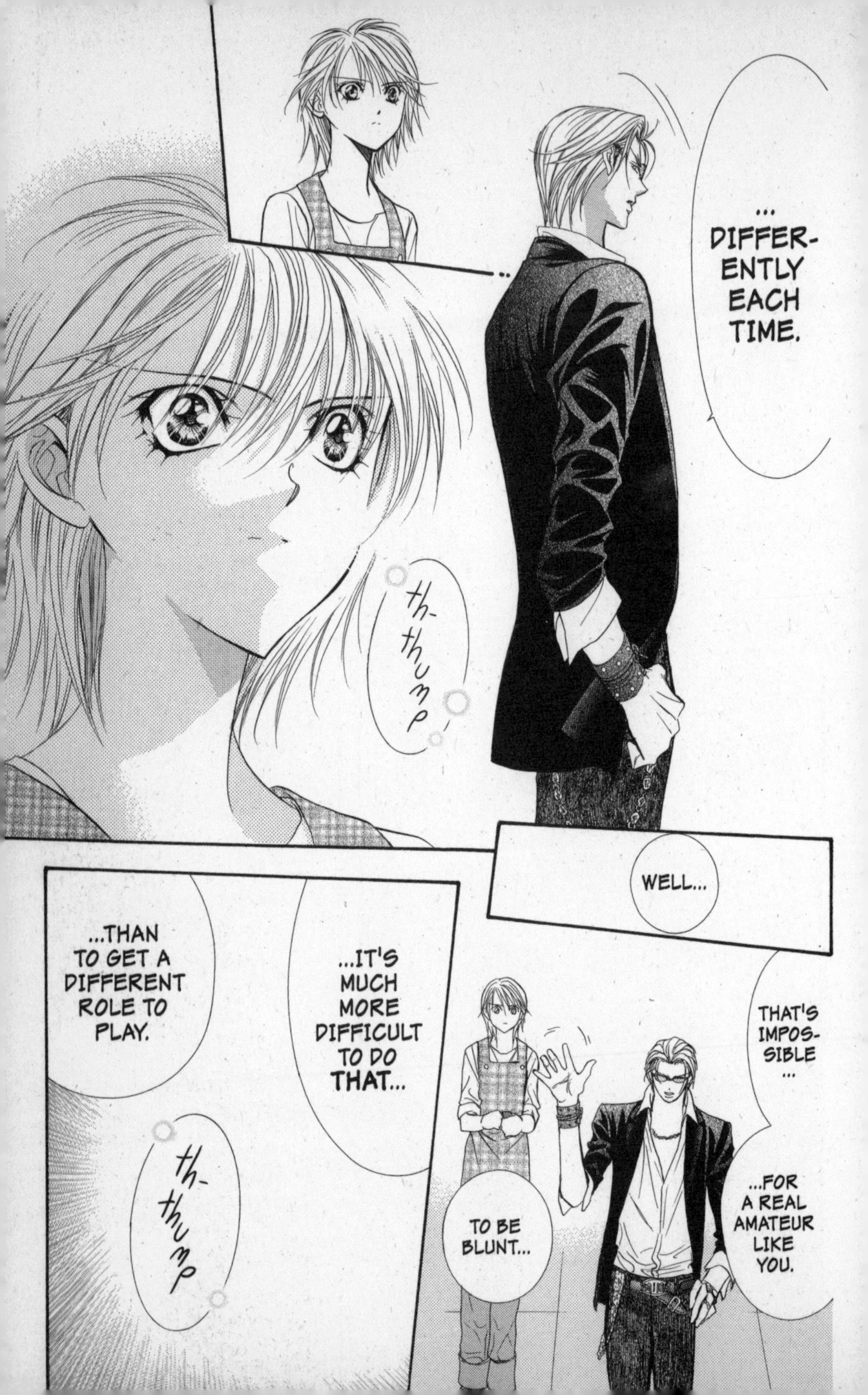

... DIFFER-ENTLY EACH TIME.
...
th-thump
WELL...
THAT'S IMPOSSIBLE...
...FOR A REAL AMATEUR LIKE YOU.
TO BE BLUNT...
...IT'S MUCH MORE DIFFICULT TO DO THAT...
...THAN TO GET A DIFFERENT ROLE TO PLAY.
th-thump

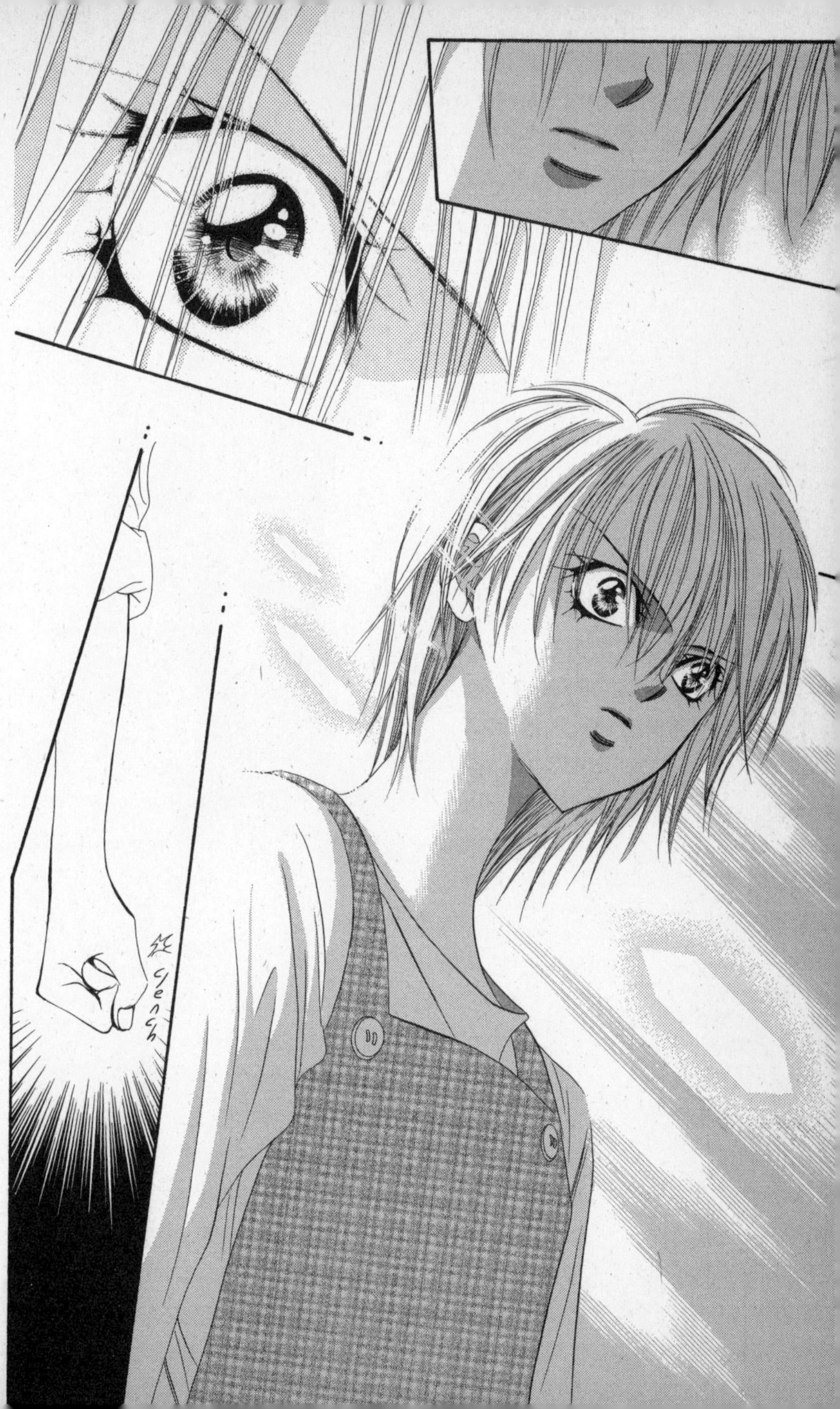
clench

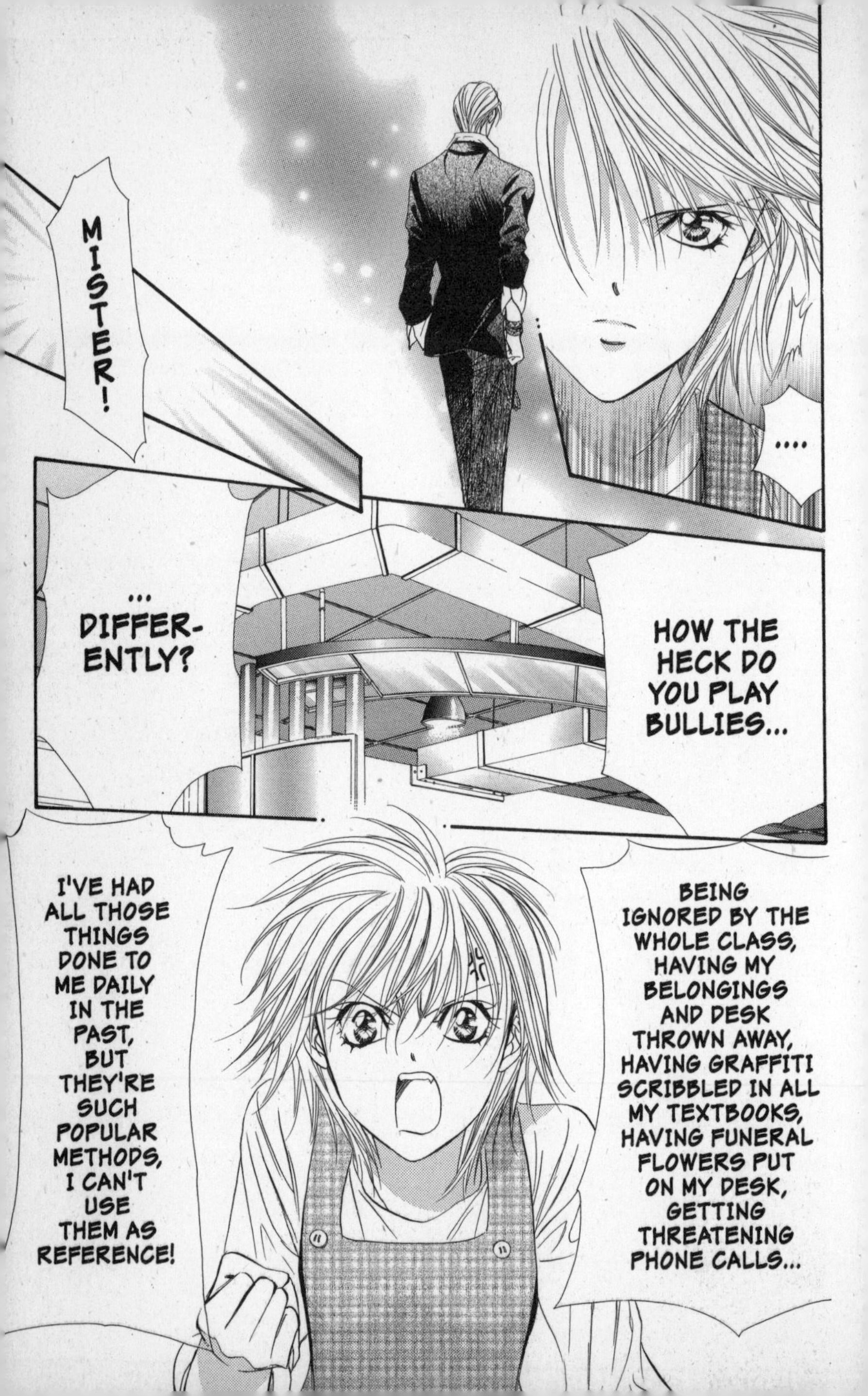
....
MISTER!
HOW THE HECK DO YOU PLAY BULLIES...
... DIFFER-ENTLY?
BEING IGNORED BY THE WHOLE CLASS, HAVING MY BELONGINGS AND DESK THROWN AWAY, HAVING GRAFFITI SCRIBBLED IN ALL MY TEXTBOOKS, HAVING FUNERAL FLOWERS PUT ON MY DESK, GETTING THREATENING PHONE CALLS...
I'VE HAD ALL THOSE THINGS DONE TO ME DAILY IN THE PAST, BUT THEY'RE SUCH POPULAR METHODS, I CAN'T USE THEM AS REFERENCE!

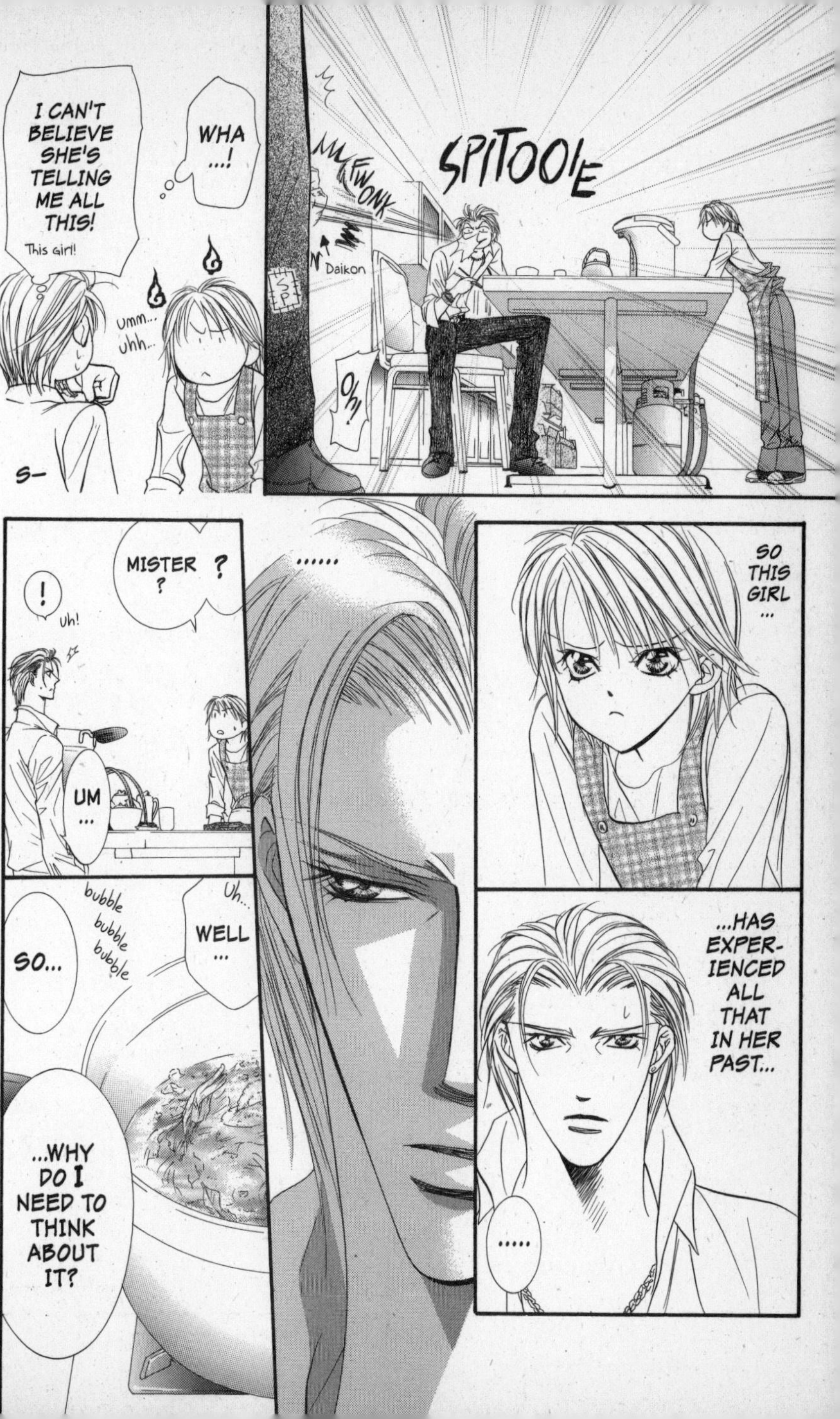
SPITOOIE
FWONK
Daikon
Oh!
WHA ...!
I CAN'T BELIEVE SHE'S TELLING ME ALL THIS!
This Girl!
Umm... uhh...
S–
SO THIS GIRL ...
...HAS EXPERIENCED ALL THAT IN HER PAST...
.....
......
MISTER ?
?
!
uh!
UM ...
Uh... WELL ...
bubble bubble bubble
SO...
...WHY DO I NEED TO THINK ABOUT IT?

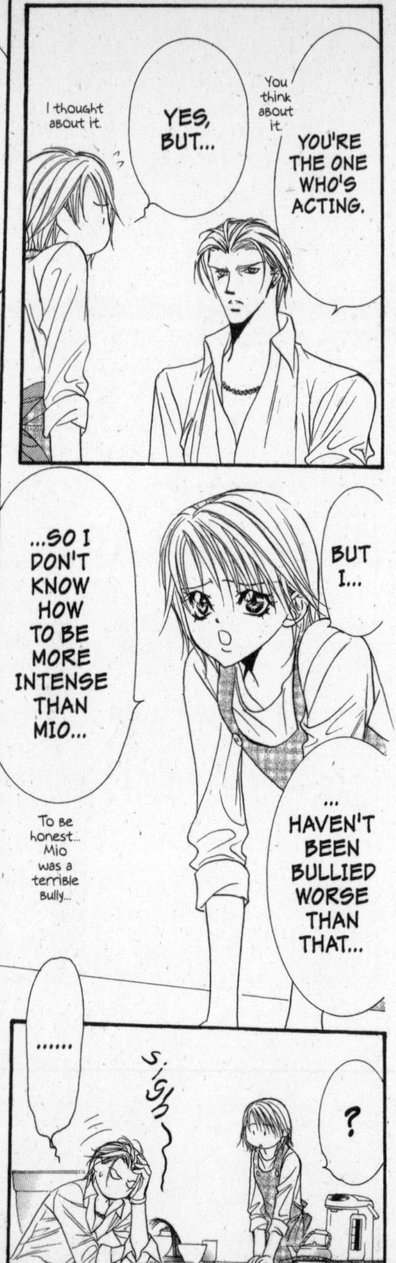
YOU'RE THE ONE WHO'S ACTING.
You think about it.
YES, BUT...
I thought about it.
BUT I...
...HAVEN'T BEEN BULLIED WORSE THAN THAT...
...SO I DON'T KNOW HOW TO BE MORE INTENSE THAN MIO...
To be honest... Mio was a terrible Bully...
?
sigh
......
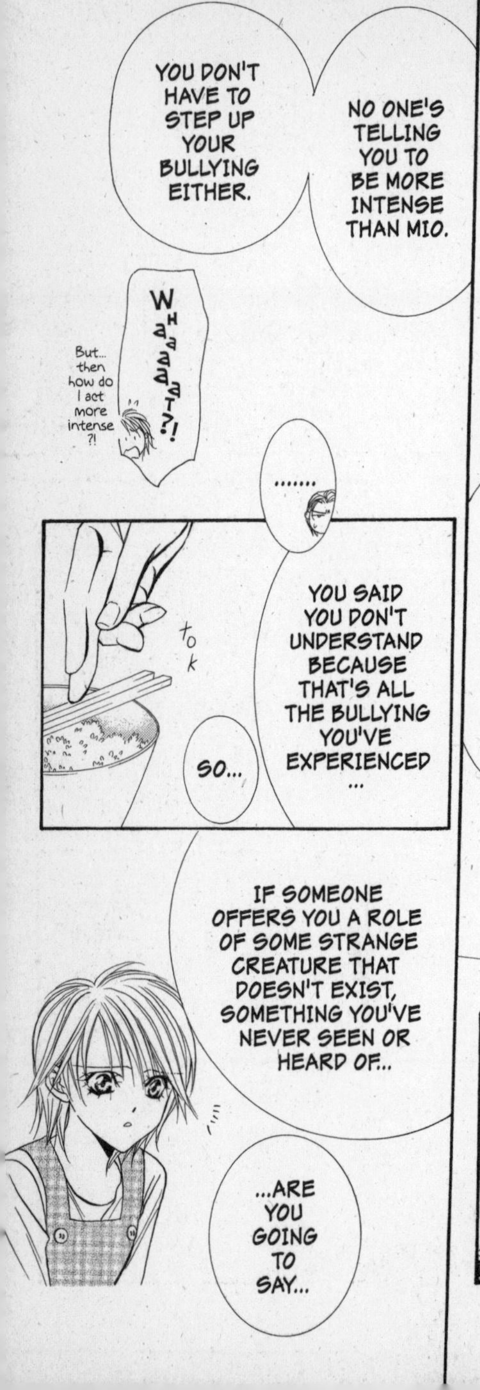
NO ONE'S TELLING YOU TO BE MORE INTENSE THAN MIO.
YOU DON'T HAVE TO STEP UP YOUR BULLYING EITHER.
Whaaaaaat?!
But... then how do I act more intense?!
......
YOU SAID YOU DON'T UNDERSTAND BECAUSE THAT'S ALL THE BULLYING YOU'VE EXPERIENCED...
tok
SO...
IF SOMEONE OFFERS YOU A ROLE OF SOME STRANGE CREATURE THAT DOESN'T EXIST, SOMETHING YOU'VE NEVER SEEN OR HEARD OF...
...ARE YOU GOING TO SAY...

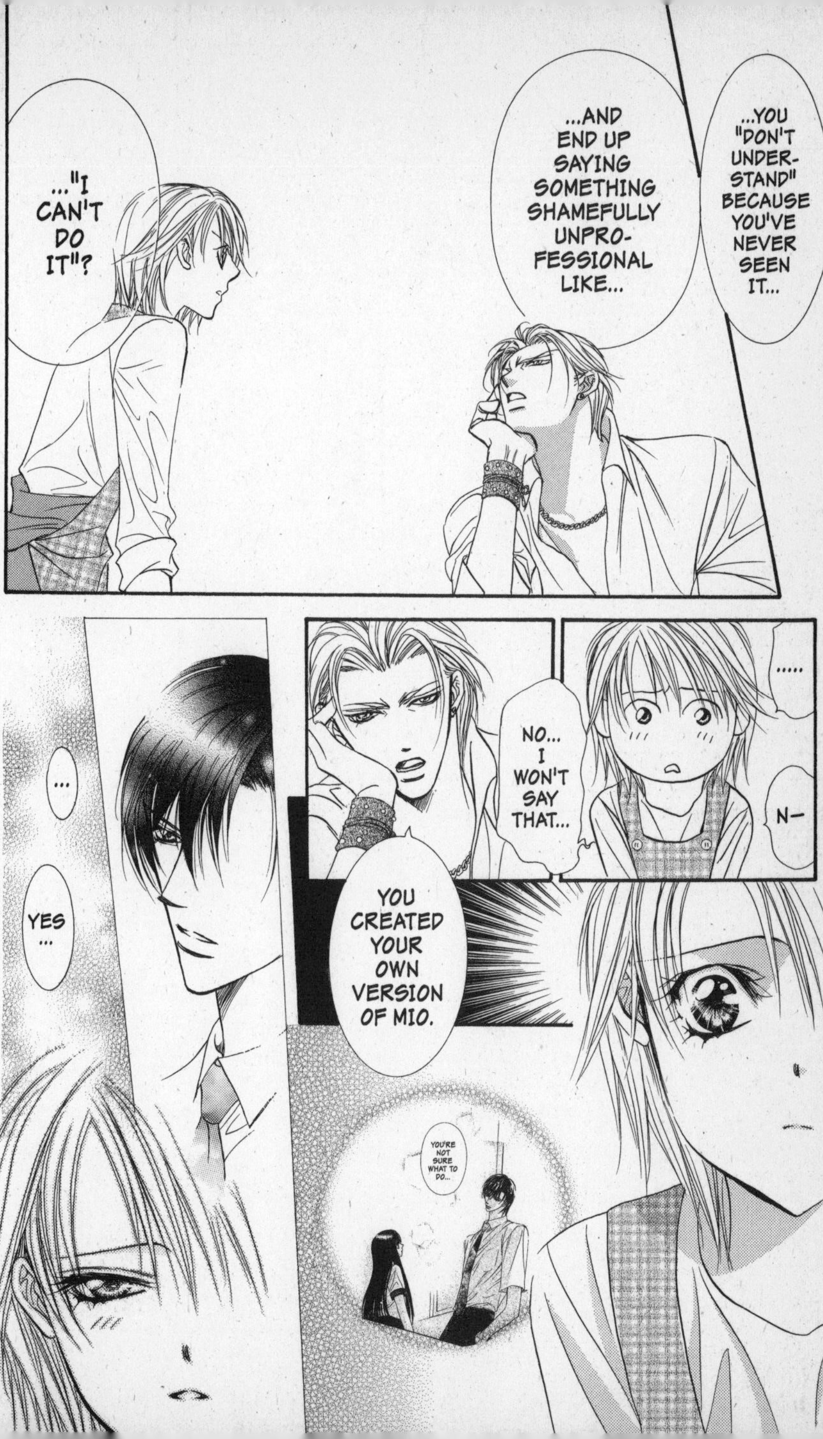
...YOU "DON'T UNDER-STAND" BECAUSE YOU'VE NEVER SEEN IT...
...AND END UP SAYING SOMETHING SHAMEFULLY UNPRO-FESSIONAL LIKE...
..."I CAN'T DO IT"?
.....
N—
NO... I WON'T SAY THAT...
YOU CREATED YOUR OWN VERSION OF MIO.
YOU'RE NOT SURE WHAT TO DO...
...
YES ...

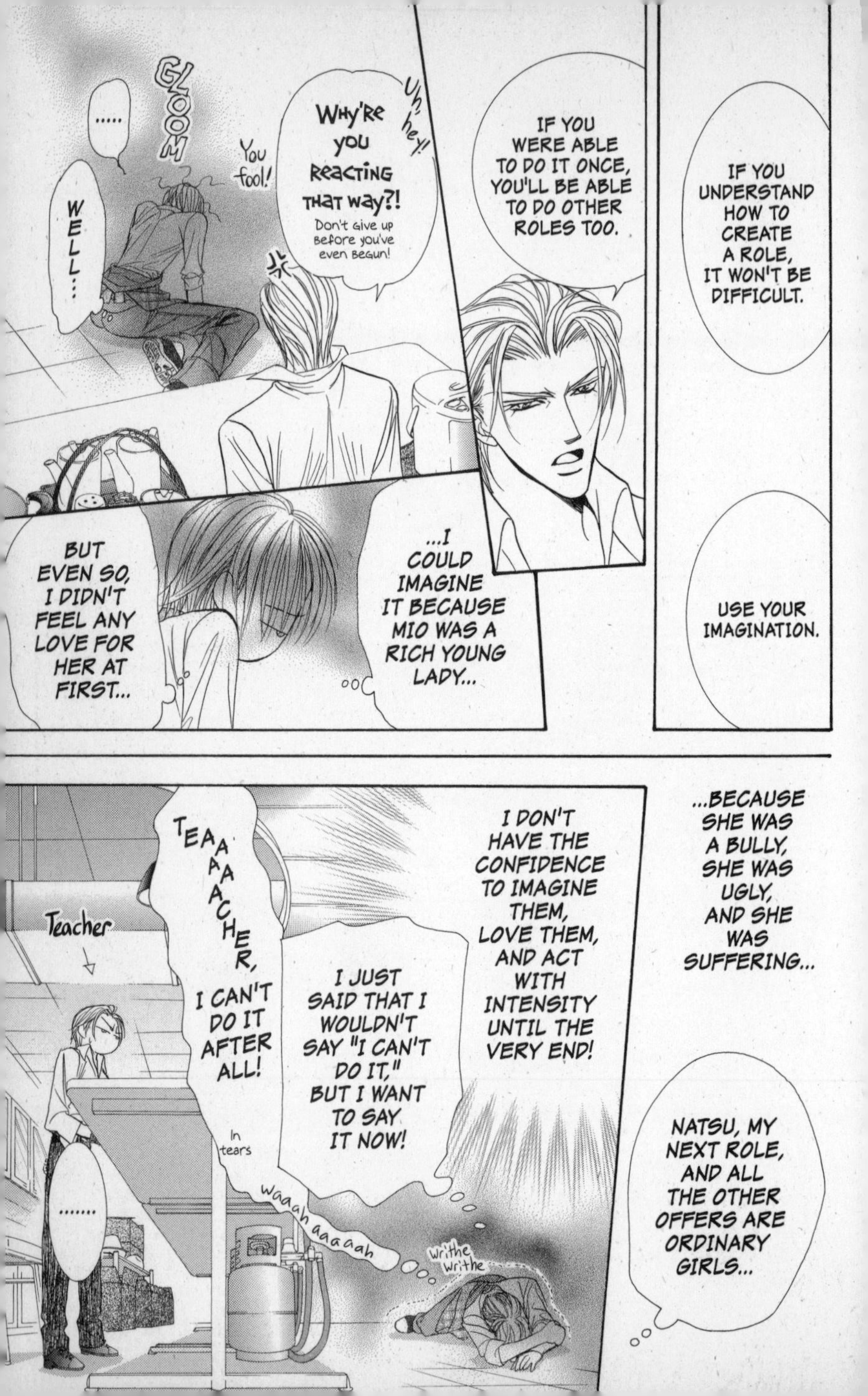
IF YOU UNDERSTAND HOW TO CREATE A ROLE, IT WON'T BE DIFFICULT.
USE YOUR IMAGINATION.
IF YOU WERE ABLE TO DO IT ONCE, YOU'LL BE ABLE TO DO OTHER ROLES TOO.
Uh, hey!!
Why're you reacting that way?!
Don't give up before you've even begun!
You fool!
GLOOM
......
WELL...
...I COULD IMAGINE IT BECAUSE MIO WAS A RICH YOUNG LADY...
BUT EVEN SO, I DIDN'T FEEL ANY LOVE FOR HER AT FIRST...
...BECAUSE SHE WAS A BULLY, SHE WAS UGLY, AND SHE WAS SUFFERING...
NATSU, MY NEXT ROLE, AND ALL THE OTHER OFFERS ARE ORDINARY GIRLS...
I DON'T HAVE THE CONFIDENCE TO IMAGINE THEM, LOVE THEM, AND ACT WITH INTENSITY UNTIL THE VERY END!
I JUST SAID THAT I WOULDN'T SAY "I CAN'T DO IT," BUT I WANT TO SAY IT NOW!
TEAAAACHER, I CAN'T DO IT AFTER ALL!
In tears
Waaah aaaaah
Writhe writhe
Teacher
....

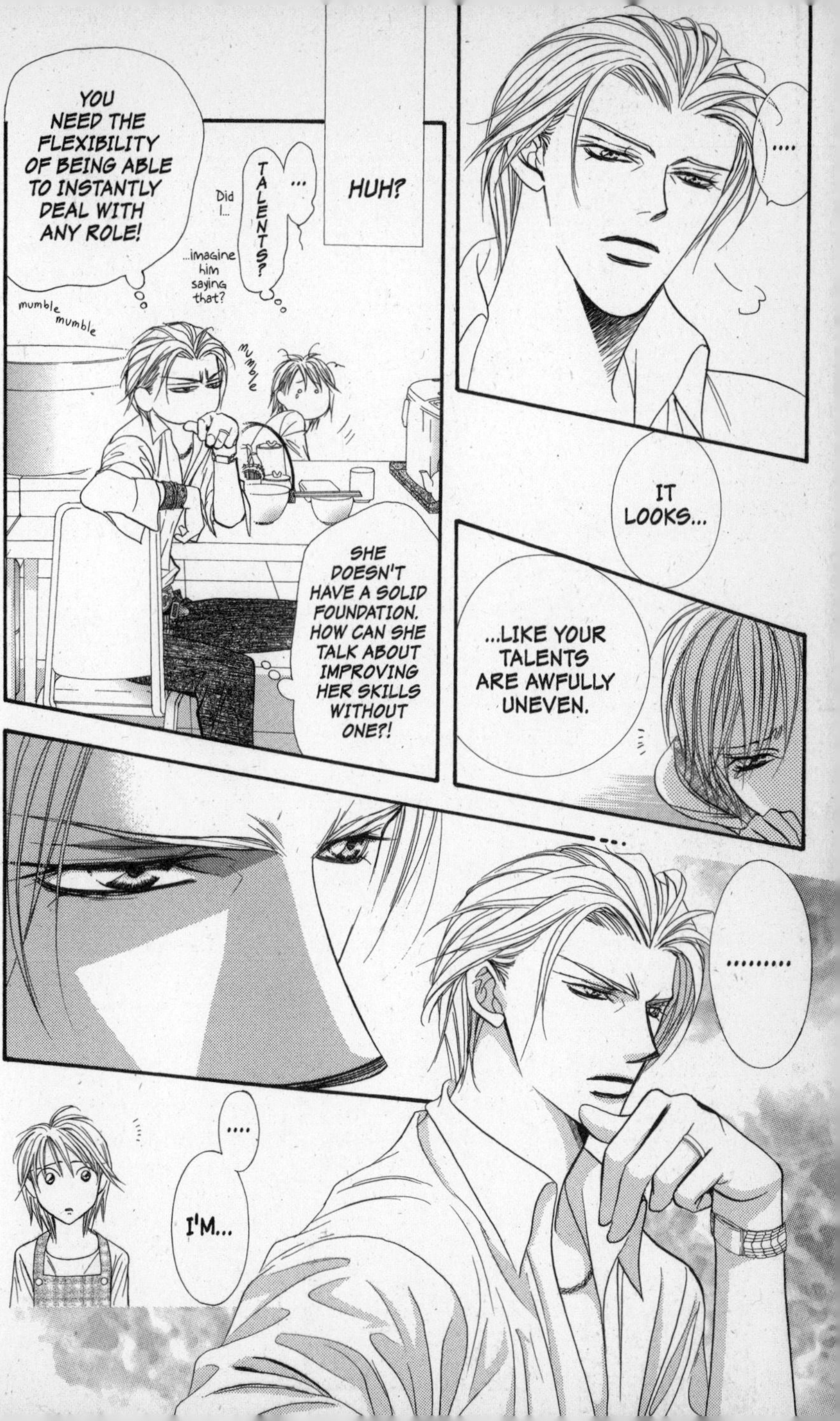
....
IT LOOKS...
...LIKE YOUR TALENTS ARE AWFULLY UNEVEN.
HUH?
... TALENTS?
Did I... ...imagine him saying that?
YOU NEED THE FLEXIBILITY OF BEING ABLE TO INSTANTLY DEAL WITH ANY ROLE!
mumble mumble
mumble
SHE DOESN'T HAVE A SOLID FOUNDATION. HOW CAN SHE TALK ABOUT IMPROVING HER SKILLS WITHOUT ONE?!
...
....
....
I'M...

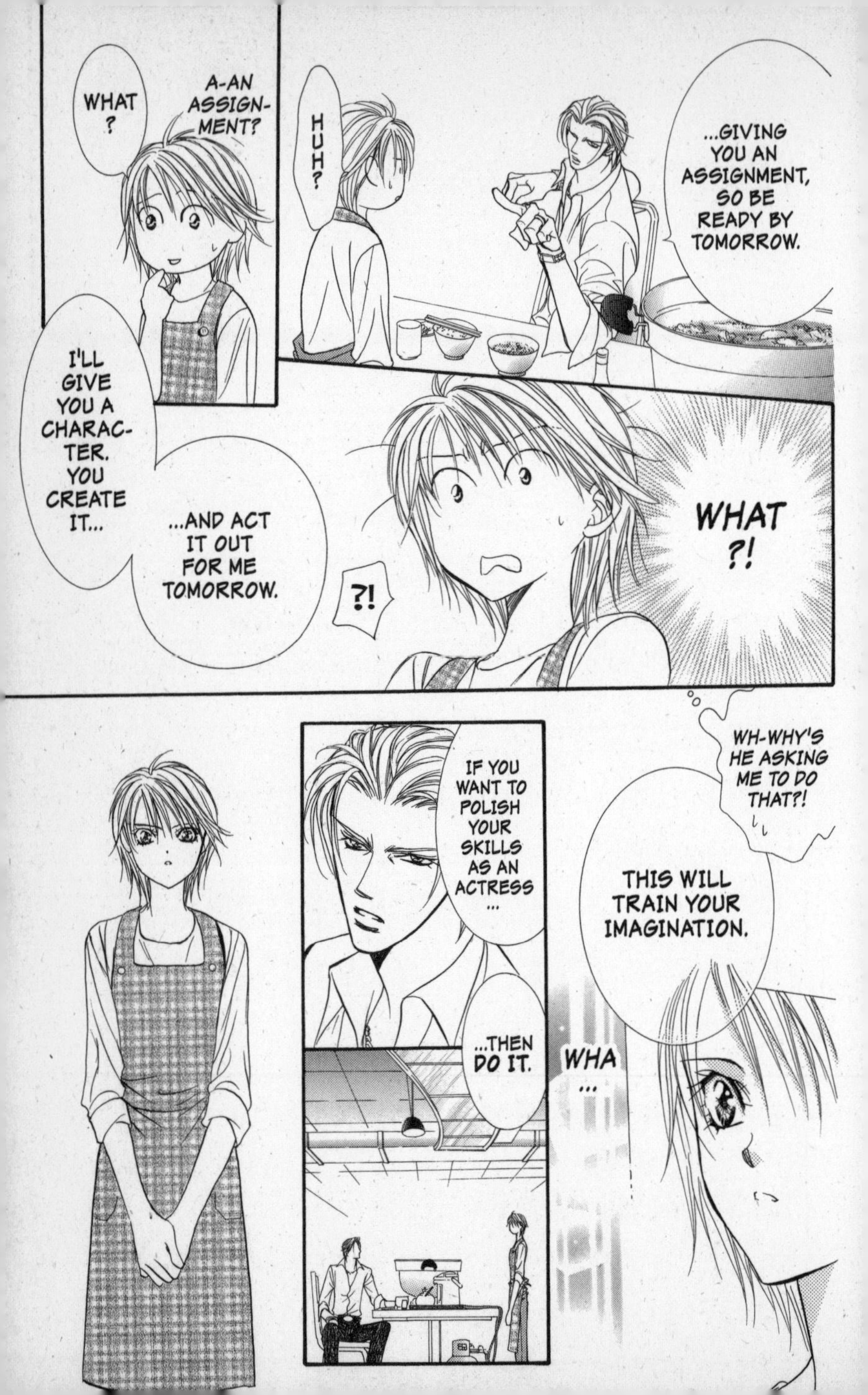
...GIVING YOU AN ASSIGNMENT, SO BE READY BY TOMORROW.
HUH?
A-AN ASSIGNMENT?
WHAT?
I'LL GIVE YOU A CHARACTER. YOU CREATE IT...
...AND ACT IT OUT FOR ME TOMORROW.
WHAT ?!
?!
WH-WHY'S HE ASKING ME TO DO THAT?!
THIS WILL TRAIN YOUR IMAGINATION.
WHA ...
IF YOU WANT TO POLISH YOUR SKILLS AS AN ACTRESS ...
...THEN DO IT.

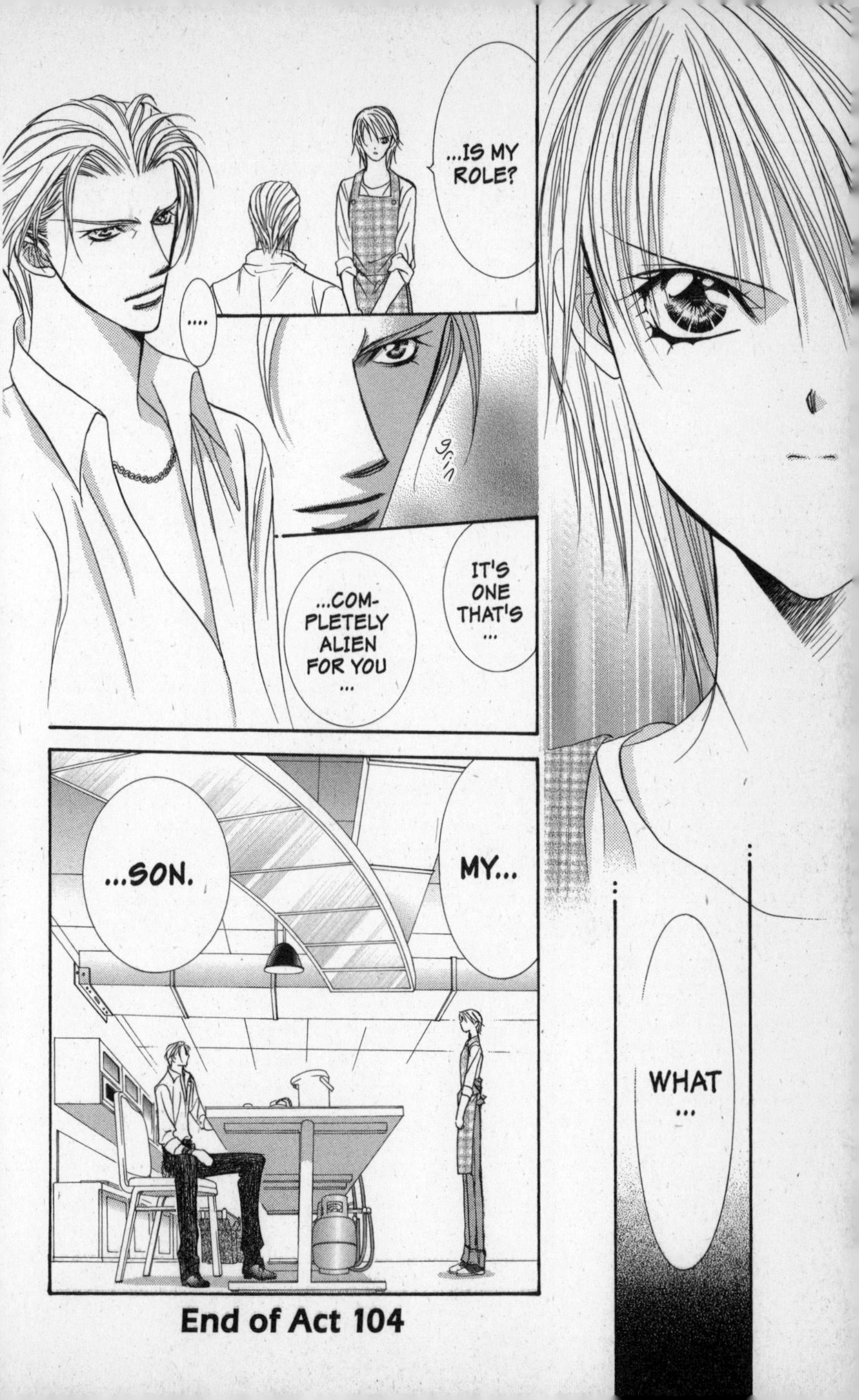
WHAT ...
...IS MY ROLE?
....
grin
IT'S ONE THAT'S ...
...COM-PLETELY ALIEN FOR YOU ...
MY...
...SON.

End of Act 104

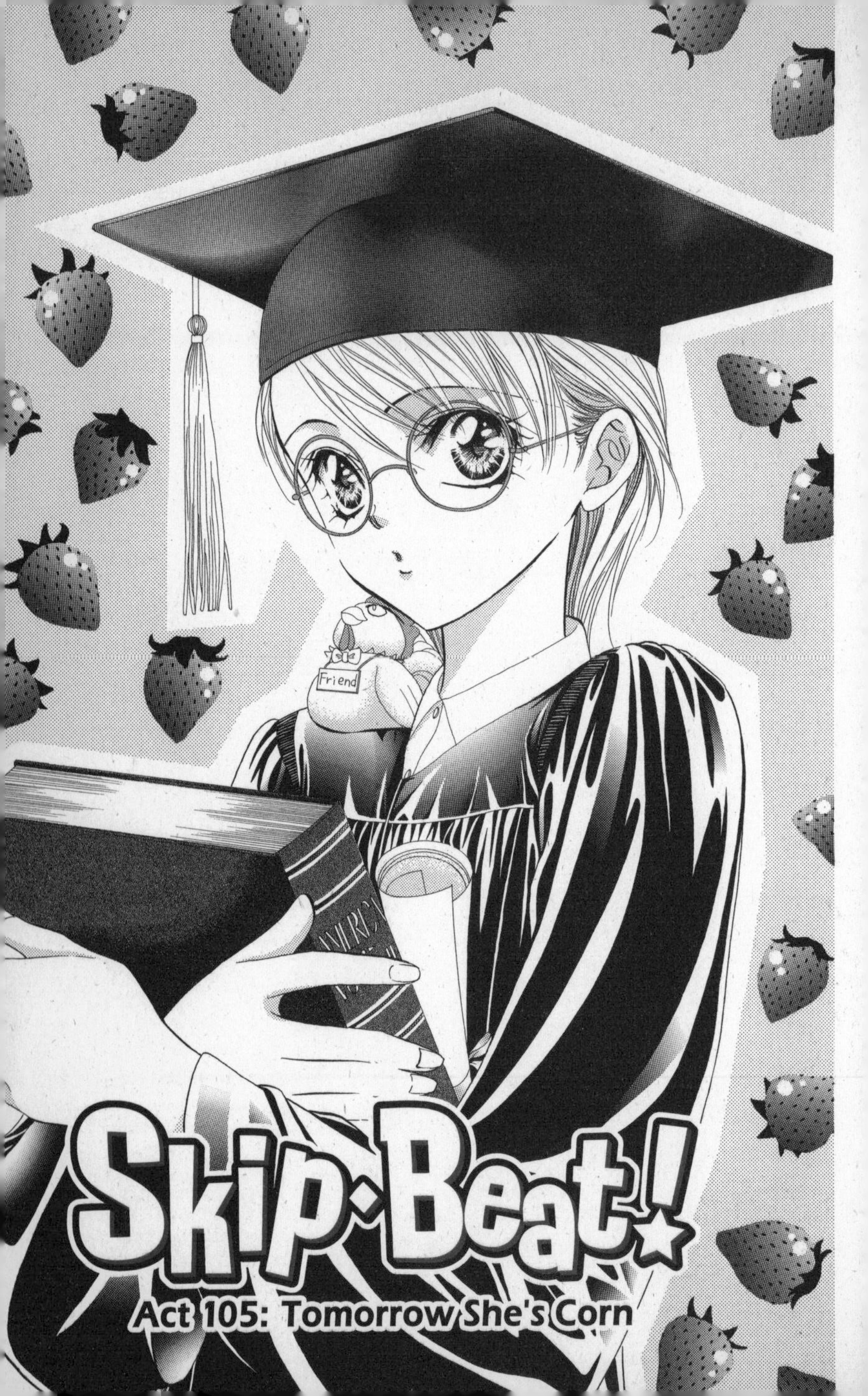
Friend
Skip·Beat!
Act 105: Tomorrow She's Corn

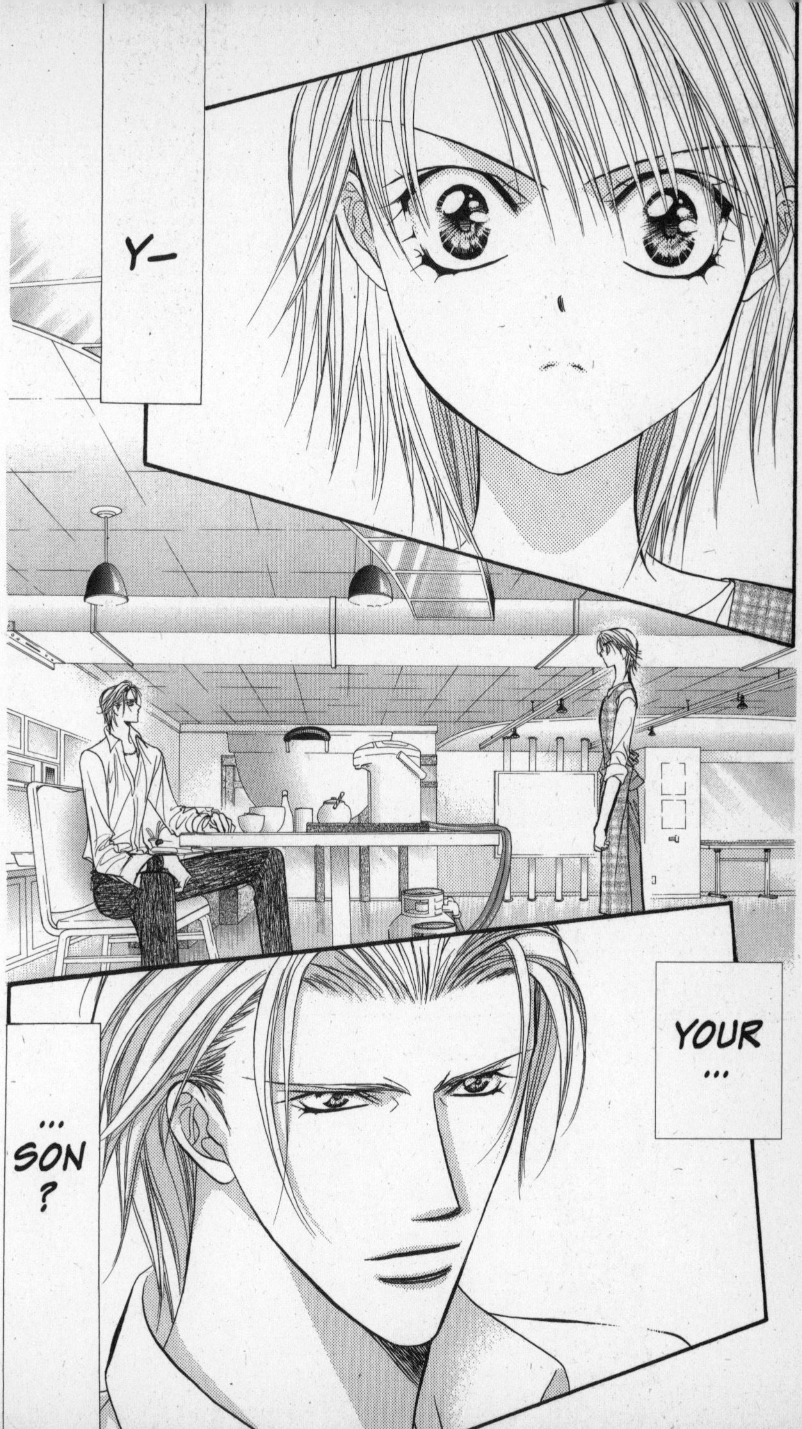
Y–
YOUR ...
... SON ?

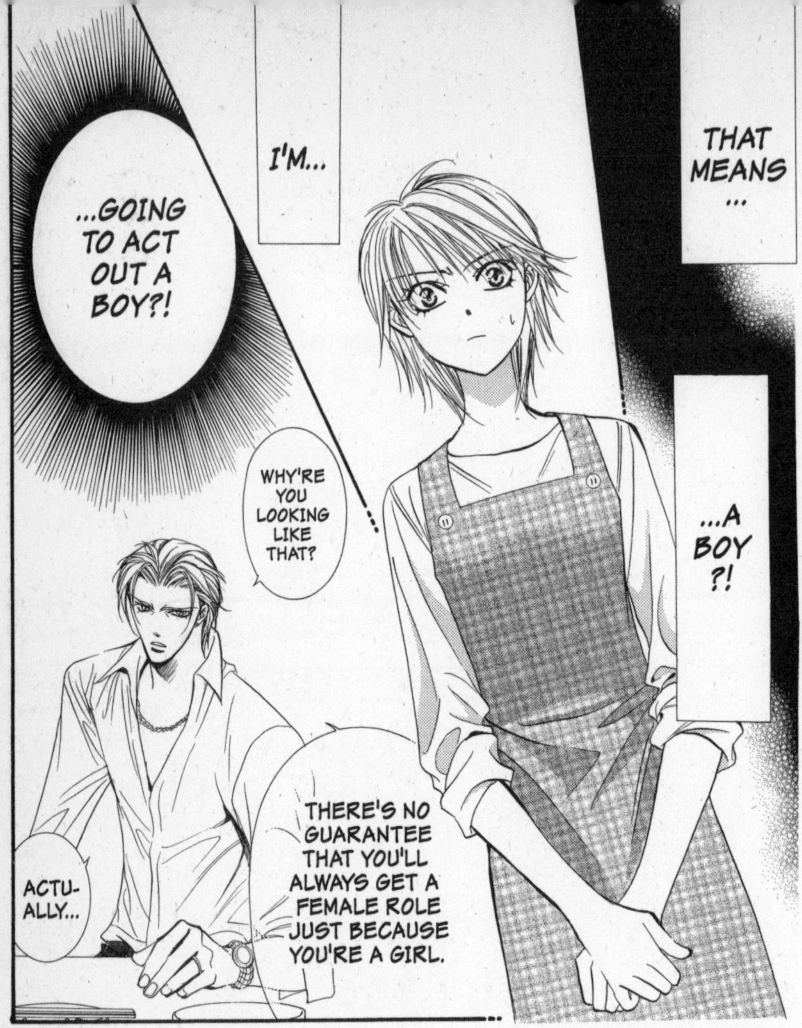
THAT MEANS ...
...A BOY ?!
I'M...
...GOING TO ACT OUT A BOY?!
WHY'RE YOU LOOKING LIKE THAT?
THERE'S NO GUARANTEE THAT YOU'LL ALWAYS GET A FEMALE ROLE JUST BECAUSE YOU'RE A GIRL.
ACTU-ALLY...
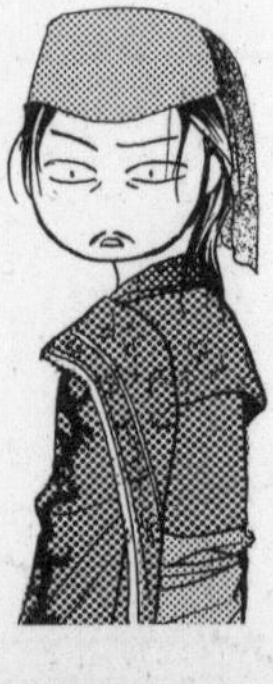

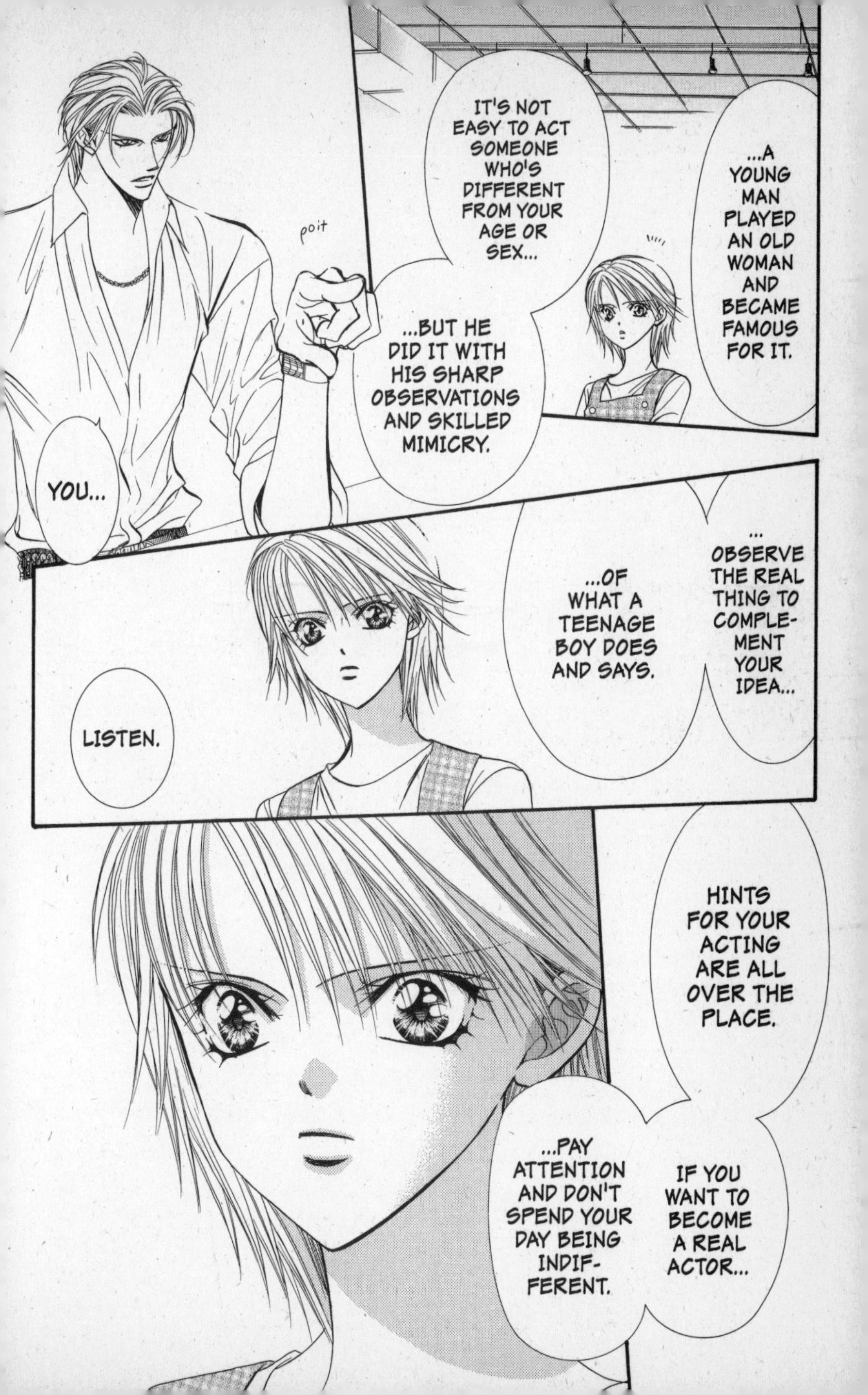
...A YOUNG MAN PLAYED AN OLD WOMAN AND BECAME FAMOUS FOR IT.
IT'S NOT EASY TO ACT SOMEONE WHO'S DIFFERENT FROM YOUR AGE OR SEX...
...BUT HE DID IT WITH HIS SHARP OBSERVATIONS AND SKILLED MIMICRY.
poit
YOU...
...OBSERVE THE REAL THING TO COMPLE-MENT YOUR IDEA...
...OF WHAT A TEENAGE BOY DOES AND SAYS.
LISTEN.
HINTS FOR YOUR ACTING ARE ALL OVER THE PLACE.
IF YOU WANT TO BECOME A REAL ACTOR...
...PAY ATTENTION AND DON'T SPEND YOUR DAY BEING INDIF-FERENT.

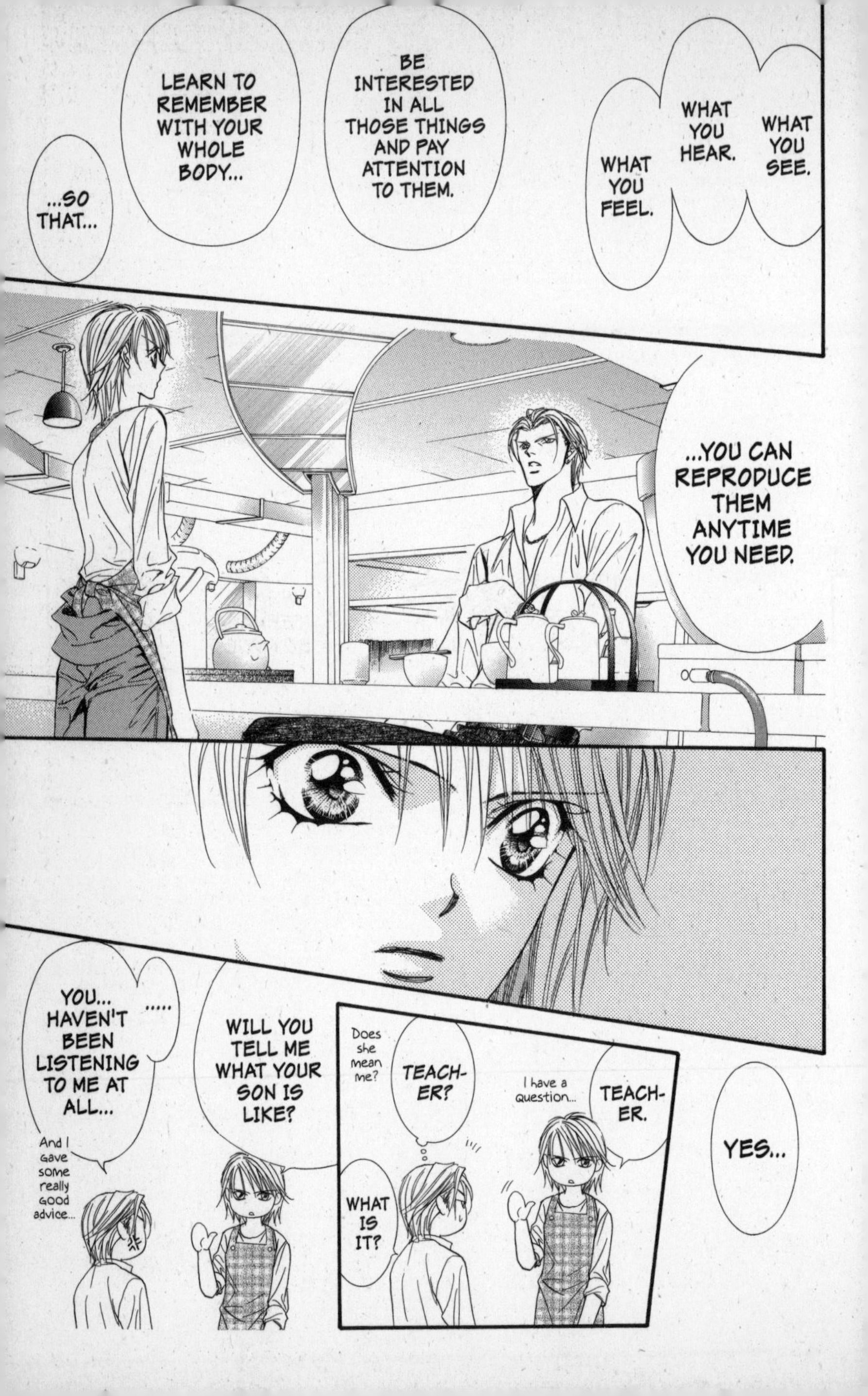
WHAT YOU SEE.
WHAT YOU HEAR.
WHAT YOU FEEL.
BE INTERESTED IN ALL THOSE THINGS AND PAY ATTENTION TO THEM.
LEARN TO REMEMBER WITH YOUR WHOLE BODY...
...SO THAT...
...YOU CAN REPRODUCE THEM ANYTIME YOU NEED.
YES...
TEACHER.
I have a question...
TEACHER?
Does she mean me?
WHAT IS IT?
WILL YOU TELL ME WHAT YOUR SON IS LIKE?
.....
YOU... HAVEN'T BEEN LISTENING TO ME AT ALL...
And I gave some really good advice...

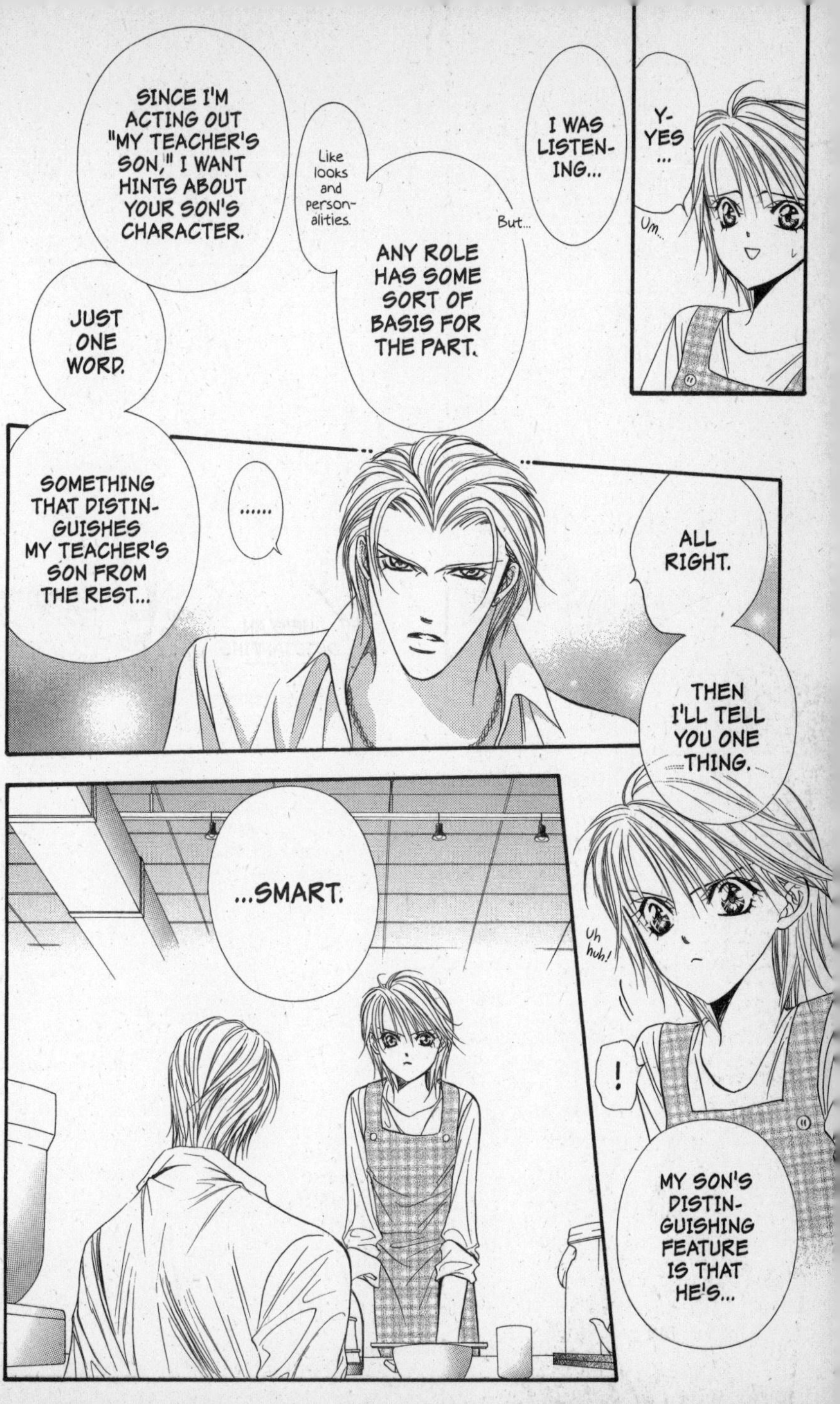
Y-YES...
Um...
I WAS LISTENING...
But...
ANY ROLE HAS SOME SORT OF BASIS FOR THE PART.
Like looks and personalities.
SINCE I'M ACTING OUT "MY TEACHER'S SON," I WANT HINTS ABOUT YOUR SON'S CHARACTER.
JUST ONE WORD.
SOMETHING THAT DISTINGUISHES MY TEACHER'S SON FROM THE REST...
......
ALL RIGHT.
THEN I'LL TELL YOU ONE THING.
Uh huh!
!
MY SON'S DISTINGUISHING FEATURE IS THAT HE'S...
...SMART.

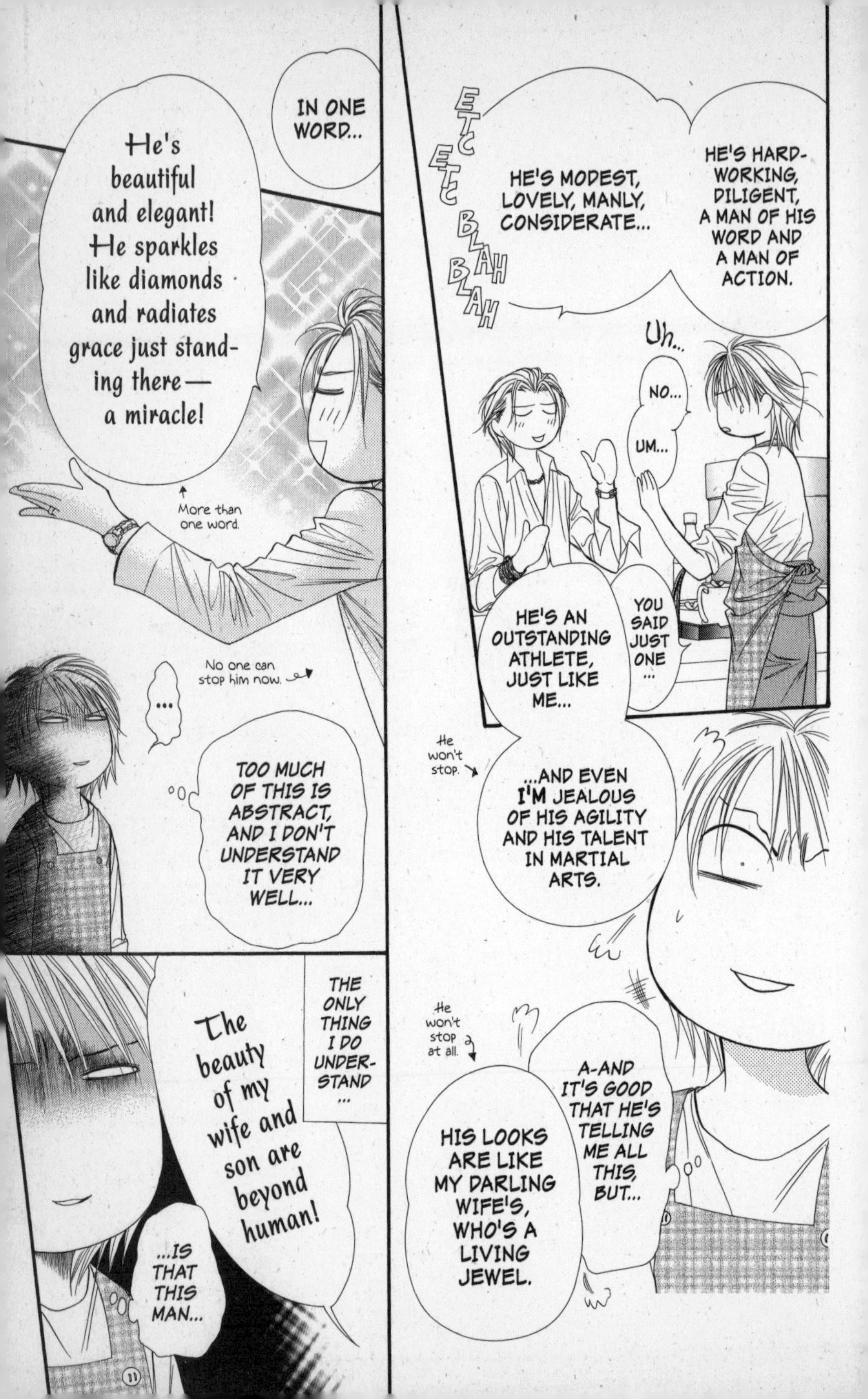
HE'S HARD-WORKING, DILIGENT, A MAN OF HIS WORD AND A MAN OF ACTION.
HE'S MODEST, LOVELY, MANLY, CONSIDERATE...
ETC ETC
BLAH BLAH
Uh...
NO...
UM...
YOU SAID JUST ONE...
HE'S AN OUTSTANDING ATHLETE, JUST LIKE ME...
He won't stop.
...AND EVEN I'M JEALOUS OF HIS AGILITY AND HIS TALENT IN MARTIAL ARTS.
A-AND IT'S GOOD THAT HE'S TELLING ME ALL THIS, BUT...
He won't stop at all.
HIS LOOKS ARE LIKE MY DARLING WIFE'S, WHO'S A LIVING JEWEL.
IN ONE WORD...
He's beautiful and elegant! He sparkles like diamonds and radiates grace just standing there—a miracle!
More than one word.
No one can stop him now.
...
TOO MUCH OF THIS IS ABSTRACT, AND I DON'T UNDERSTAND IT VERY WELL...
THE ONLY THING I DO UNDERSTAND...
The beauty of my wife and son are beyond human!
...IS THAT THIS MAN...

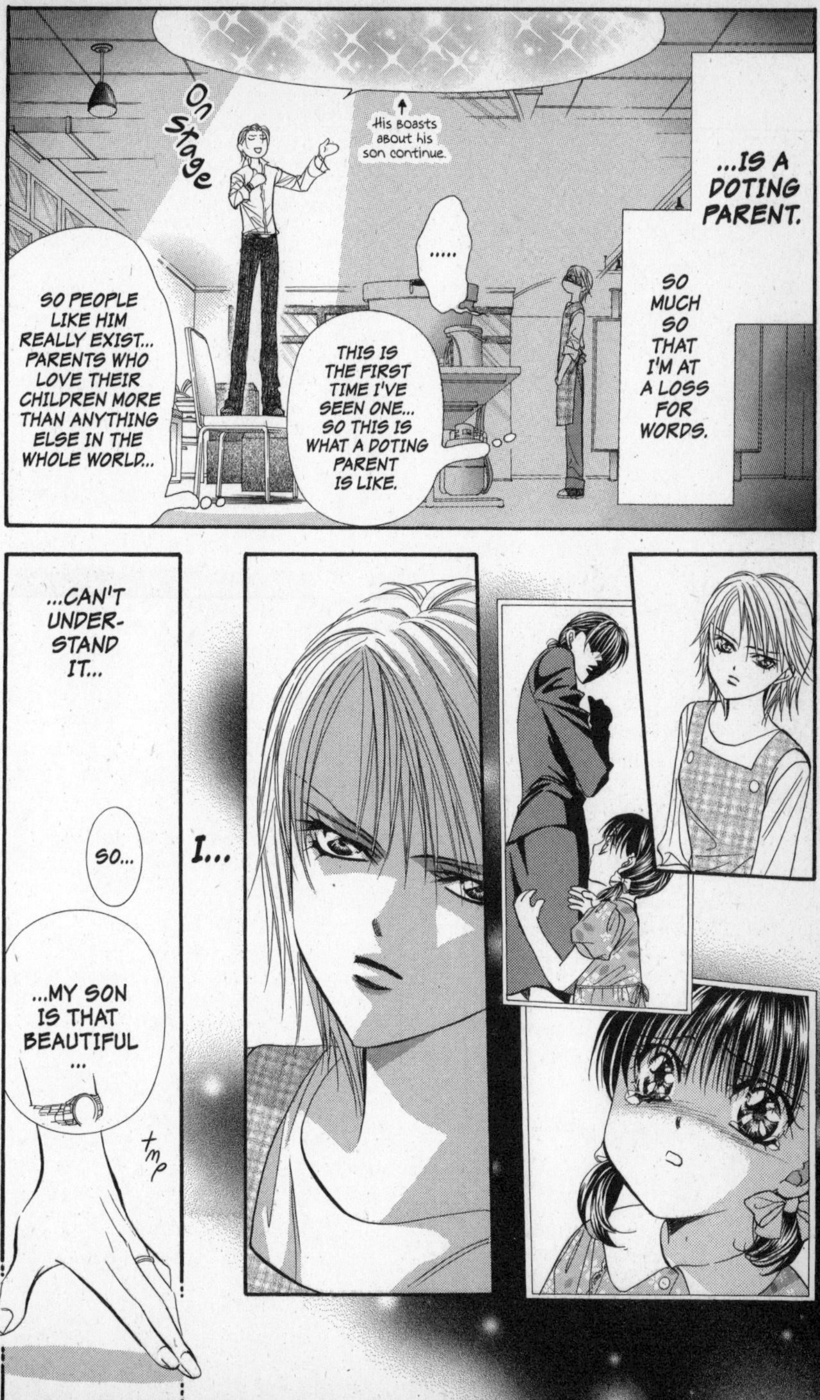
...IS A DOTING PARENT.
SO MUCH SO THAT I'M AT A LOSS FOR WORDS.
His boasts about his son continue.
On Stage
.....
THIS IS THE FIRST TIME I'VE SEEN ONE... SO THIS IS WHAT A DOTING PARENT IS LIKE.
SO PEOPLE LIKE HIM REALLY EXIST... PARENTS WHO LOVE THEIR CHILDREN MORE THAN ANYTHING ELSE IN THE WHOLE WORLD...
I...
...CAN'T UNDER-STAND IT...
SO...
...MY SON IS THAT BEAUTIFUL ...
tmp

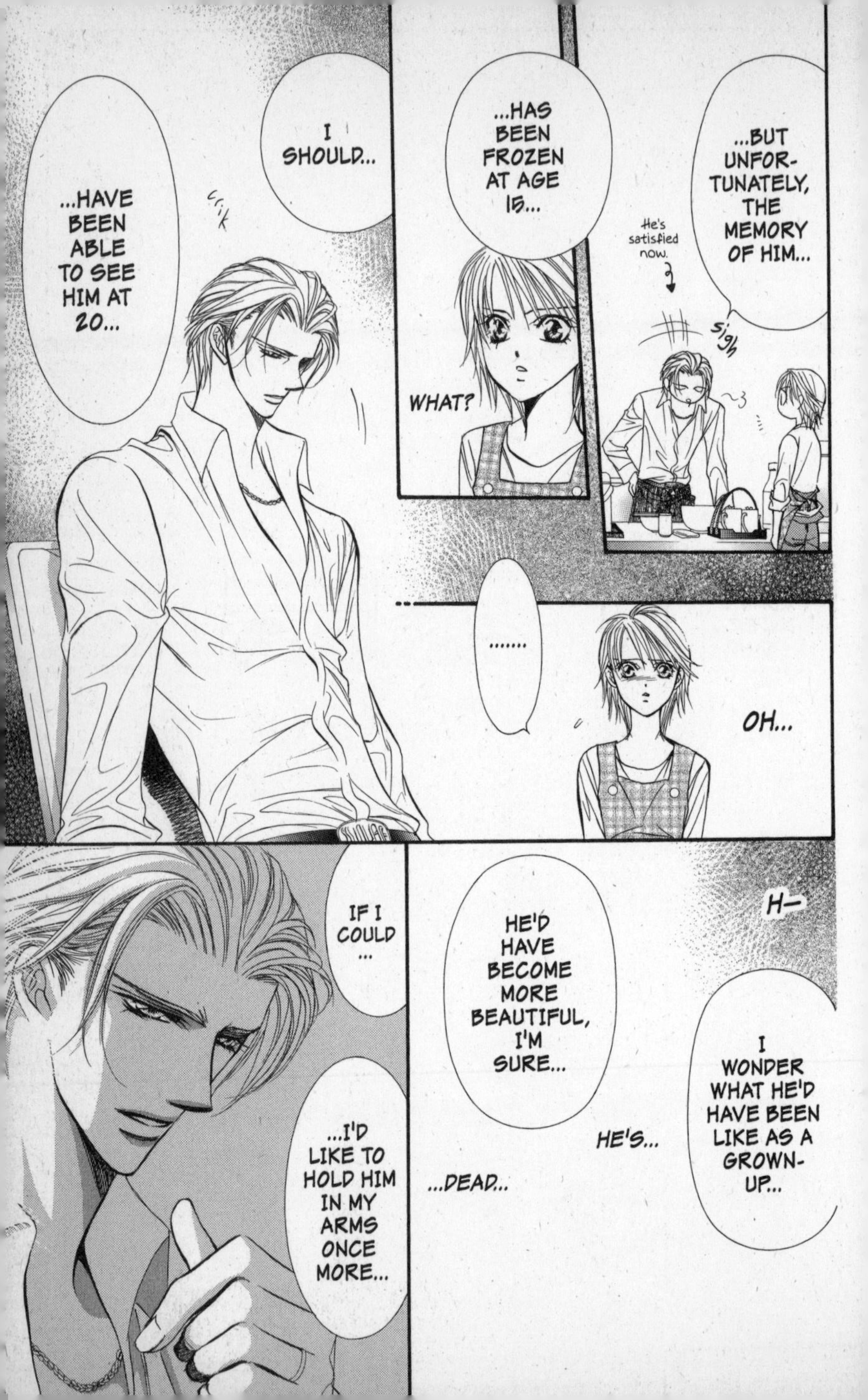
...BUT UNFORTUNATELY, THE MEMORY OF HIM...
He's satisfied now.
sigh
...HAS BEEN FROZEN AT AGE 15...
WHAT?
....
OH...
I SHOULD...
...HAVE BEEN ABLE TO SEE HIM AT 20...
crik
H—
I WONDER WHAT HE'D HAVE BEEN LIKE AS A GROWN-UP...
HE'D HAVE BECOME MORE BEAUTIFUL, I'M SURE...
HE'S...
...DEAD...
IF I COULD...
...I'D LIKE TO HOLD HIM IN MY ARMS ONCE MORE...

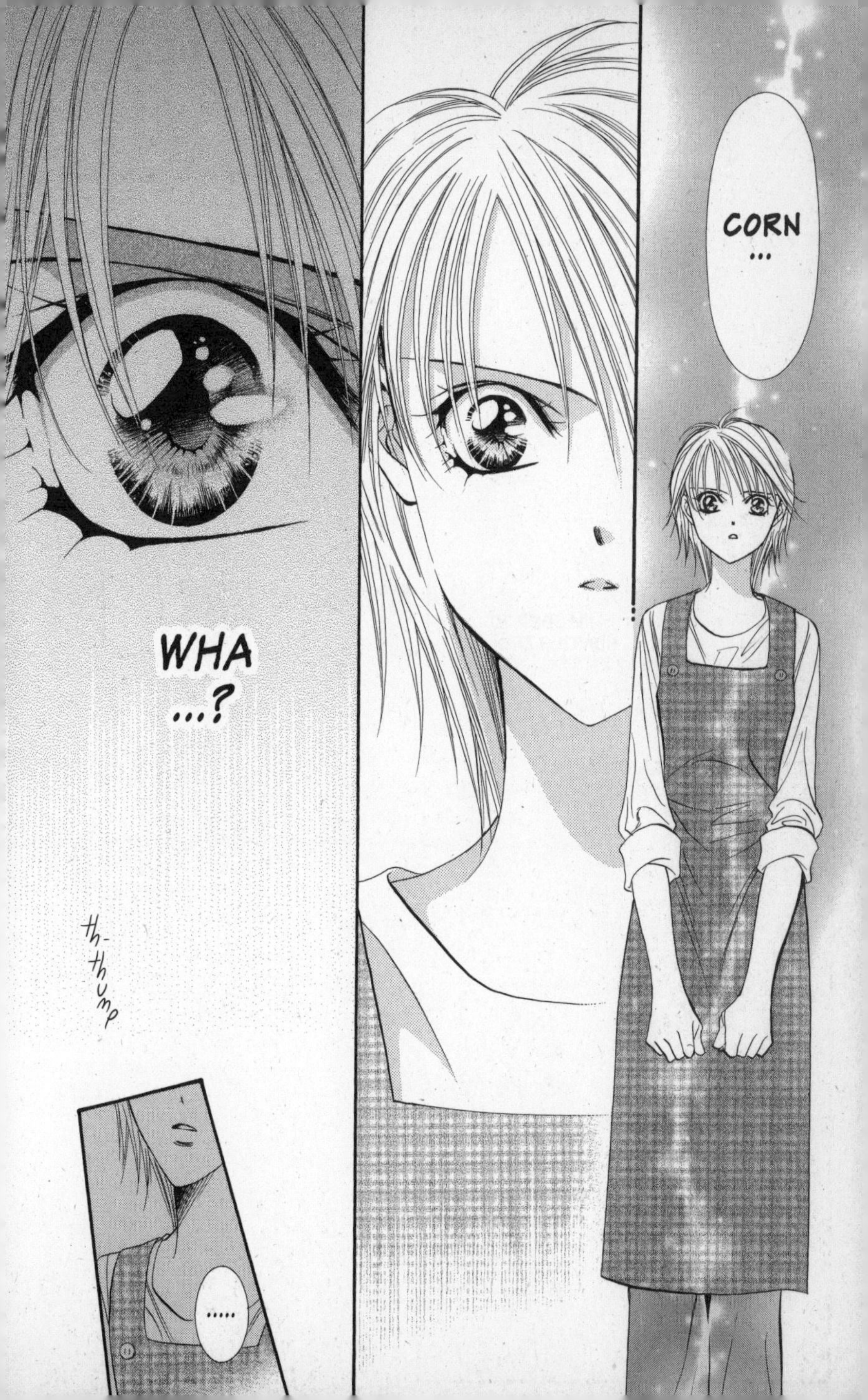
CORN
...
WHA
...?
th-thump
.....

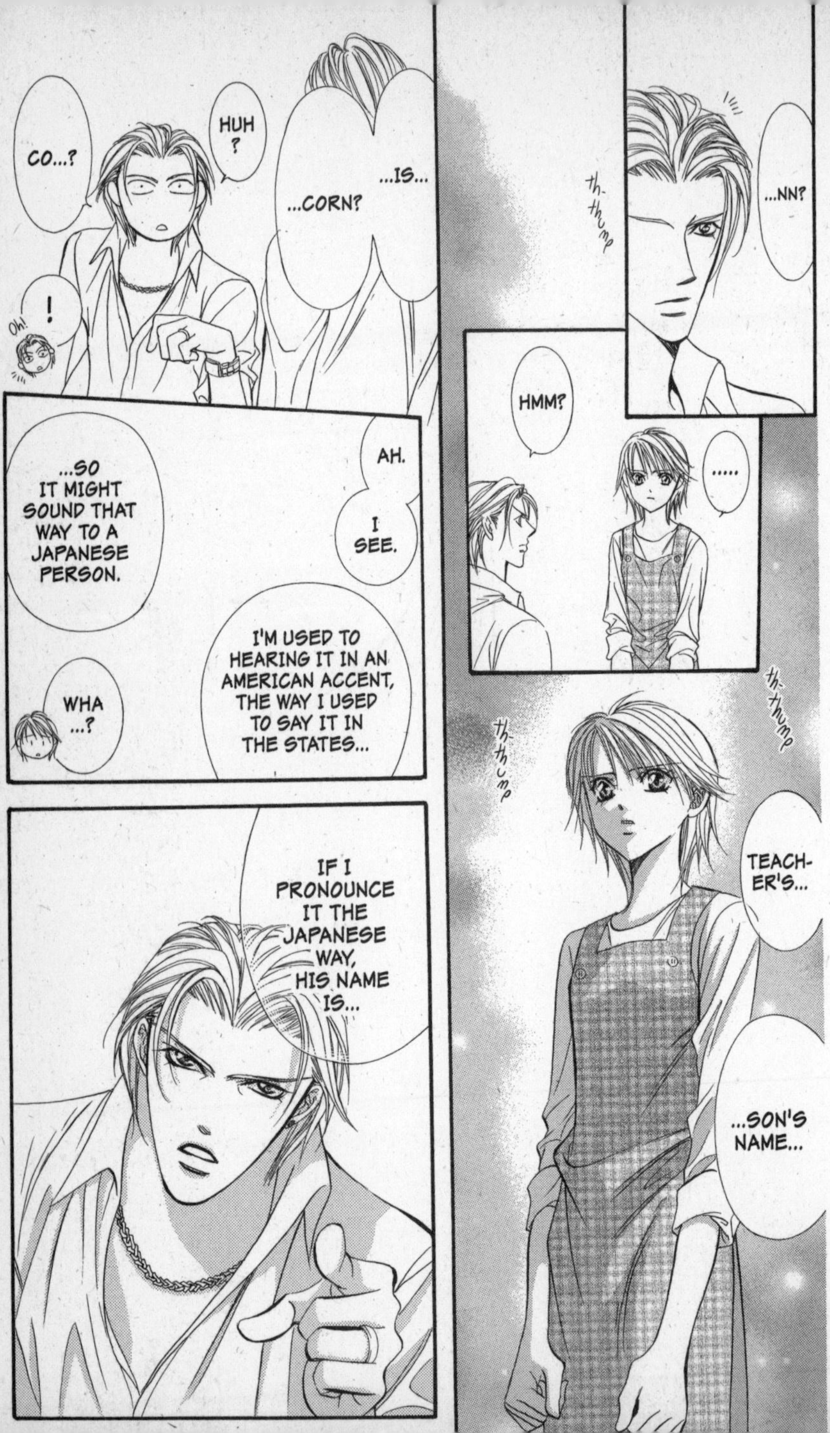
th-thump
...NN?
.....
HMM?
th-thump
th-thump
TEACHER'S...
...SON'S NAME...
...IS...
...CORN?
HUH?
CO...?
!
Oh!
AH.
I SEE.
...SO IT MIGHT SOUND THAT WAY TO A JAPANESE PERSON.
I'M USED TO HEARING IT IN AN AMERICAN ACCENT, THE WAY I USED TO SAY IT IN THE STATES...
WHA ...?
IF I PRONOUNCE IT THE JAPANESE WAY, HIS NAME IS...

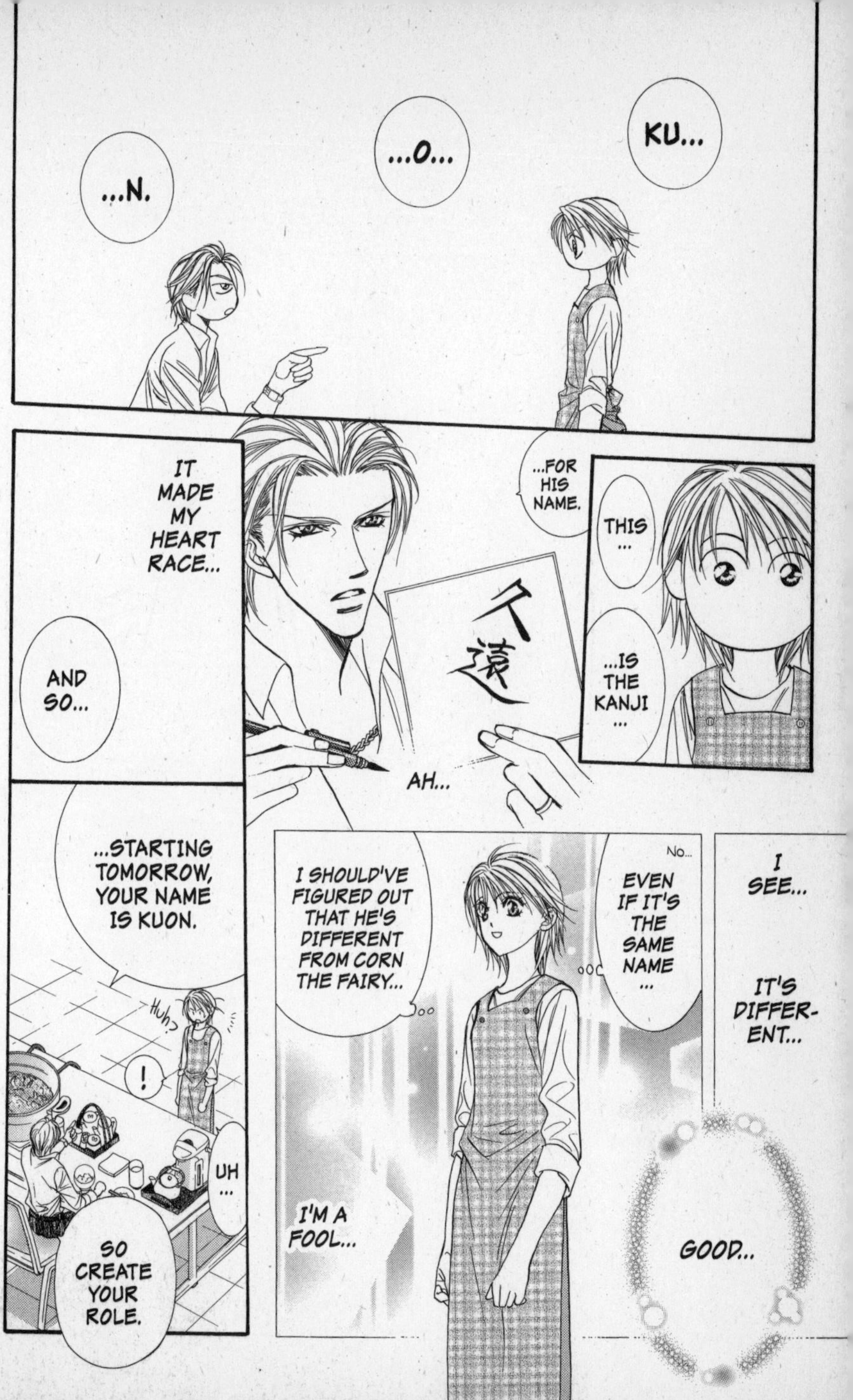
KU...
...O...
...N.
THIS ...
...IS THE KANJI ...
...FOR HIS NAME.
久遠
AH...
I SEE...
IT'S DIFFER-ENT...
No...
EVEN IF IT'S THE SAME NAME ...
I SHOULD'VE FIGURED OUT THAT HE'S DIFFERENT FROM CORN THE FAIRY...
I'M A FOOL...
GOOD...
IT MADE MY HEART RACE...
AND SO...
...STARTING TOMORROW, YOUR NAME IS KUON.
Huh?
!
UH ...
SO CREATE YOUR ROLE.

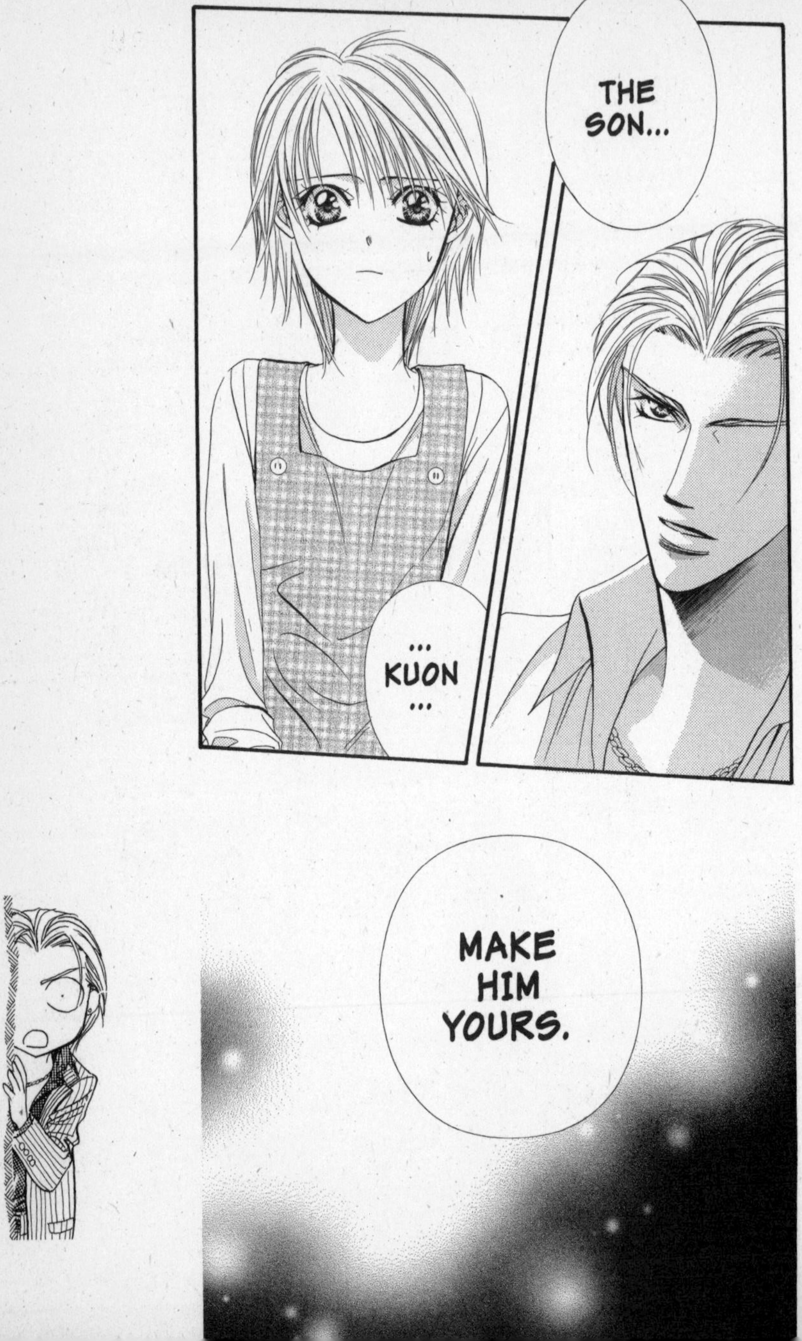
THE SON...
...KUON...
MAKE HIM YOURS.

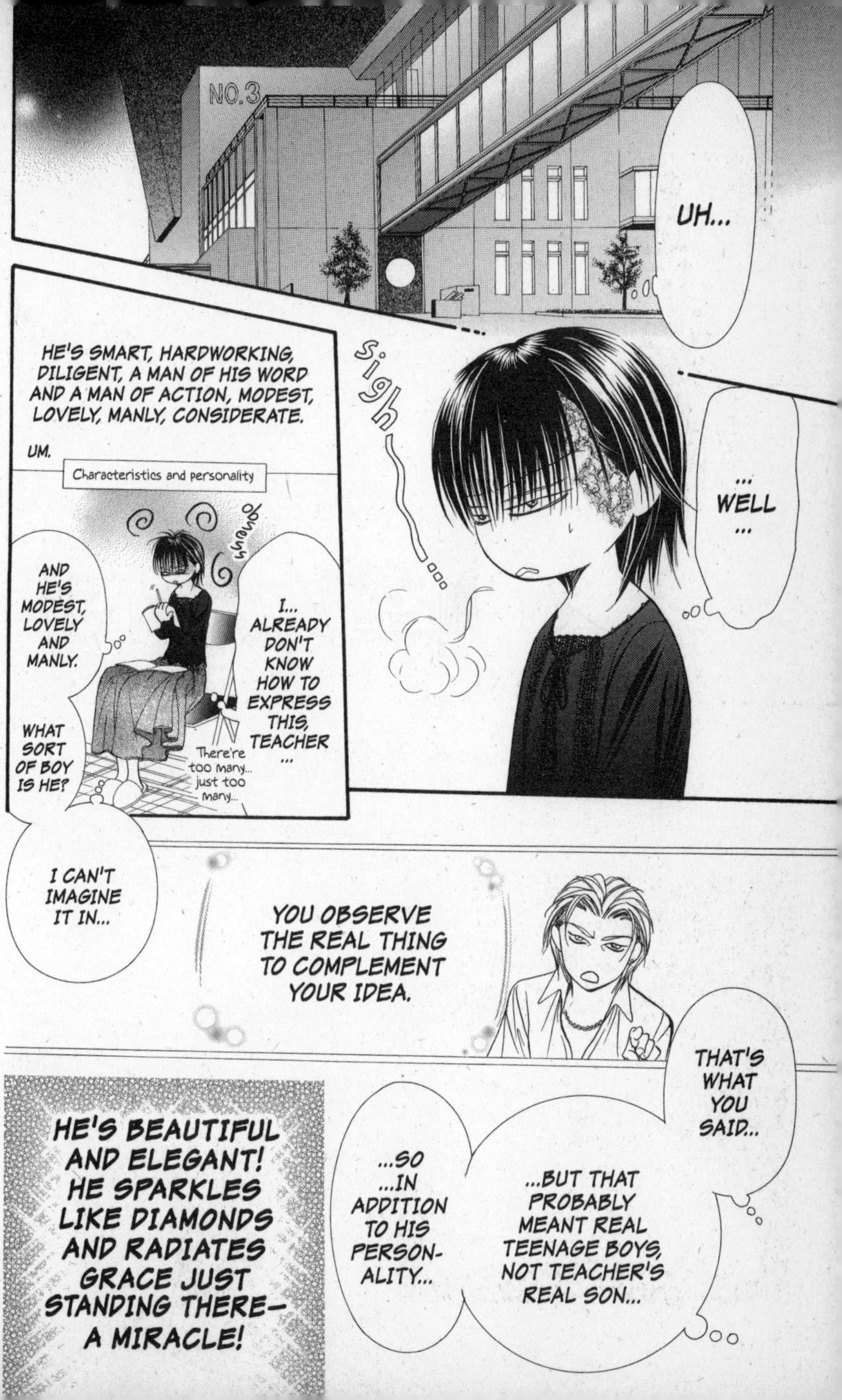
UH...
...WELL...
sigh
HE'S SMART, HARDWORKING, DILIGENT, A MAN OF HIS WORD AND A MAN OF ACTION, MODEST, LOVELY, MANLY, CONSIDERATE.
UM.
Characteristics and personality
I... ALREADY DON'T KNOW HOW TO EXPRESS THIS, TEACHER...
AND HE'S MODEST, LOVELY AND MANLY.
There're too many... just too many...
WHAT SORT OF BOY IS HE?
I CAN'T IMAGINE IT IN...
YOU OBSERVE THE REAL THING TO COMPLEMENT YOUR IDEA.
THAT'S WHAT YOU SAID...
...BUT THAT PROBABLY MEANT REAL TEENAGE BOYS, NOT TEACHER'S REAL SON...
...SO ...IN ADDITION TO HIS PERSON-ALITY...
HE'S BEAUTIFUL AND ELEGANT! HE SPARKLES LIKE DIAMONDS AND RADIATES GRACE JUST STANDING THERE—A MIRACLE!

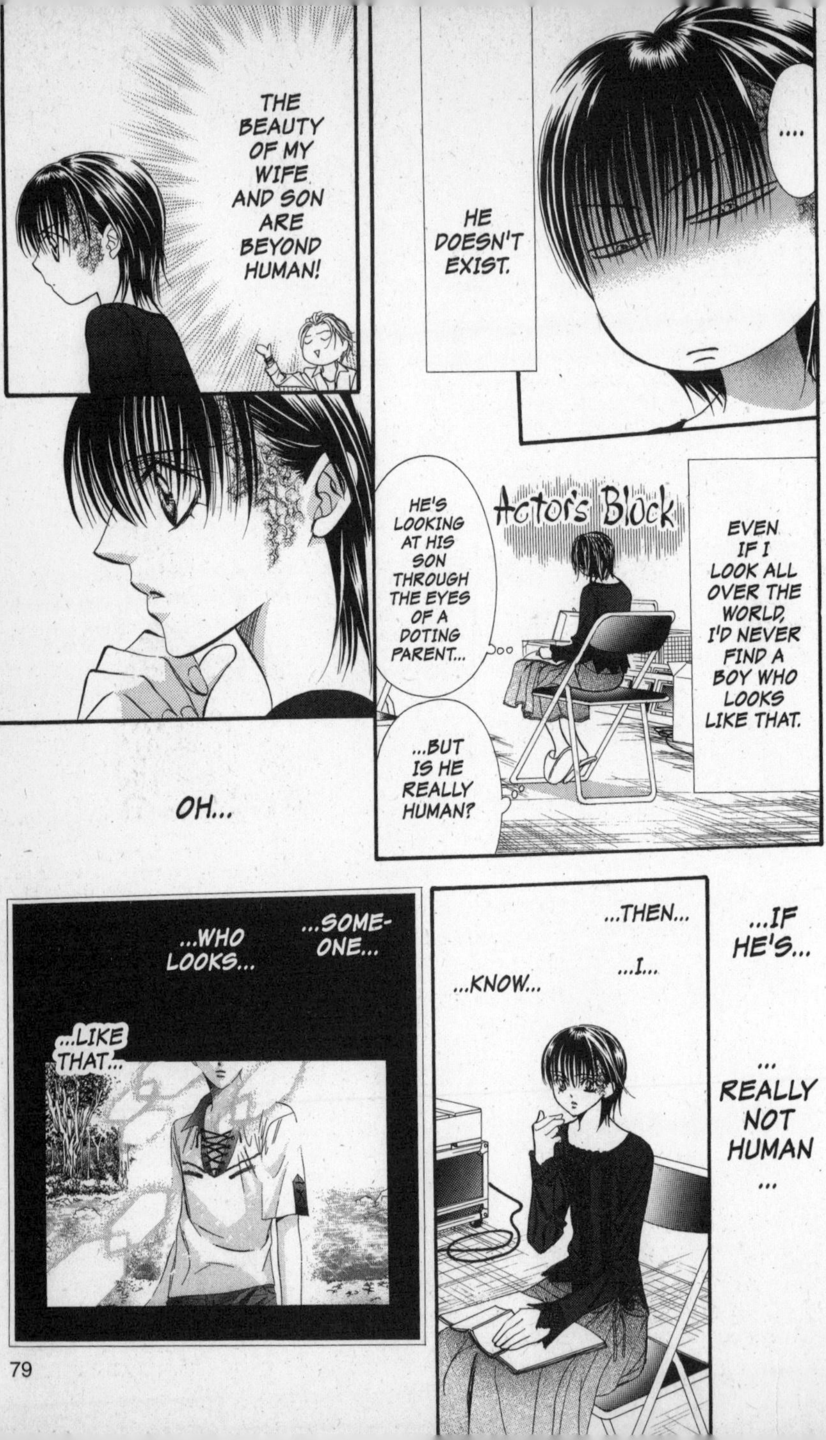
....
HE DOESN'T EXIST.
THE BEAUTY OF MY WIFE AND SON ARE BEYOND HUMAN!
EVEN IF I LOOK ALL OVER THE WORLD, I'D NEVER FIND A BOY WHO LOOKS LIKE THAT.
Actor's Block
HE'S LOOKING AT HIS SON THROUGH THE EYES OF A DOTING PARENT...
...BUT IS HE REALLY HUMAN?
OH...
...IF HE'S...
... REALLY NOT HUMAN ...
...THEN...
...I...
...KNOW...
...SOME-ONE...
...WHO LOOKS...
...LIKE THAT...

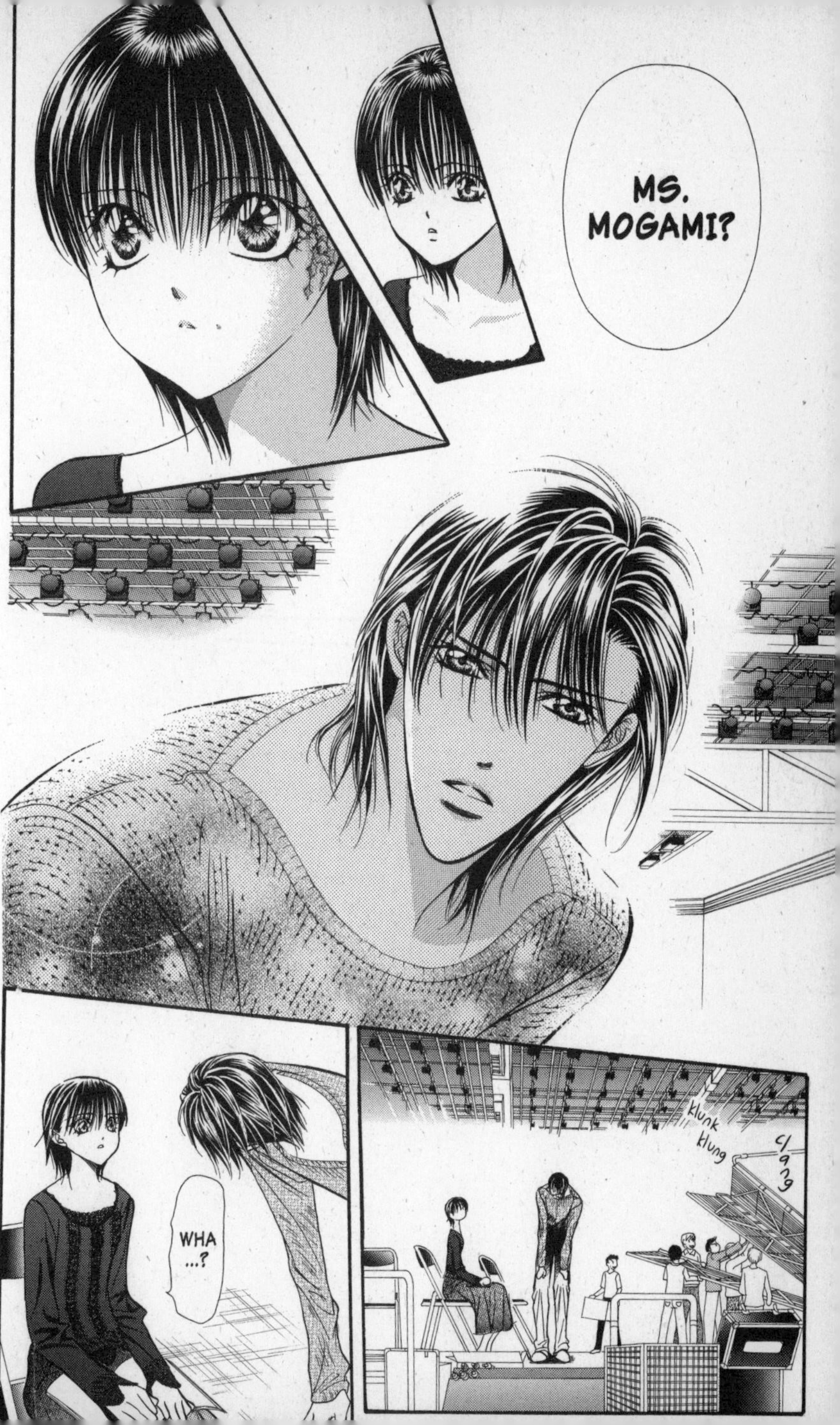
MS. MOGAMI?
klunk
klung
clang
WHA ...?

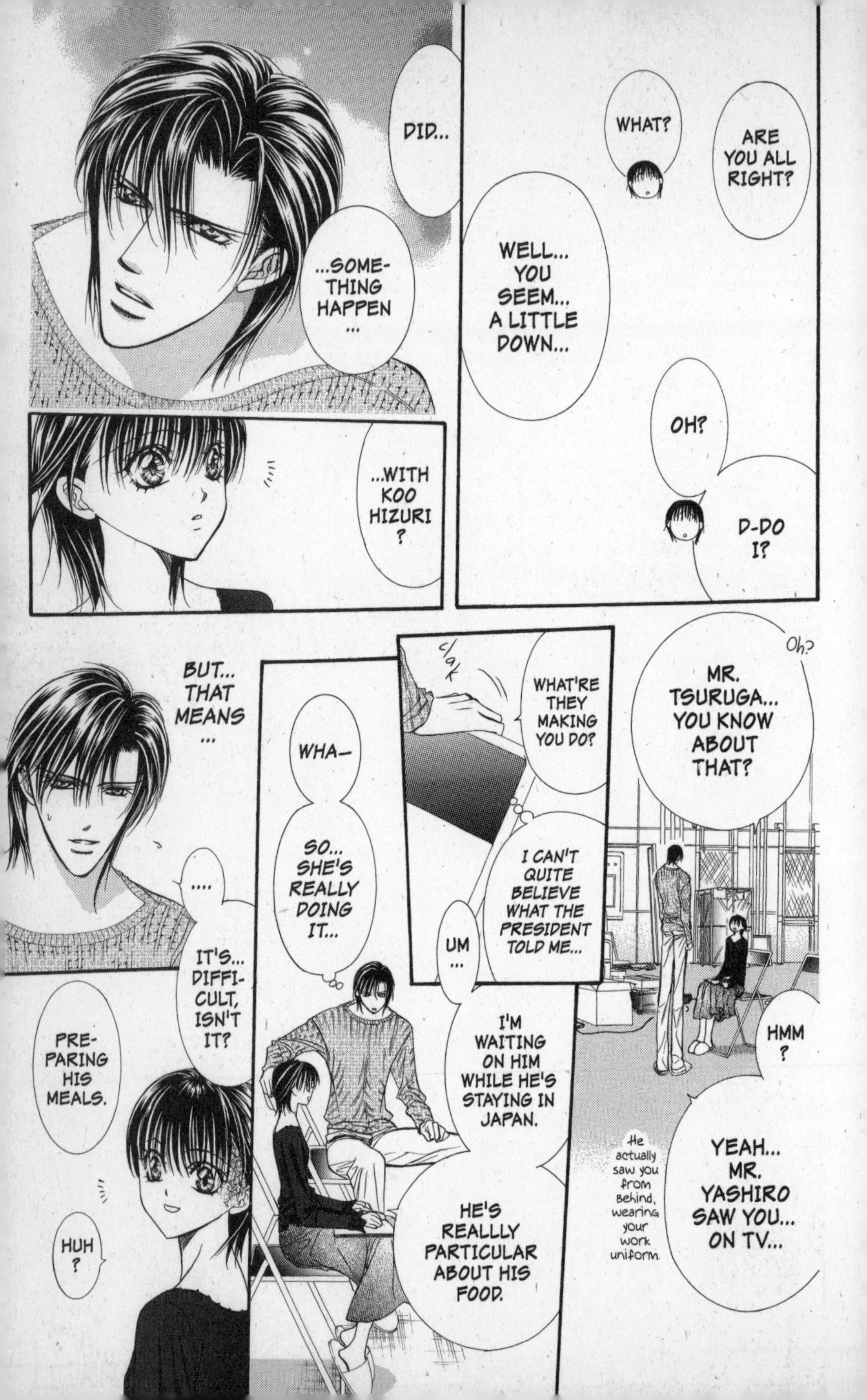
ARE YOU ALL RIGHT?
WHAT?
WELL... YOU SEEM... A LITTLE DOWN...
OH?
D-DO I?
DID...
...SOME-THING HAPPEN...
...WITH KOO HIZURI?
Oh?
MR. TSURUGA... YOU KNOW ABOUT THAT?
HMM?
YEAH... MR. YASHIRO SAW YOU... ON TV...
He actually saw you from behind, wearing your work uniform.
clak
WHAT'RE THEY MAKING YOU DO?
I CAN'T QUITE BELIEVE WHAT THE PRESIDENT TOLD ME...
UM...
I'M WAITING ON HIM WHILE HE'S STAYING IN JAPAN.
HE'S REALLLY PARTICULAR ABOUT HIS FOOD.
WHA—
SO... SHE'S REALLY DOING IT...
BUT... THAT MEANS...
....
IT'S... DIFFICULT, ISN'T IT?
HUH?
PRE-PARING HIS MEALS.

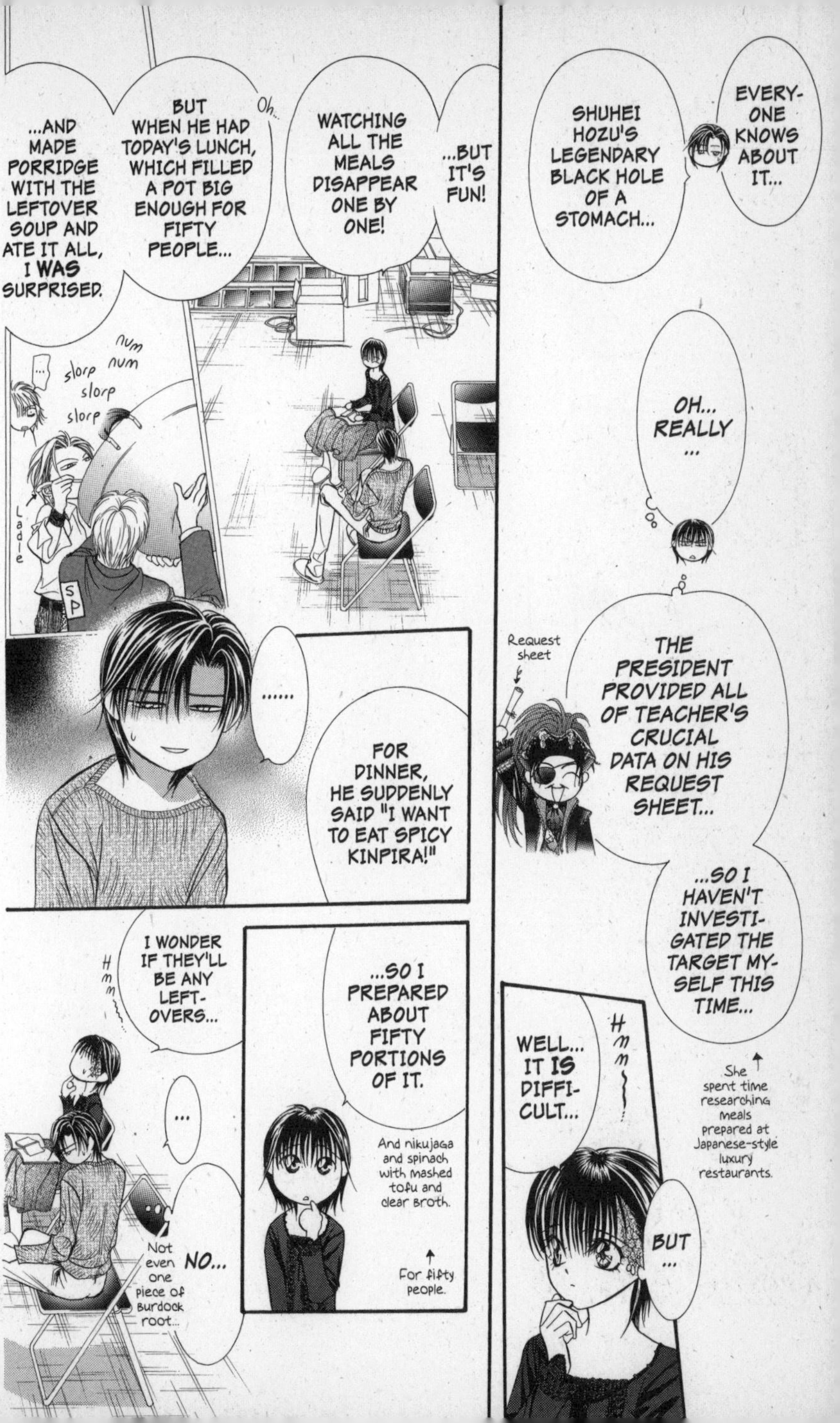
EVERY-ONE KNOWS ABOUT IT...
SHUHEI HOZU'S LEGENDARY BLACK HOLE OF A STOMACH...
OH... REALLY ...
Request sheet
THE PRESIDENT PROVIDED ALL OF TEACHER'S CRUCIAL DATA ON HIS REQUEST SHEET...
...SO I HAVEN'T INVESTIGATED THE TARGET MYSELF THIS TIME...
She spent time researching meals prepared at Japanese-style luxury restaurants.
Hmm~
WELL... IT IS DIFFICULT...
BUT ...
...BUT IT'S FUN!
WATCHING ALL THE MEALS DISAPPEAR ONE BY ONE!
Oh...
BUT WHEN HE HAD TODAY'S LUNCH, WHICH FILLED A POT BIG ENOUGH FOR FIFTY PEOPLE...
...AND MADE PORRIDGE WITH THE LEFTOVER SOUP AND ATE IT ALL, I WAS SURPRISED.
num num
slorp slorp slorp
...
Ladle
SP
......
FOR DINNER, HE SUDDENLY SAID "I WANT TO EAT SPICY KINPIRA!"
...SO I PREPARED ABOUT FIFTY PORTIONS OF IT.
And nikujaga and spinach with mashed tofu and clear broth.
For fifty people.
I WONDER IF THEY'LL BE ANY LEFT-OVERS...
Hmm~
...
NO...
Not even one piece of burdock root...

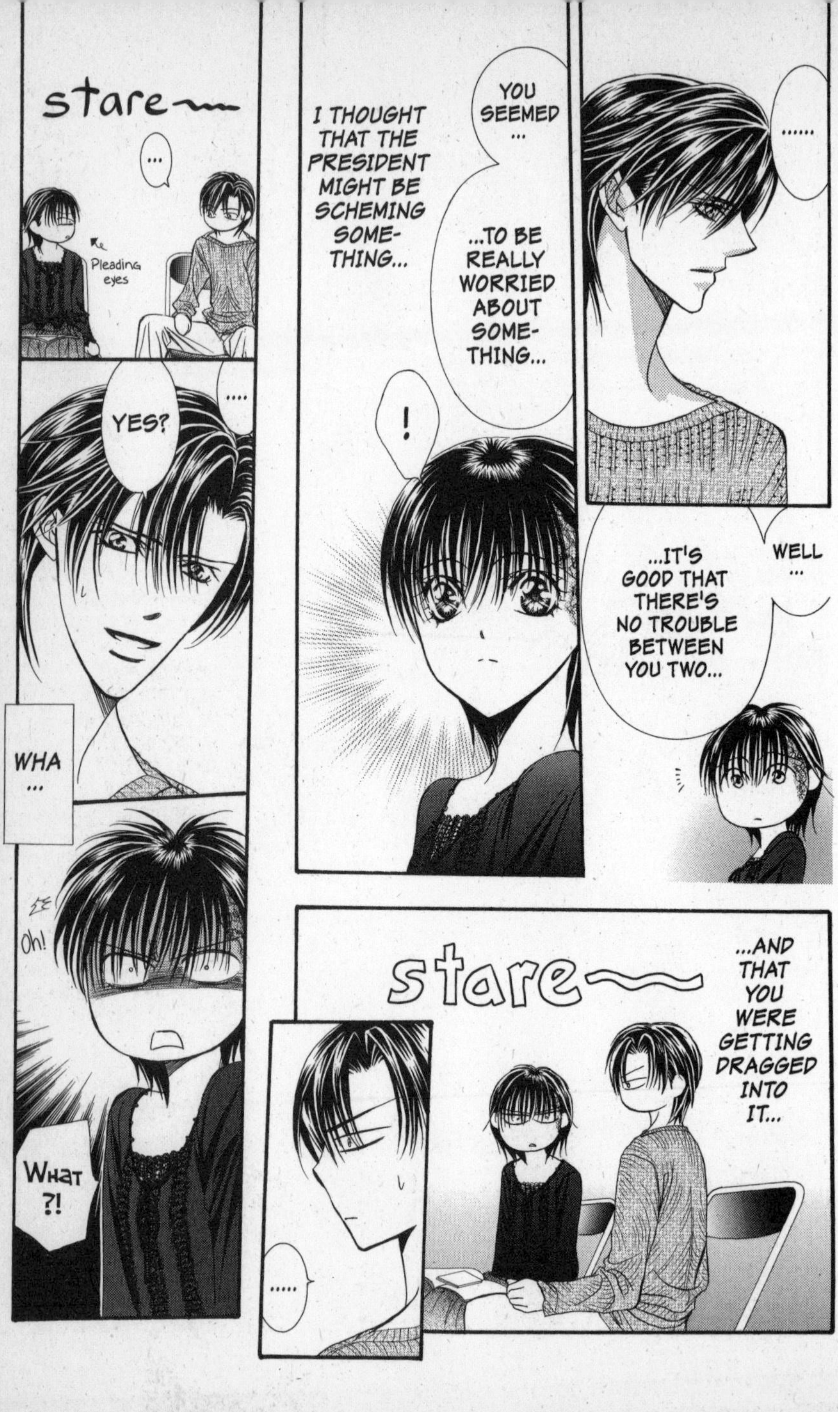

......
WELL ...
...IT'S GOOD THAT THERE'S NO TROUBLE BETWEEN YOU TWO...
I THOUGHT THAT THE PRESIDENT MIGHT BE SCHEMING SOME-THING...
YOU SEEMED ...
...TO BE REALLY WORRIED ABOUT SOME-THING...
!
stare
...AND THAT YOU WERE GETTING DRAGGED INTO IT...
.....
stare
...
Pleading eyes
....
YES?
WHA ...
Oh!
What ?!

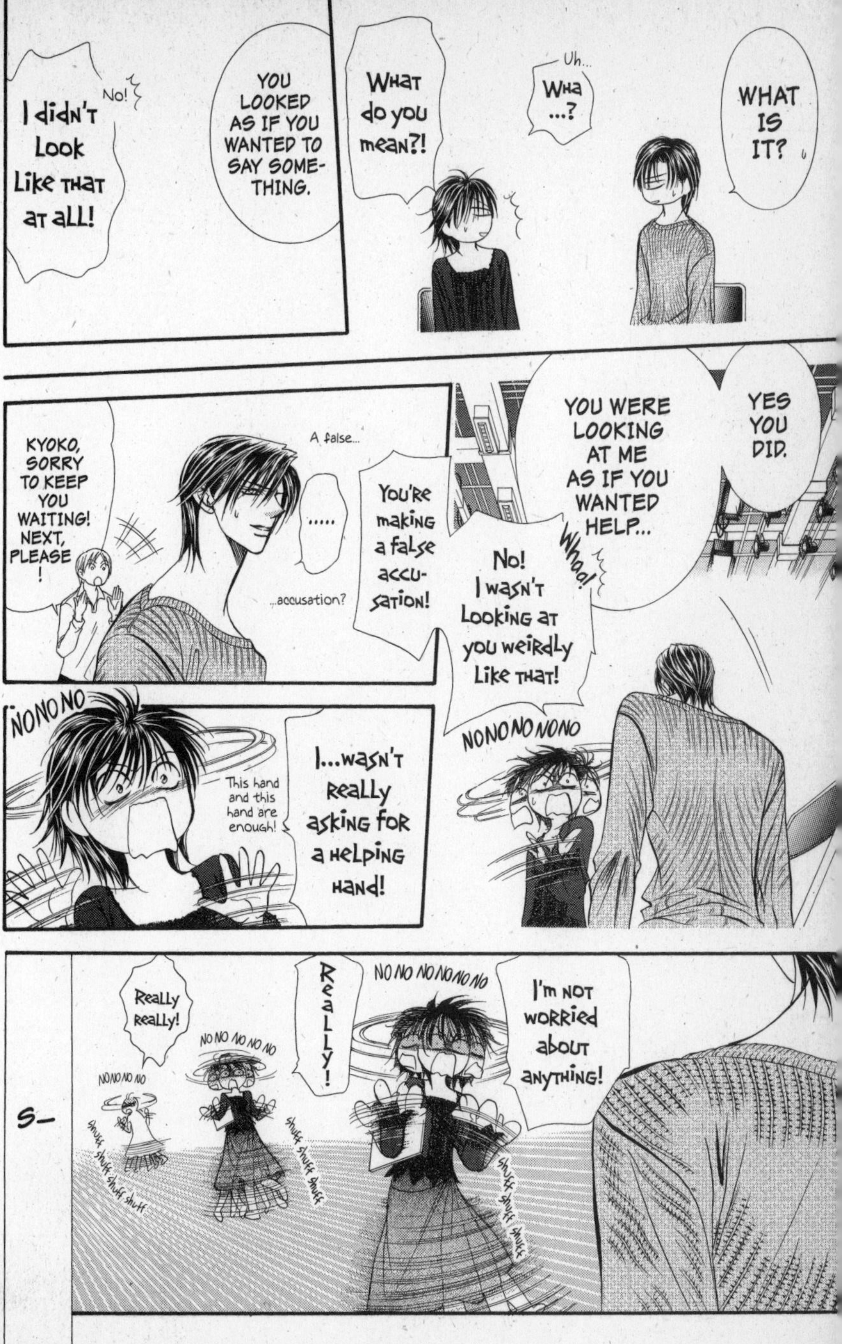
WHAT IS IT?
Uh...
WHA ...?
What do you mean?!
YOU LOOKED AS IF YOU WANTED TO SAY SOME-THING.
No!
I didn't look like that at all!
YES YOU DID.
YOU WERE LOOKING AT ME AS IF YOU WANTED HELP...
Whoa!
No! I wasn't looking at you weirdly like that!
NONONONONO
You're making a false accu-sation!
A false...
.....
...accusation?
KYOKO, SORRY TO KEEP YOU WAITING! NEXT, PLEASE!
I...wasn't really asking for a helping hand!
This hand and this hand are enough!
NONONO
I'm not worried about anything!
NO NO NO NO NO NO
Really!
shuff shuff shuff
shuff shuff shuff
Really really!
NO NO NO NO NO
shuff shuff shuff
NONONO NO
shuff shuff shuff shuff
S—

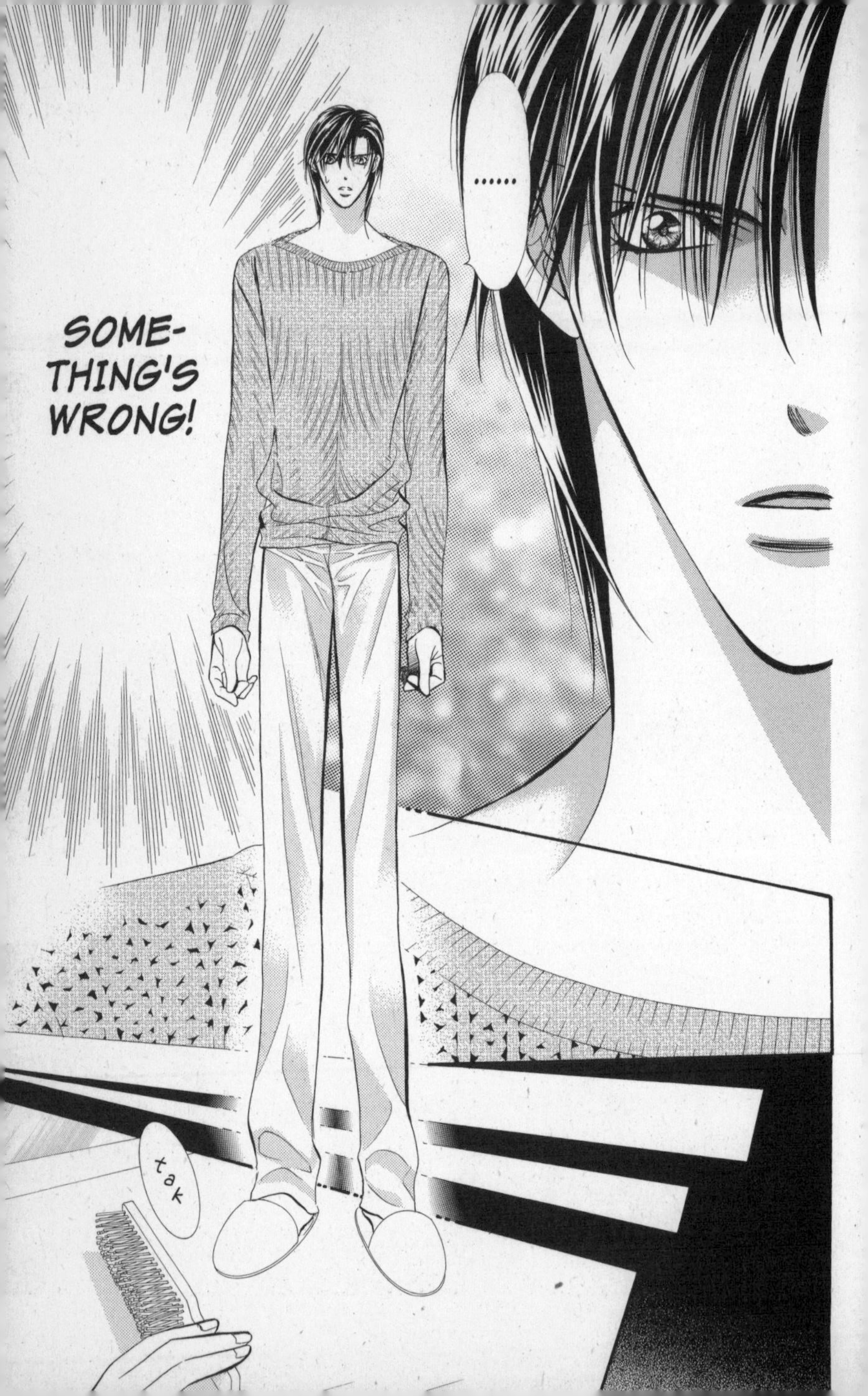
......
SOME-THING'S WRONG!
tak

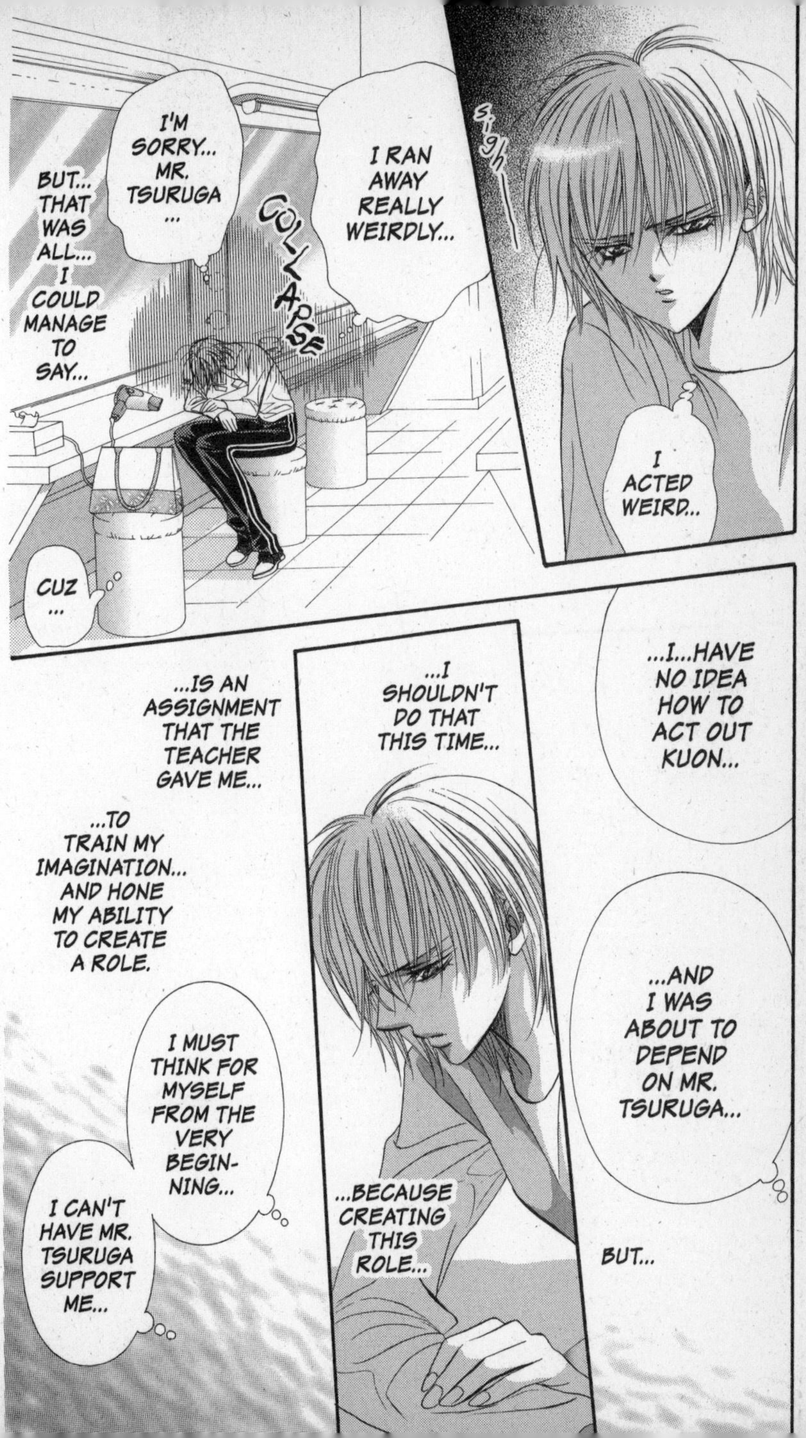
SIGH
I ACTED WEIRD...
I RAN AWAY REALLY WEIRDLY...
I'M SORRY... MR. TSURUGA...
BUT... THAT WAS ALL... I COULD MANAGE TO SAY...
COLLAPSE
CUZ...
...I...HAVE NO IDEA HOW TO ACT OUT KUON...
...AND I WAS ABOUT TO DEPEND ON MR. TSURUGA...
BUT...
...I SHOULDN'T DO THAT THIS TIME...
...BECAUSE CREATING THIS ROLE...
...IS AN ASSIGNMENT THAT THE TEACHER GAVE ME...
...TO TRAIN MY IMAGINATION... AND HONE MY ABILITY TO CREATE A ROLE.
I MUST THINK FOR MYSELF FROM THE VERY BEGIN-NING...
I CAN'T HAVE MR. TSURUGA SUPPORT ME...

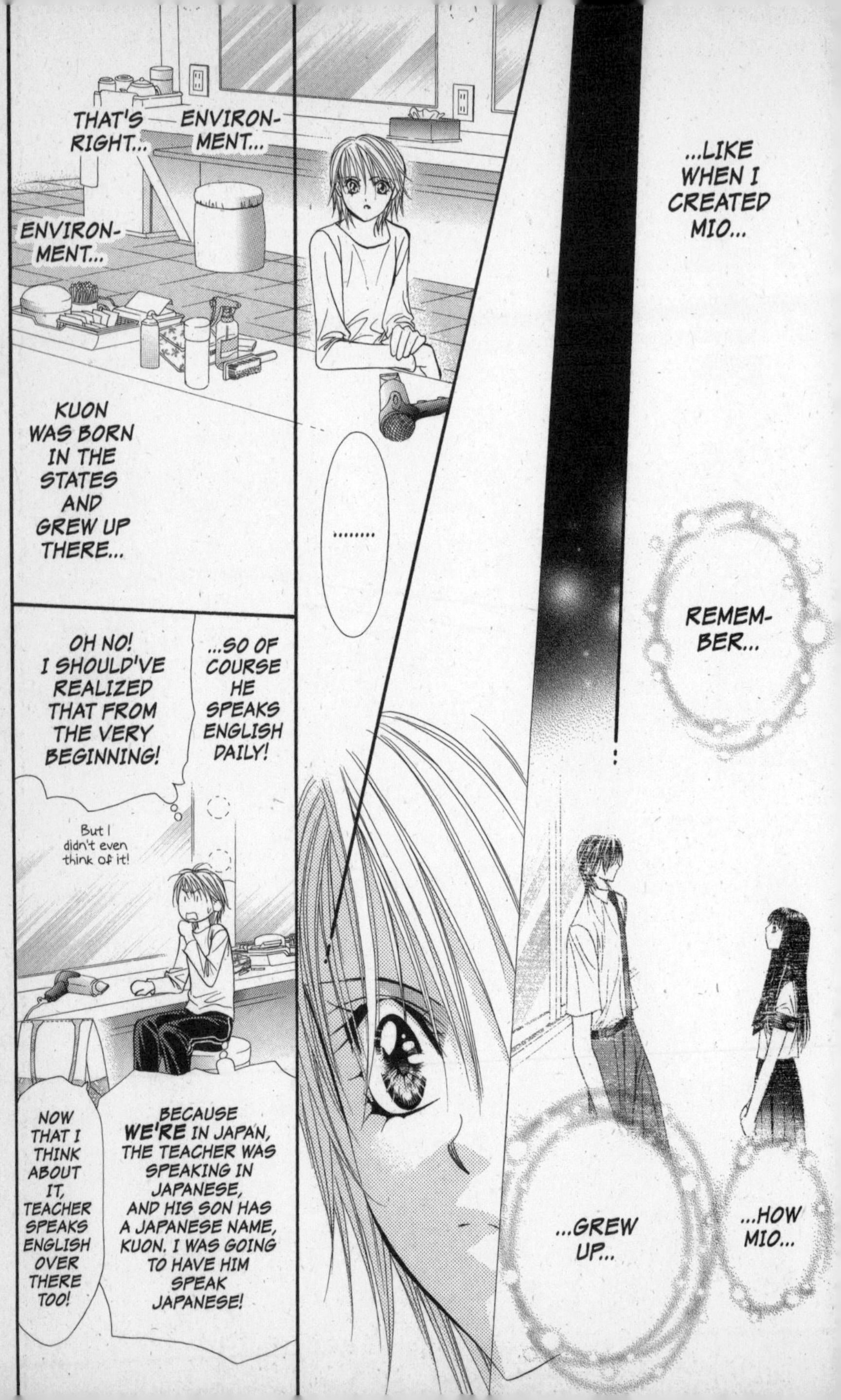
ENVIRON-MENT...
THAT'S RIGHT...
ENVIRON-MENT...
KUON WAS BORN IN THE STATES AND GREW UP THERE...
...SO OF COURSE HE SPEAKS ENGLISH DAILY!
OH NO! I SHOULD'VE REALIZED THAT FROM THE VERY BEGINNING!
But I didn't even think of it!
BECAUSE **WE'RE** IN JAPAN, THE TEACHER WAS SPEAKING IN JAPANESE, AND HIS SON HAS A JAPANESE NAME, KUON. I WAS GOING TO HAVE HIM SPEAK JAPANESE!
NOW THAT I THINK ABOUT IT, TEACHER SPEAKS ENGLISH OVER THERE TOO!
....
REMEM-BER...
...LIKE WHEN I CREATED MIO...
...HOW MIO...
...GREW UP...

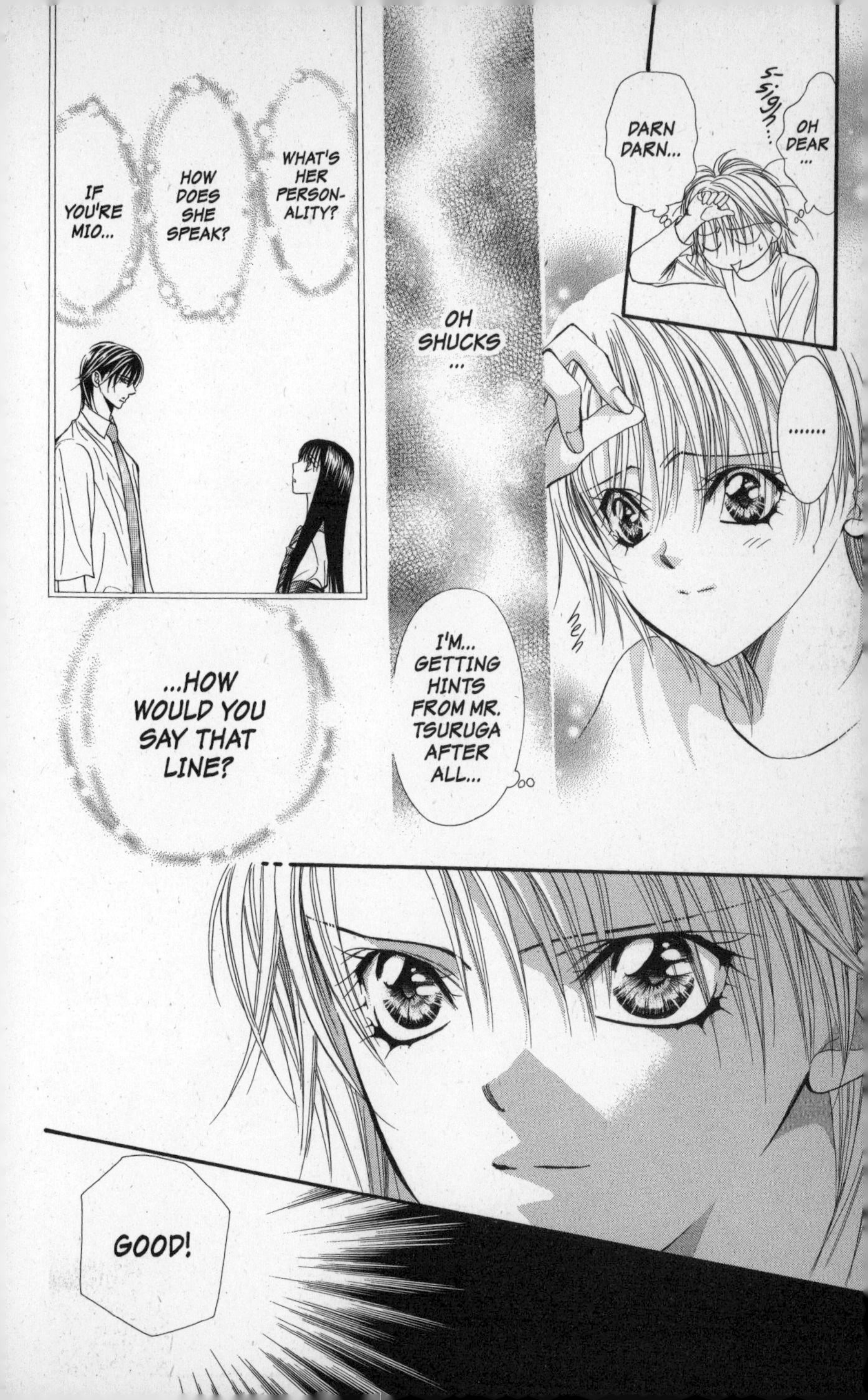
s-sigh...
OH DEAR ...
DARN DARN...
....
heh
OH SHUCKS ...
I'M... GETTING HINTS FROM MR. TSURUGA AFTER ALL...
WHAT'S HER PERSONALITY?
HOW DOES SHE SPEAK?
IF YOU'RE MIO...
...HOW WOULD YOU SAY THAT LINE?
GOOD!

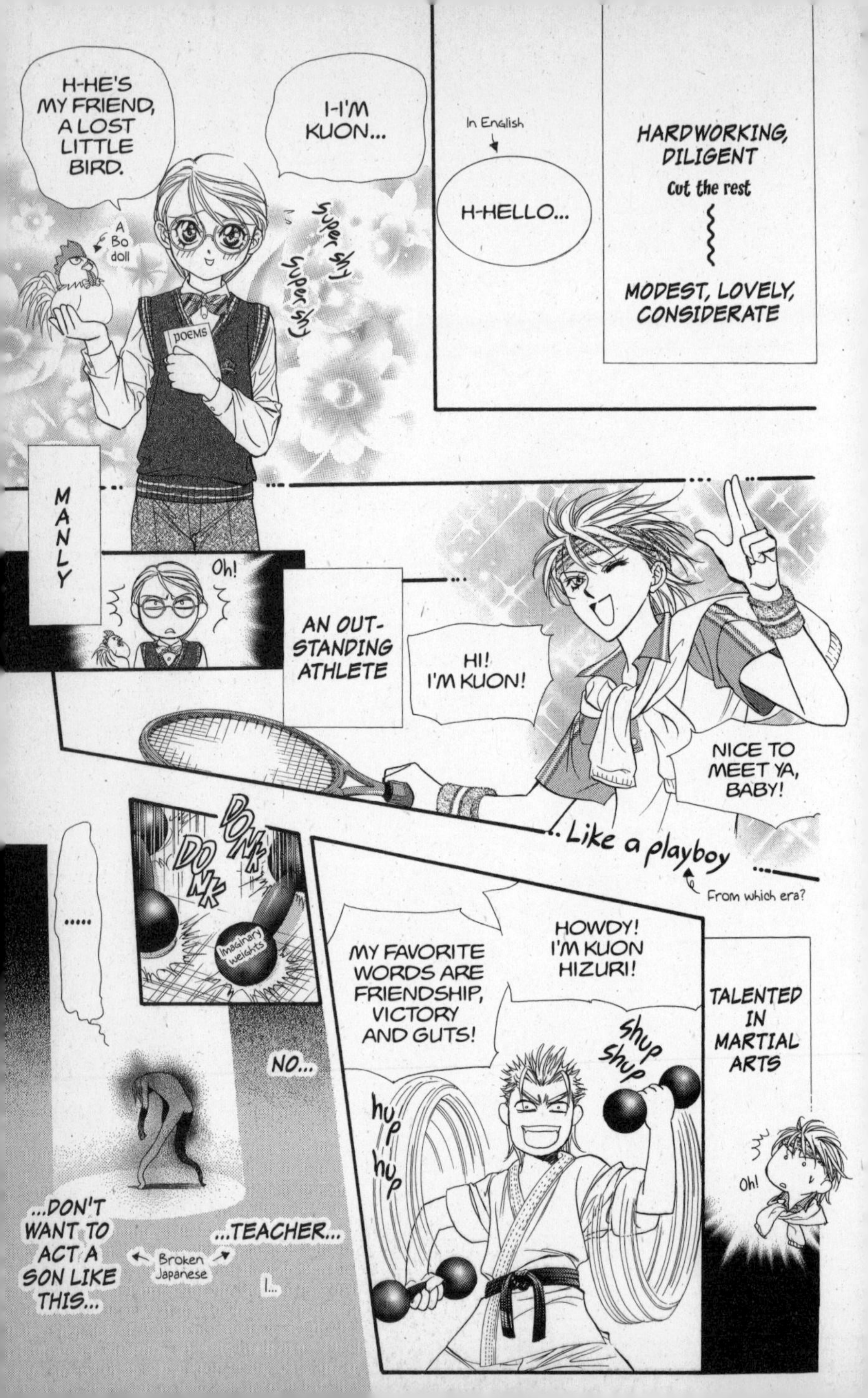

HARDWORKING, DILIGENT
Cut the rest
MODEST, LOVELY, CONSIDERATE
In English
H-HELLO...
I-I'M KUON...
H-HE'S MY FRIEND, A LOST LITTLE BIRD.
A Bo doll
POEMS
super shy super shy
AN OUT-STANDING ATHLETE
HI! I'M KUON!
NICE TO MEET YA, BABY!
...Like a playboy...
From which era?
MANLY
Oh!
TALENTED IN MARTIAL ARTS
Oh!
HOWDY! I'M KUON HIZURI!
MY FAVORITE WORDS ARE FRIENDSHIP, VICTORY AND GUTS!
shup shup
hup hup
DONK DONK
Imaginary weights
......
NO...
...TEACHER...
I...
...DON'T WANT TO ACT A SON LIKE THIS...
Broken Japanese

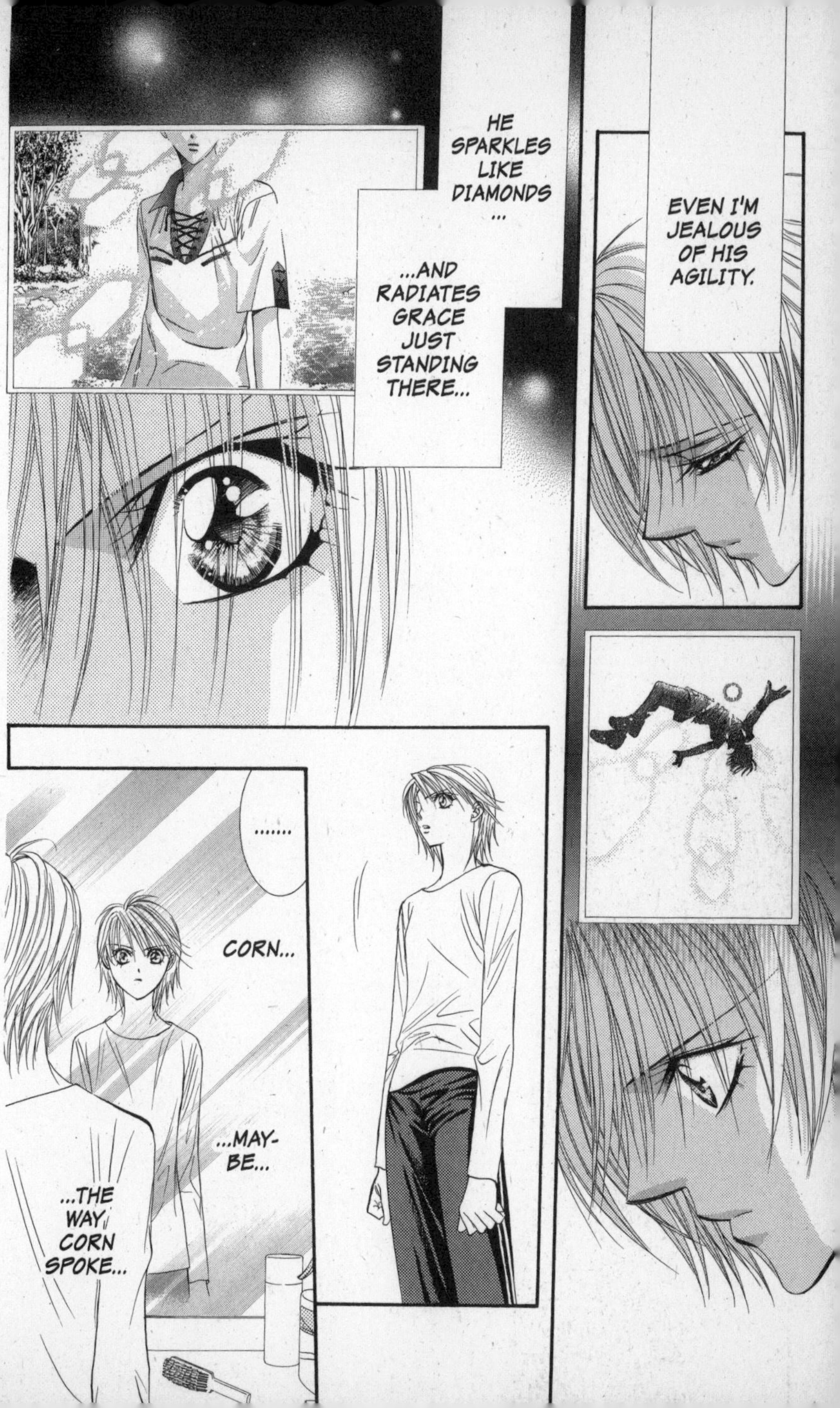
EVEN I'M JEALOUS OF HIS AGILITY.
HE SPARKLES LIKE DIAMONDS ...
...AND RADIATES GRACE JUST STANDING THERE...
....
CORN...
...MAY-BE...
...THE WAY CORN SPOKE...

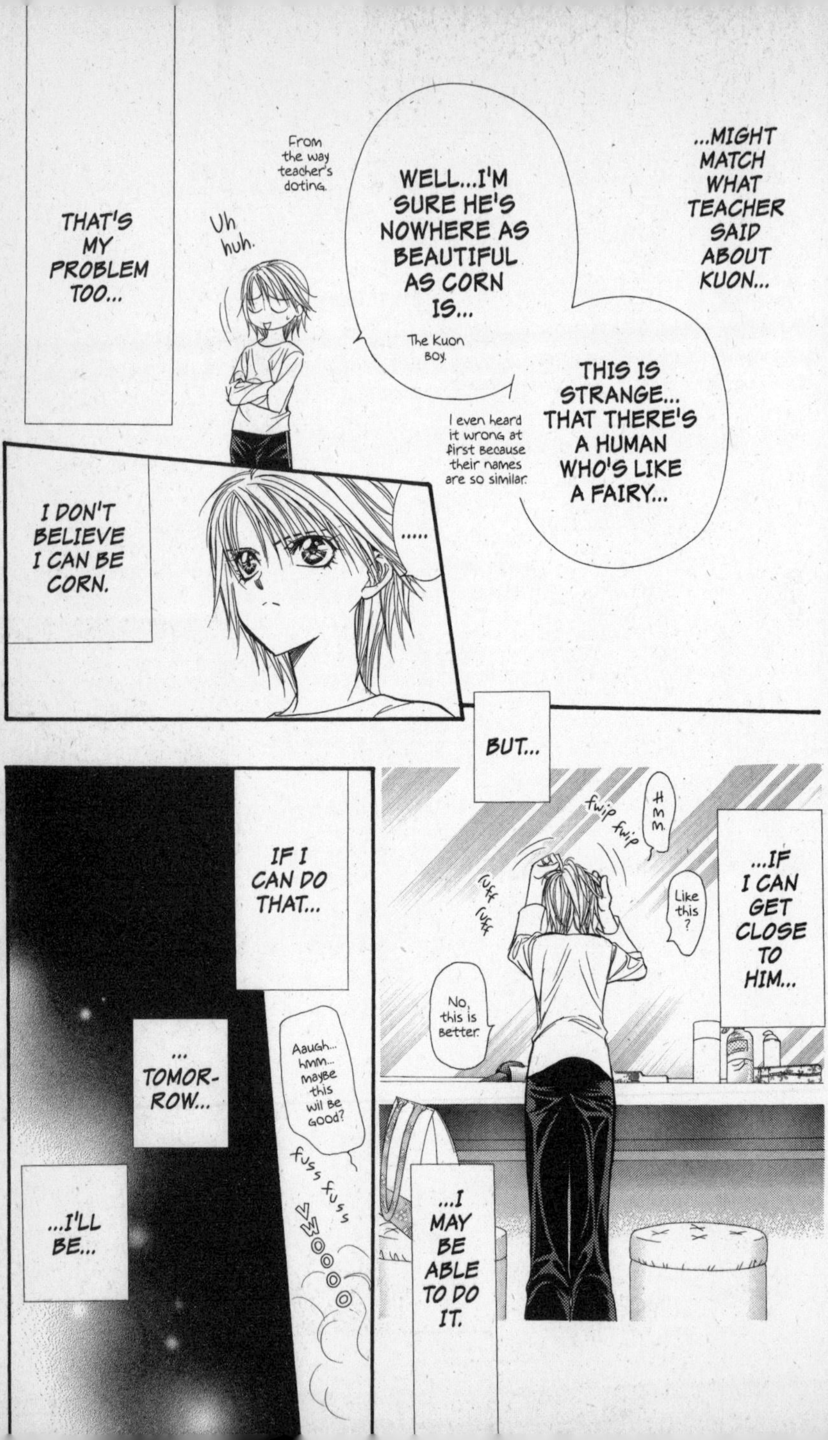
...MIGHT MATCH WHAT TEACHER SAID ABOUT KUON...
WELL...I'M SURE HE'S NOWHERE AS BEAUTIFUL AS CORN IS...
The Kuon boy.
From the way teacher's doting.
Uh huh.
THIS IS STRANGE... THAT THERE'S A HUMAN WHO'S LIKE A FAIRY...
I even heard it wrong at first because their names are so similar.
THAT'S MY PROBLEM TOO...
.....
I DON'T BELIEVE I CAN BE CORN.
BUT...
HMM.
fwip fwip
...IF I CAN GET CLOSE TO HIM...
Like this?
ruff ruff
No, this is better.
...I MAY BE ABLE TO DO IT.
IF I CAN DO THAT...
Aaugh... hmm... maybe this wil be good?
fuss fuss
VWOOOO
...TOMORROW...
...I'LL BE...

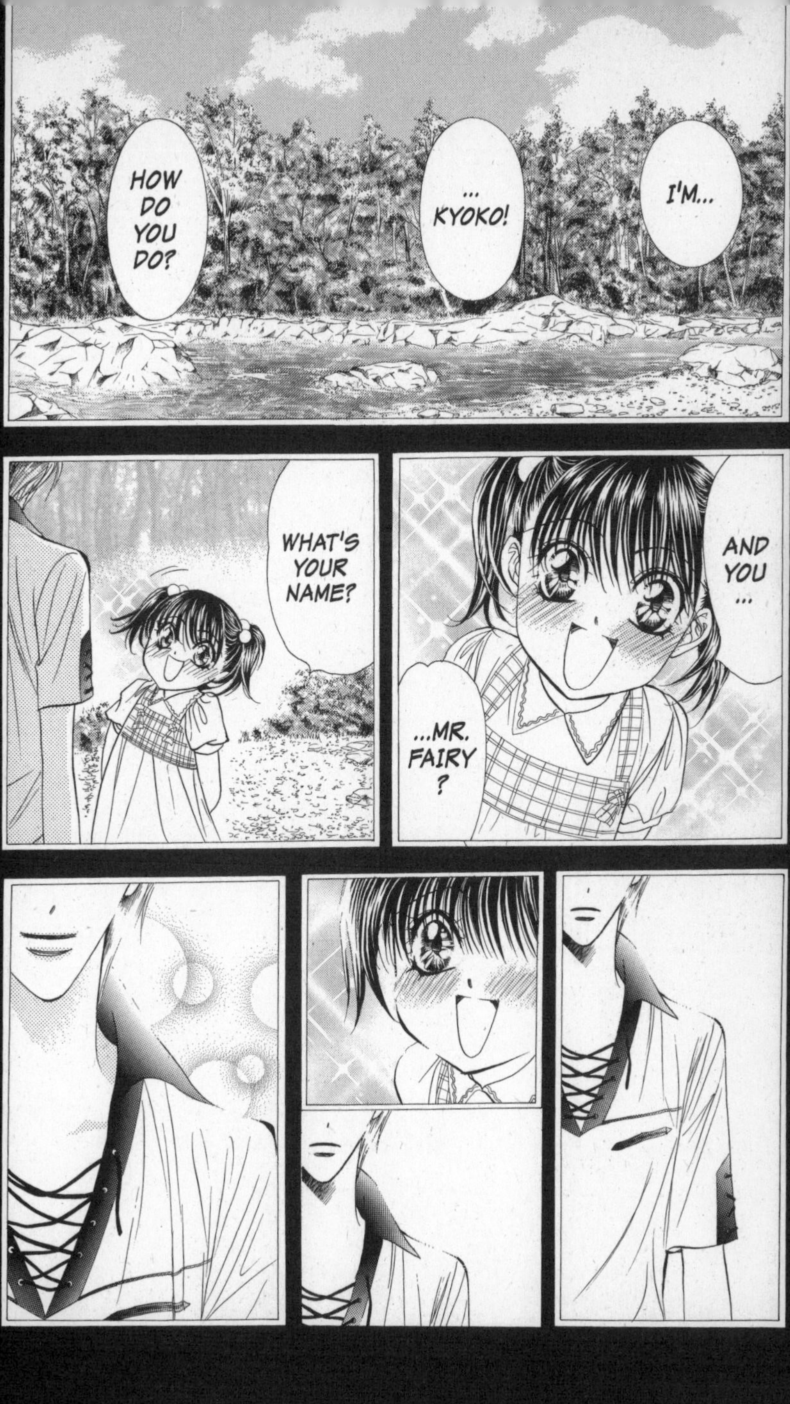
I'M...
...KYOKO!
HOW DO YOU DO?
AND YOU ...
...MR. FAIRY ?
WHAT'S YOUR NAME?

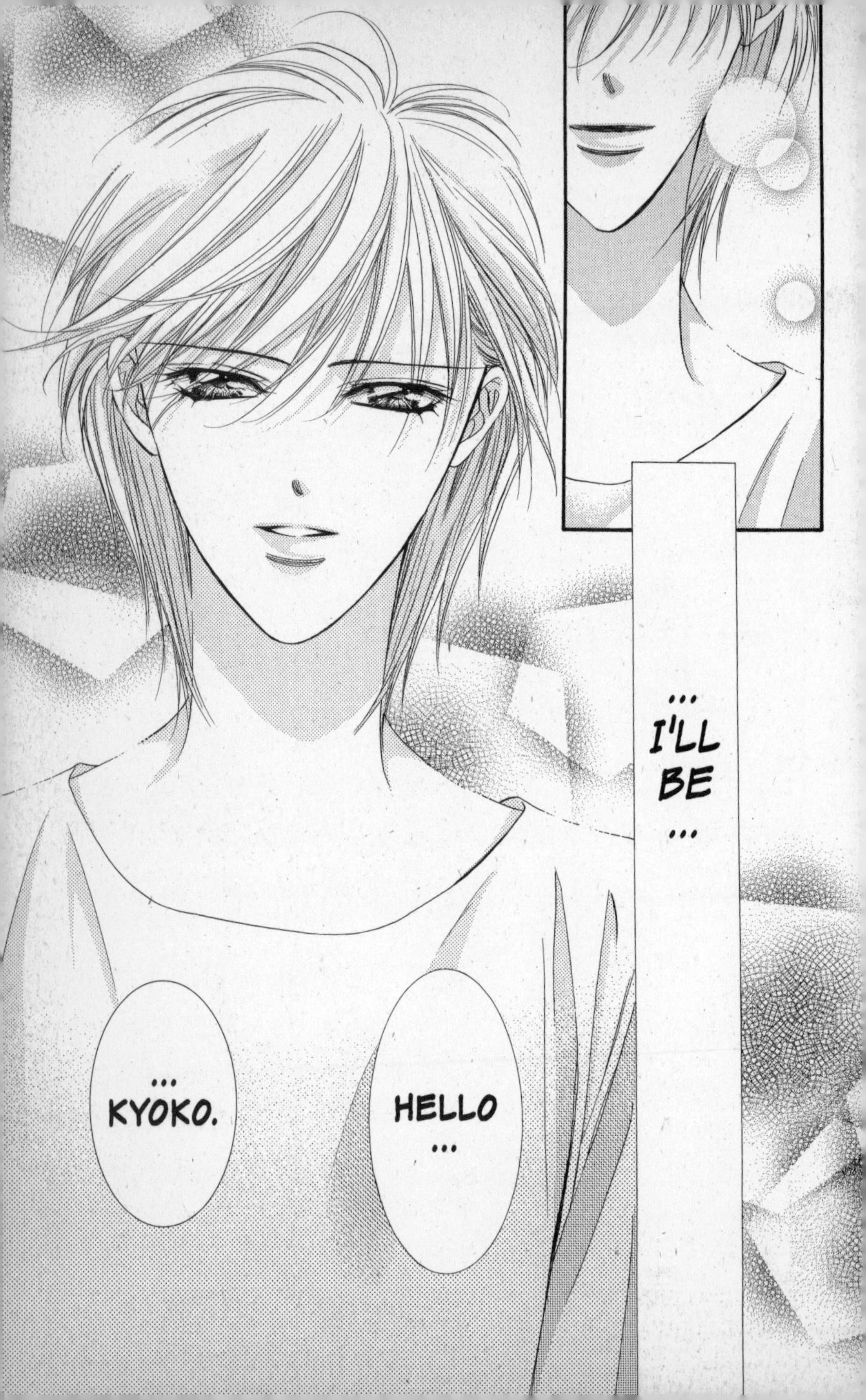
... I'LL BE ...
HELLO ...
... KYOKO.

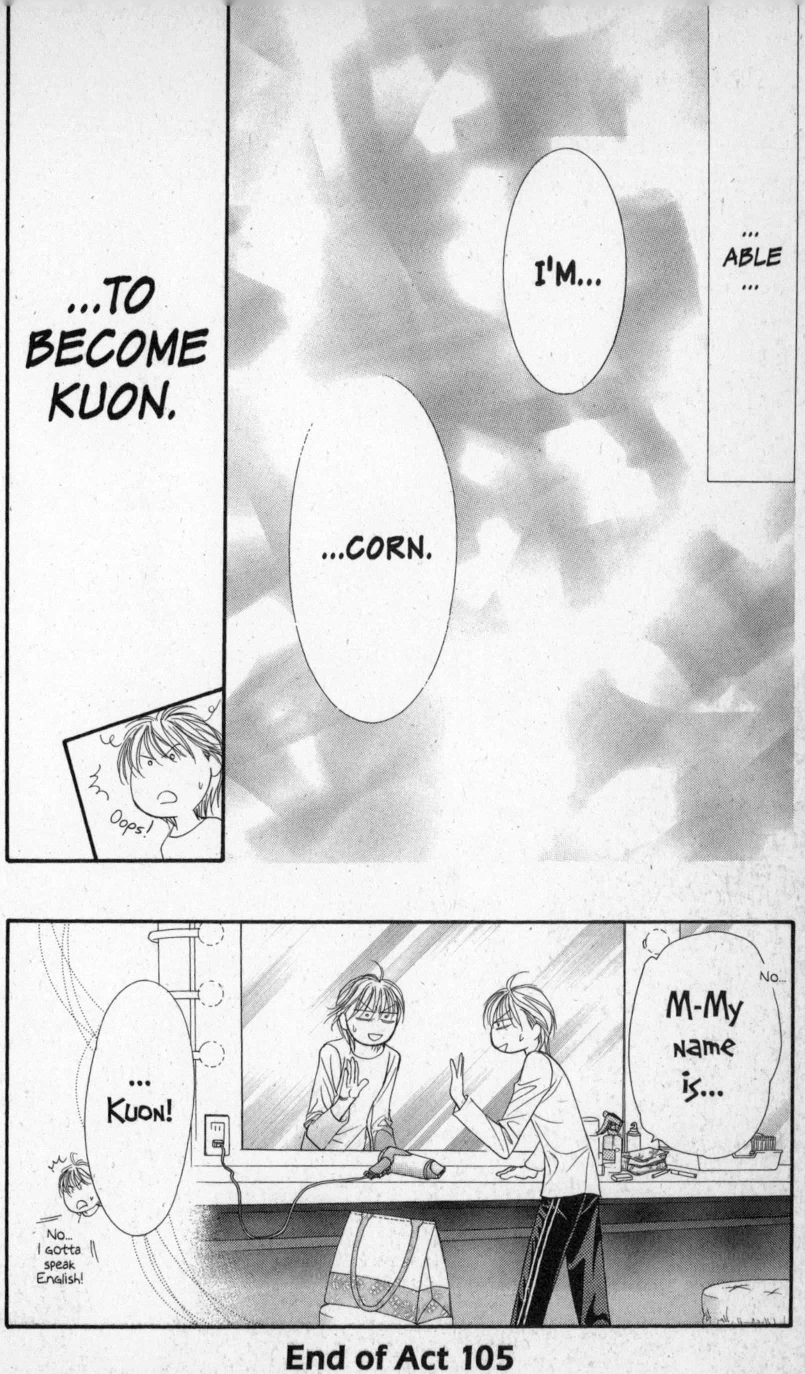
... ABLE ...
I'M...
...CORN.
...TO BECOME KUON.
Oops!
No...
M-My name is...
... KUON!
No... I gotta speak English!

End of Act 105

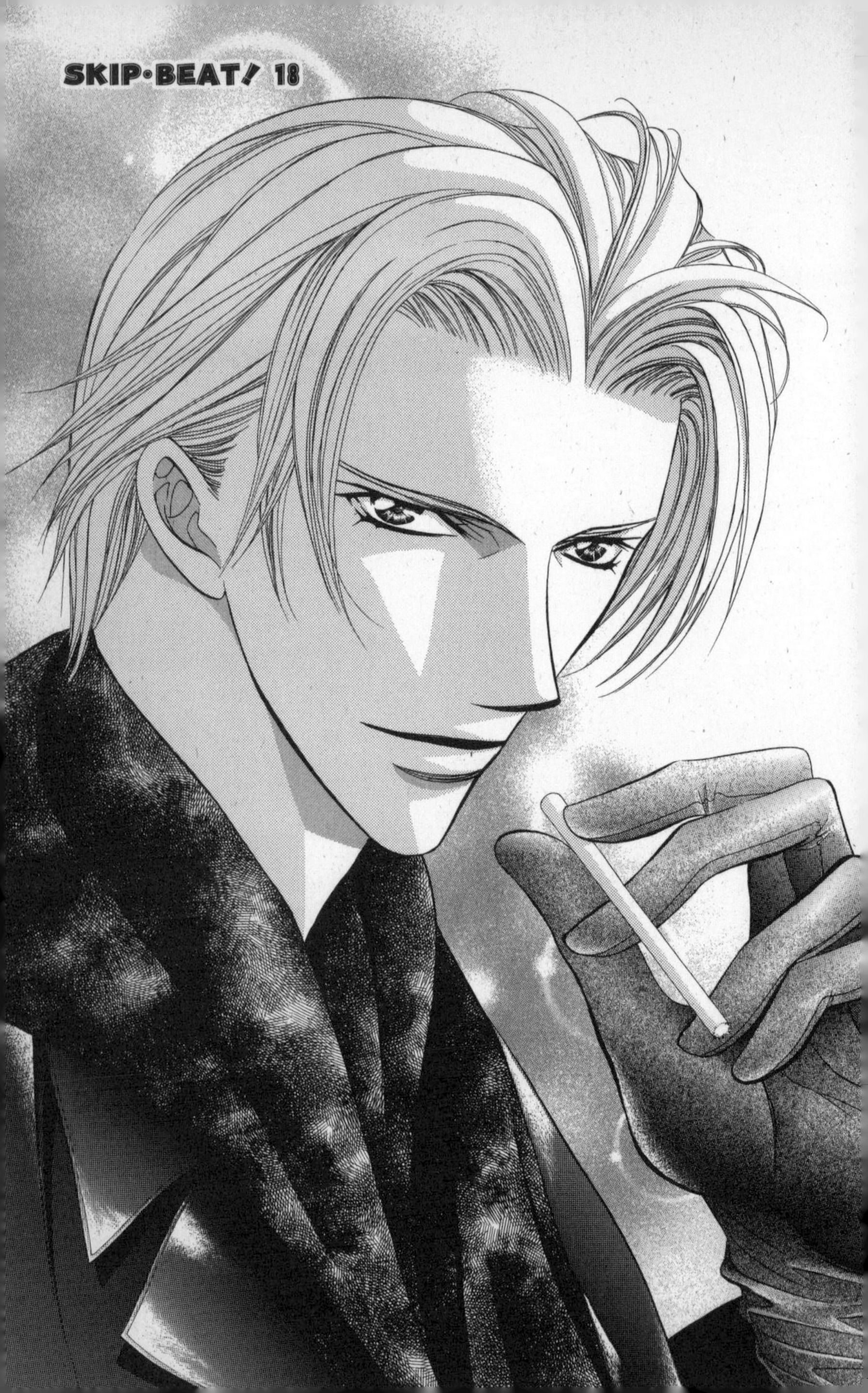
SKIP·BEAT! 18

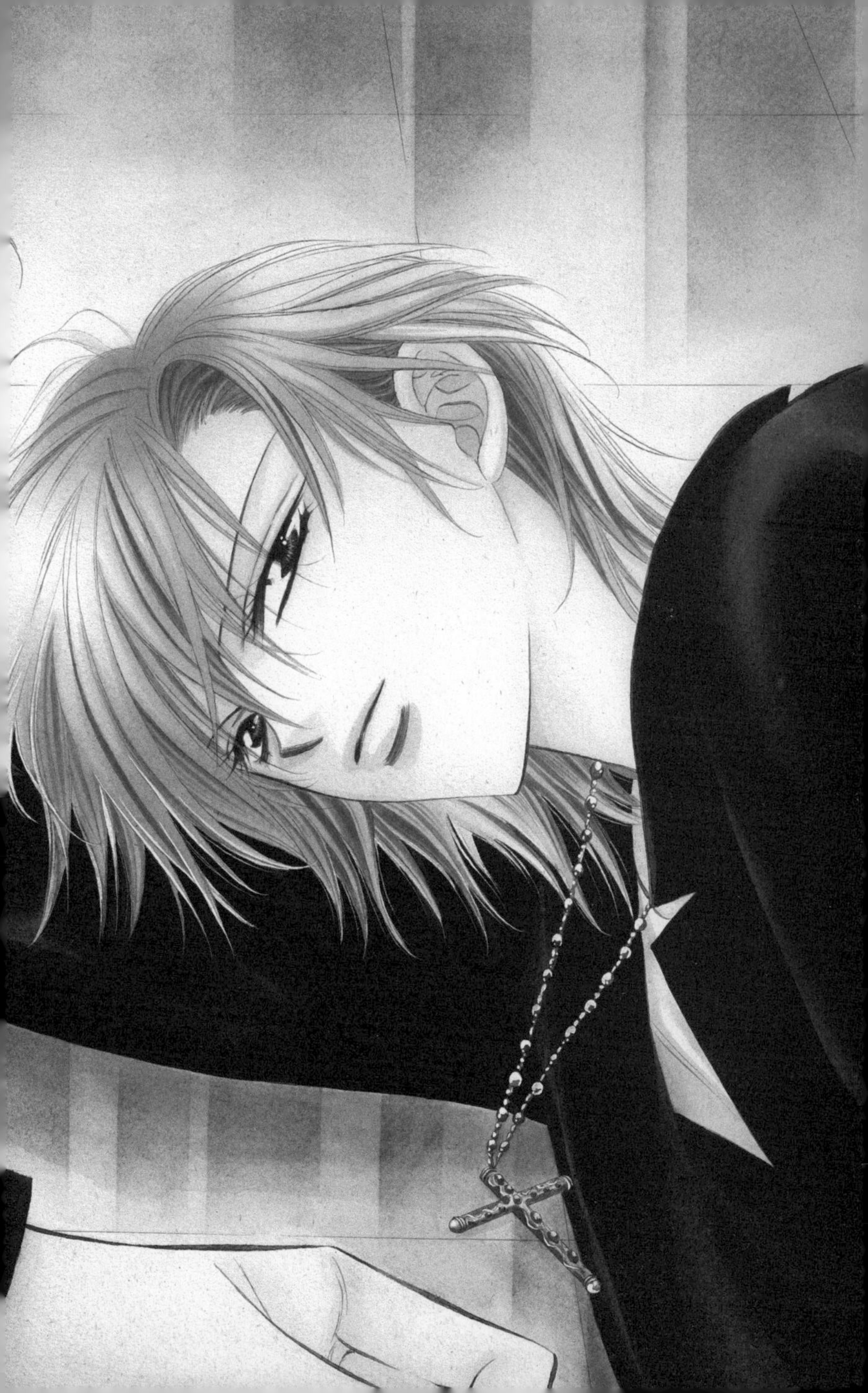

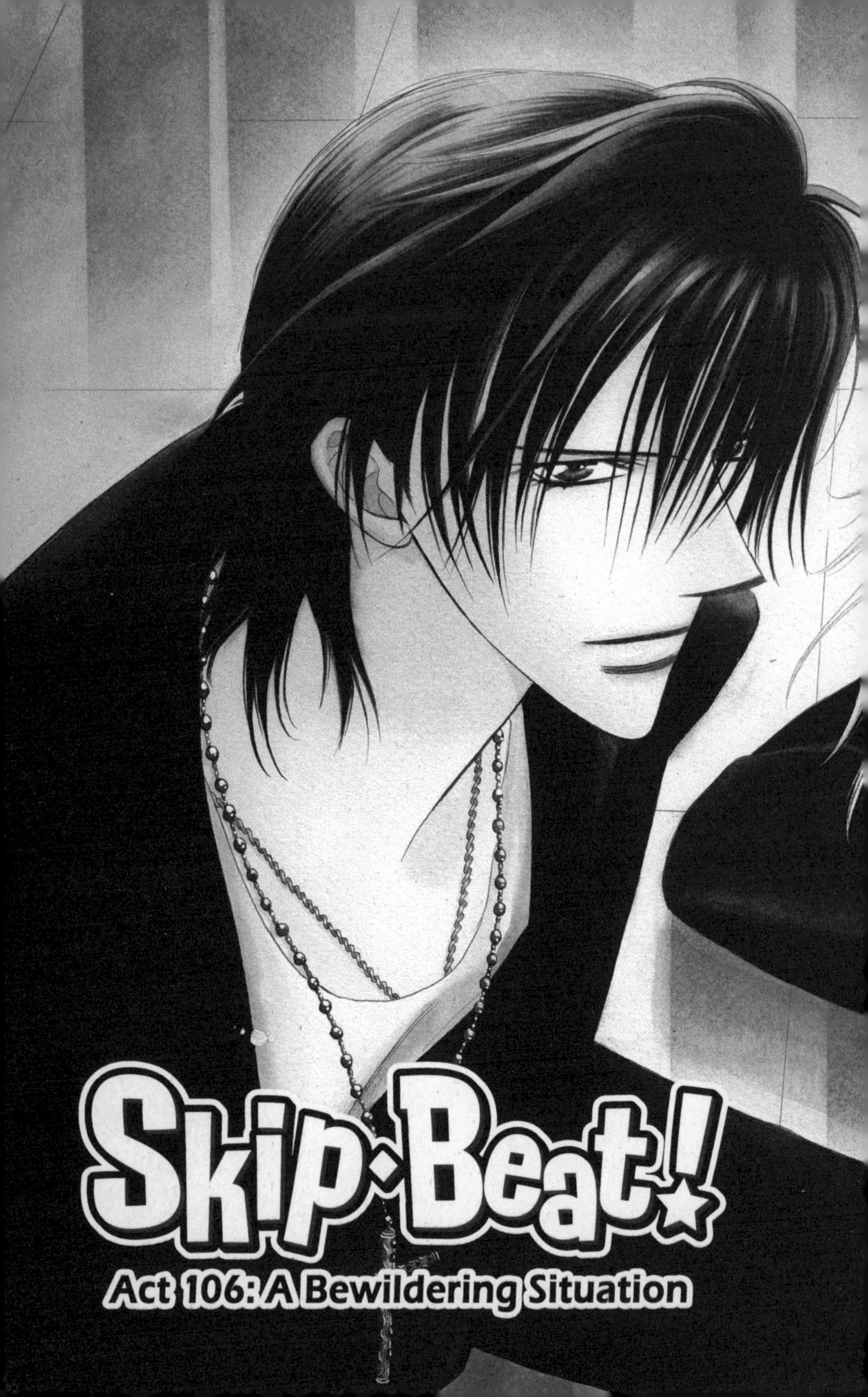
Skip·Beat!
Act 106: A Bewildering Situation

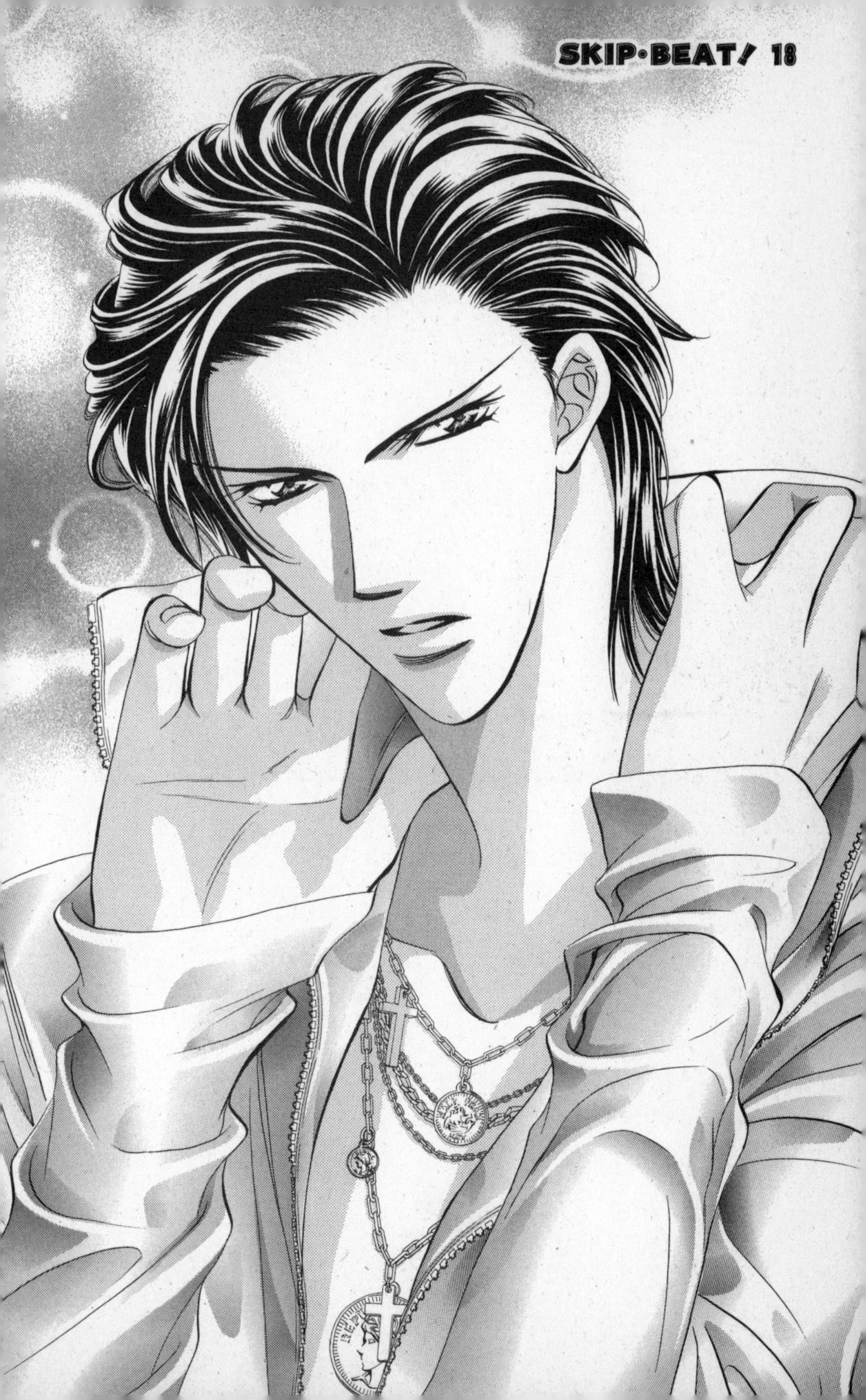

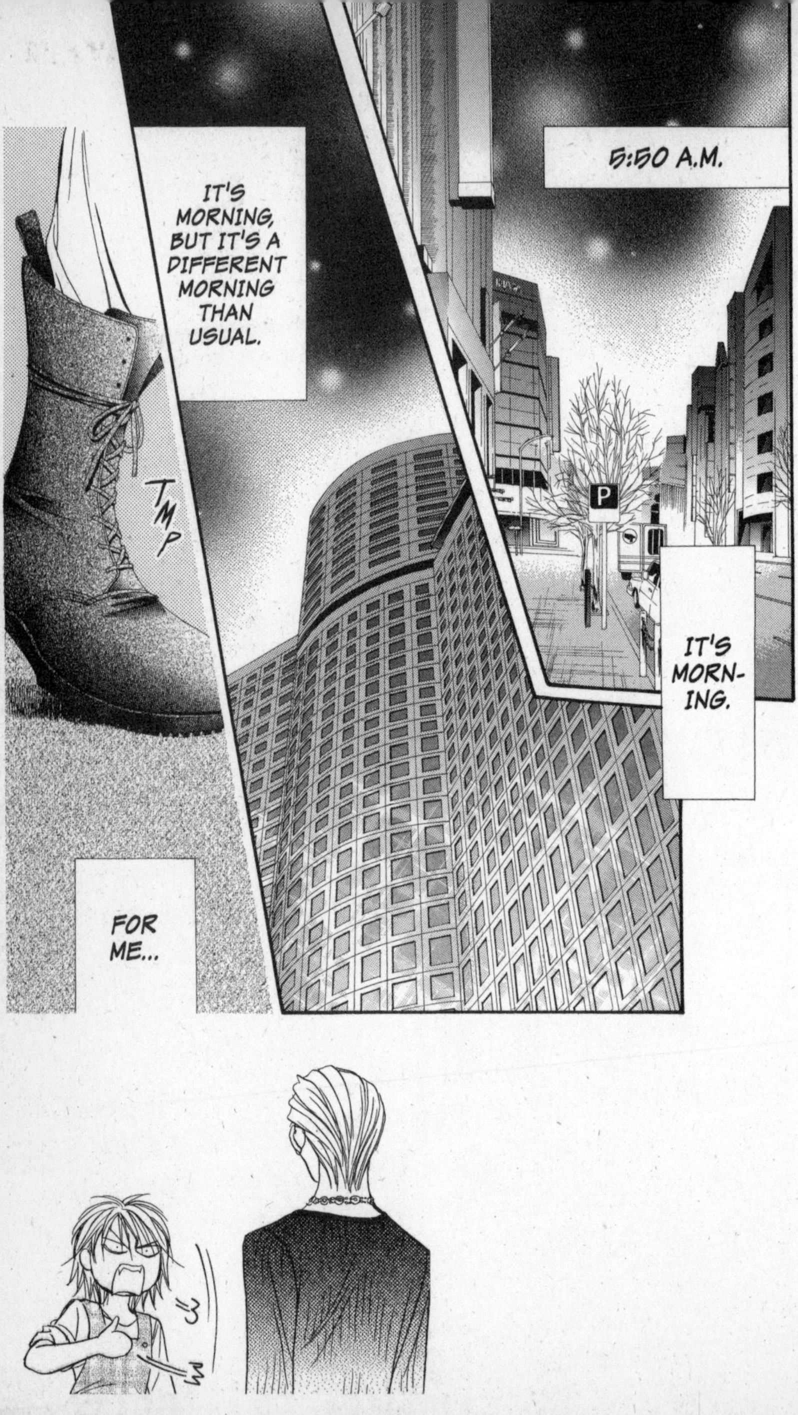
5:50 A.M.
IT'S MORNING.
IT'S MORNING, BUT IT'S A DIFFERENT MORNING THAN USUAL.
TMP
FOR ME...

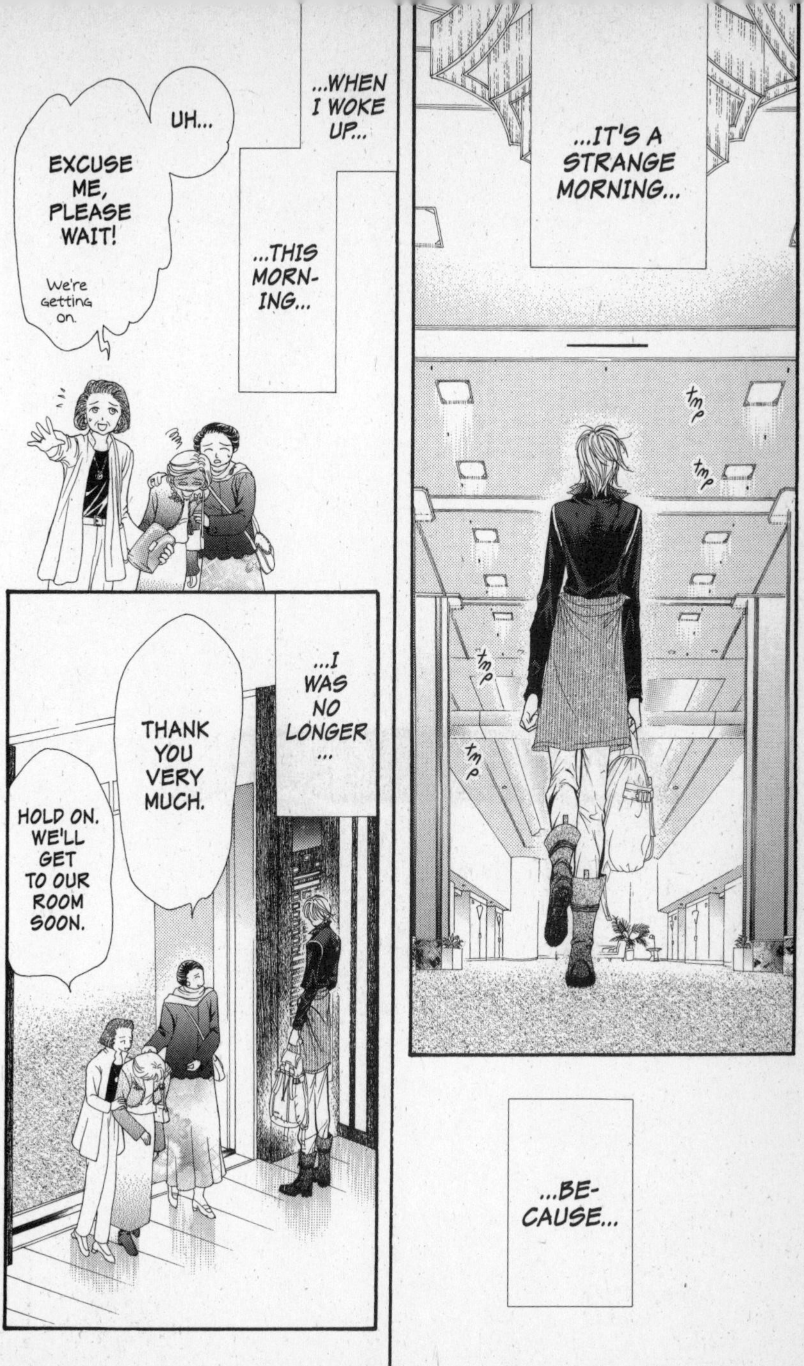
...IT'S A STRANGE MORNING...
tmp
tmp
tmp
tmp
...BE-CAUSE...
...WHEN I WOKE UP...
...THIS MORN-ING...
UH...
EXCUSE ME, PLEASE WAIT!
We're getting on.
...I WAS NO LONGER...
THANK YOU VERY MUCH.
HOLD ON. WE'LL GET TO OUR ROOM SOON.

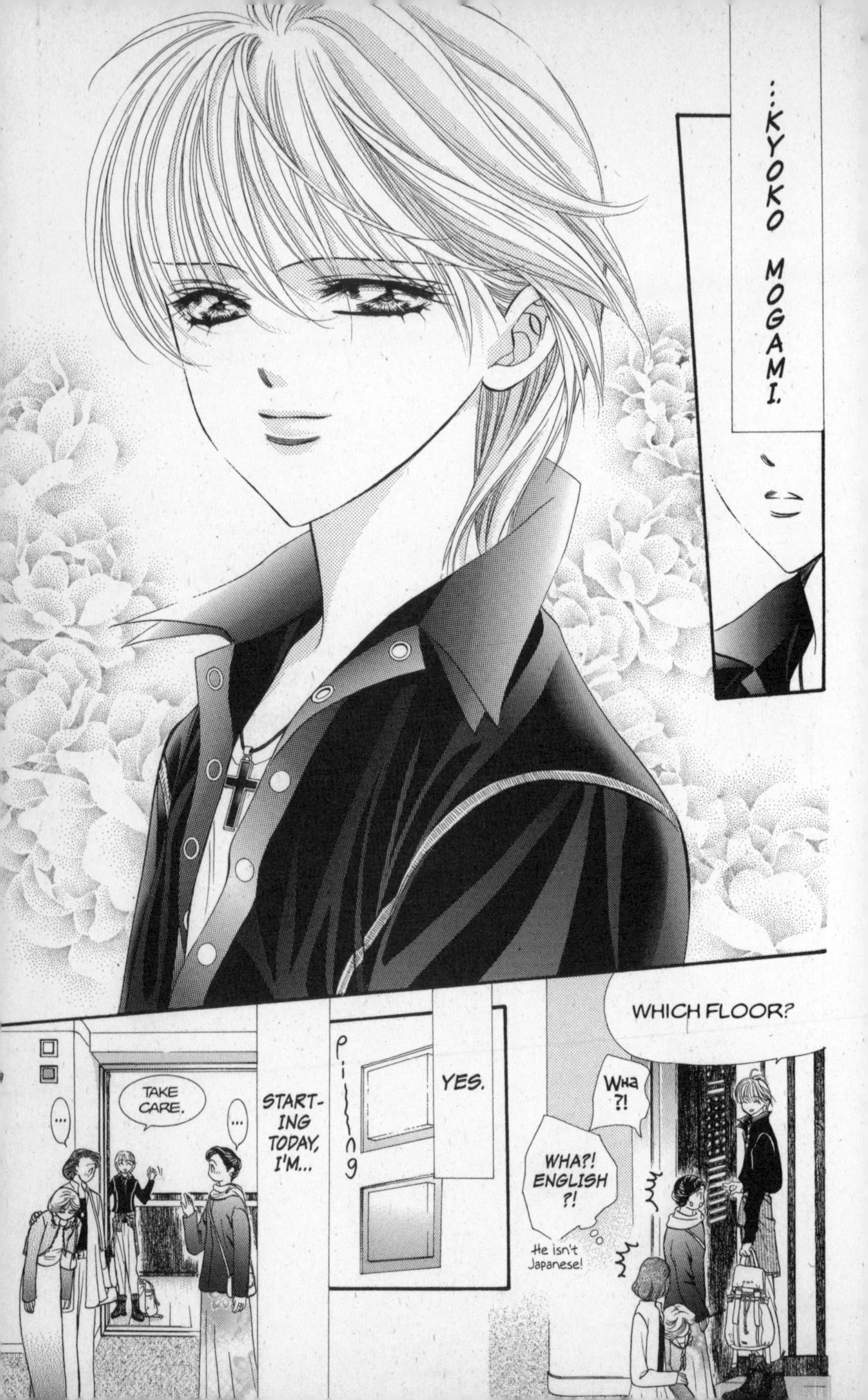
...KYOKO MOGAMI.
WHICH FLOOR?
Wha ?!
WHA?! ENGLISH ?!
He isn't Japanese!
YES.
START-ING TODAY, I'M...
Pi---ng
TAKE CARE.
...
...

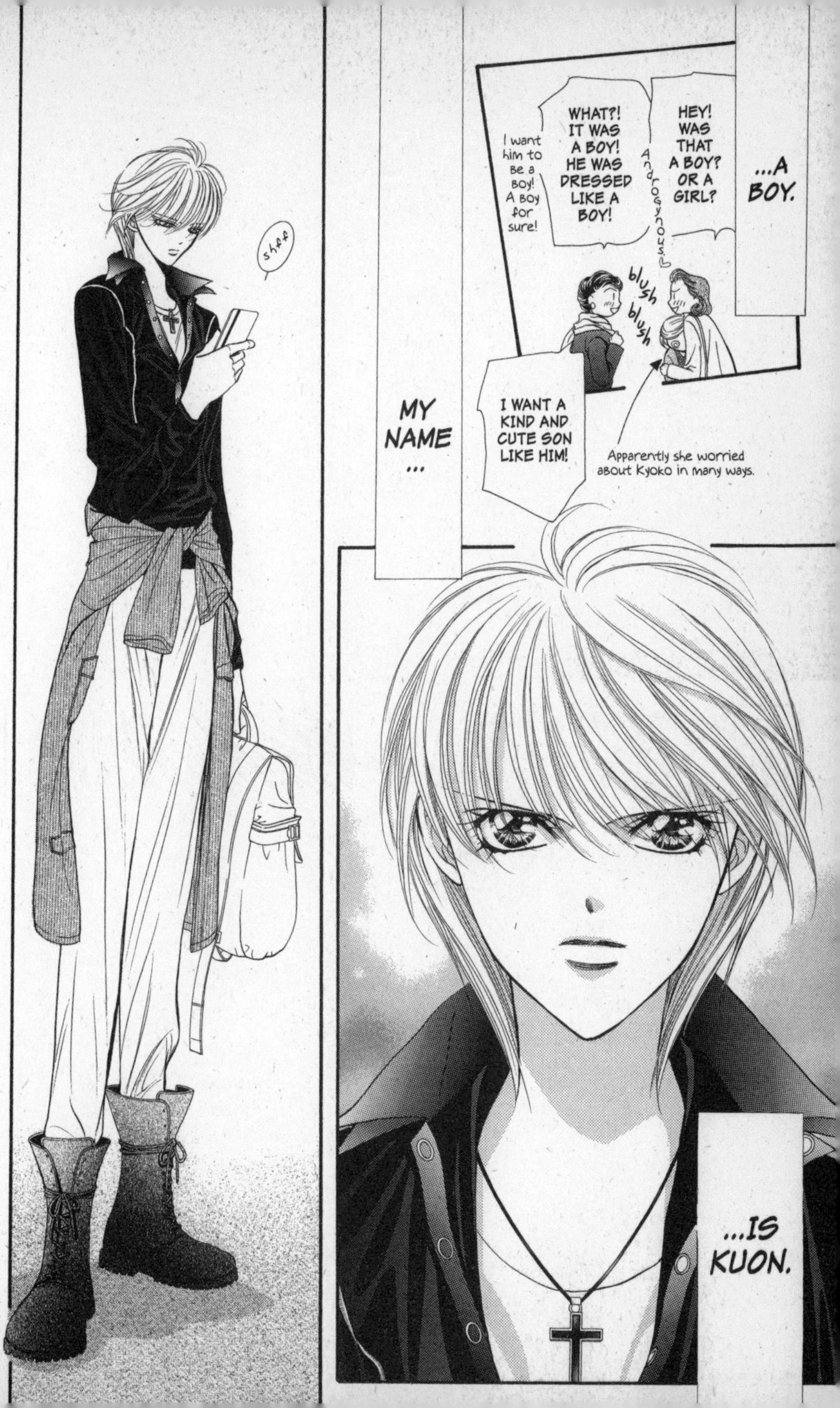

...A BOY.
HEY! WAS THAT A BOY? OR A GIRL?
Androgynous
WHAT?! IT WAS A BOY! HE WAS DRESSED LIKE A BOY!
I want him to be a boy! A boy for sure!
blush blush
I WANT A KIND AND CUTE SON LIKE HIM!
Apparently she worried about Kyoko in many ways.
MY NAME ...
...IS KUON.
shff

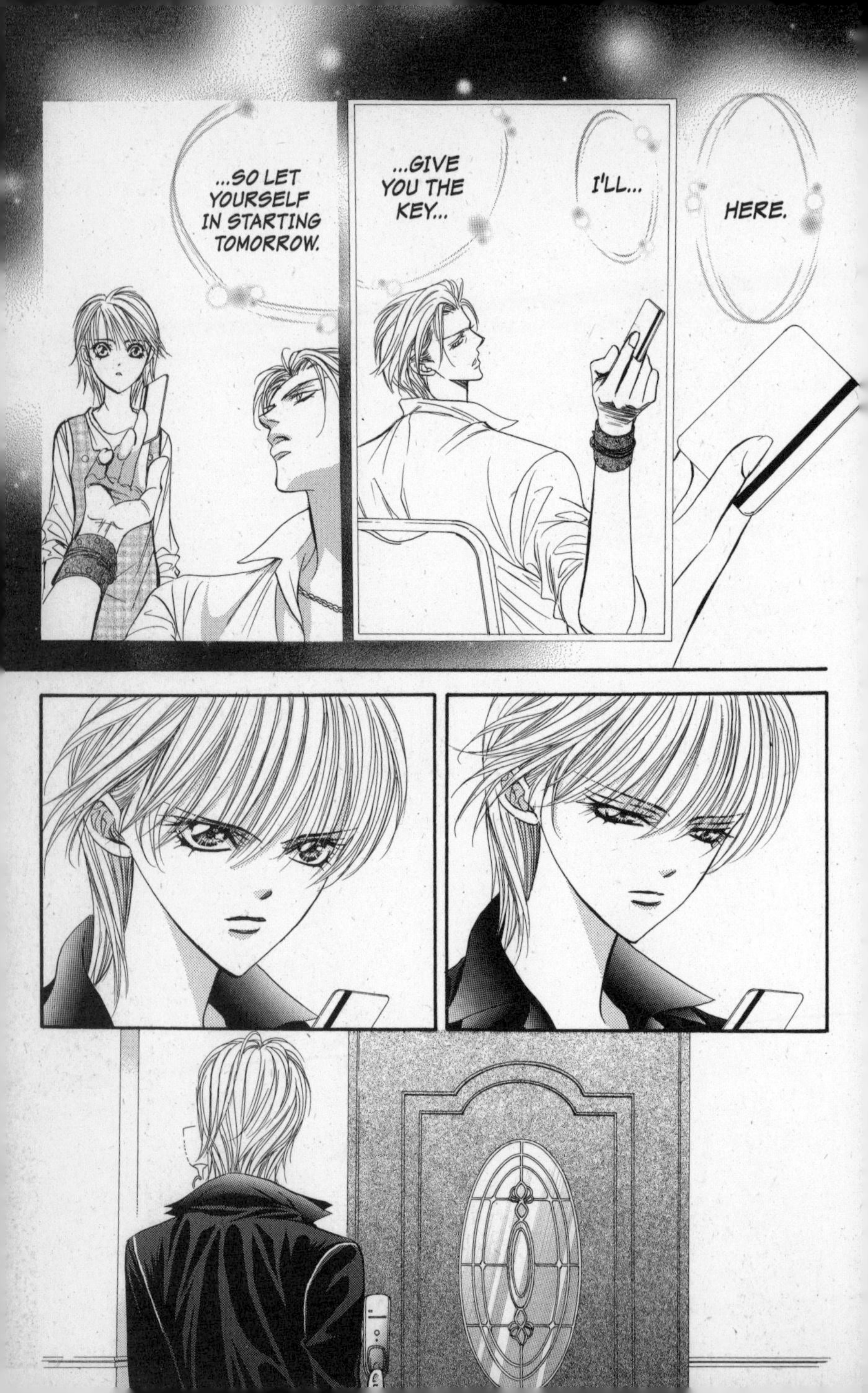
HERE.
I'LL...
...GIVE YOU THE KEY...
...SO LET YOURSELF IN STARTING TOMORROW.

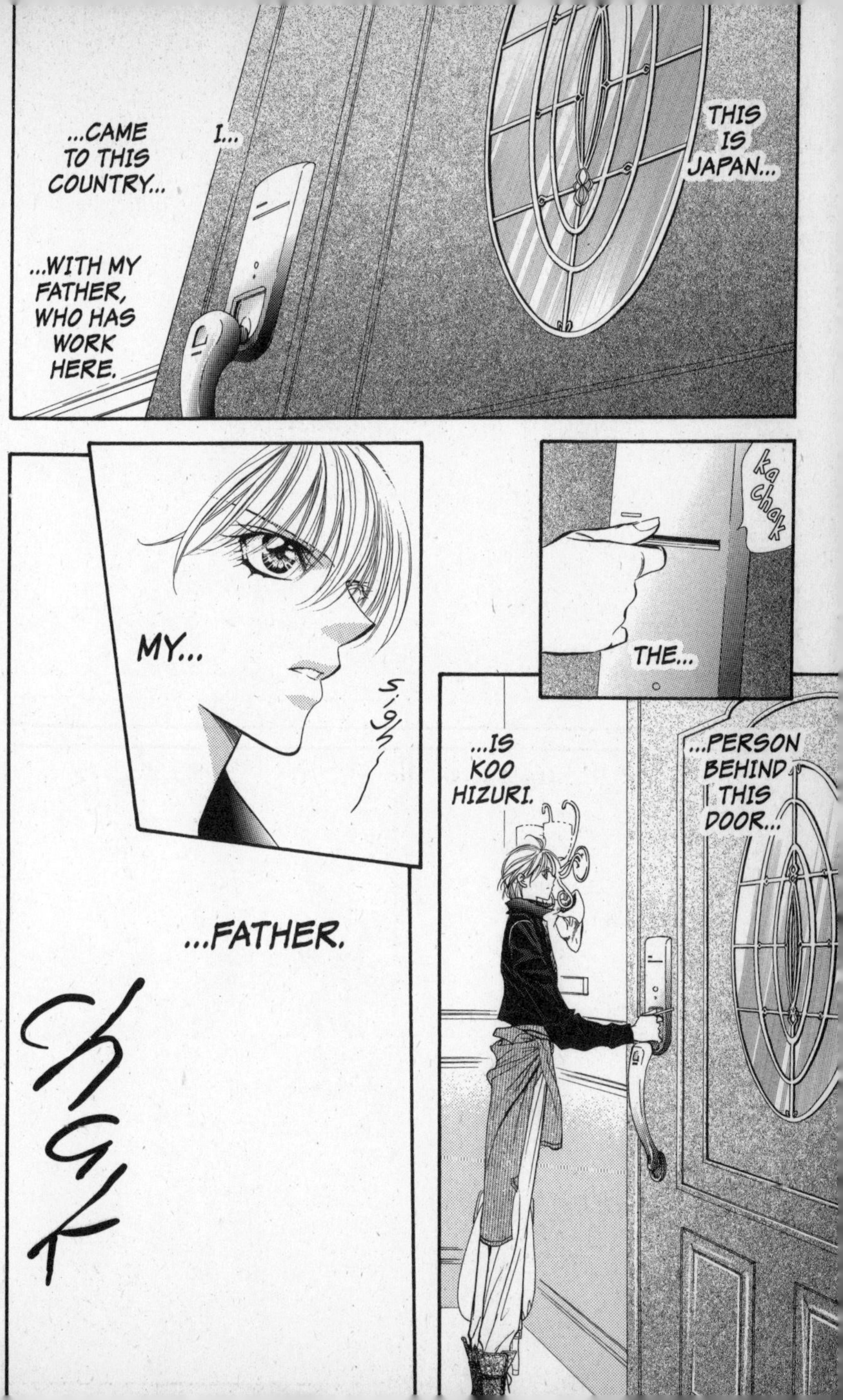
THIS IS JAPAN...
I...
...CAME TO THIS COUNTRY...
...WITH MY FATHER, WHO HAS WORK HERE.
ka chak
THE...
...PERSON BEHIND THIS DOOR...
...IS KOO HIZURI.
MY...
sigh
...FATHER.
CHGK

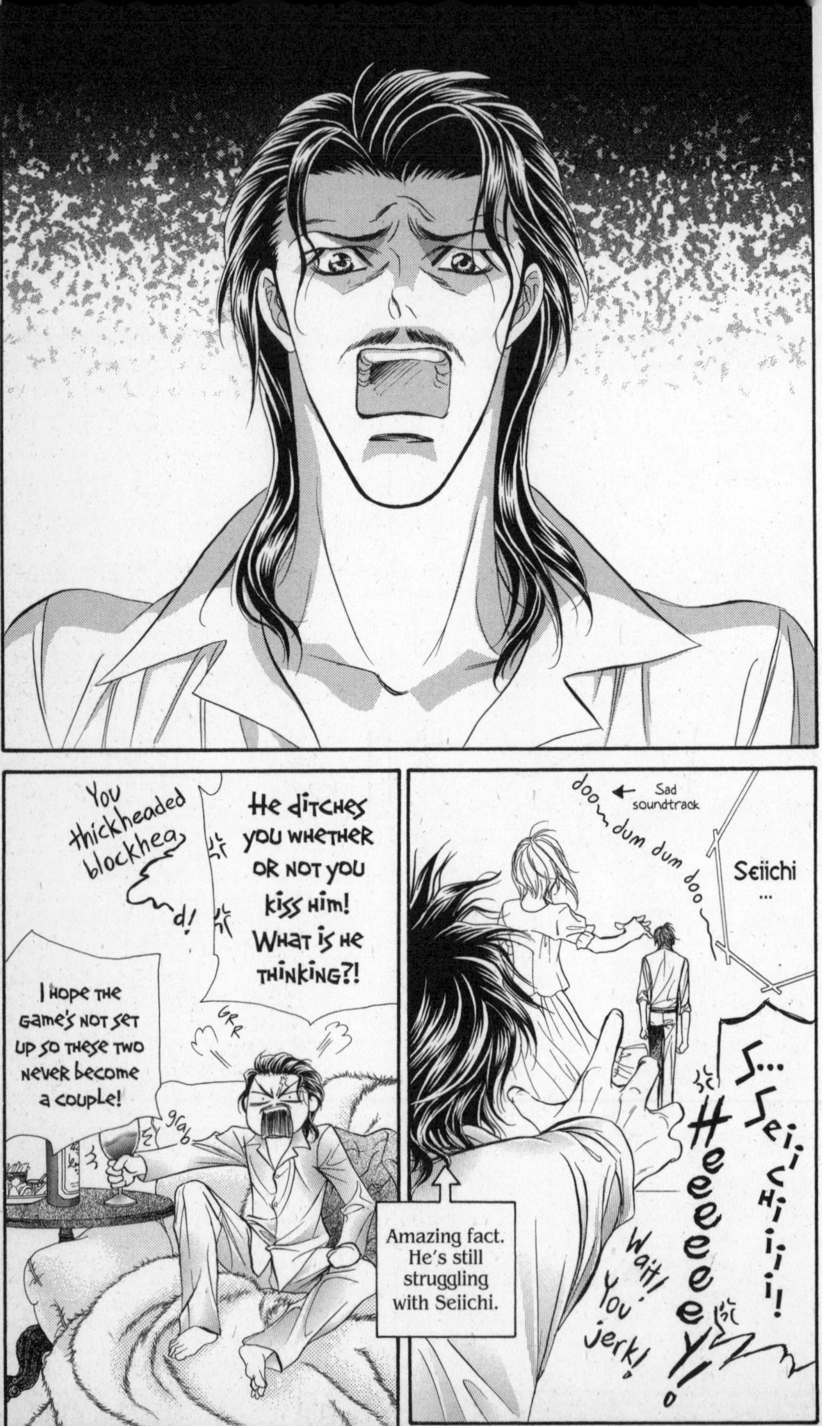
doo dum dum doo
Sad soundtrack
Seiichi ...
S... Seiichiiiii!
Heeeeeey!
Wait! You jerk!
Amazing fact. He's still struggling with Seiichi.
He ditches you whether or not you kiss him! What is he thinking?!
You thickheaded blockhea d!
GRR
I hope the game's not set up so these two never become a couple!
grab

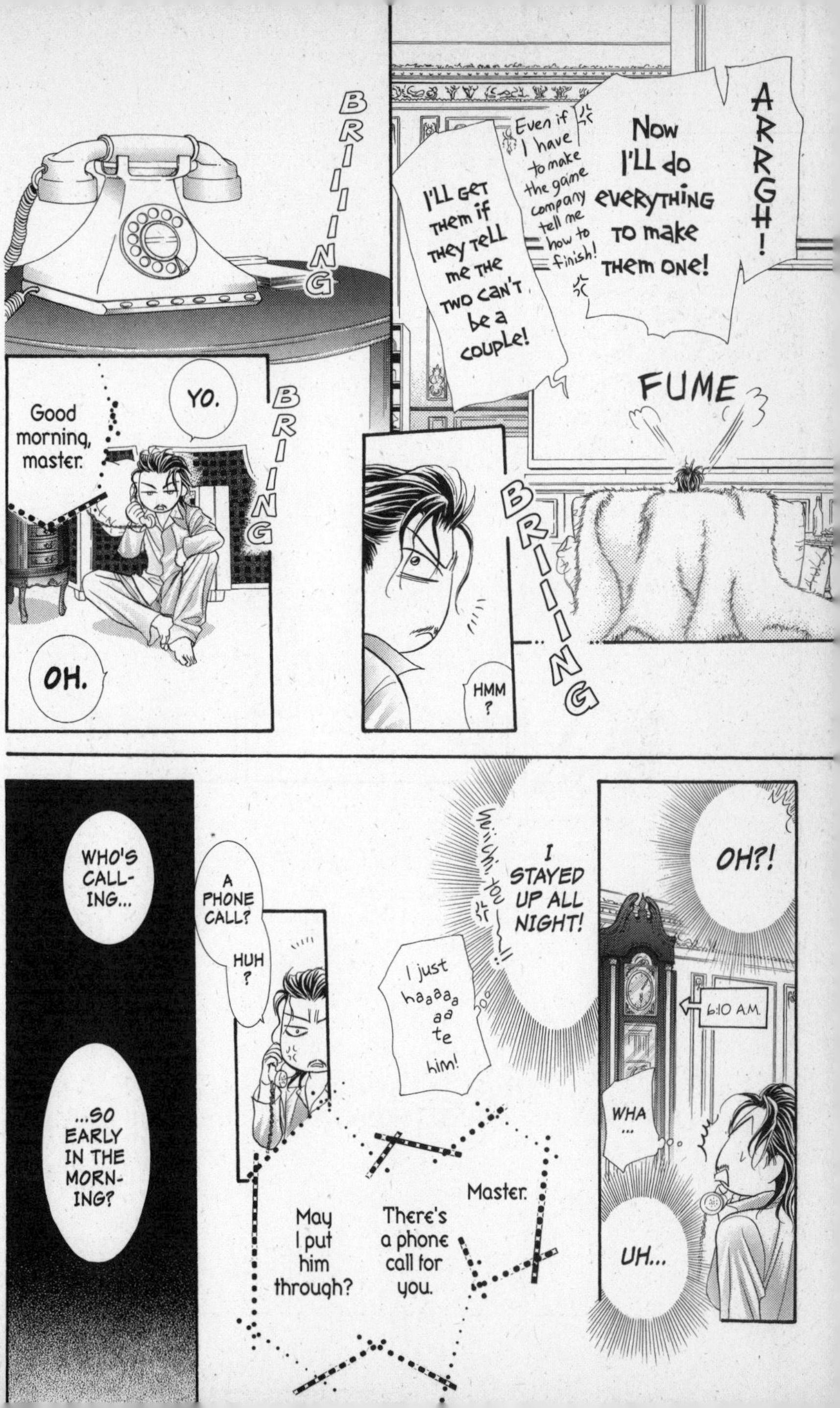
ARRGH!
Now I'll do everything to make them one!
Even if I have to make the game company tell me how to finish!
I'll get them if they tell me the two can't be a couple!
FUME
BRIIIING
BRIIIING
HMM?
BRIING
YO.
Good morning, master.
OH.
OH?!
6:10 A.M.
WHA...
UH...
I STAYED UP ALL NIGHT!
Seiichi, you~!!
I just haaaaaaate him!
Master.
There's a phone call for you.
May I put him through?
A PHONE CALL?
HUH?
WHO'S CALLING...
...SO EARLY IN THE MORNING?

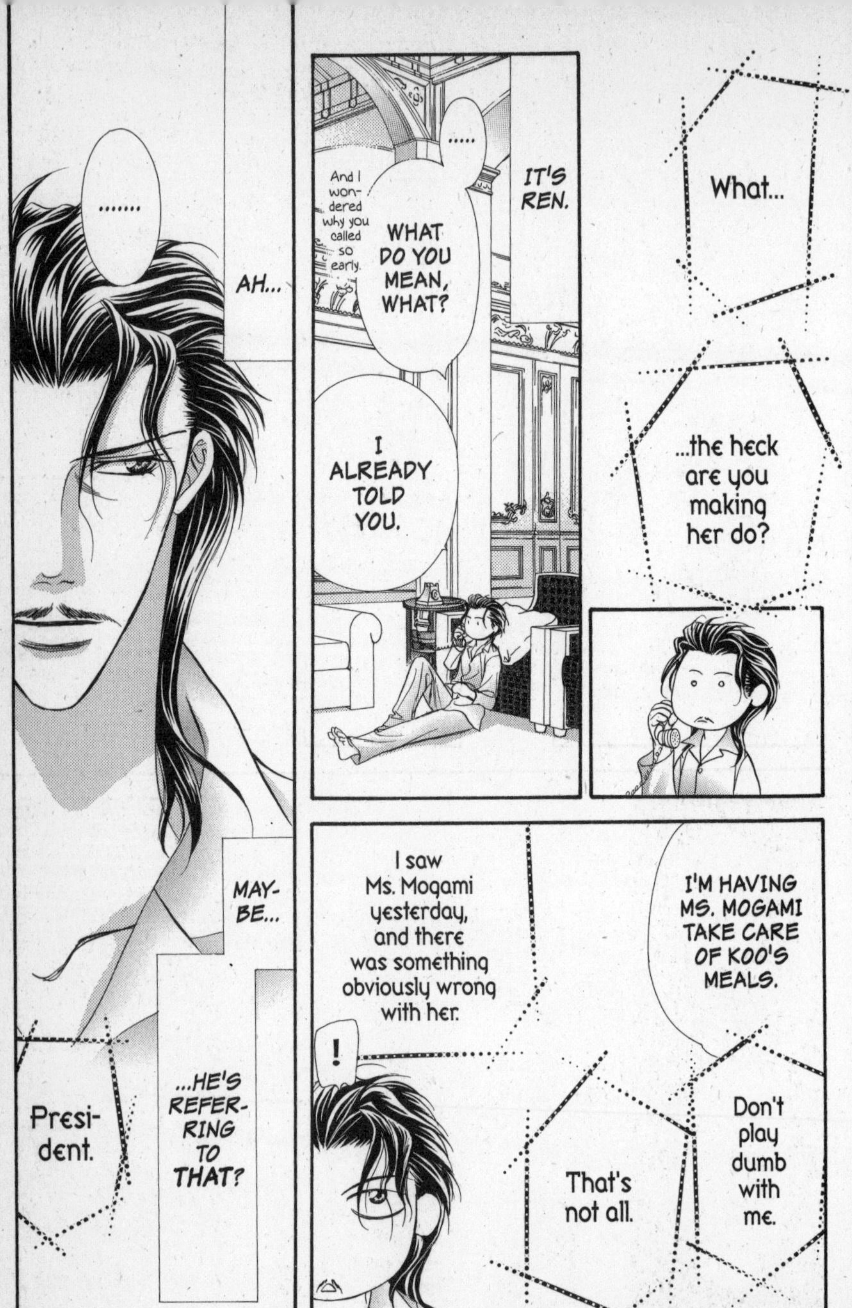
What...
...the heck are you making her do?
IT'S REN.
.....
WHAT DO YOU MEAN, WHAT?
And I wondered why you called so early.
I ALREADY TOLD YOU.
I'M HAVING MS. MOGAMI TAKE CARE OF KOO'S MEALS.
I saw Ms. Mogami yesterday, and there was something obviously wrong with her.
Don't play dumb with me.
That's not all.
!
AH...
....
MAY-BE...
...HE'S REFERRING TO THAT?
President.

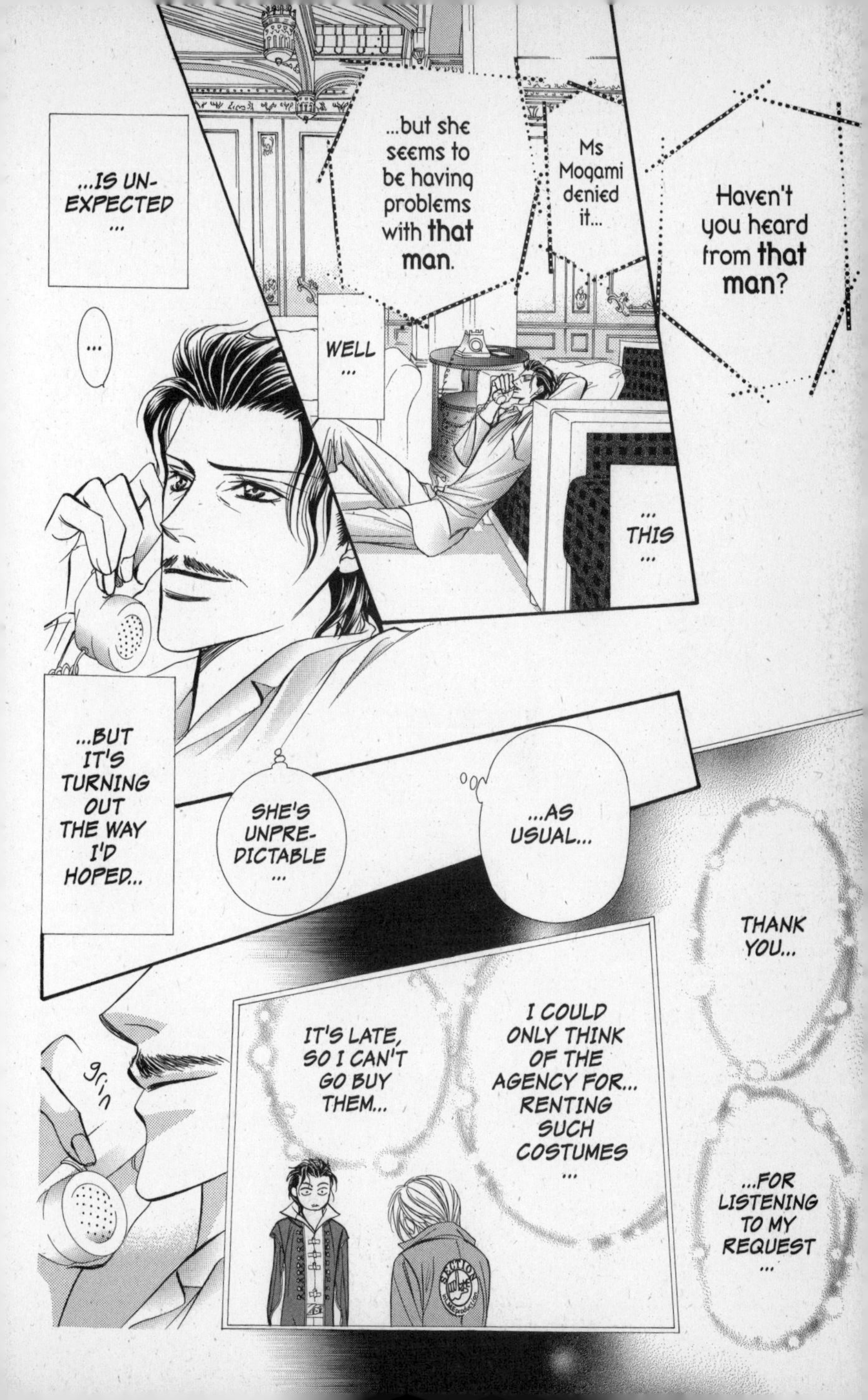
Haven't you heard from that man?
Ms Mogami denied it...
...but she seems to be having problems with that man.
WELL...
...THIS...
...IS UN-EXPECTED...
...
...AS USUAL...
SHE'S UNPRE-DICTABLE...
...BUT IT'S TURNING OUT THE WAY I'D HOPED...
THANK YOU...
...FOR LISTENING TO MY REQUEST...
I COULD ONLY THINK OF THE AGENCY FOR... RENTING SUCH COSTUMES...
IT'S LATE, SO I CAN'T GO BUY THEM...
grin

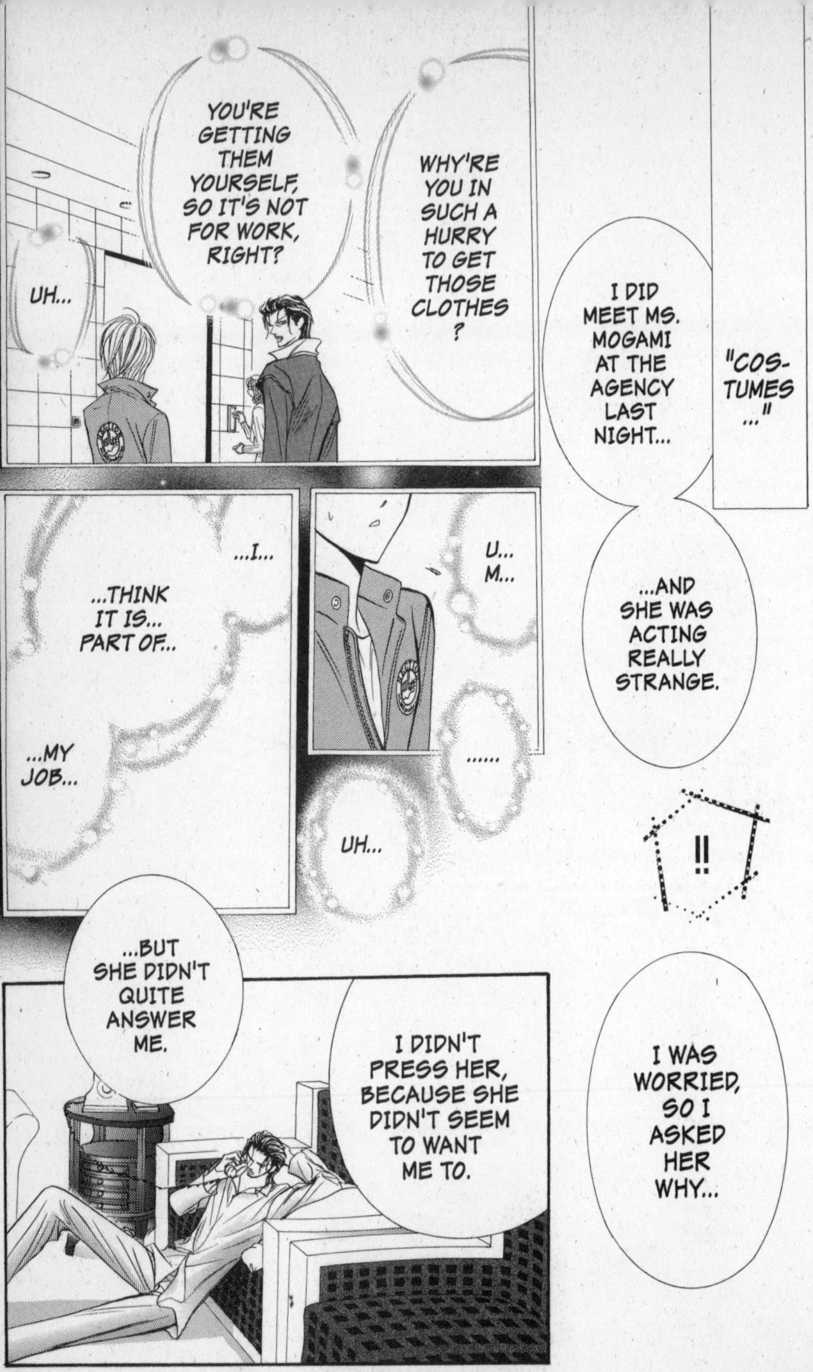
"COS-TUMES..."
I DID MEET MS. MOGAMI AT THE AGENCY LAST NIGHT...
...AND SHE WAS ACTING REALLY STRANGE.
WHY'RE YOU IN SUCH A HURRY TO GET THOSE CLOTHES?
YOU'RE GETTING THEM YOURSELF, SO IT'S NOT FOR WORK, RIGHT?
UH...
U... M...
......
UH...
...I...
...THINK IT IS... PART OF...
...MY JOB...
!!
I WAS WORRIED, SO I ASKED HER WHY...
...BUT SHE DIDN'T QUITE ANSWER ME.
I DIDN'T PRESS HER, BECAUSE SHE DIDN'T SEEM TO WANT ME TO.

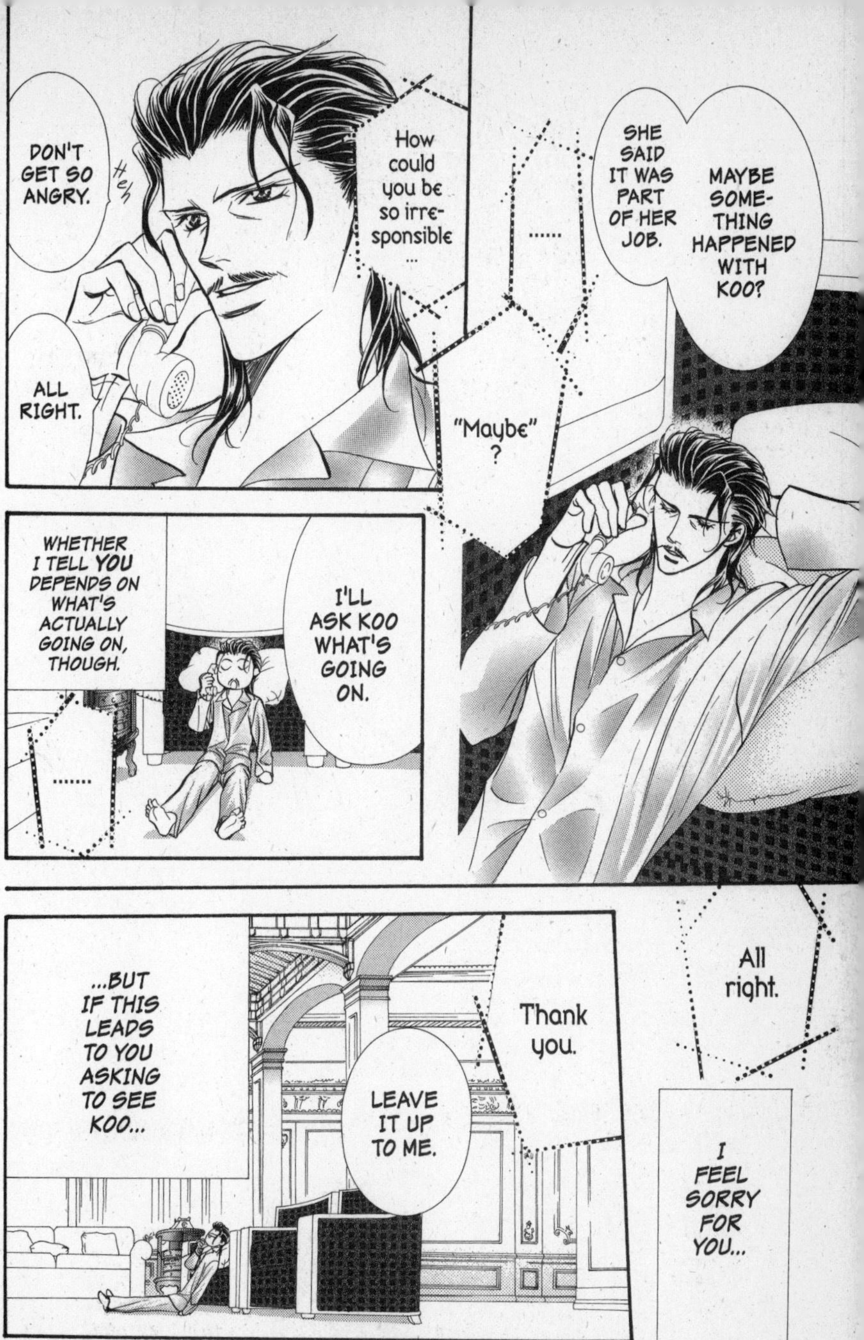
MAYBE SOME-THING HAPPENED WITH KOO?
SHE SAID IT WAS PART OF HER JOB.
.....
"Maybe" ?
How could you be so irre-sponsible ...
DON'T GET SO ANGRY.
Heh
ALL RIGHT.
I'LL ASK KOO WHAT'S GOING ON.
WHETHER I TELL YOU DEPENDS ON WHAT'S ACTUALLY GOING ON, THOUGH.
......
All right.
I FEEL SORRY FOR YOU...
Thank you.
LEAVE IT UP TO ME.
...BUT IF THIS LEADS TO YOU ASKING TO SEE KOO...

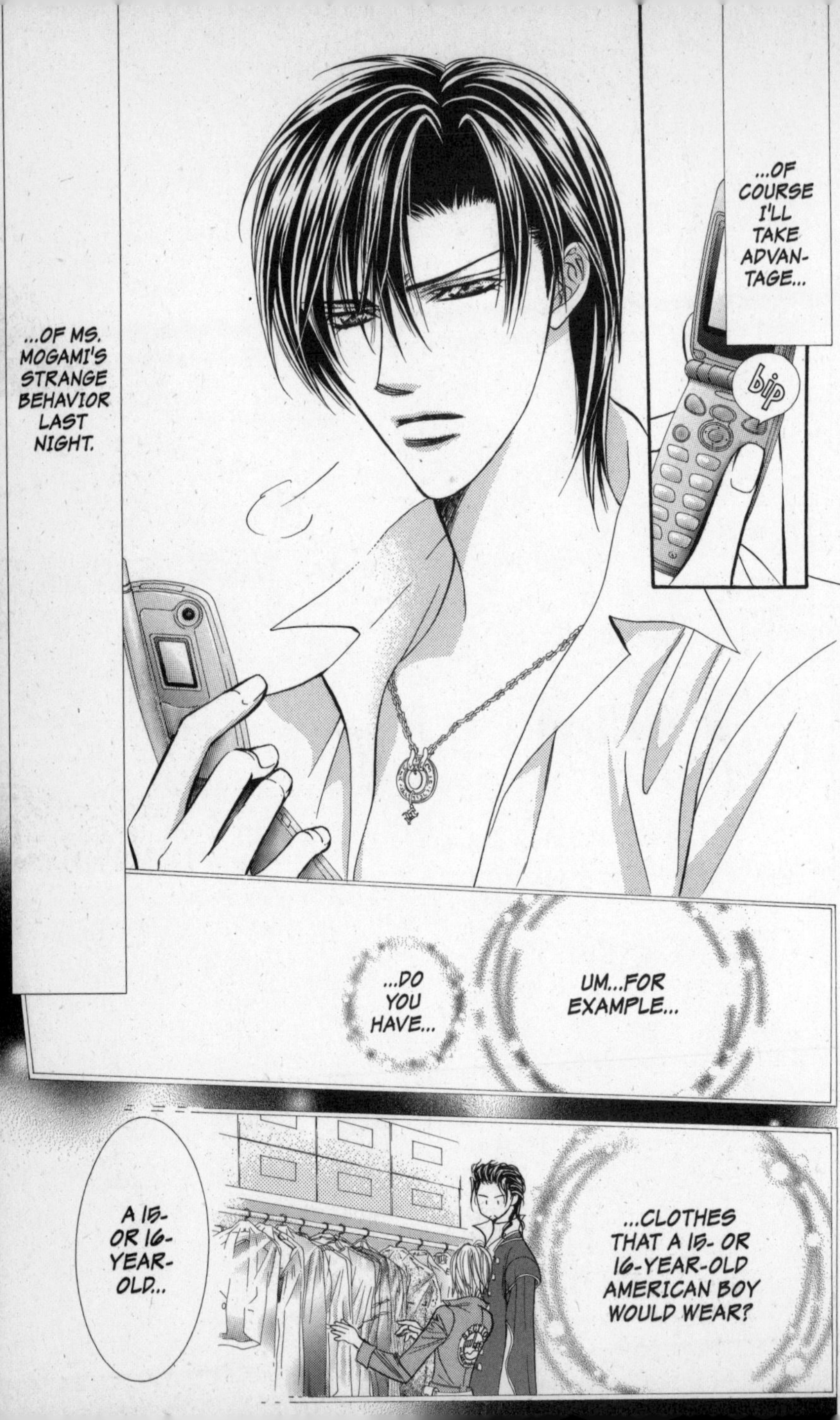
...OF COURSE I'LL TAKE ADVAN-TAGE...
bip
...OF MS. MOGAMI'S STRANGE BEHAVIOR LAST NIGHT.
UM...FOR EXAMPLE...
...DO YOU HAVE...
...CLOTHES THAT A 15- OR 16-YEAR-OLD AMERICAN BOY WOULD WEAR?
A 15- OR 16-YEAR-OLD...

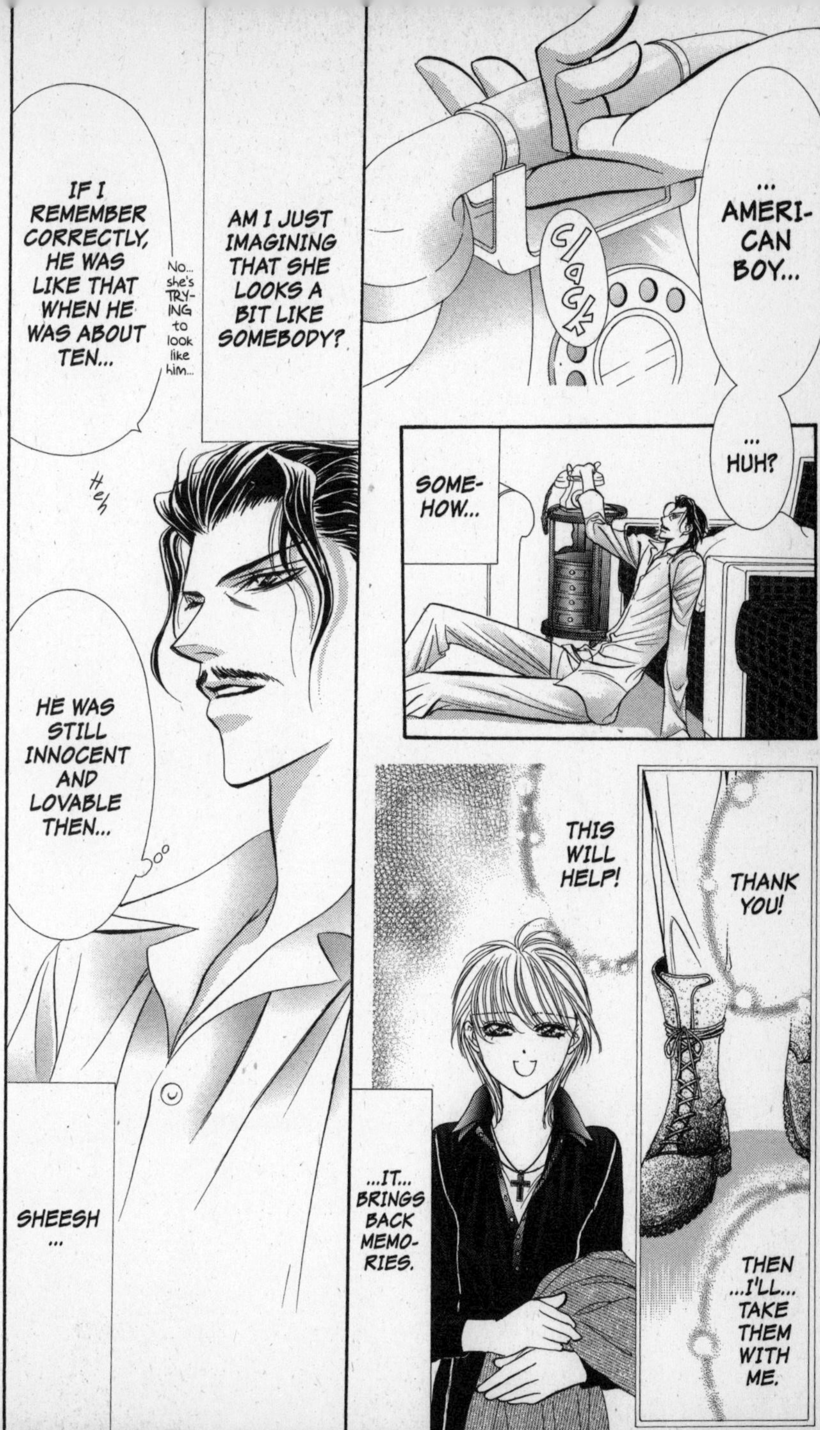

clack
...AMERI-CAN BOY...
...HUH?
SOME-HOW...
THANK YOU!
THEN ...I'LL... TAKE THEM WITH ME.
THIS WILL HELP!
...IT... BRINGS BACK MEMO-RIES.
AM I JUST IMAGINING THAT SHE LOOKS A BIT LIKE SOMEBODY?
IF I REMEMBER CORRECTLY, HE WAS LIKE THAT WHEN HE WAS ABOUT TEN...
No... she's TRY-ING to look like him...
Heh
HE WAS STILL INNOCENT AND LOVABLE THEN...
SHEESH...

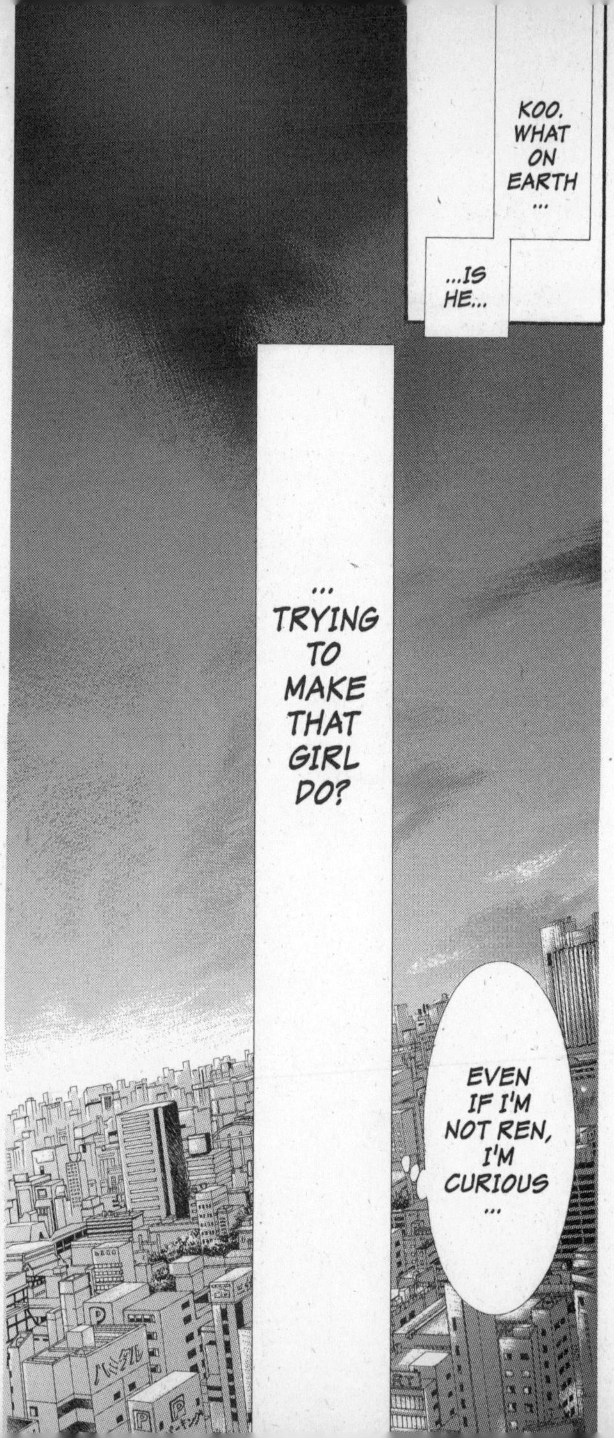
KOO. WHAT ON EARTH...
...IS HE...
...TRYING TO MAKE THAT GIRL DO?
EVEN IF I'M NOT REN, I'M CURIOUS...
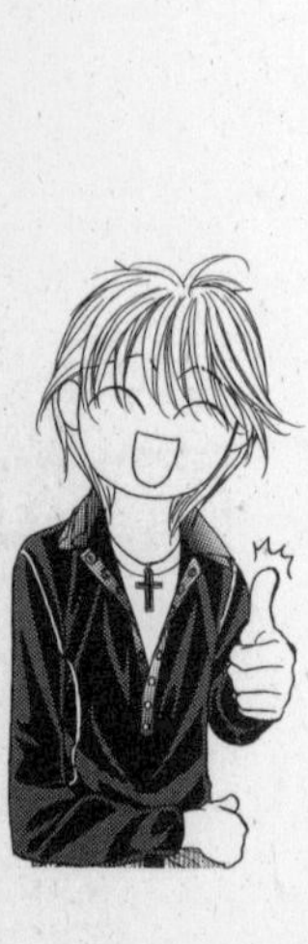

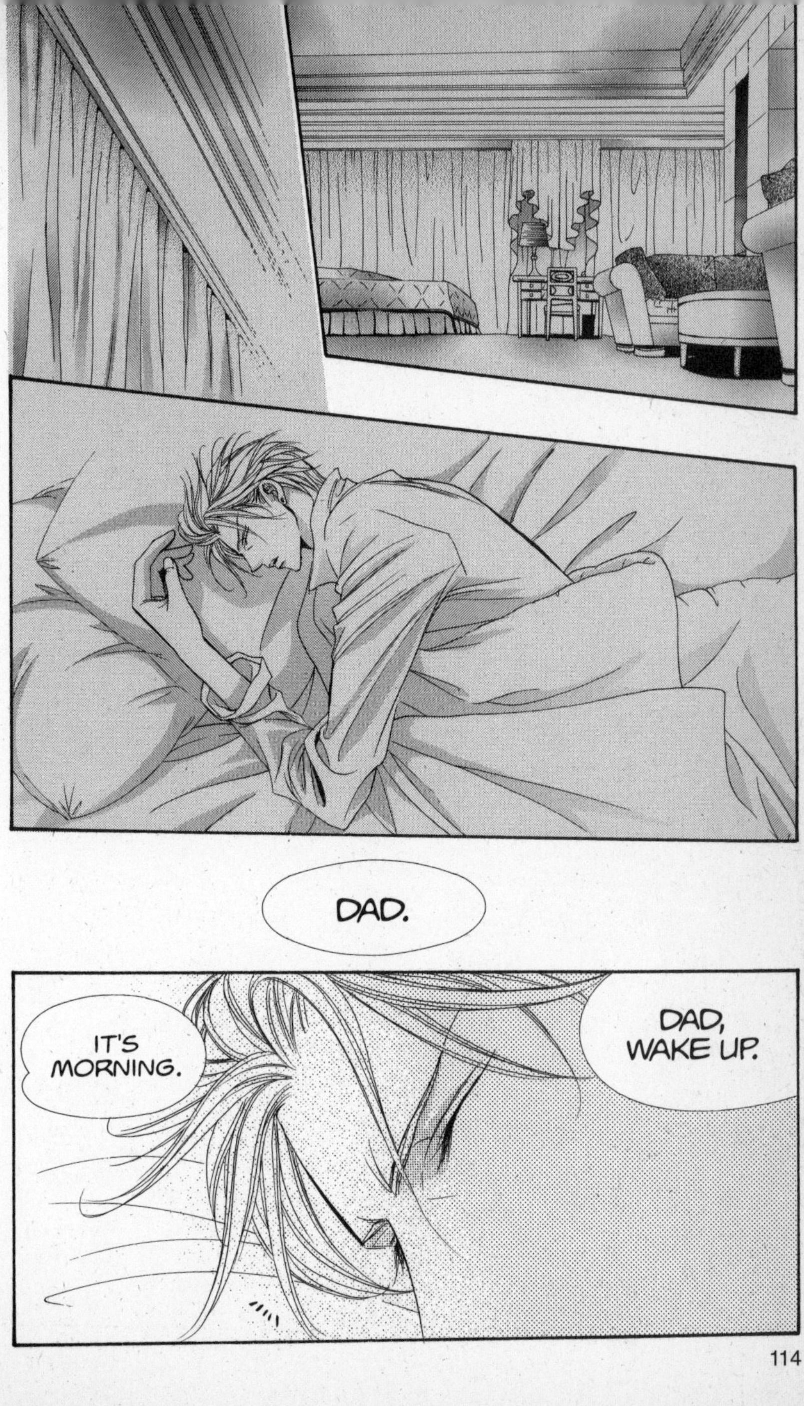
DAD.
DAD, WAKE UP.
IT'S MORNING.

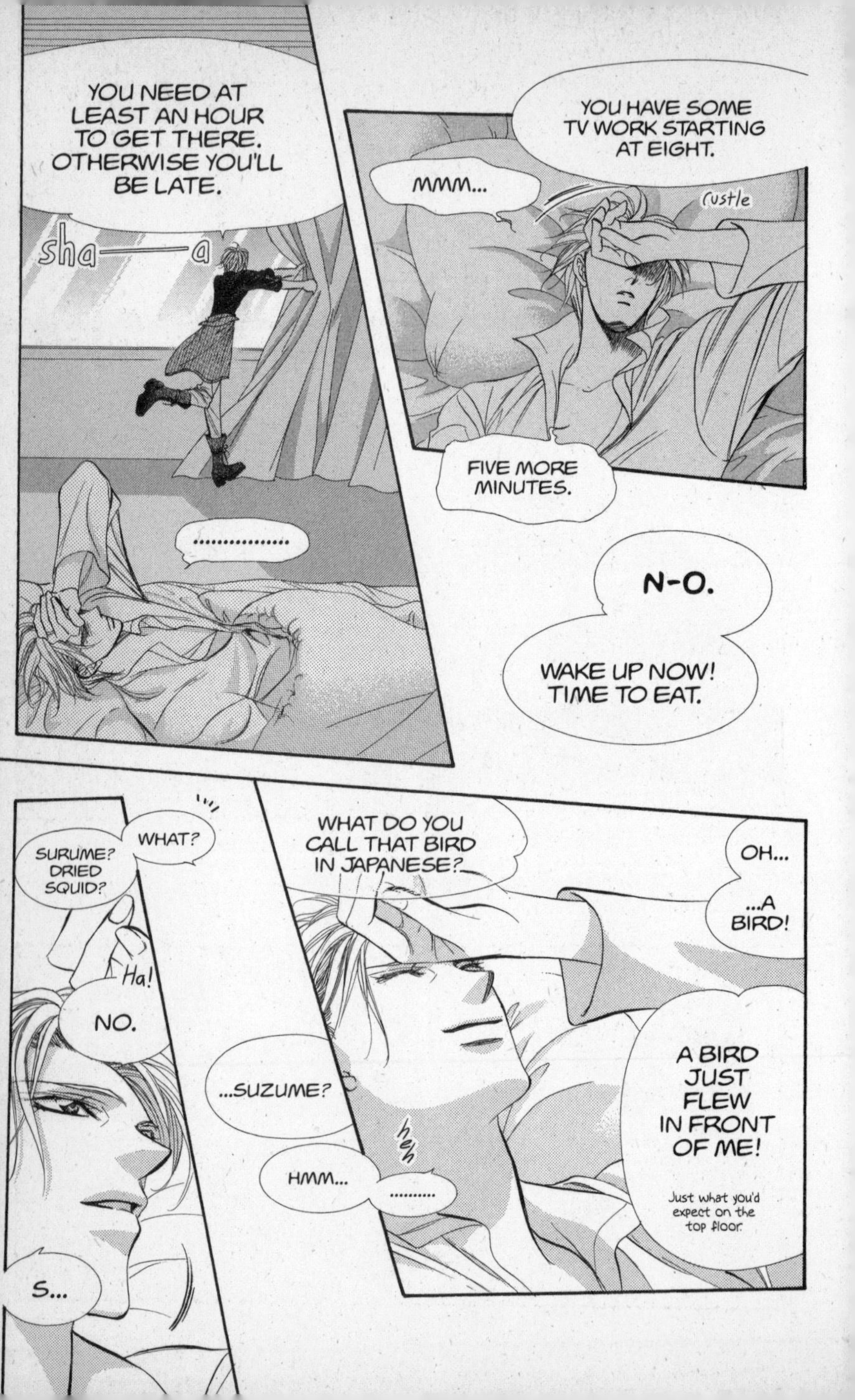

YOU HAVE SOME TV WORK STARTING AT EIGHT.
MMM...
rustle
FIVE MORE MINUTES.
N-O.
WAKE UP NOW! TIME TO EAT.
YOU NEED AT LEAST AN HOUR TO GET THERE. OTHERWISE YOU'LL BE LATE.
sha——a
....
OH...
...A BIRD!
A BIRD JUST FLEW IN FRONT OF ME!
Just what you'd expect on the top floor.
WHAT DO YOU CALL THAT BIRD IN JAPANESE?
...SUZUME?
heh
HMM...
....
WHAT?
SURUME? DRIED SQUID?
Ha!
NO.
S...

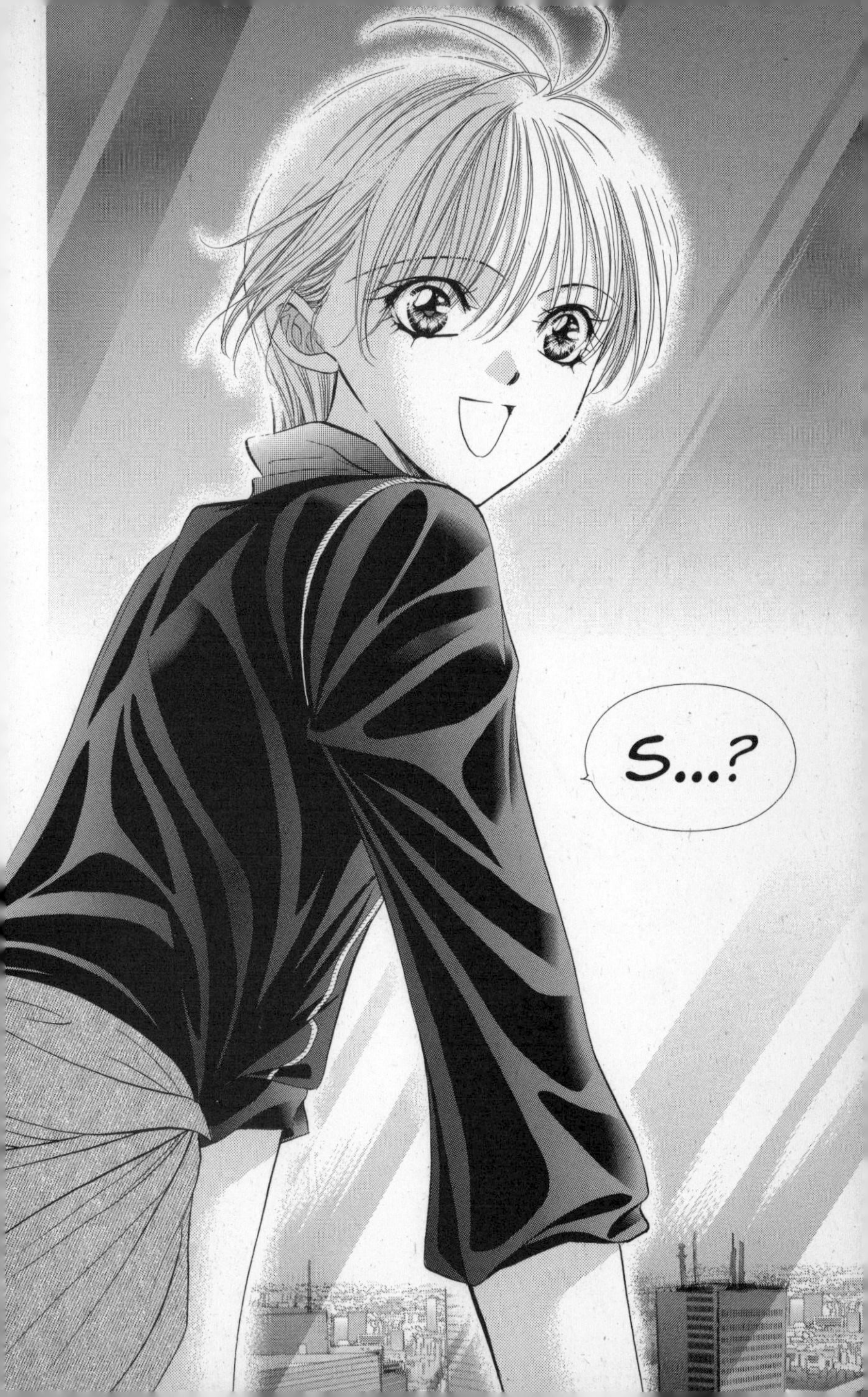
S...?

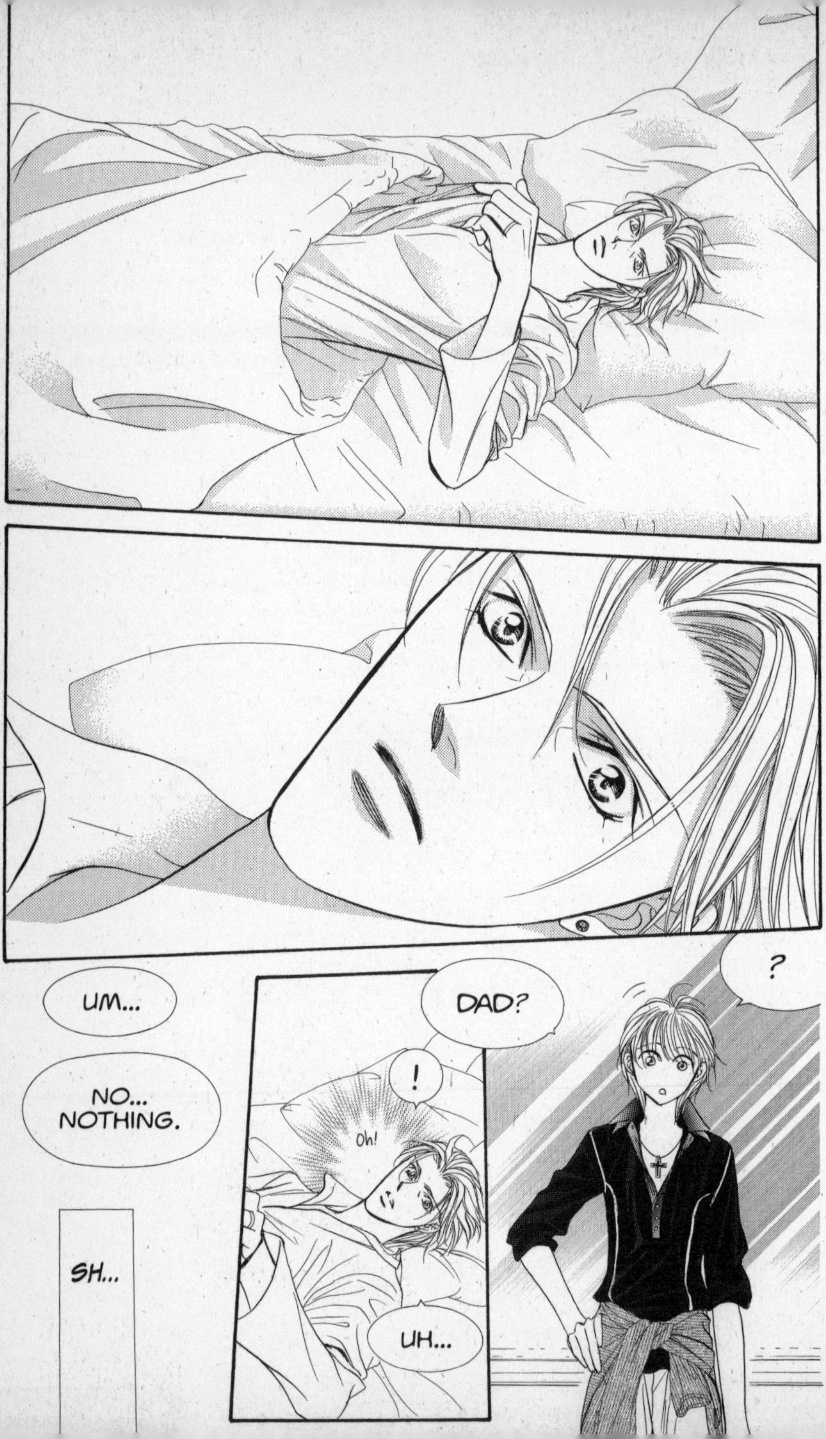
?
DAD?
!
Oh!
UH...
UM...
NO... NOTHING.
SH...

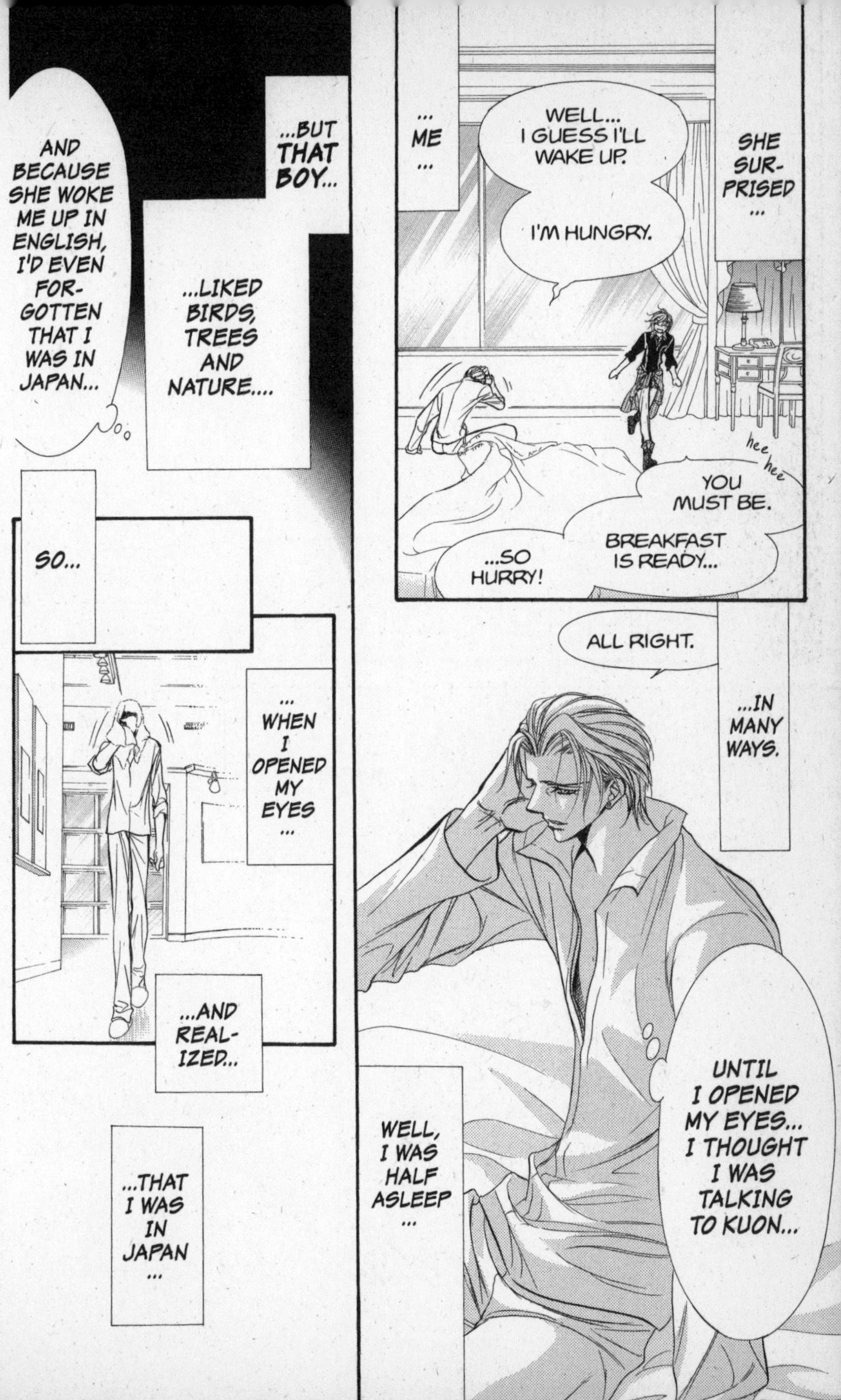
SHE SURPRISED...
WELL... I GUESS I'LL WAKE UP.
I'M HUNGRY.
...ME...
hee hee
YOU MUST BE.
BREAKFAST IS READY...
...SO HURRY!
...IN MANY WAYS.
ALL RIGHT.
UNTIL I OPENED MY EYES... I THOUGHT I WAS TALKING TO KUON...
WELL, I WAS HALF ASLEEP...
...BUT THAT BOY...
...LIKED BIRDS, TREES AND NATURE....
AND BECAUSE SHE WOKE ME UP IN ENGLISH, I'D EVEN FORGOTTEN THAT I WAS IN JAPAN...
SO...
...WHEN I OPENED MY EYES...
...AND REALIZED...
...THAT I WAS IN JAPAN...

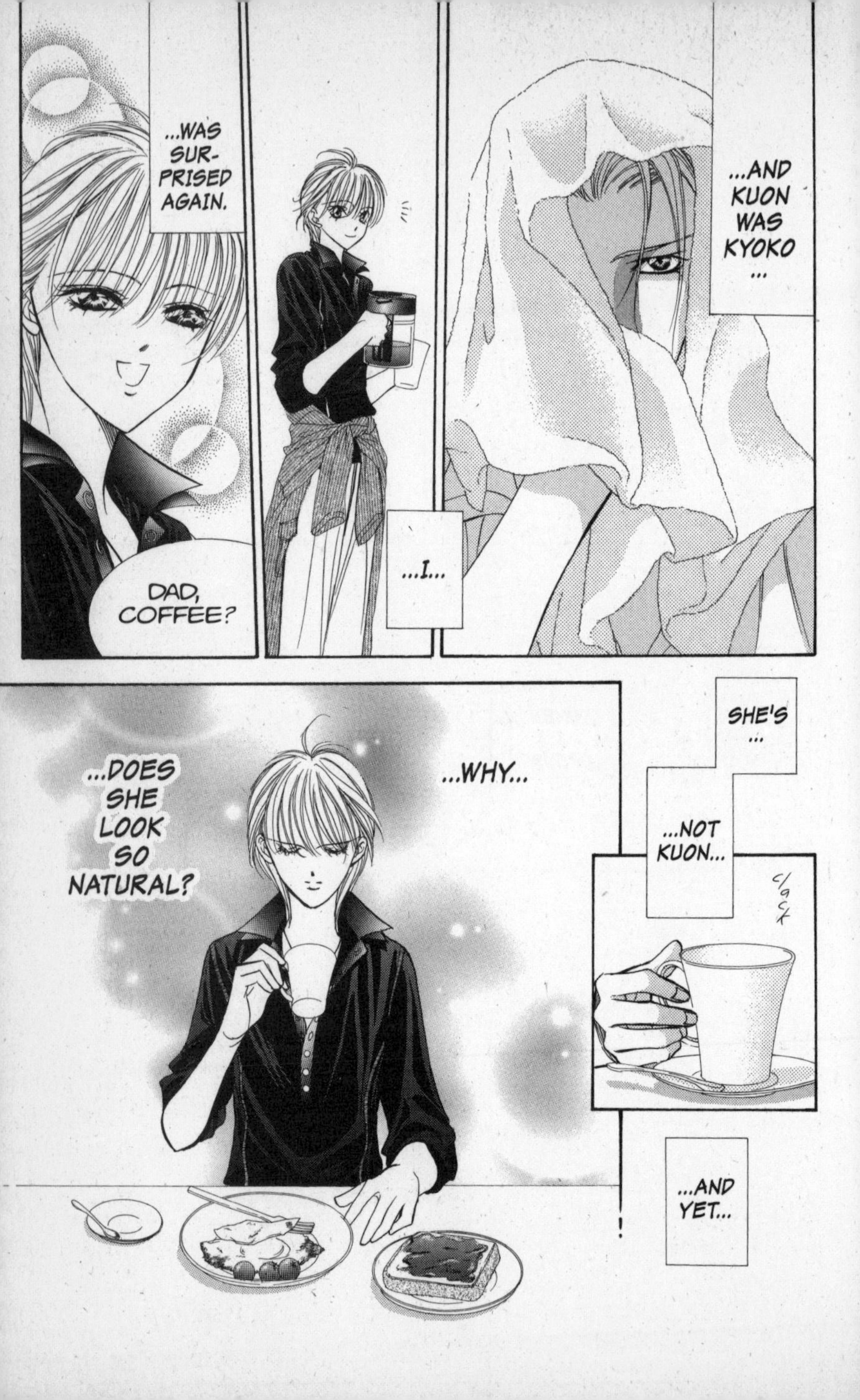
...AND KUON WAS KYOKO ...
...I...
...WAS SUR-PRISED AGAIN.
DAD, COFFEE?
SHE'S ...
...NOT KUON...
clack
...AND YET...
...WHY...
...DOES SHE LOOK SO NATURAL?

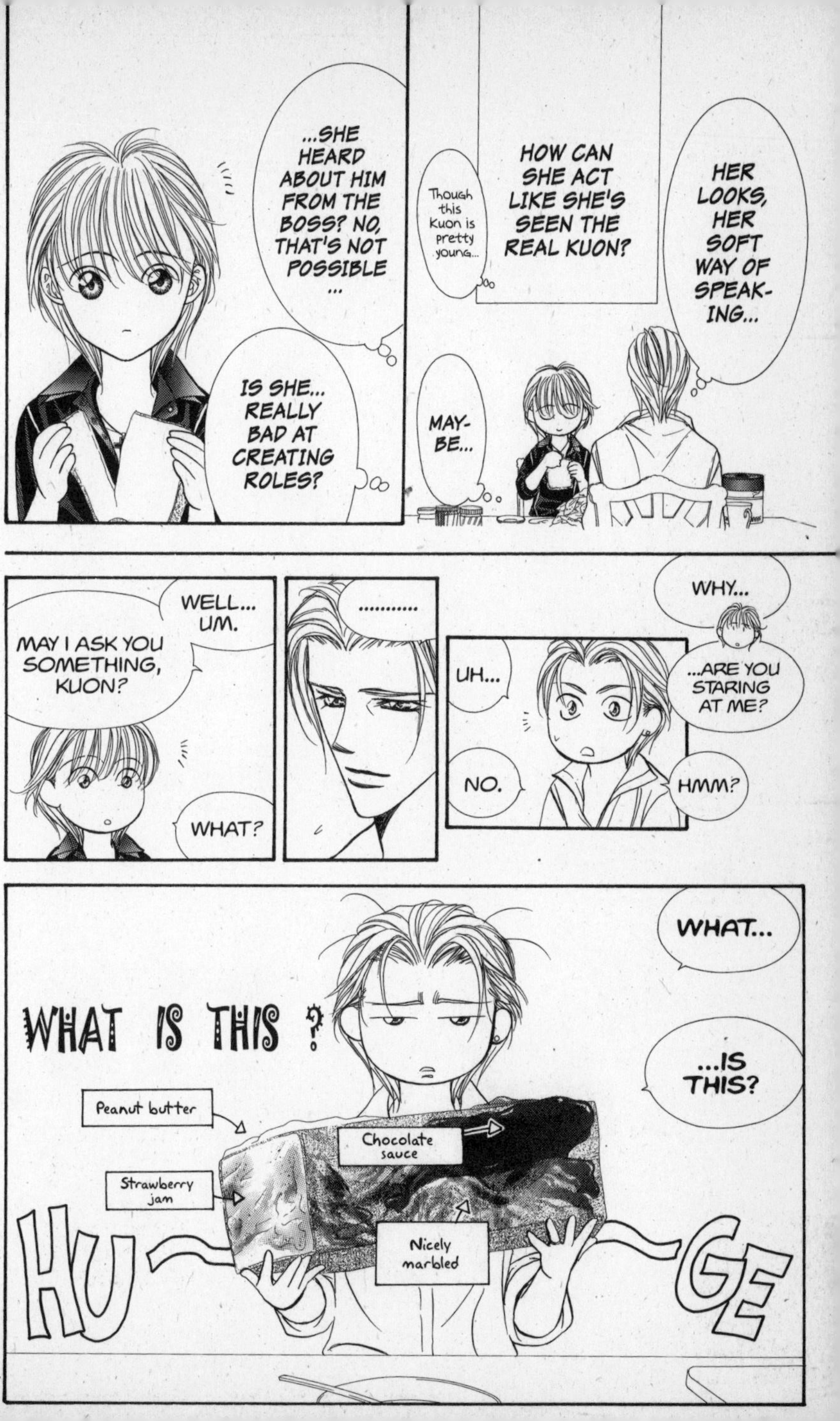
HER LOOKS, HER SOFT WAY OF SPEAK-ING...
HOW CAN SHE ACT LIKE SHE'S SEEN THE REAL KUON?
Though this Kuon is pretty young...
MAY-BE...
...SHE HEARD ABOUT HIM FROM THE BOSS? NO, THAT'S NOT POSSIBLE ...
IS SHE... REALLY BAD AT CREATING ROLES?
WHY...
...ARE YOU STARING AT ME?
HMM?
UH...
NO.
....
WELL... UM.
MAY I ASK YOU SOMETHING, KUON?
WHAT?
WHAT...
...IS THIS?
WHAT IS THIS?
Peanut butter
Chocolate sauce
Strawberry jam
Nicely marbled
HU~~GE

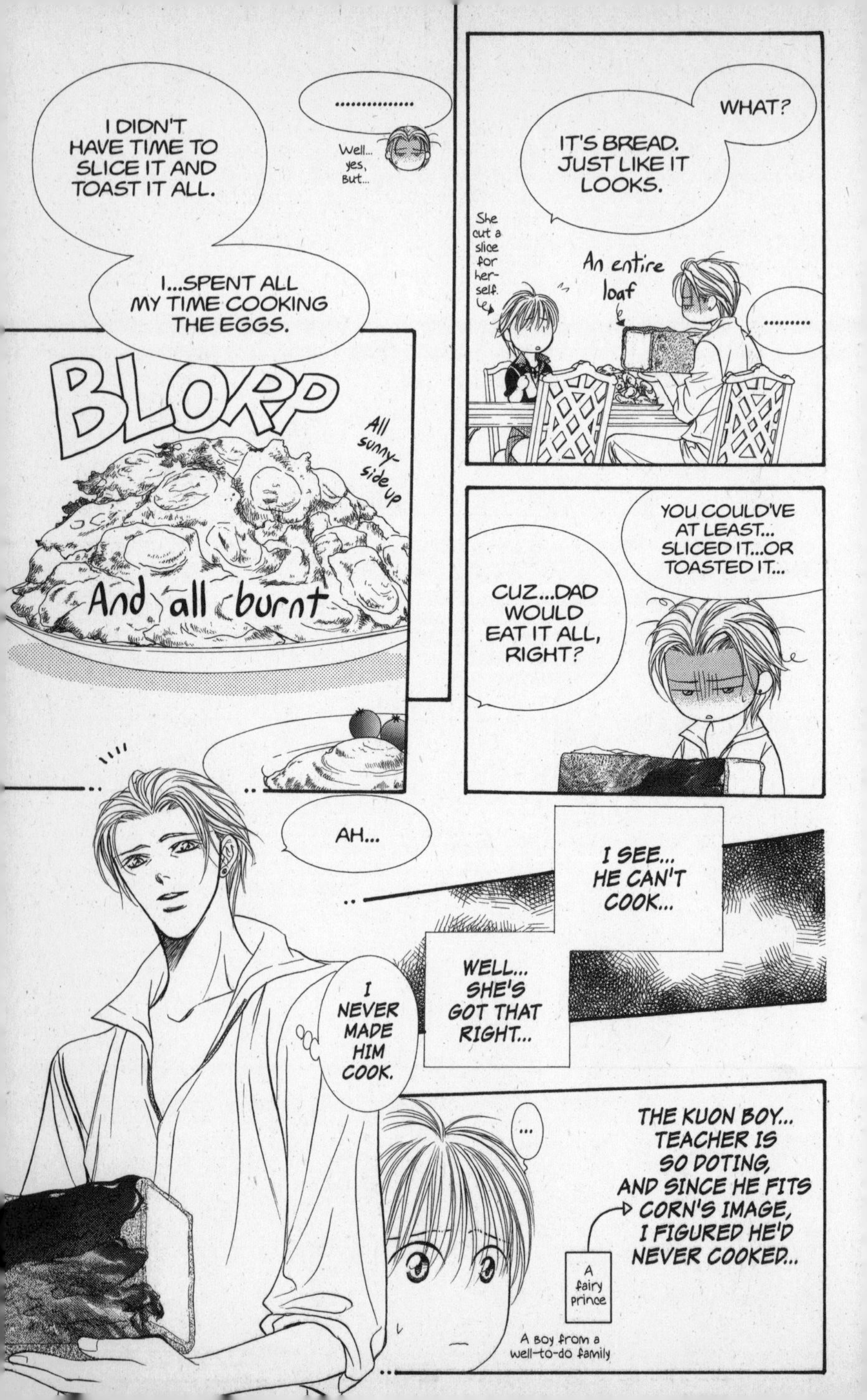
WHAT?
IT'S BREAD. JUST LIKE IT LOOKS.
She cut a slice for her-self.
An entire loaf
....
....
Well... yes, but...
I DIDN'T HAVE TIME TO SLICE IT AND TOAST IT ALL.
I...SPENT ALL MY TIME COOKING THE EGGS.
BLORP
All sunny-side up
And all burnt
YOU COULD'VE AT LEAST... SLICED IT...OR TOASTED IT...
CUZ...DAD WOULD EAT IT ALL, RIGHT?
AH...
I SEE... HE CAN'T COOK...
WELL... SHE'S GOT THAT RIGHT...
I NEVER MADE HIM COOK.
THE KUON BOY... TEACHER IS SO DOTING, AND SINCE HE FITS CORN'S IMAGE, I FIGURED HE'D NEVER COOKED...
...
A fairy prince
A boy from a well-to-do family

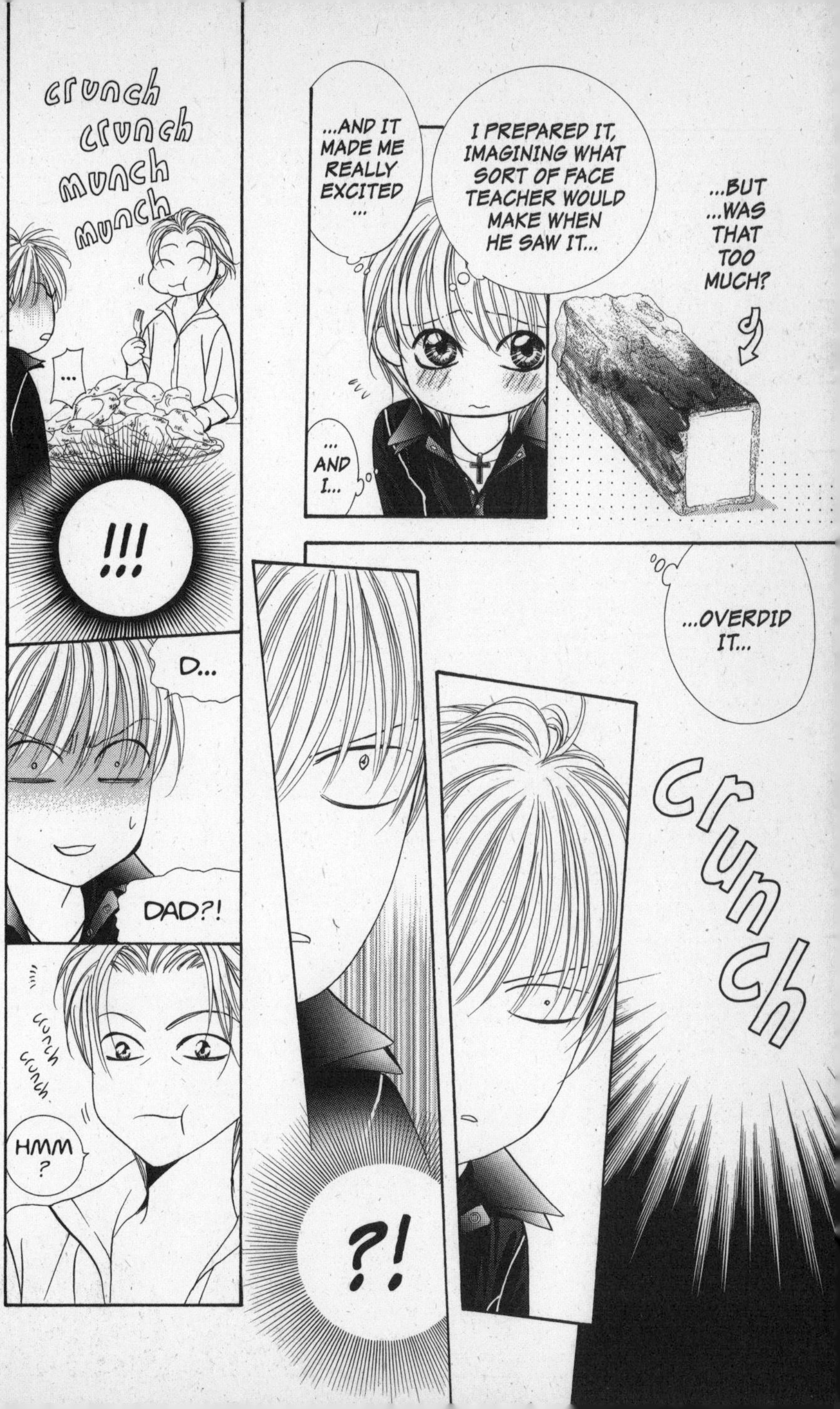
I PREPARED IT, IMAGINING WHAT SORT OF FACE TEACHER WOULD MAKE WHEN HE SAW IT...
...AND IT MADE ME REALLY EXCITED ...
...BUT ...WAS THAT TOO MUCH?
... AND I...
...OVERDID IT...
CRUNCH
?!
crunch crunch munch munch
...
!!!
D...
DAD?!
crunch crunch
HMM ?

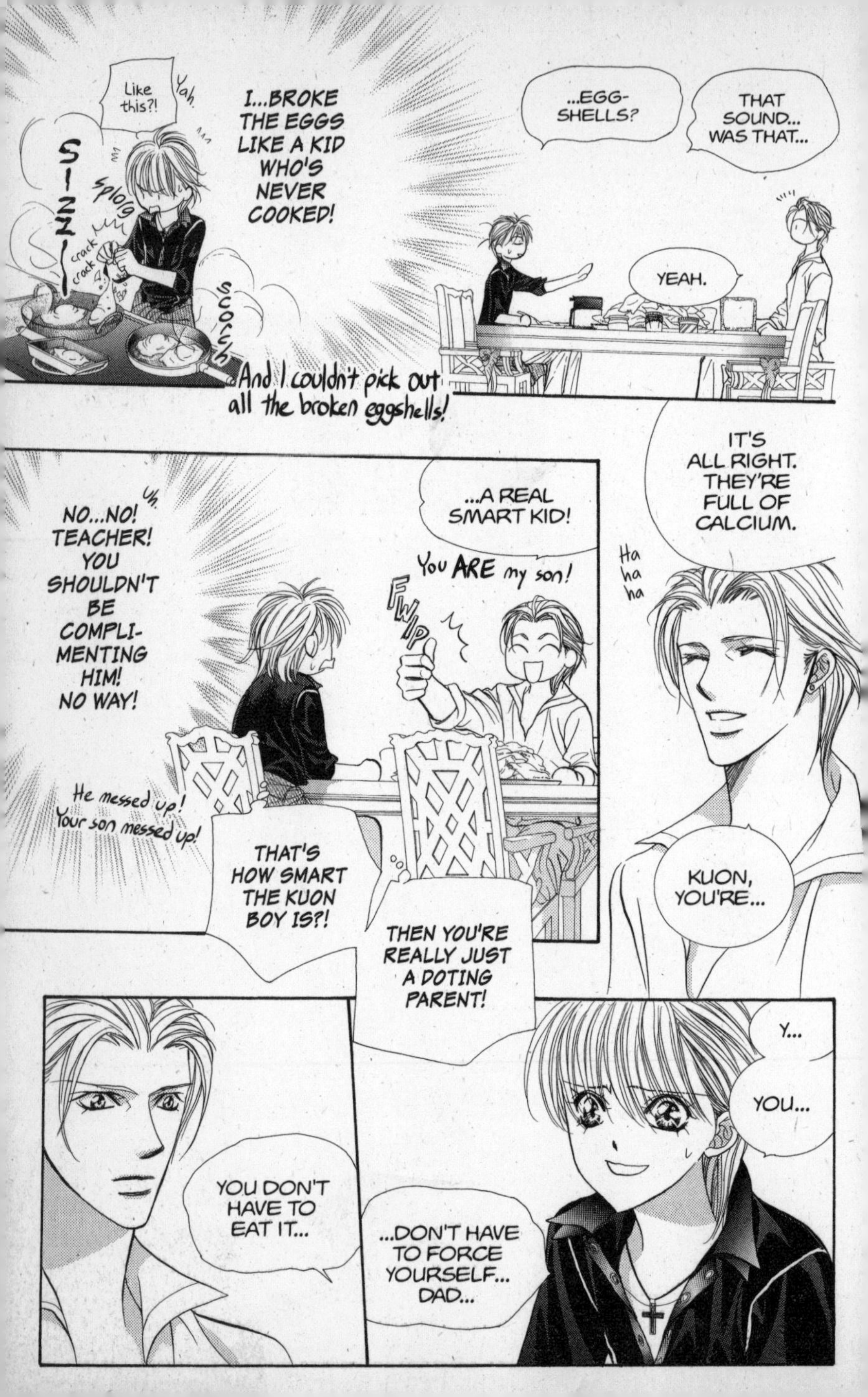
THAT SOUND... WAS THAT...
...EGG-SHELLS?
YEAH.
I...BROKE THE EGGS LIKE A KID WHO'S NEVER COOKED!
Yah.
Like this?!
SIZZ
splorg
crack crack
SCORCH
And I couldn't pick out all the broken eggshells!
IT'S ALL RIGHT. THEY'RE FULL OF CALCIUM.
Ha ha ha
KUON, YOU'RE...
...A REAL SMART KID!
You ARE my son!
FWIP
Uh.
NO...NO! TEACHER! YOU SHOULDN'T BE COMPLIMENTING HIM! NO WAY!
He messed up! Your son messed up!
THAT'S HOW SMART THE KUON BOY IS?!
THEN YOU'RE REALLY JUST A DOTING PARENT!
Y...
YOU...
YOU DON'T HAVE TO EAT IT...
...DON'T HAVE TO FORCE YOURSELF... DAD...

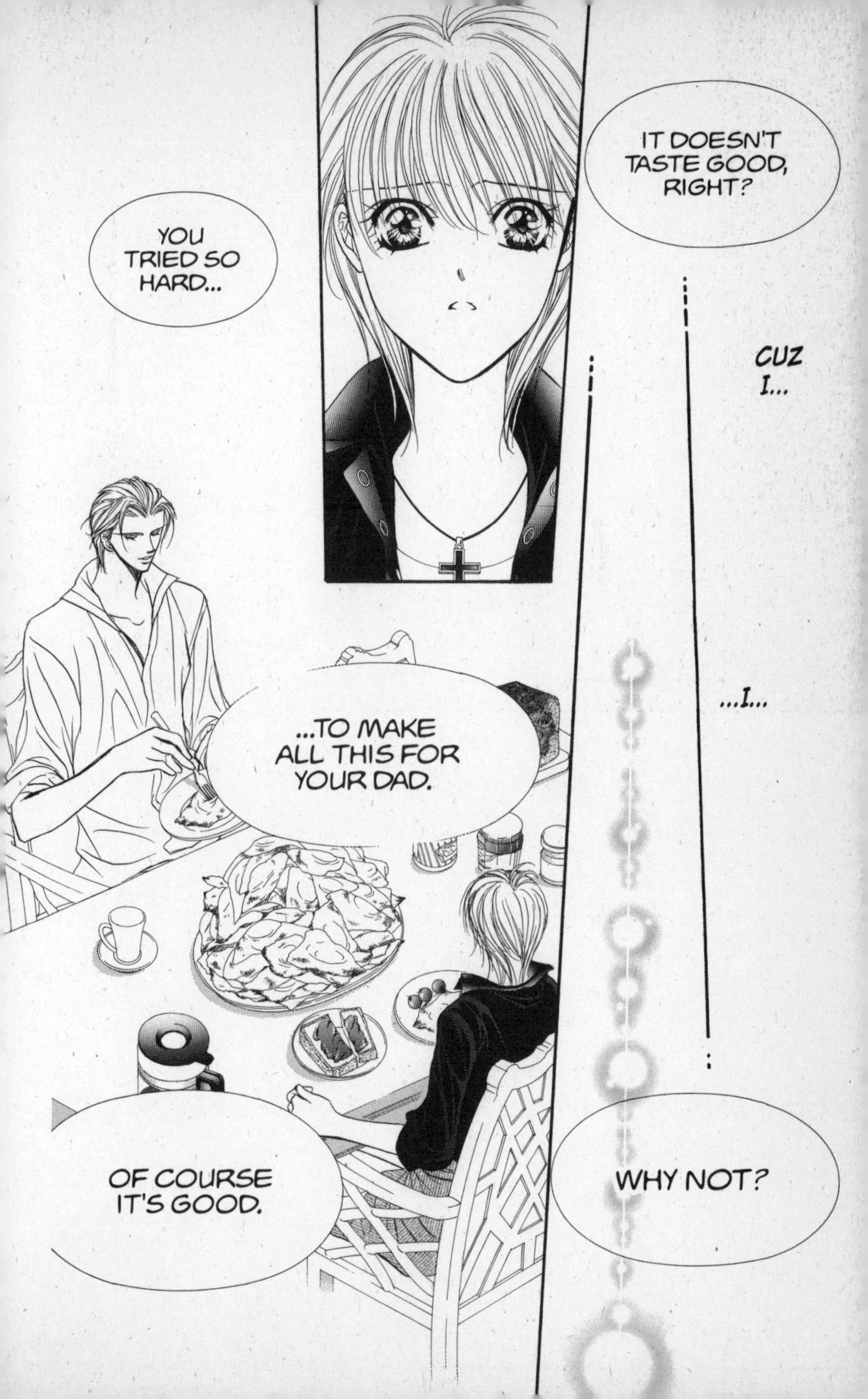
IT DOESN'T TASTE GOOD, RIGHT?
CUZ I...
...I...
WHY NOT?
YOU TRIED SO HARD...
...TO MAKE ALL THIS FOR YOUR DAD.
OF COURSE IT'S GOOD.

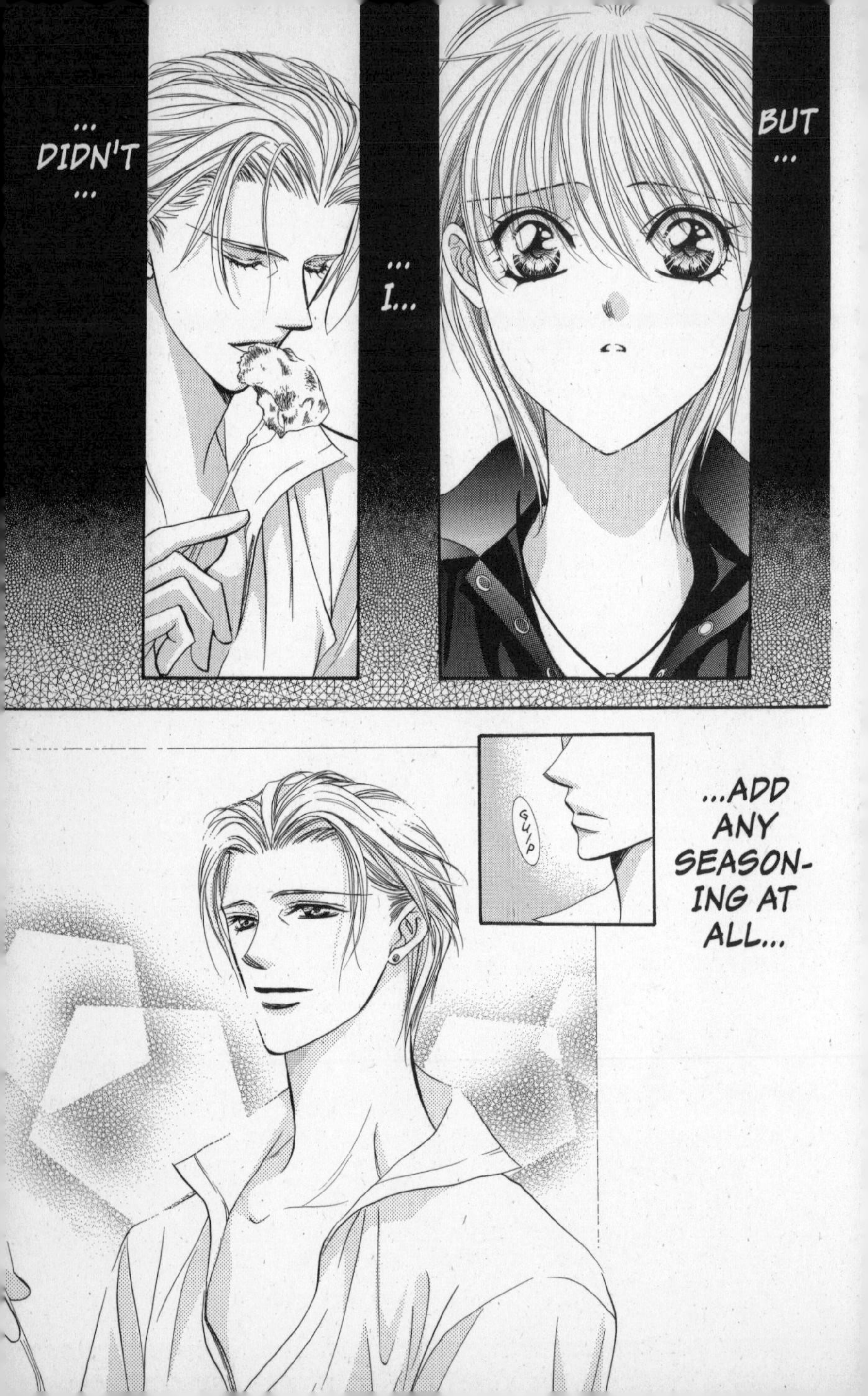
BUT ...
... I...
... DIDN'T ...
GULP
...ADD ANY SEASON-ING AT ALL...

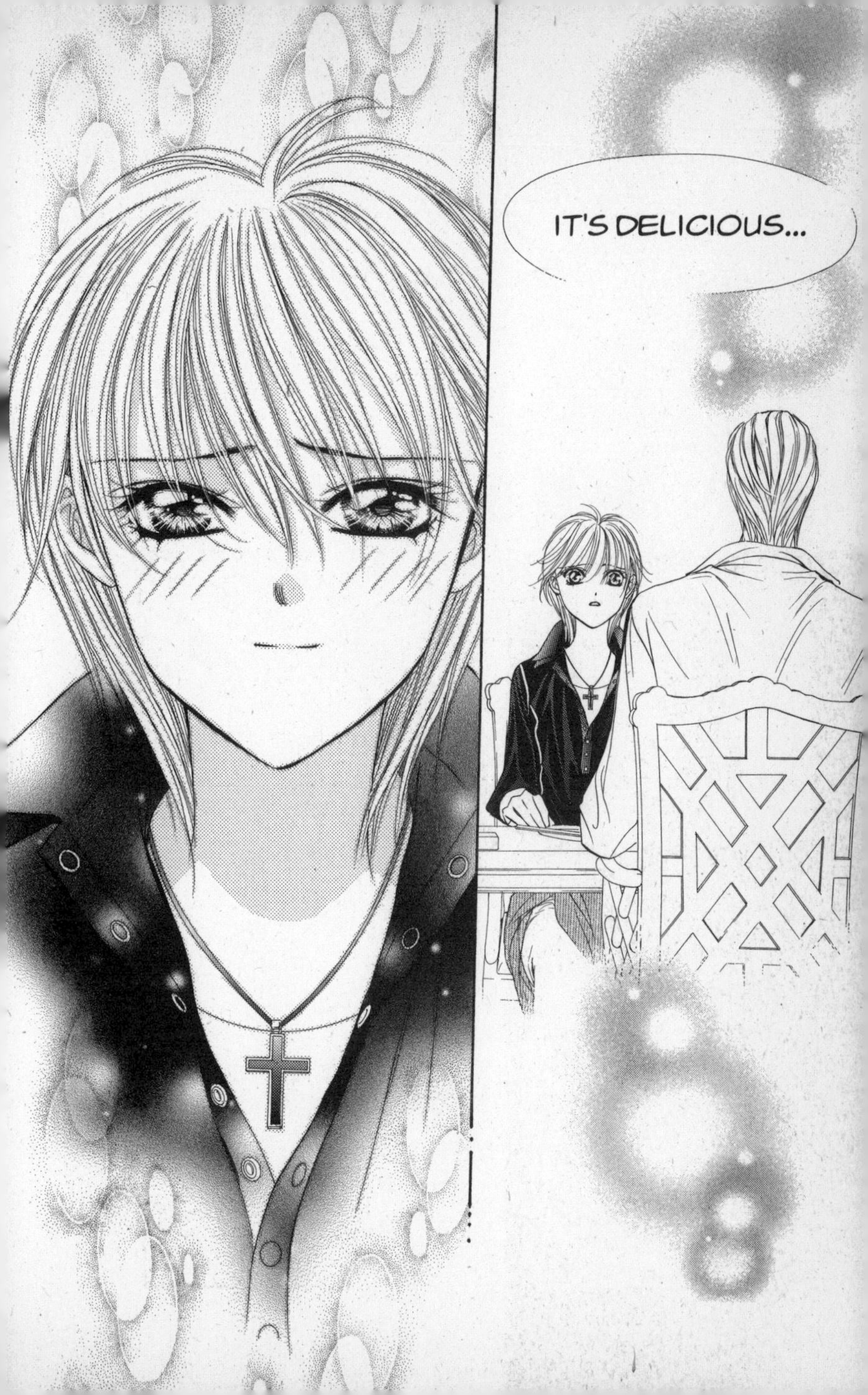
IT'S DELICIOUS...

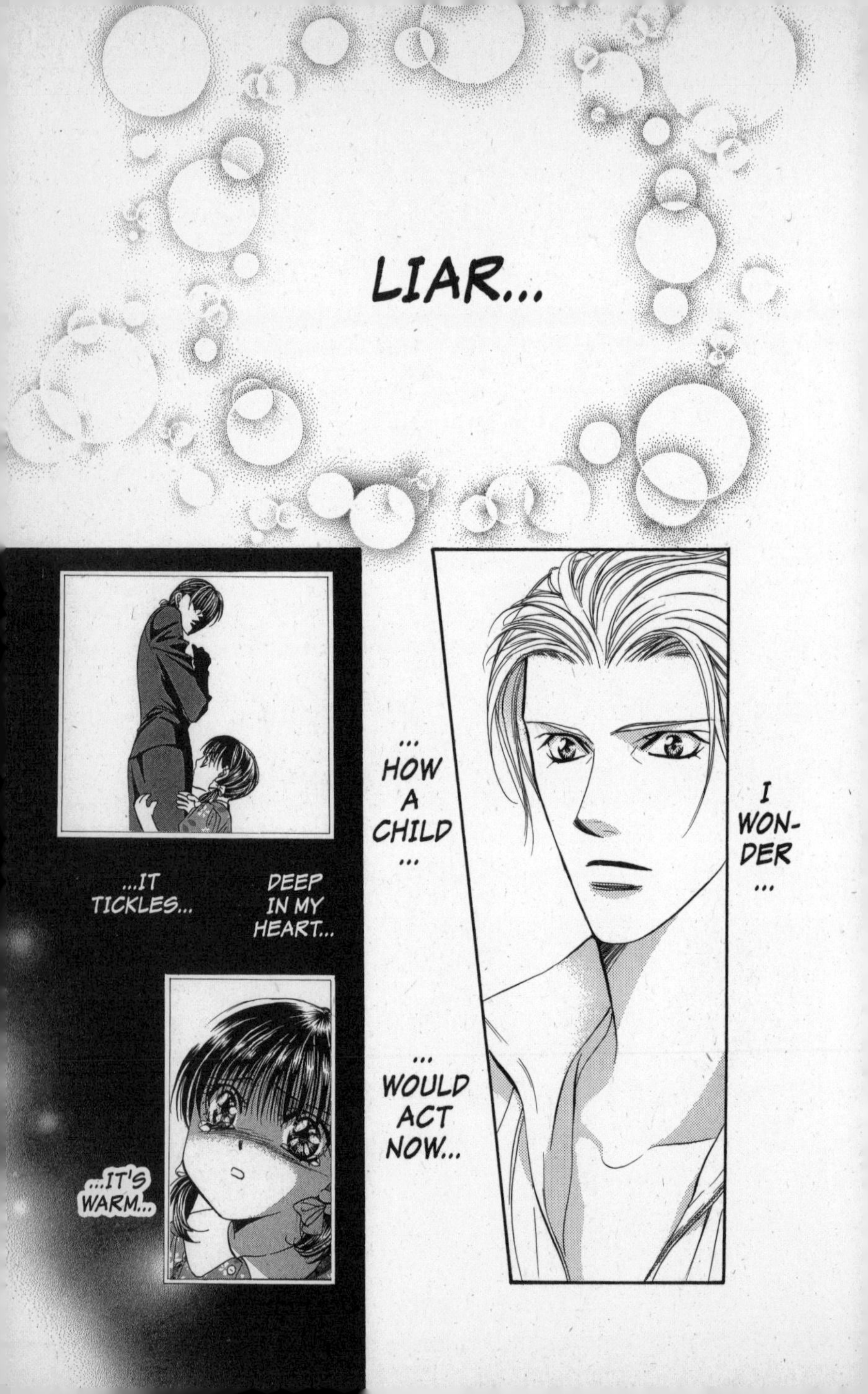
LIAR...
I WON-DER ...
... HOW A CHILD ...
... WOULD ACT NOW...
DEEP IN MY HEART...
...IT TICKLES...
...IT'S WARM...

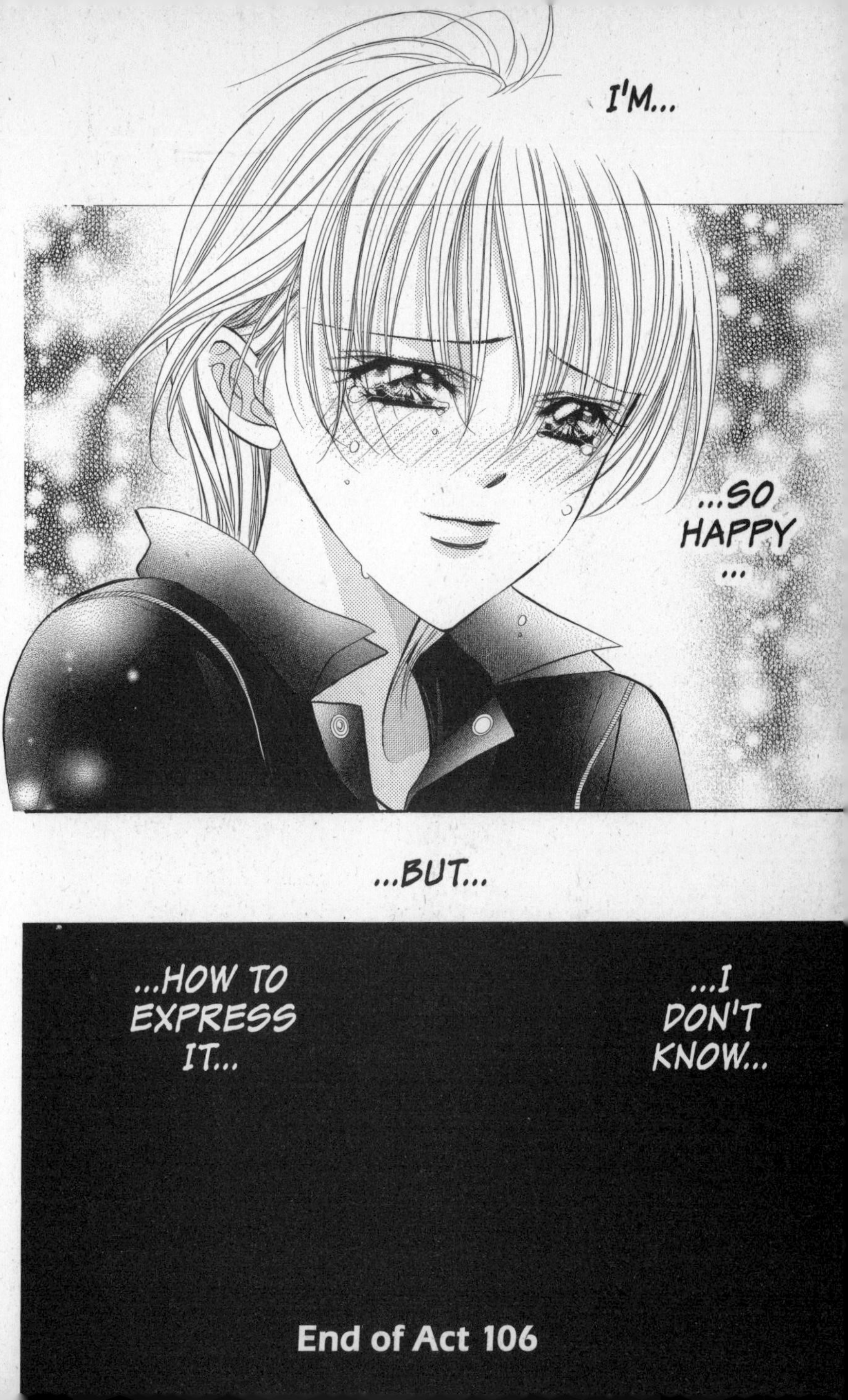
I'M...
...SO HAPPY ...
...BUT...
...I DON'T KNOW...
...HOW TO EXPRESS IT...
End of Act 106

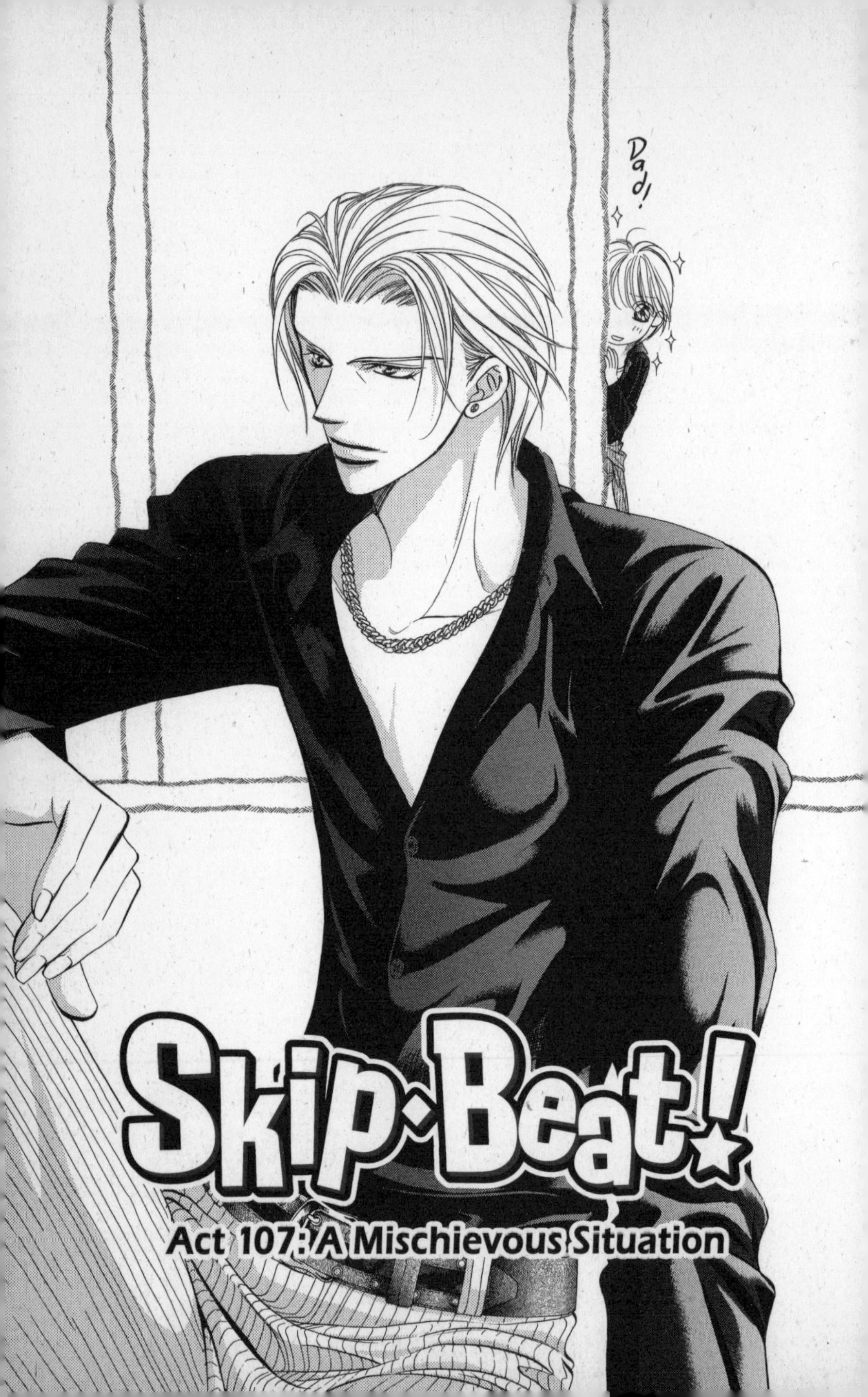
Dad!
Skip·Beat!
Act 107: A Mischievous Situation

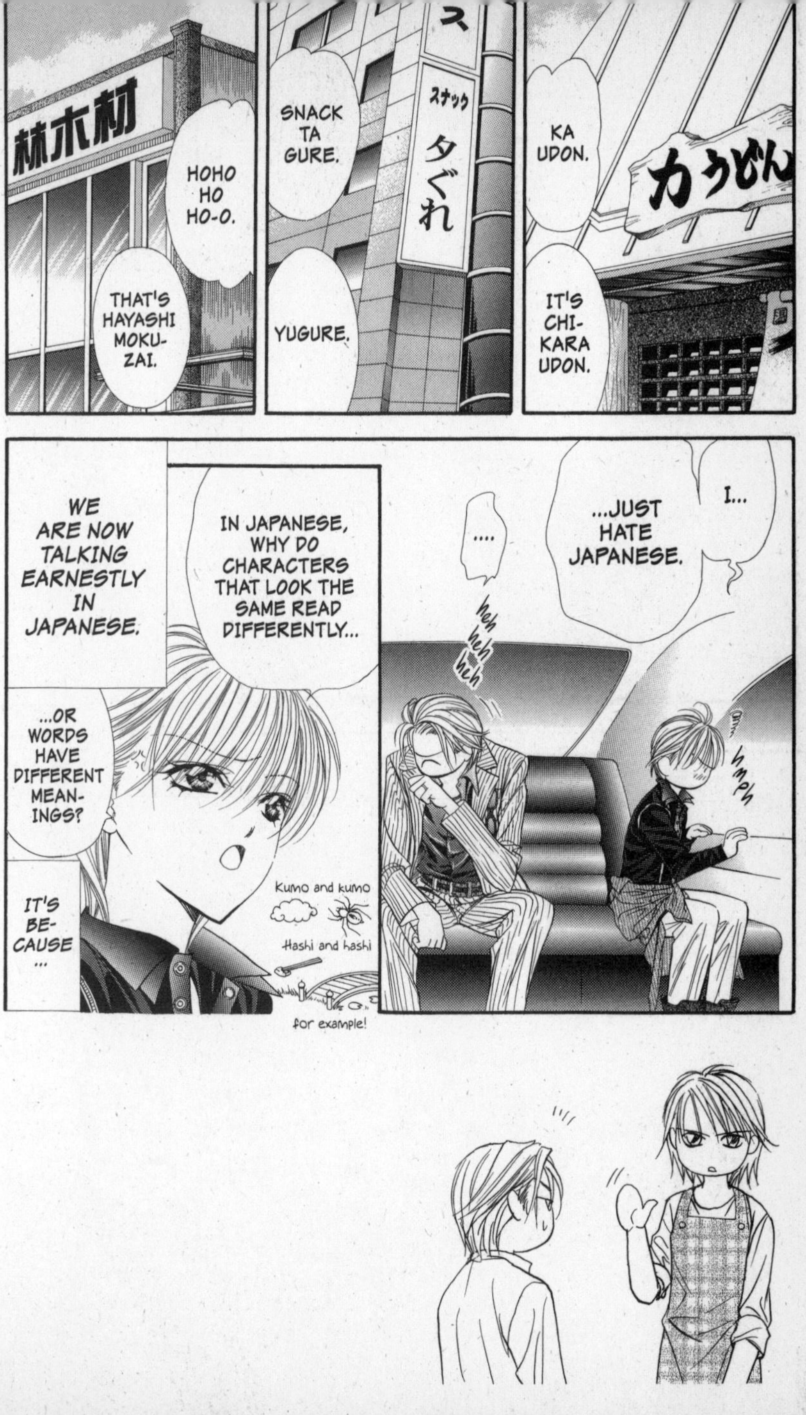
カうどん
KA UDON.
IT'S CHI-KARA UDON.
スナック 夕ぐれ
SNACK TA GURE.
YUGURE.
林木材
HOHO HO HO-O.
THAT'S HAYASHI MOKU-ZAI.
I...
...JUST HATE JAPANESE.
....
heh heh heh
hmph
WE ARE NOW TALKING EARNESTLY IN JAPANESE.
IN JAPANESE, WHY DO CHARACTERS THAT LOOK THE SAME READ DIFFERENTLY...
...OR WORDS HAVE DIFFERENT MEAN-INGS?
IT'S BE-CAUSE ...
Kumo and kumo
Hashi and hashi
for example!

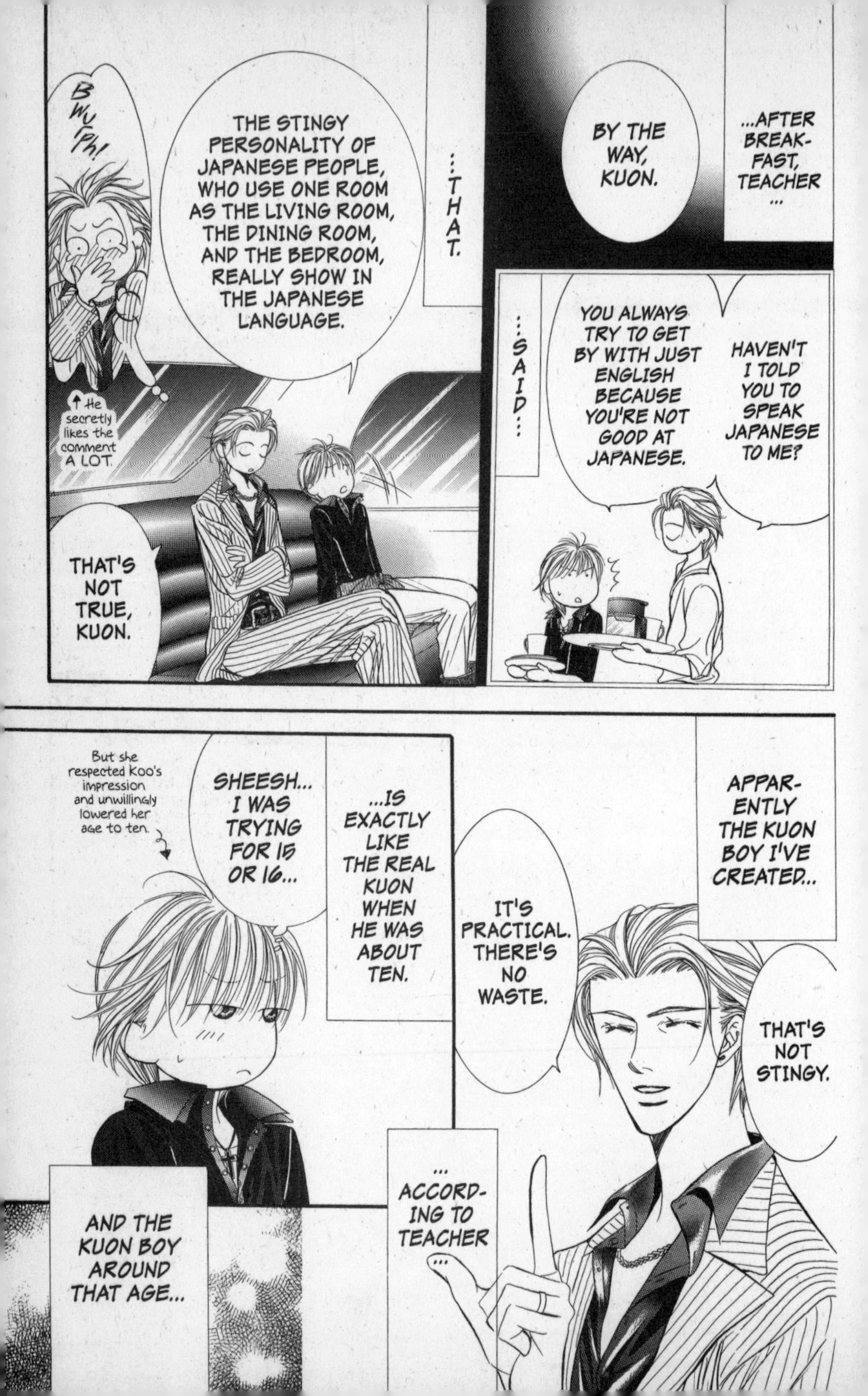
...AFTER BREAK- FAST, TEACHER ...
BY THE WAY, KUON.
HAVEN'T I TOLD YOU TO SPEAK JAPANESE TO ME?
YOU ALWAYS TRY TO GET BY WITH JUST ENGLISH BECAUSE YOU'RE NOT GOOD AT JAPANESE.
...SAID...
...THAT.
THE STINGY PERSONALITY OF JAPANESE PEOPLE, WHO USE ONE ROOM AS THE LIVING ROOM, THE DINING ROOM, AND THE BEDROOM, REALLY SHOW IN THE JAPANESE LANGUAGE.
BWUPH!
↑He secretly likes the comment A LOT.
THAT'S NOT TRUE, KUON.
APPAR- ENTLY THE KUON BOY I'VE CREATED...
THAT'S NOT STINGY.
IT'S PRACTICAL. THERE'S NO WASTE.
... ACCORD- ING TO TEACHER ...
SHEESH... I WAS TRYING FOR 15 OR 16...
But she respected Koo's impression and unwillingly lowered her age to ten.
AND THE KUON BOY AROUND THAT AGE...
...IS EXACTLY LIKE THE REAL KUON WHEN HE WAS ABOUT TEN.

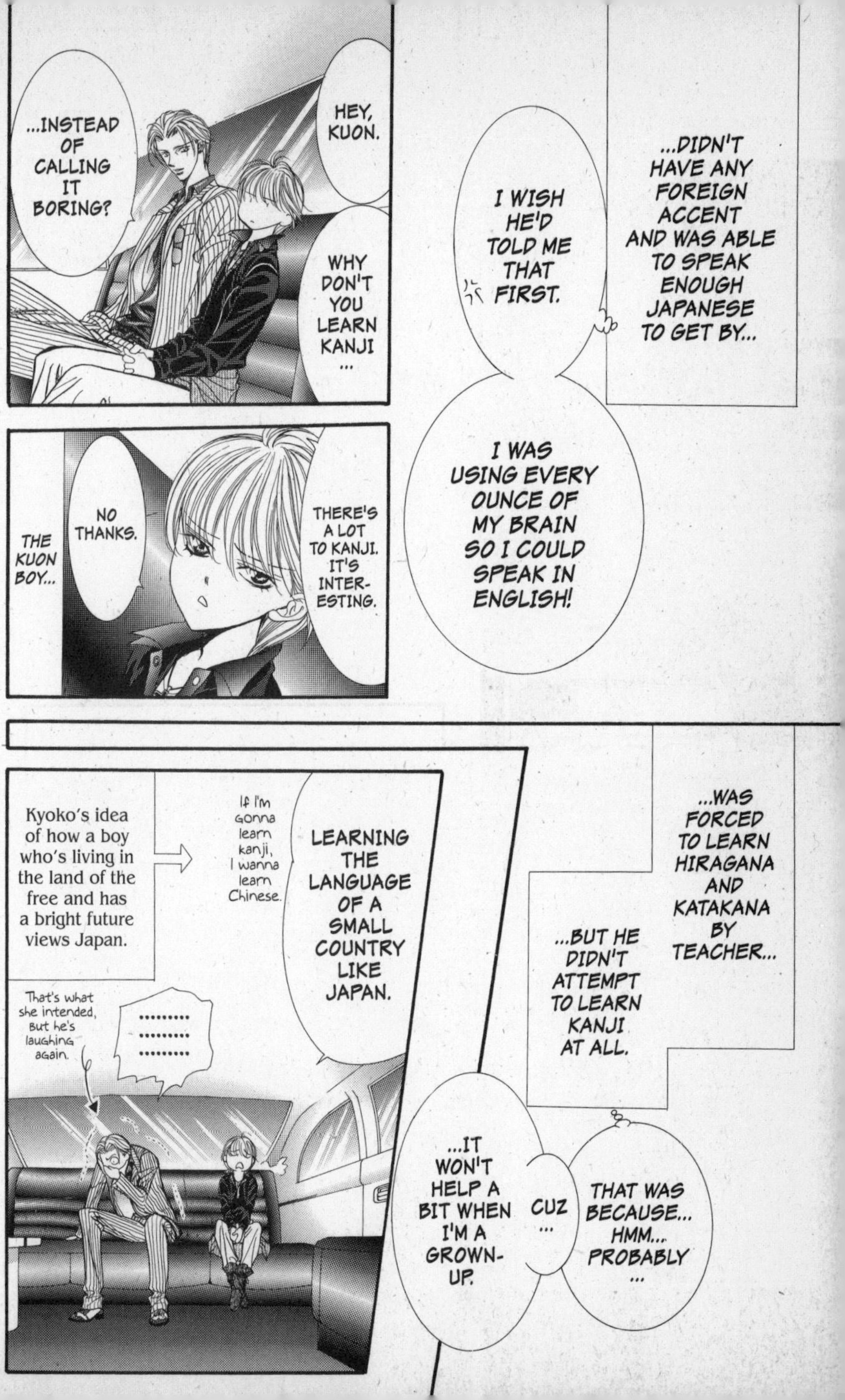
...DIDN'T HAVE ANY FOREIGN ACCENT AND WAS ABLE TO SPEAK ENOUGH JAPANESE TO GET BY...
I WISH HE'D TOLD ME THAT FIRST.
I WAS USING EVERY OUNCE OF MY BRAIN SO I COULD SPEAK IN ENGLISH!
HEY, KUON.
WHY DON'T YOU LEARN KANJI...
...INSTEAD OF CALLING IT BORING?
THERE'S A LOT TO KANJI. IT'S INTERESTING.
NO THANKS.
THE KUON BOY...
...WAS FORCED TO LEARN HIRAGANA AND KATAKANA BY TEACHER...
...BUT HE DIDN'T ATTEMPT TO LEARN KANJI AT ALL.
THAT WAS BECAUSE... HMM... PROBABLY...
CUZ...
...IT WON'T HELP A BIT WHEN I'M A GROWN-UP.
LEARNING THE LANGUAGE OF A SMALL COUNTRY LIKE JAPAN.
If I'm gonna learn kanji, I wanna learn Chinese.
Kyoko's idea of how a boy who's living in the land of the free and has a bright future views Japan.
....
....
....
That's what she intended, but he's laughing again.

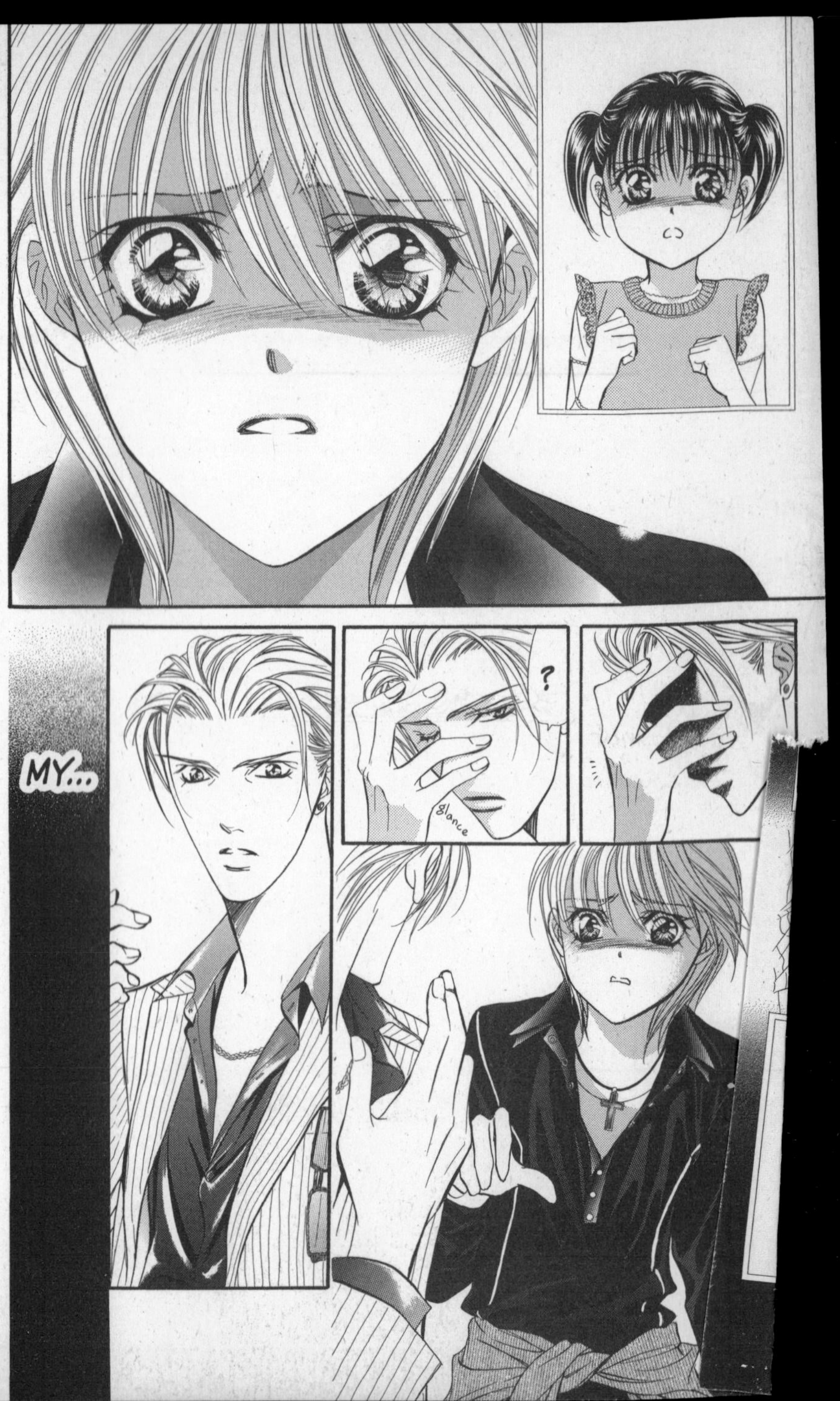
?
glance
MY...
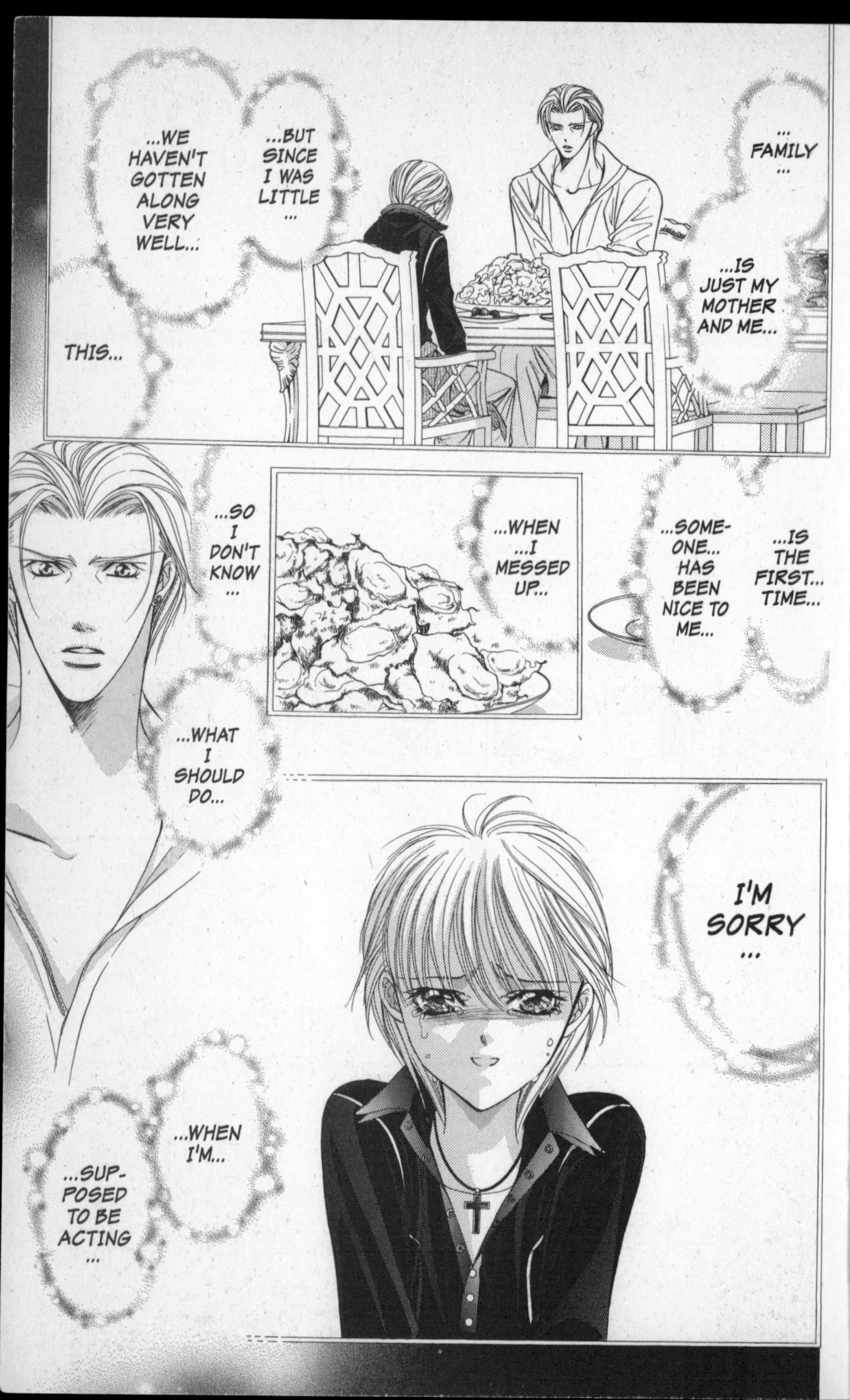
... FAMILY ...
...IS JUST MY MOTHER AND ME...
...BUT SINCE I WAS LITTLE ...
...WE HAVEN'T GOTTEN ALONG VERY WELL...
THIS...
...IS THE FIRST... TIME...
...SOME-ONE... HAS BEEN NICE TO ME...
...WHEN ...I MESSED UP...
...SO I DON'T KNOW ...
...WHAT I SHOULD DO...
I'M SORRY ...
...WHEN I'M...
...SUP-POSED TO BE ACTING ...

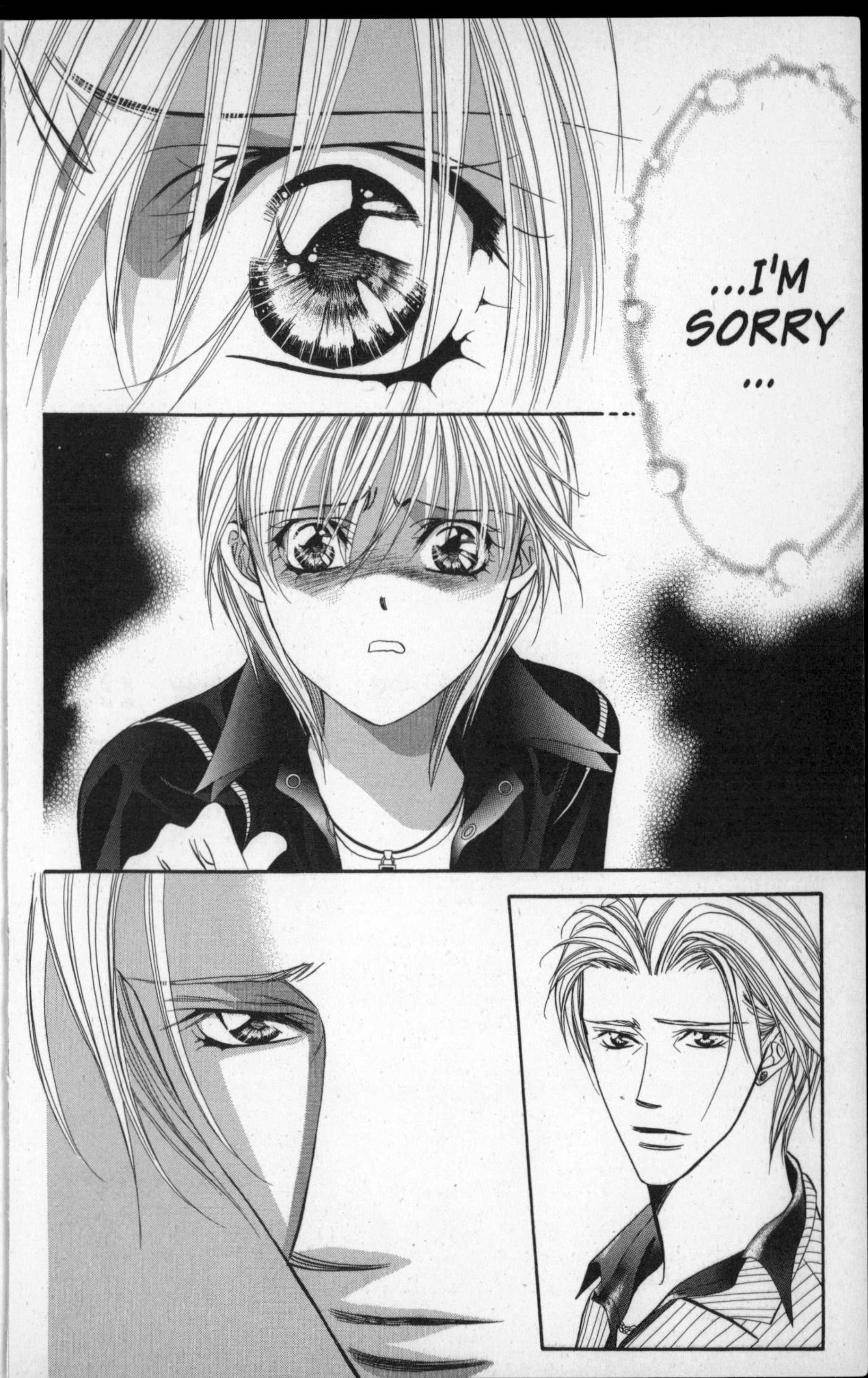
...I'M SORRY ...

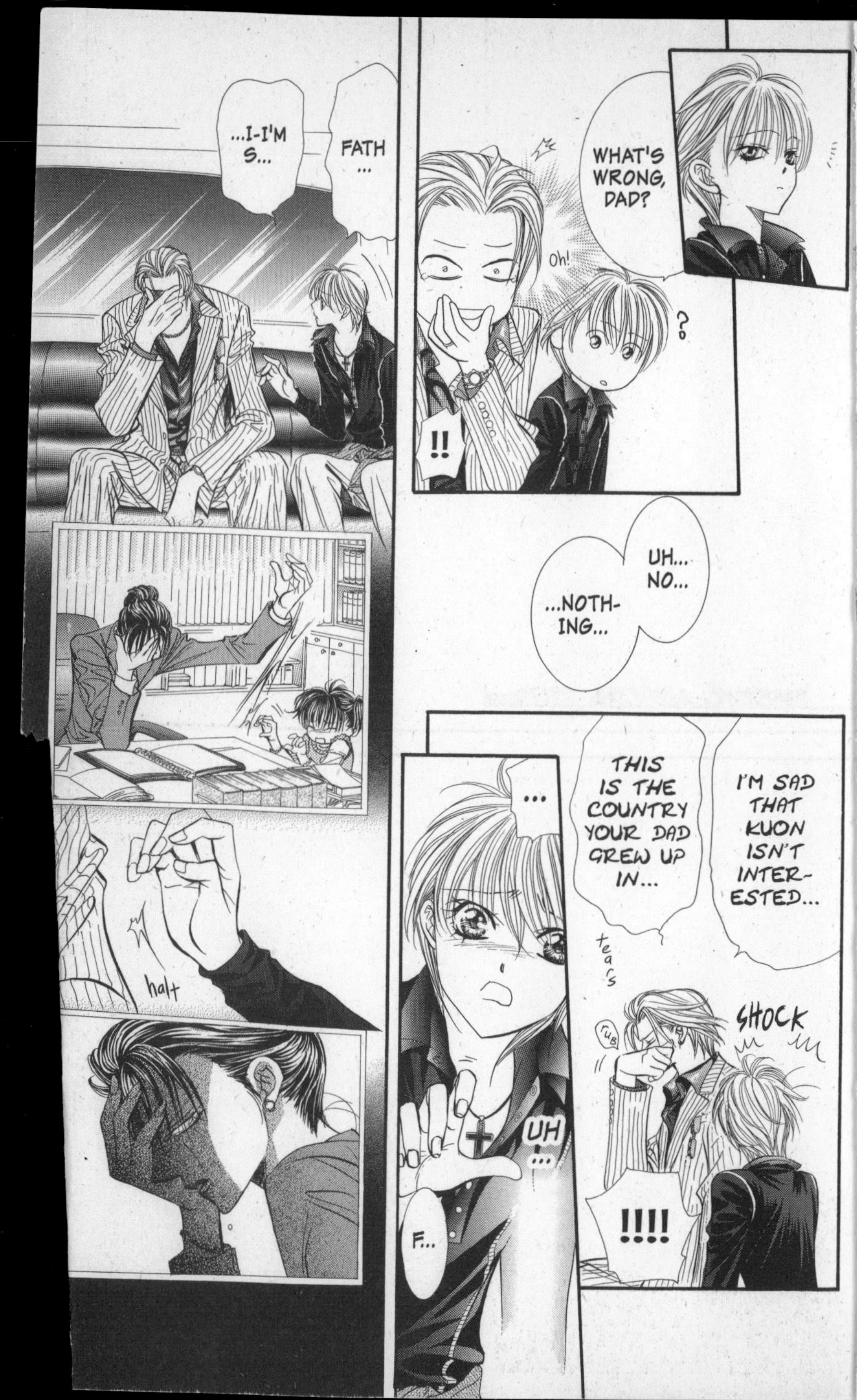
WHAT'S WRONG, DAD?
Oh!
?
!!
UH... NO...
...NOTH-ING...
I'M SAD THAT KUON ISN'T INTER-ESTED...
THIS IS THE COUNTRY YOUR DAD GREW UP IN...
...
tears
rub
SHOCK
UH ...
!!!!
F...
FATH ...
...I-I'M S...
halt

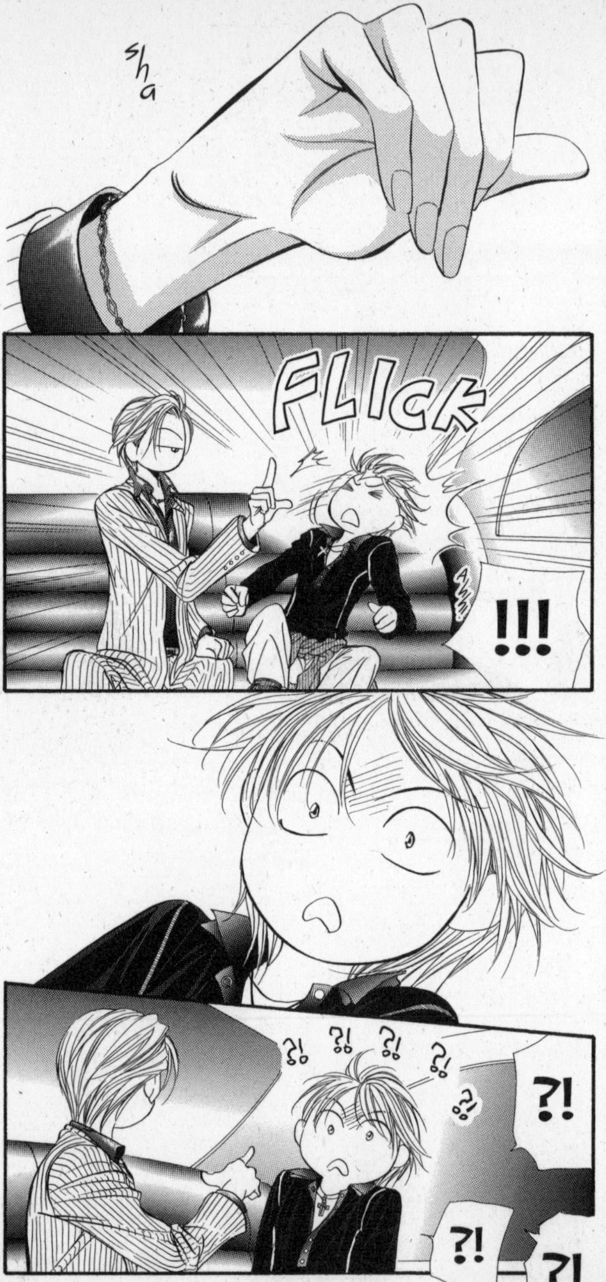
sha
FLICK
AHH!
!!!
?!
?!
?!
?! ?! ?! ?! ?!

The proprie-tress-to-be

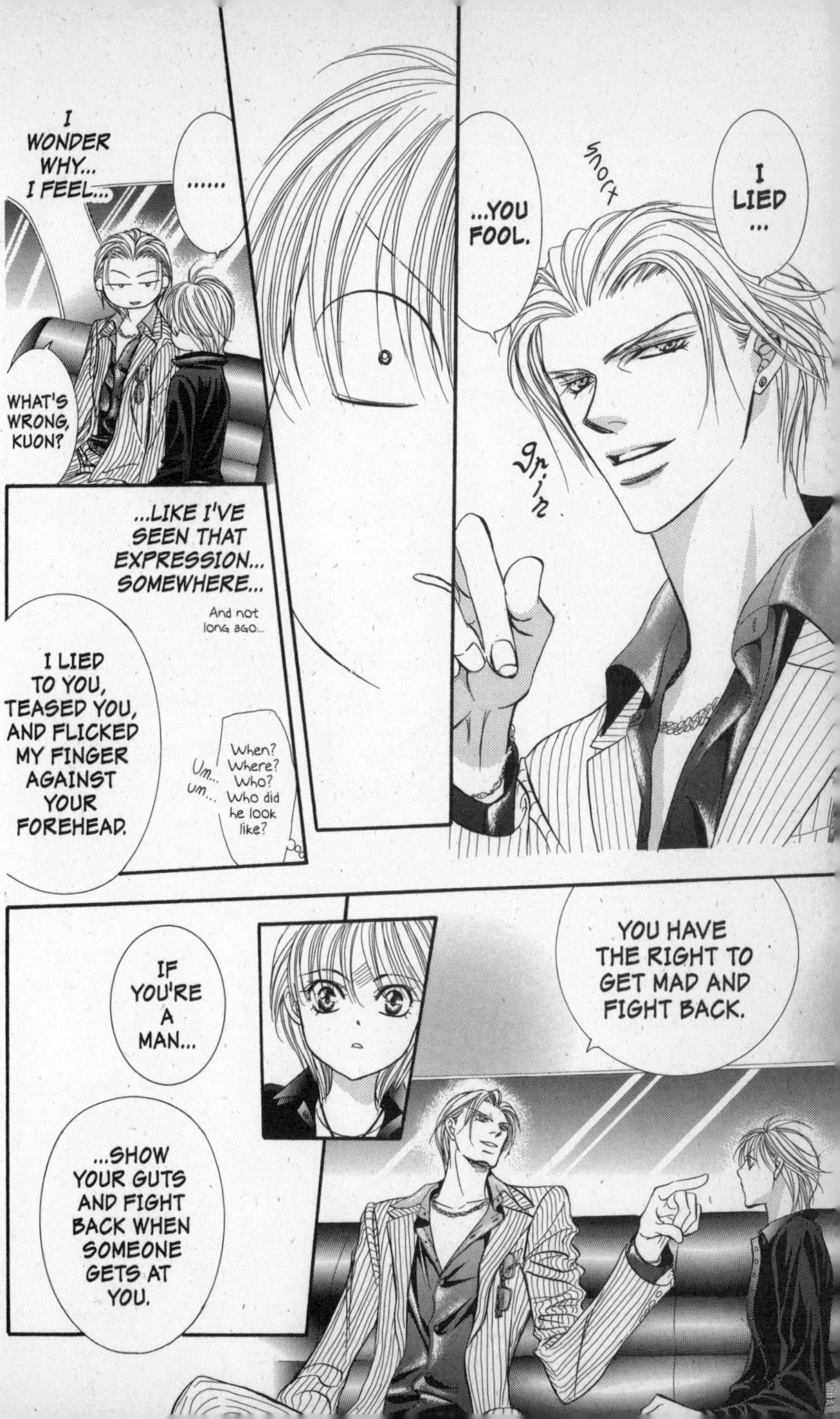
I LIED ...
snort
...YOU FOOL.
grin
......
I WONDER WHY... I FEEL...
WHAT'S WRONG, KUON?
...LIKE I'VE SEEN THAT EXPRESSION... SOMEWHERE...
And not long ago...
When? Where? Who? Who did he look like?
Um... um...
I LIED TO YOU, TEASED YOU, AND FLICKED MY FINGER AGAINST YOUR FOREHEAD.
YOU HAVE THE RIGHT TO GET MAD AND FIGHT BACK.
IF YOU'RE A MAN...
...SHOW YOUR GUTS AND FIGHT BACK WHEN SOMEONE GETS AT YOU.

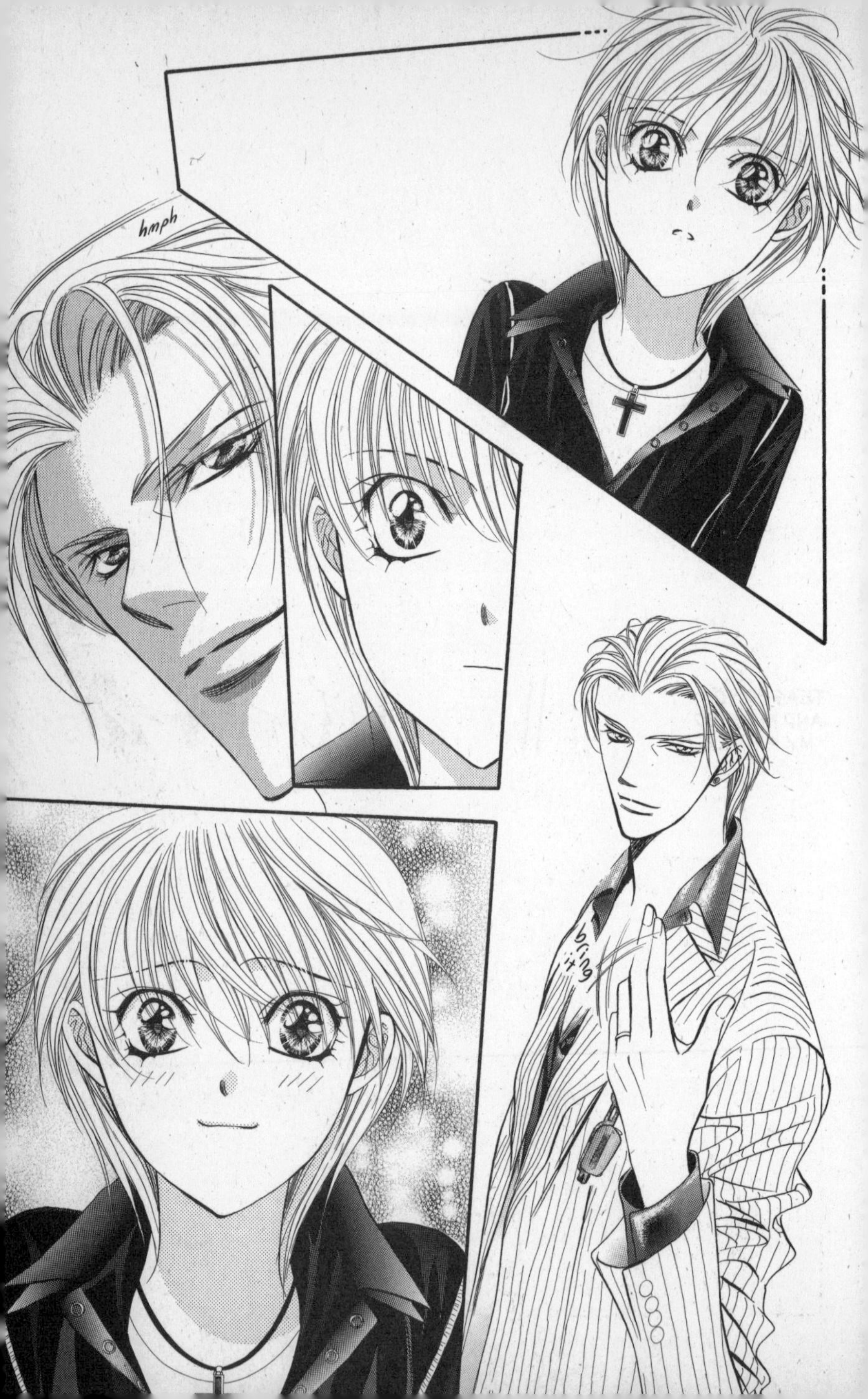
hmph
bring it

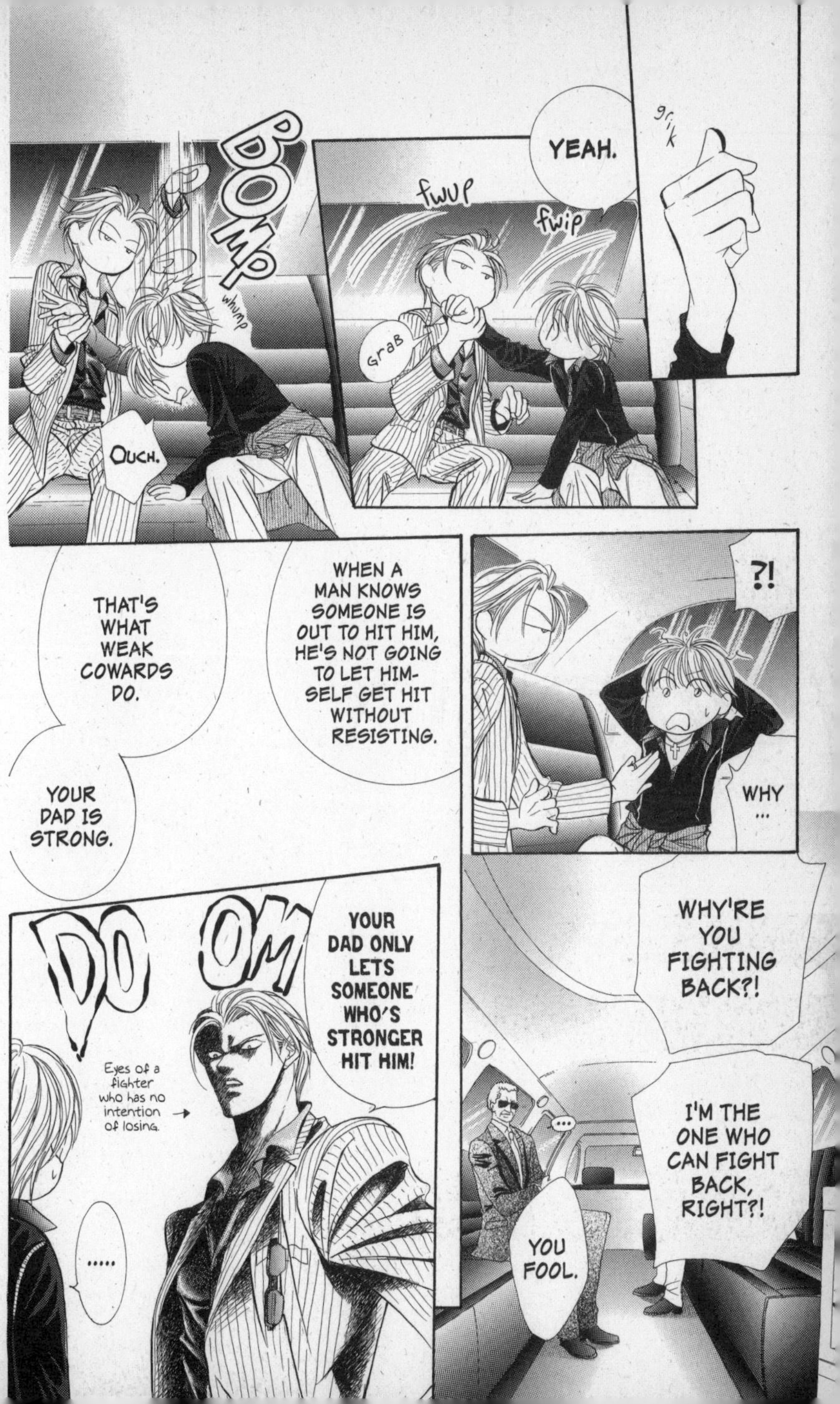
YEAH.
grik
fwup
fwip
GRAB
BOMP
whump
OUCH.
?!
WHY ...
WHEN A MAN KNOWS SOMEONE IS OUT TO HIT HIM, HE'S NOT GOING TO LET HIM-SELF GET HIT WITHOUT RESISTING.
THAT'S WHAT WEAK COWARDS DO.
YOUR DAD IS STRONG.
WHY'RE YOU FIGHTING BACK?!
I'M THE ONE WHO CAN FIGHT BACK, RIGHT?!
...
YOU FOOL.
DOOM
YOUR DAD ONLY LETS SOMEONE WHO'S STRONGER HIT HIM!
Eyes of a fighter who has no intention of losing.
.....

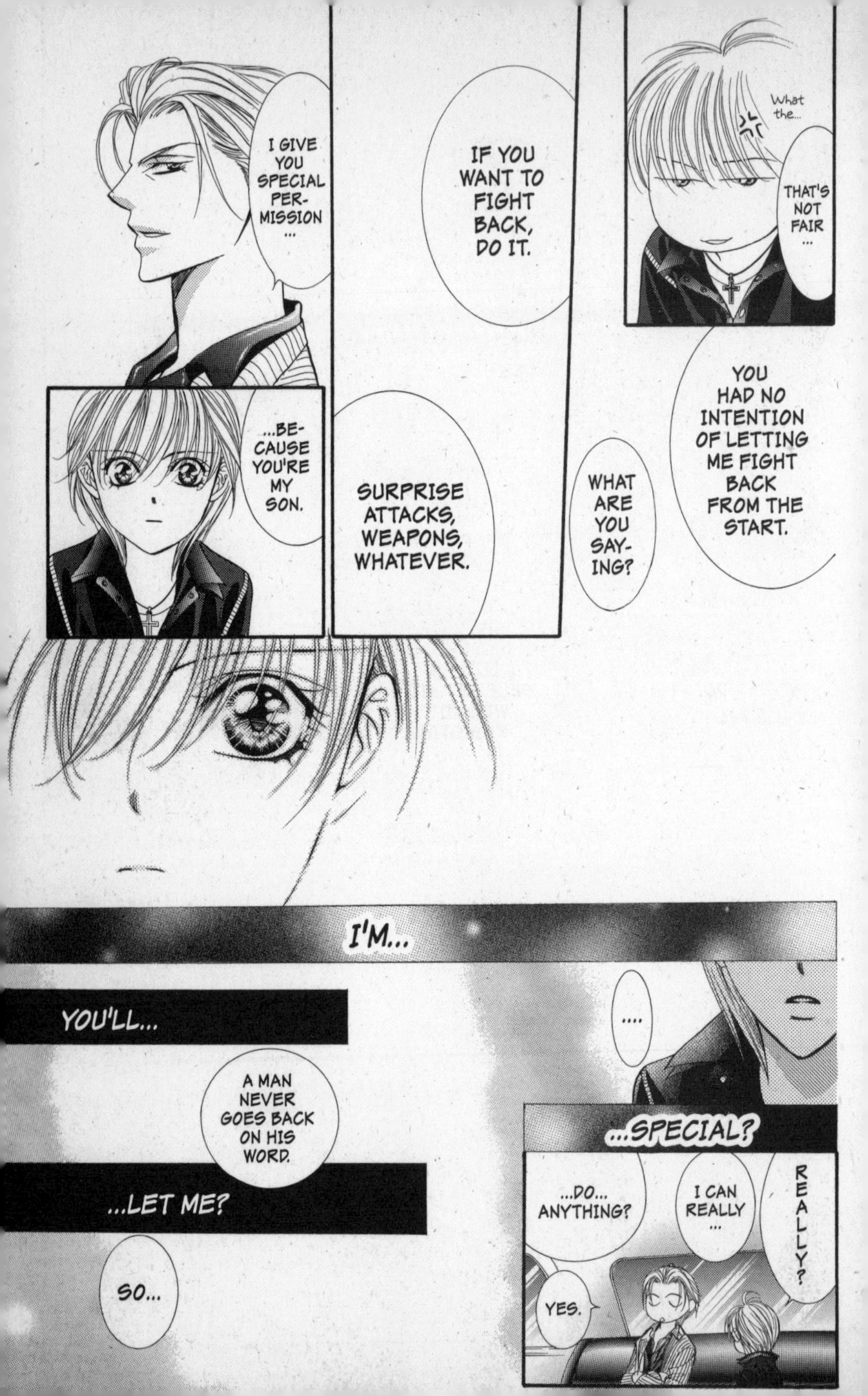
What the...
THAT'S NOT FAIR...
YOU HAD NO INTENTION OF LETTING ME FIGHT BACK FROM THE START.
WHAT ARE YOU SAYING?
IF YOU WANT TO FIGHT BACK, DO IT.
SURPRISE ATTACKS, WEAPONS, WHATEVER.
I GIVE YOU SPECIAL PER-MISSION...
...BE-CAUSE YOU'RE MY SON.
I'M...
....
YOU'LL...
A MAN NEVER GOES BACK ON HIS WORD.
...LET ME?
SO...
...SPECIAL?
REALLY?
I CAN REALLY...
...DO... ANYTHING?
YES.

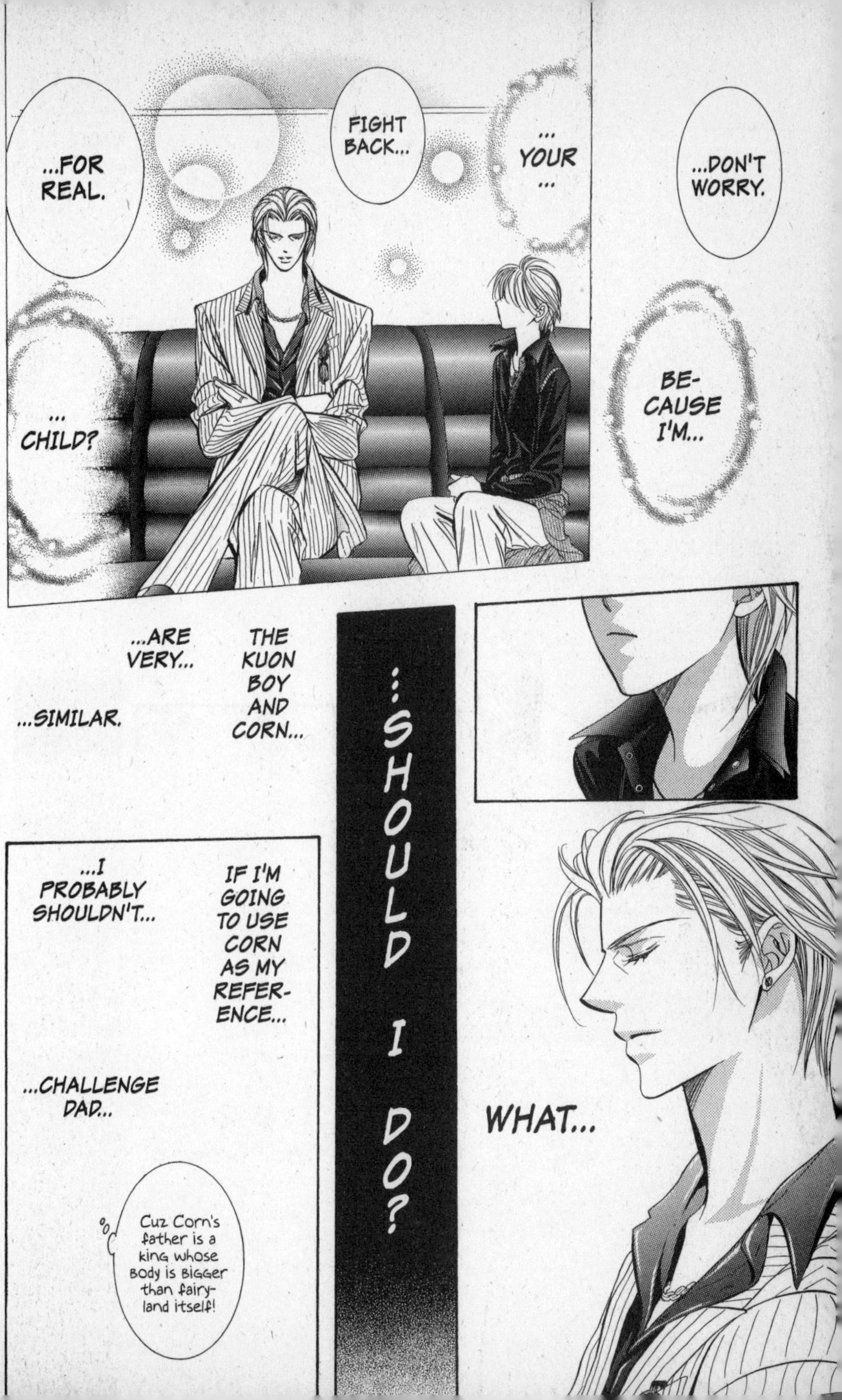
...DON'T WORRY.
BE-CAUSE I'M...
... YOUR ...
... CHILD?
FIGHT BACK...
...FOR REAL.
THE KUON BOY AND CORN...
...ARE VERY...
...SIMILAR.
WHAT...
...SHOULD I DO?
IF I'M GOING TO USE CORN AS MY REFER-ENCE...
...I PROBABLY SHOULDN'T...
...CHALLENGE DAD...
Cuz Corn's father is a king whose body is bigger than fairy-land itself!

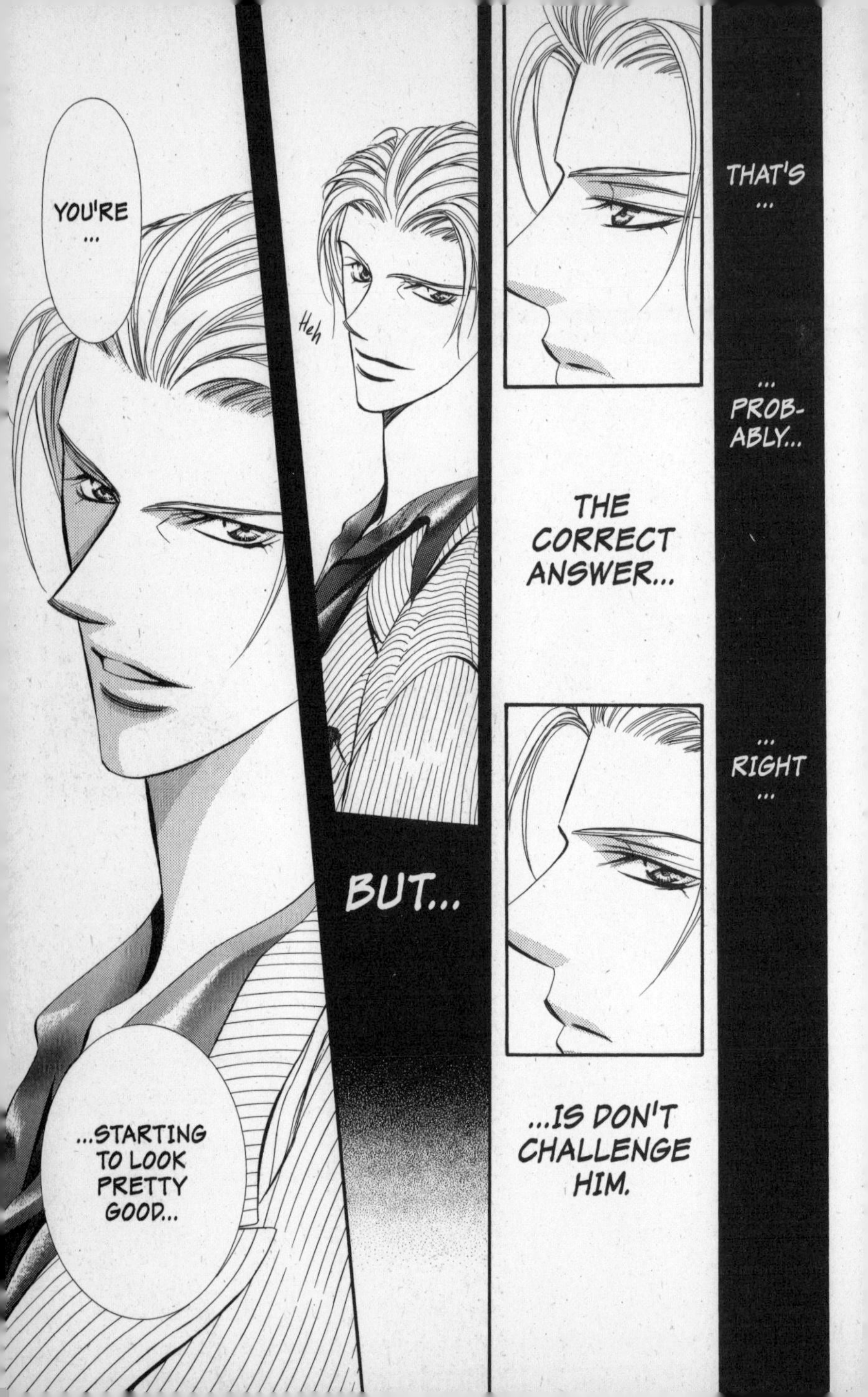
THAT'S ...
... PROB-ABLY...
... RIGHT ...
THE CORRECT ANSWER...
...IS DON'T CHALLENGE HIM.
BUT...
Heh
YOU'RE ...
...STARTING TO LOOK PRETTY GOOD...

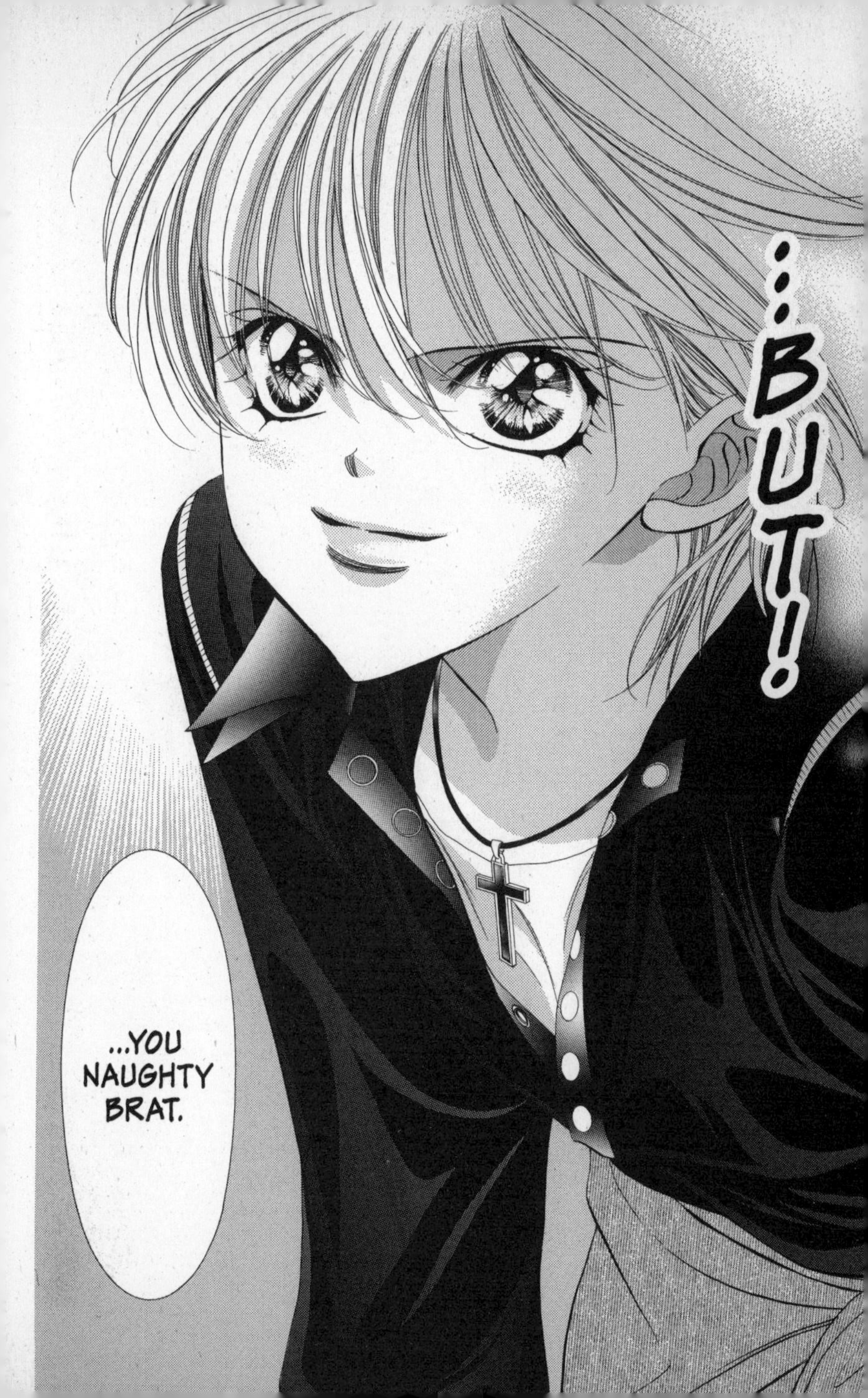
...BUT!
...YOU NAUGHTY BRAT.

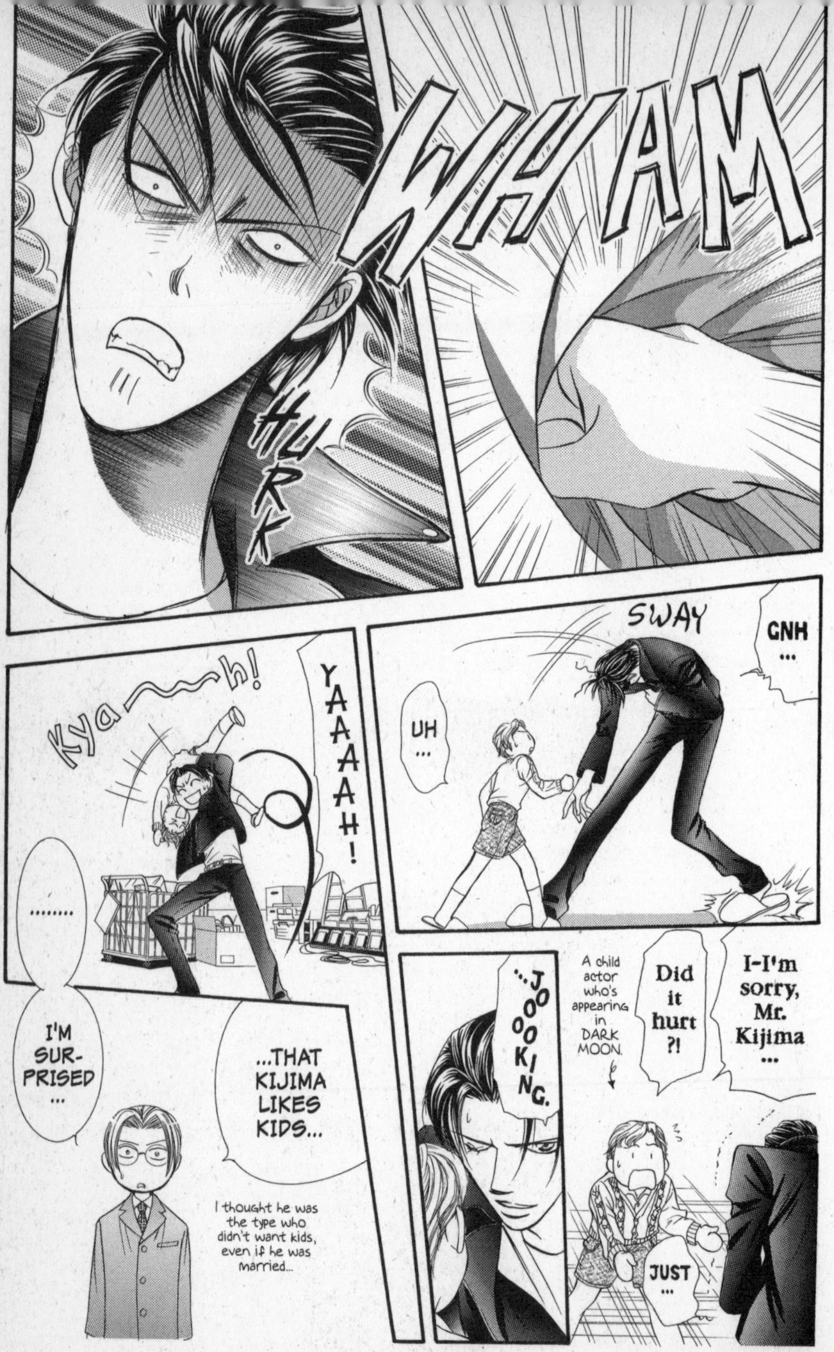
WHAM
HURK
SWAY
GNH ...
UH ...
Kya~~h!
YAAAAAH!
....
I-I'm sorry, Mr. Kijima ...
Did it hurt ?!
A child actor who's appearing in DARK MOON.
...JOOOOOKING.
JUST ...
I'M SURPRISED ...
...THAT KIJIMA LIKES KIDS...
I thought he was the type who didn't want kids, even if he was married...

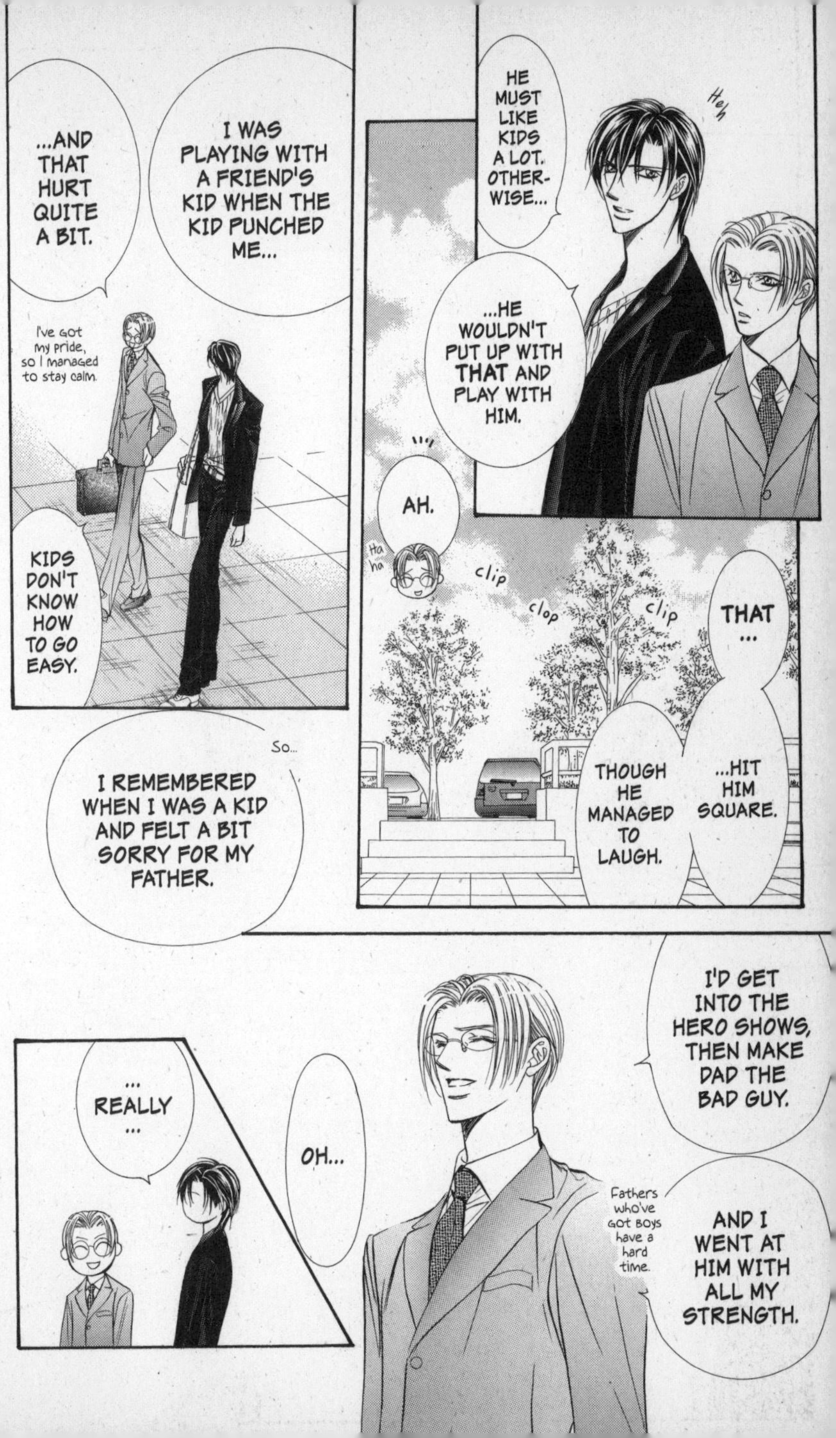
Heh
HE MUST LIKE KIDS A LOT. OTHER-WISE...
...HE WOULDN'T PUT UP WITH THAT AND PLAY WITH HIM.
AH.
Ha ha
clip
clop
clip
THAT...
...HIT HIM SQUARE.
THOUGH HE MANAGED TO LAUGH.
I WAS PLAYING WITH A FRIEND'S KID WHEN THE KID PUNCHED ME...
...AND THAT HURT QUITE A BIT.
I've got my pride, so I managed to stay calm.
KIDS DON'T KNOW HOW TO GO EASY.
So...
I REMEMBERED WHEN I WAS A KID AND FELT A BIT SORRY FOR MY FATHER.
I'D GET INTO THE HERO SHOWS, THEN MAKE DAD THE BAD GUY.
Fathers who've got boys have a hard time.
AND I WENT AT HIM WITH ALL MY STRENGTH.
OH...
...REALLY...

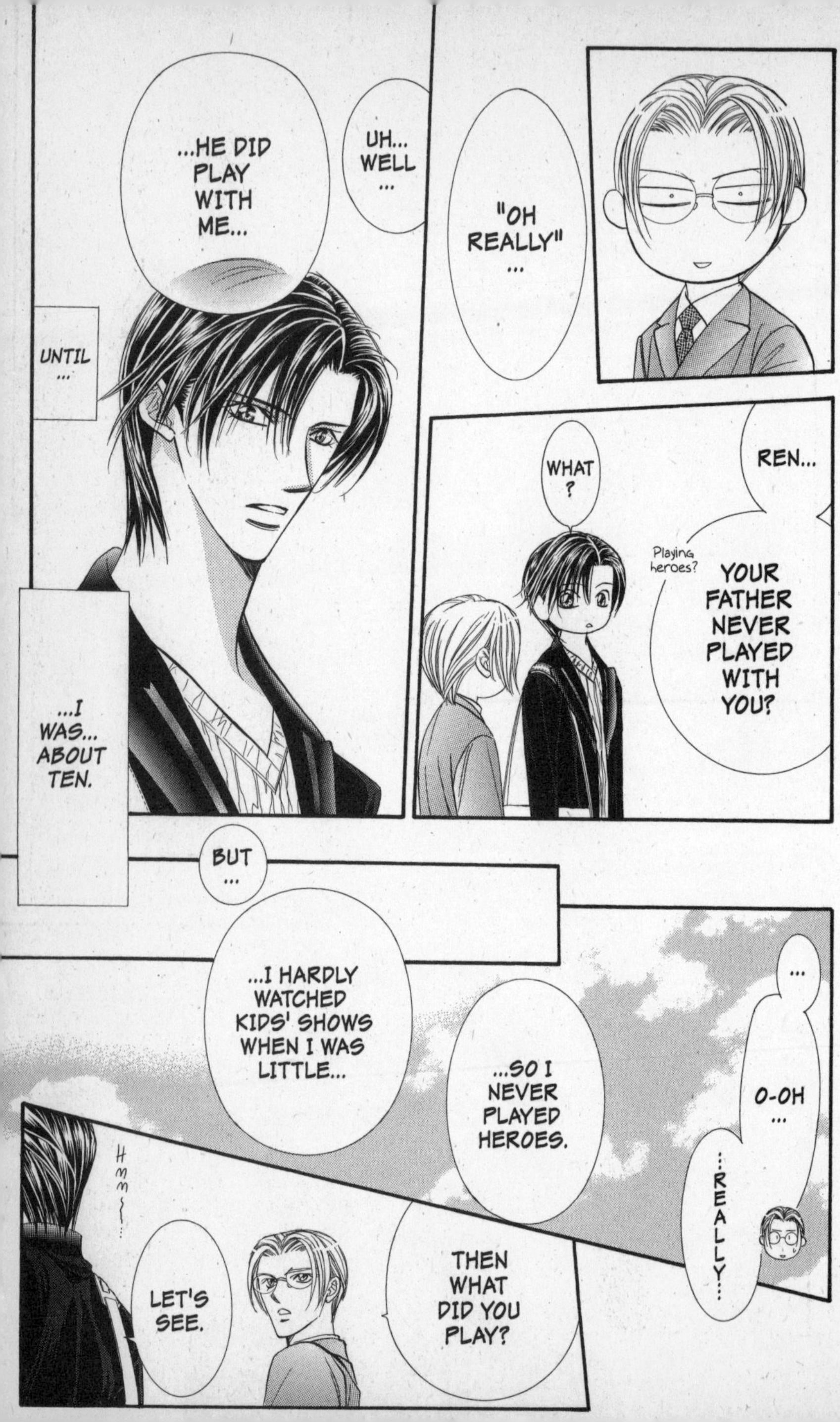
"OH REALLY" ...
REN...
YOUR FATHER NEVER PLAYED WITH YOU?
Playing heroes?
WHAT?
UH... WELL...
...HE DID PLAY WITH ME...
UNTIL...
...I WAS... ABOUT TEN.
BUT...
...I HARDLY WATCHED KIDS' SHOWS WHEN I WAS LITTLE...
...SO I NEVER PLAYED HEROES.
...
O-OH...
...REALLY...
THEN WHAT DID YOU PLAY?
LET'S SEE.
Hmm~...

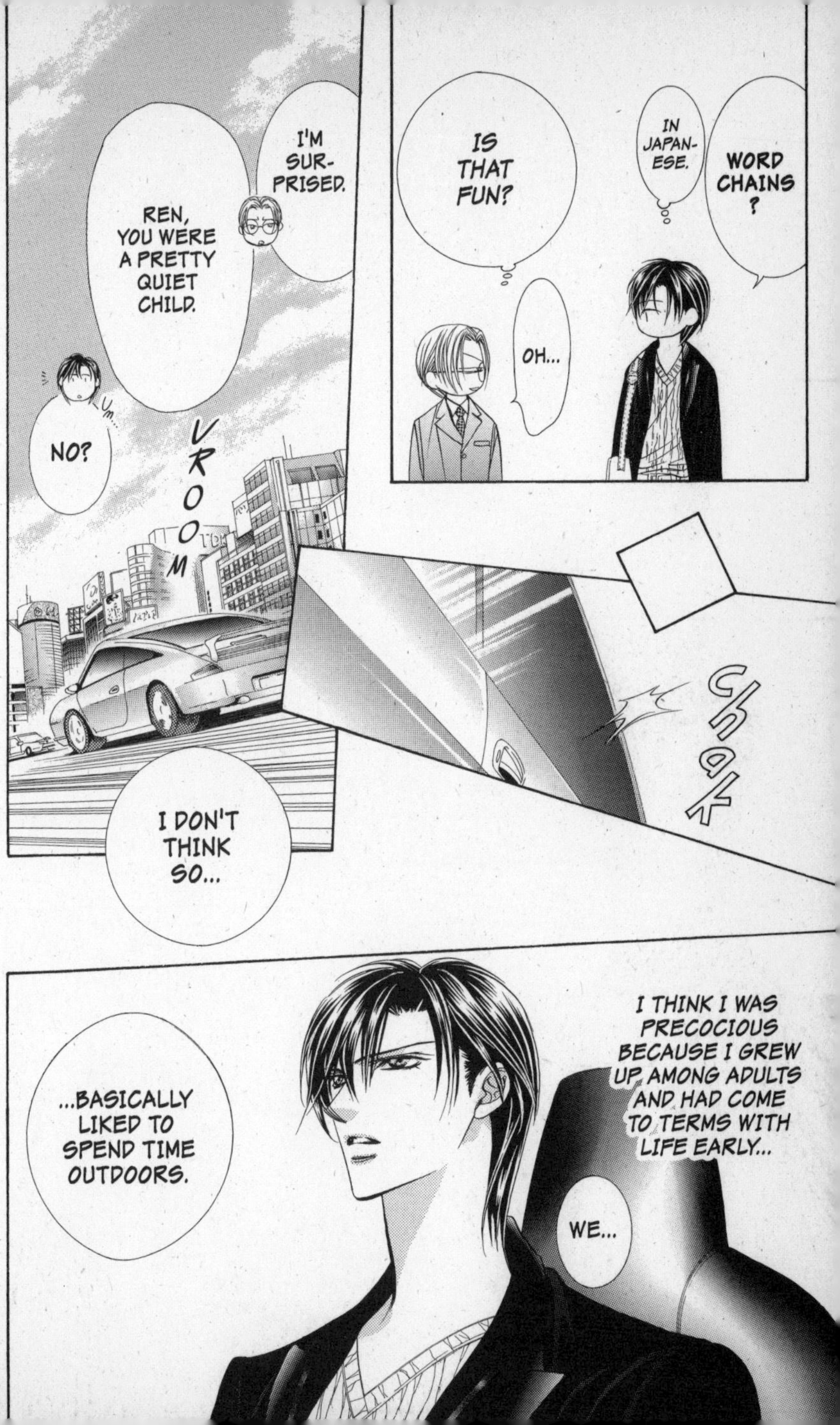
WORD CHAINS?
IN JAPANESE.
IS THAT FUN?
OH...
CHAK
I'M SURPRISED.
REN, YOU WERE A PRETTY QUIET CHILD.
Um...
NO?
VROOOM
I DON'T THINK SO...
I THINK I WAS PRECOCIOUS BECAUSE I GREW UP AMONG ADULTS AND HAD COME TO TERMS WITH LIFE EARLY...
WE...
...BASICALLY LIKED TO SPEND TIME OUTDOORS.

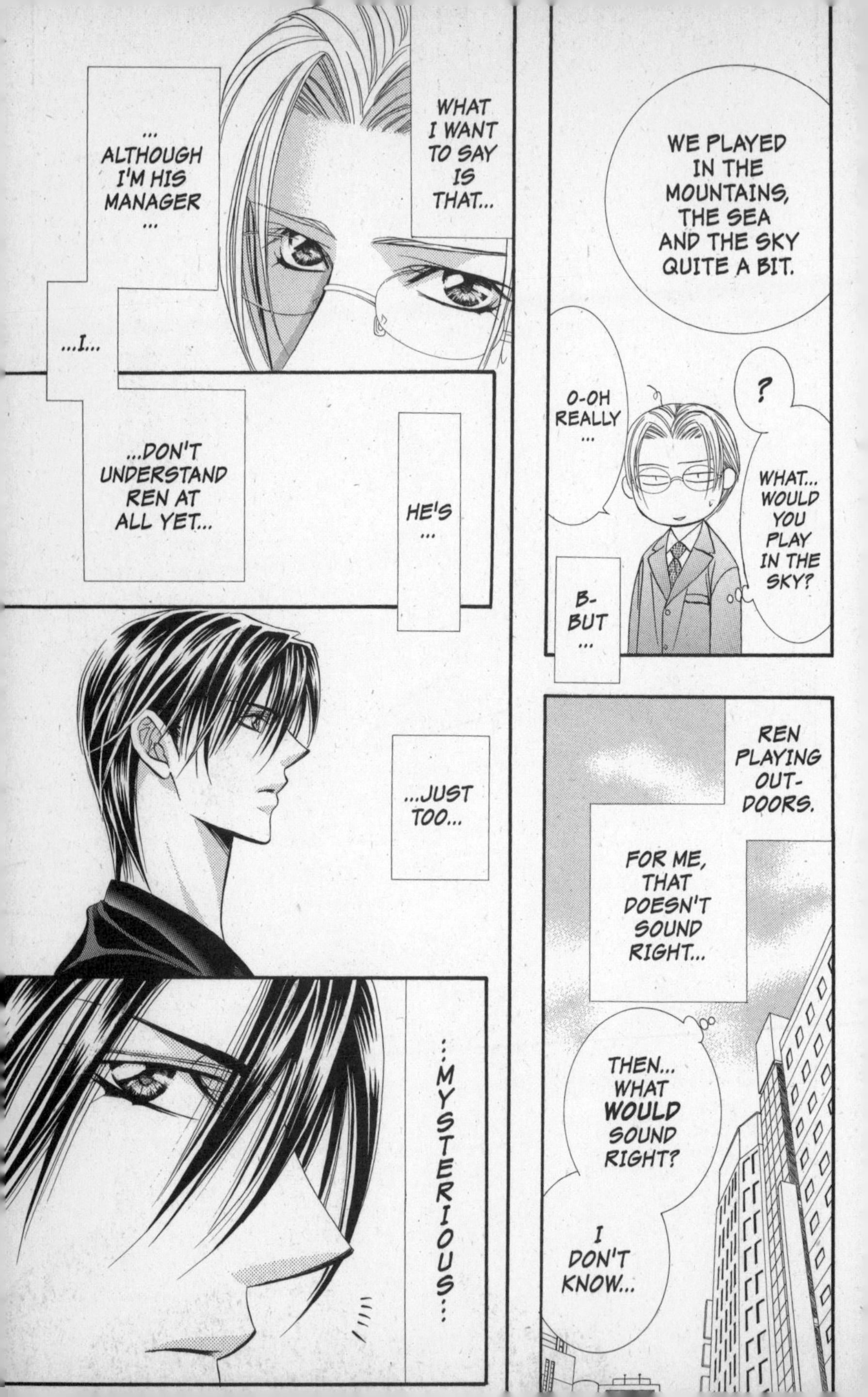
WE PLAYED IN THE MOUNTAINS, THE SEA AND THE SKY QUITE A BIT.
?
WHAT... WOULD YOU PLAY IN THE SKY?
O-OH REALLY ...
B-BUT ...
REN PLAYING OUT-DOORS.
FOR ME, THAT DOESN'T SOUND RIGHT...
THEN... WHAT **WOULD** SOUND RIGHT?
I DON'T KNOW...
WHAT I WANT TO SAY IS THAT...
... ALTHOUGH I'M HIS MANAGER ...
...I...
...DON'T UNDERSTAND REN AT ALL YET...
HE'S ...
...JUST TOO...
...MYSTERIOUS...

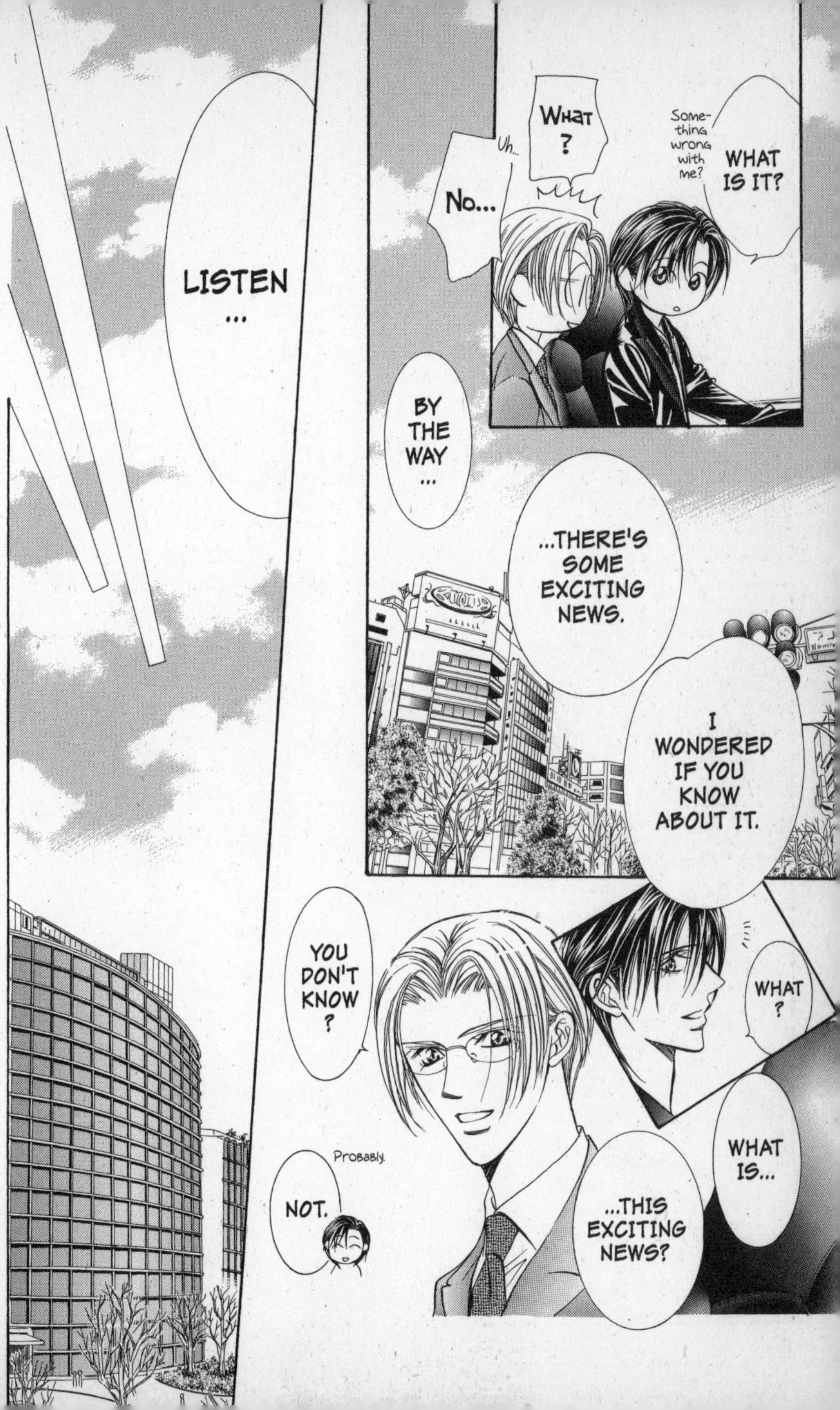
WHAT IS IT?
Something wrong with me?
WHAT ?
Uh...
No...
BY THE WAY ...
...THERE'S SOME EXCITING NEWS.
I WONDERED IF YOU KNOW ABOUT IT.
WHAT ?
WHAT IS...
...THIS EXCITING NEWS?
YOU DON'T KNOW ?
Probably.
NOT.
LISTEN ...

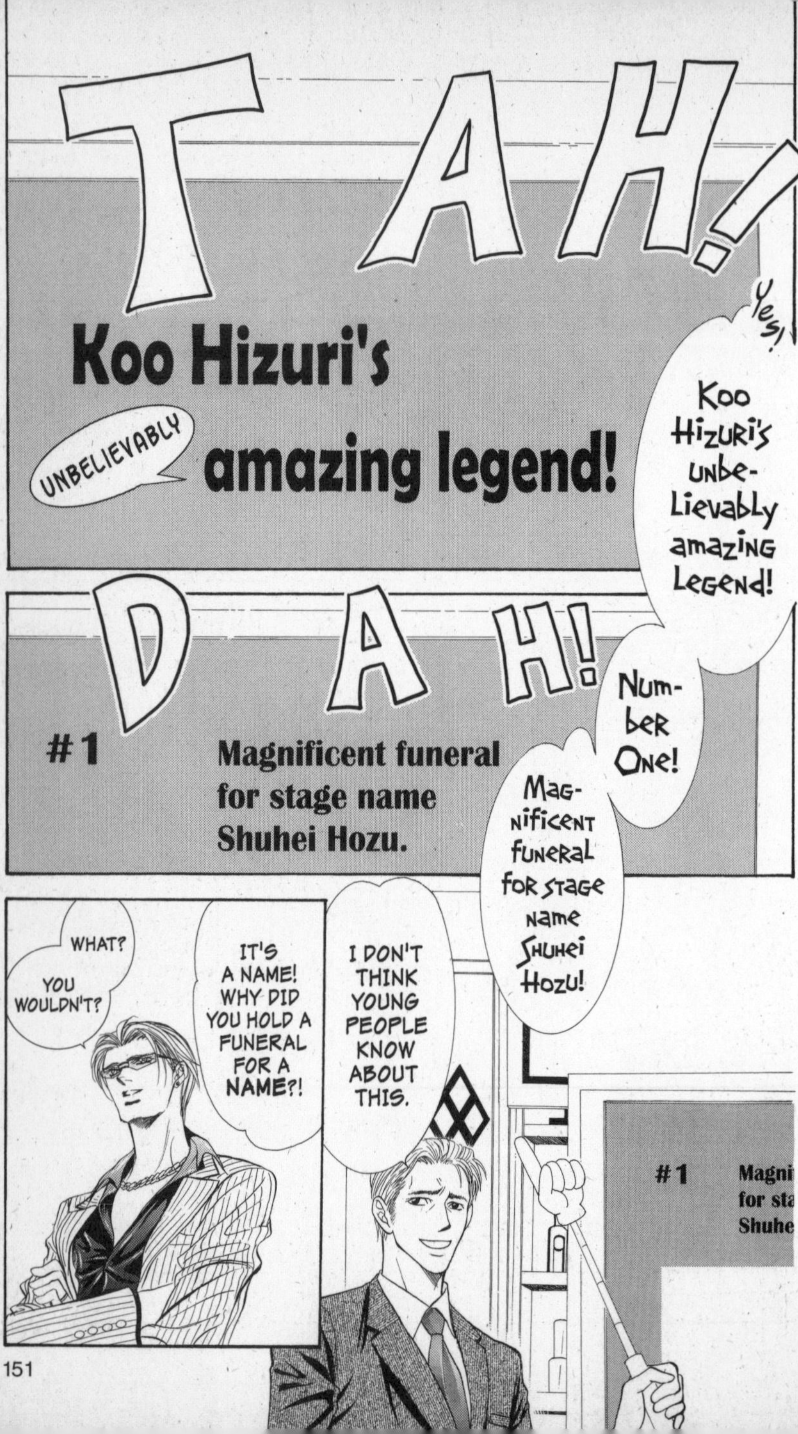
TAH!
Koo Hizuri's UNBELIEVABLY amazing legend!
Yes!
Koo Hizuri's unbelievably amazing legend!
DAH!
#1 Magnificent funeral for stage name Shuhei Hozu.
Number One!
Magnificent funeral for stage name Shuhei Hozu!
I DON'T THINK YOUNG PEOPLE KNOW ABOUT THIS.
IT'S A NAME! WHY DID YOU HOLD A FUNERAL FOR A NAME?!
WHAT?
YOU WOULDN'T?

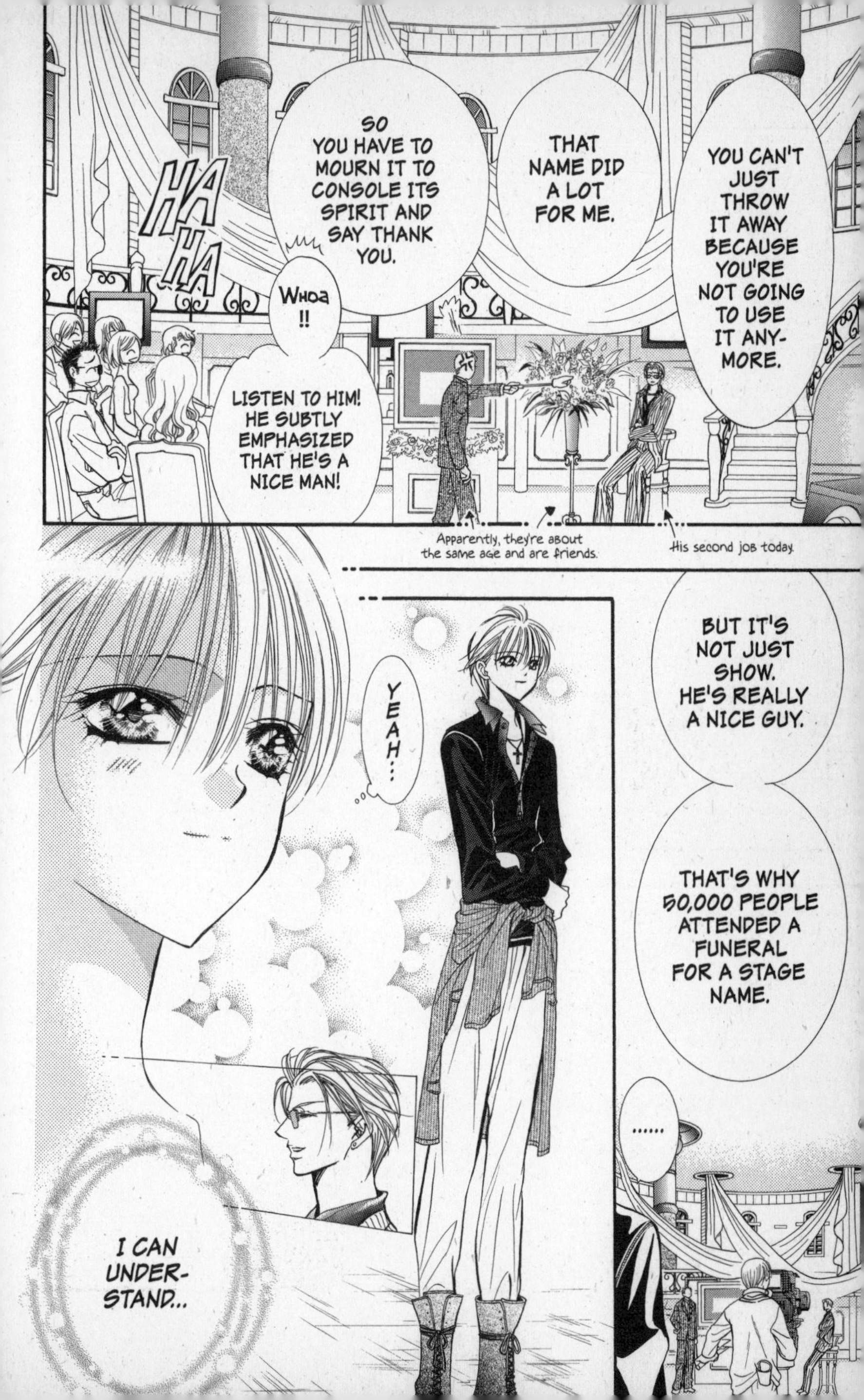
YOU CAN'T JUST THROW IT AWAY BECAUSE YOU'RE NOT GOING TO USE IT ANY-MORE.
THAT NAME DID A LOT FOR ME.
SO YOU HAVE TO MOURN IT TO CONSOLE ITS SPIRIT AND SAY THANK YOU.
HA HA
WHOA !!
LISTEN TO HIM! HE SUBTLY EMPHASIZED THAT HE'S A NICE MAN!
His second job today.
Apparently, they're about the same age and are friends.
BUT IT'S NOT JUST SHOW. HE'S REALLY A NICE GUY.
THAT'S WHY 50,000 PEOPLE ATTENDED A FUNERAL FOR A STAGE NAME.
......
YEAH...
I CAN UNDER-STAND...

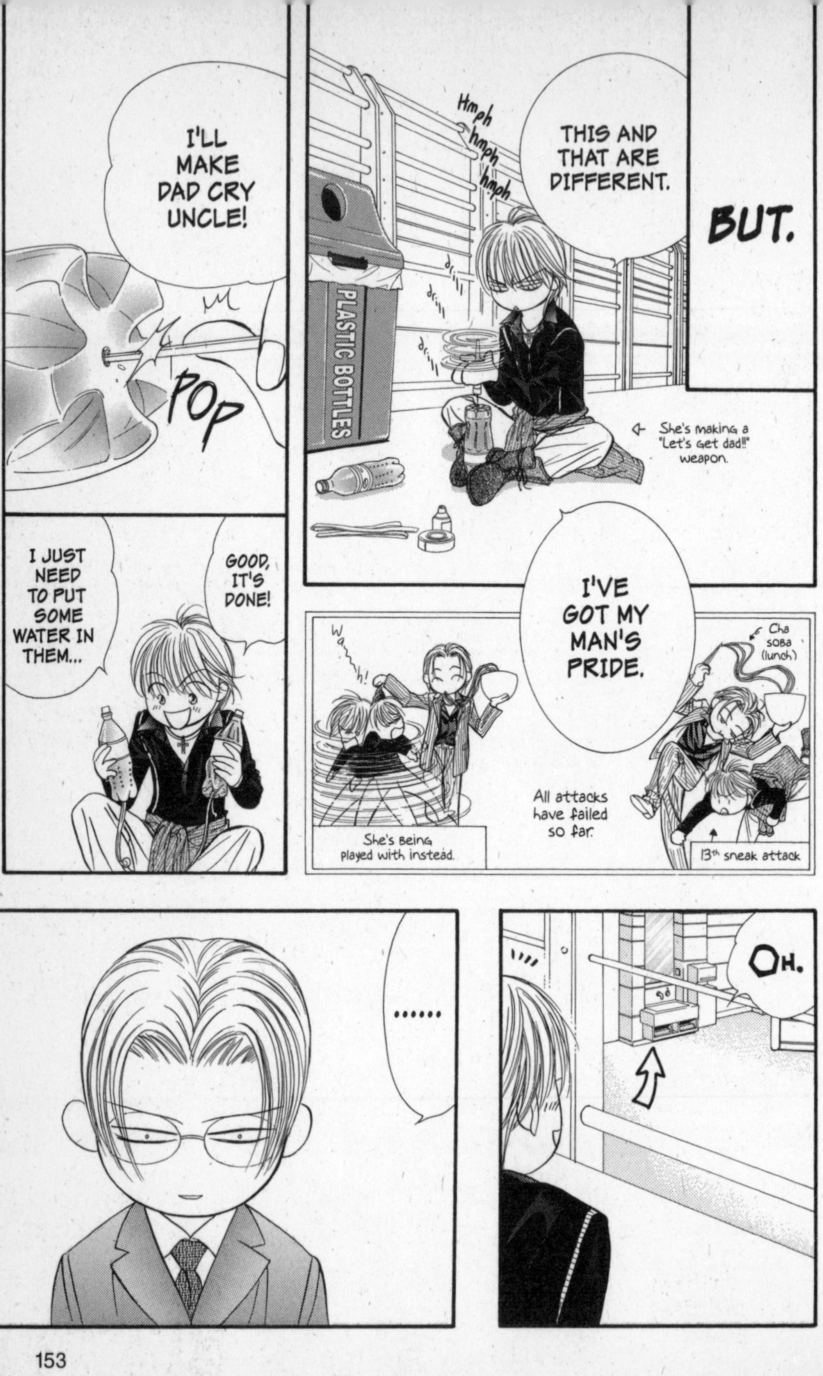
BUT.
THIS AND THAT ARE DIFFERENT.
Hmph hmph hmph
drill drill drill
PLASTIC BOTTLES
She's making a "Let's Get dad!!" weapon.
I'LL MAKE DAD CRY UNCLE!
POP
I'VE GOT MY MAN'S PRIDE.
Cha soba (lunch)
13th sneak attack
All attacks have failed so far.
Waaah!
She's being played with instead.
GOOD, IT'S DONE!
I JUST NEED TO PUT SOME WATER IN THEM...
OH.
......

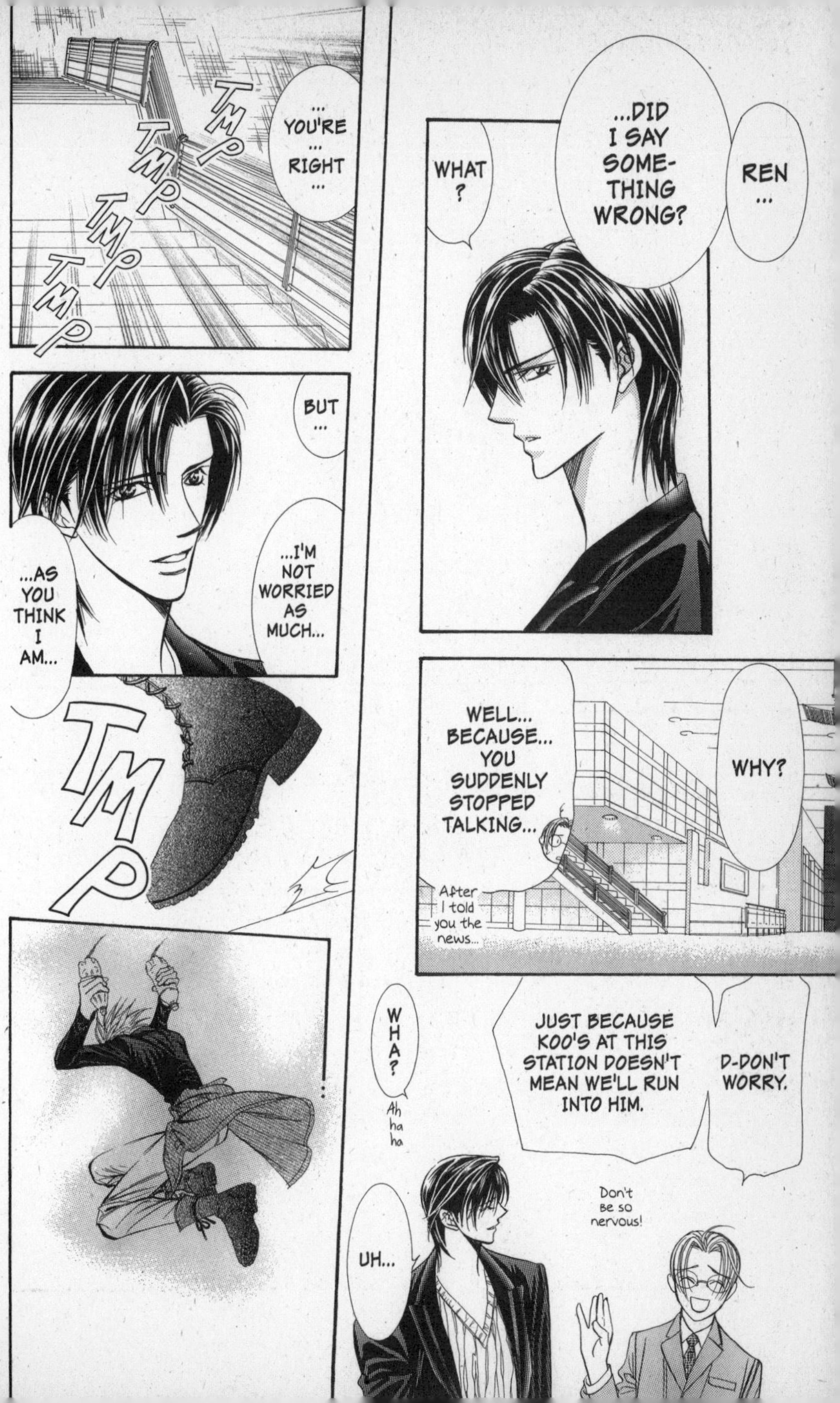
REN ...
...DID I SAY SOME-THING WRONG?
WHAT ?
WHY?
WELL... BECAUSE... YOU SUDDENLY STOPPED TALKING...
After I told you the news...
D-DON'T WORRY.
JUST BECAUSE KOO'S AT THIS STATION DOESN'T MEAN WE'LL RUN INTO HIM.
WHA ?
Ah ha ha
Don't be so nervous!
UH...
... YOU'RE ... RIGHT ...
TMP TMP TMP TMP
BUT ...
...I'M NOT WORRIED AS MUCH...
...AS YOU THINK I AM...
TMP

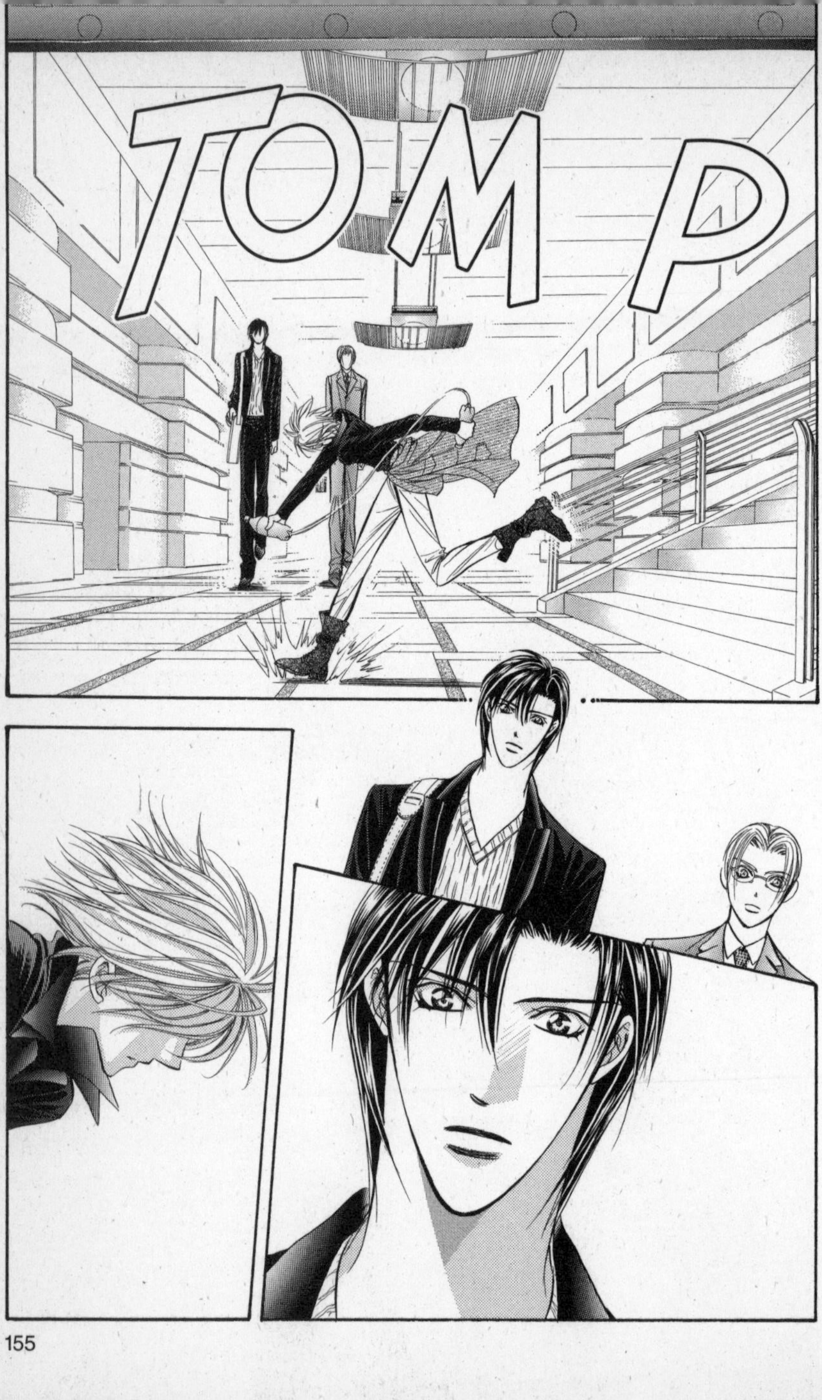
TOMP

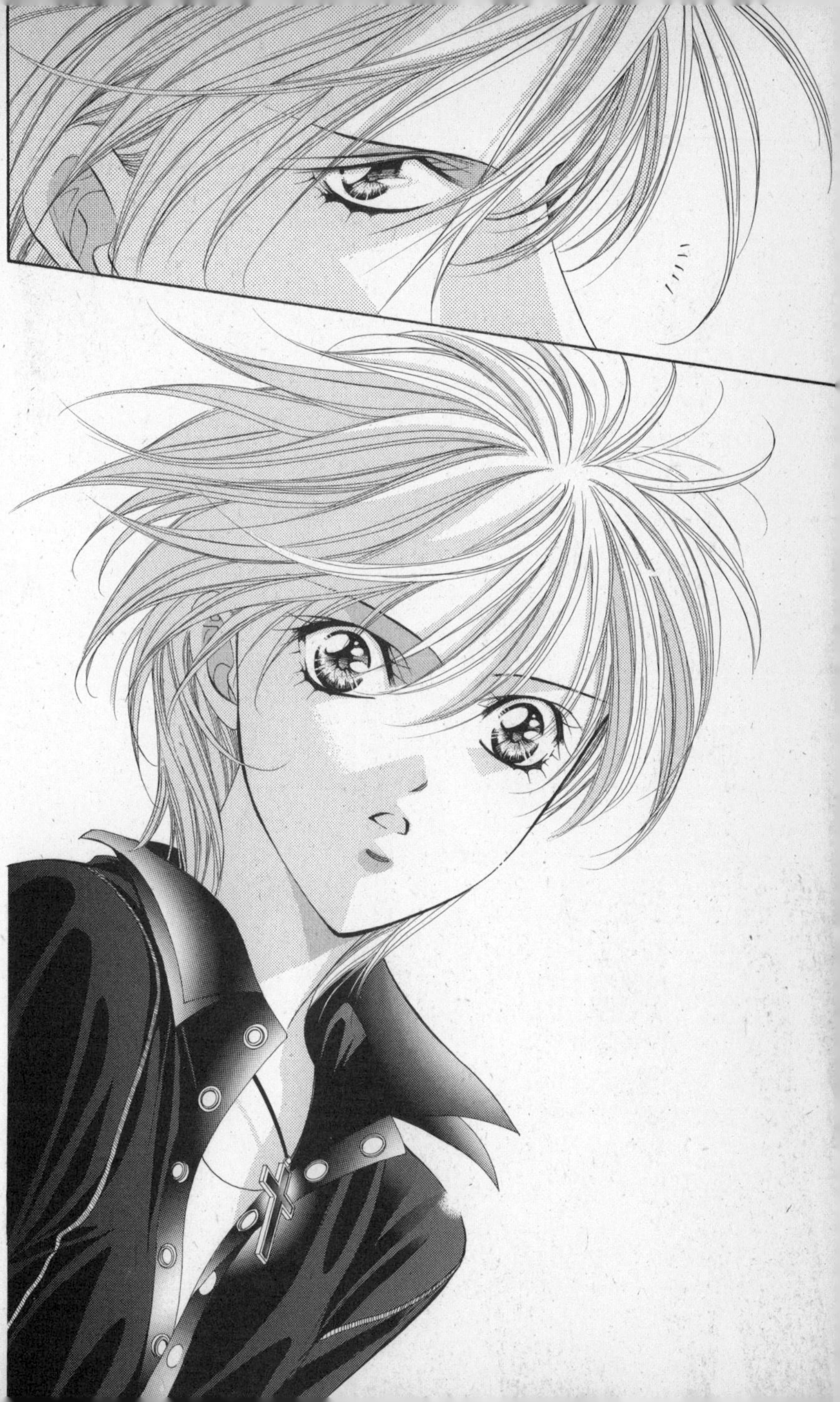

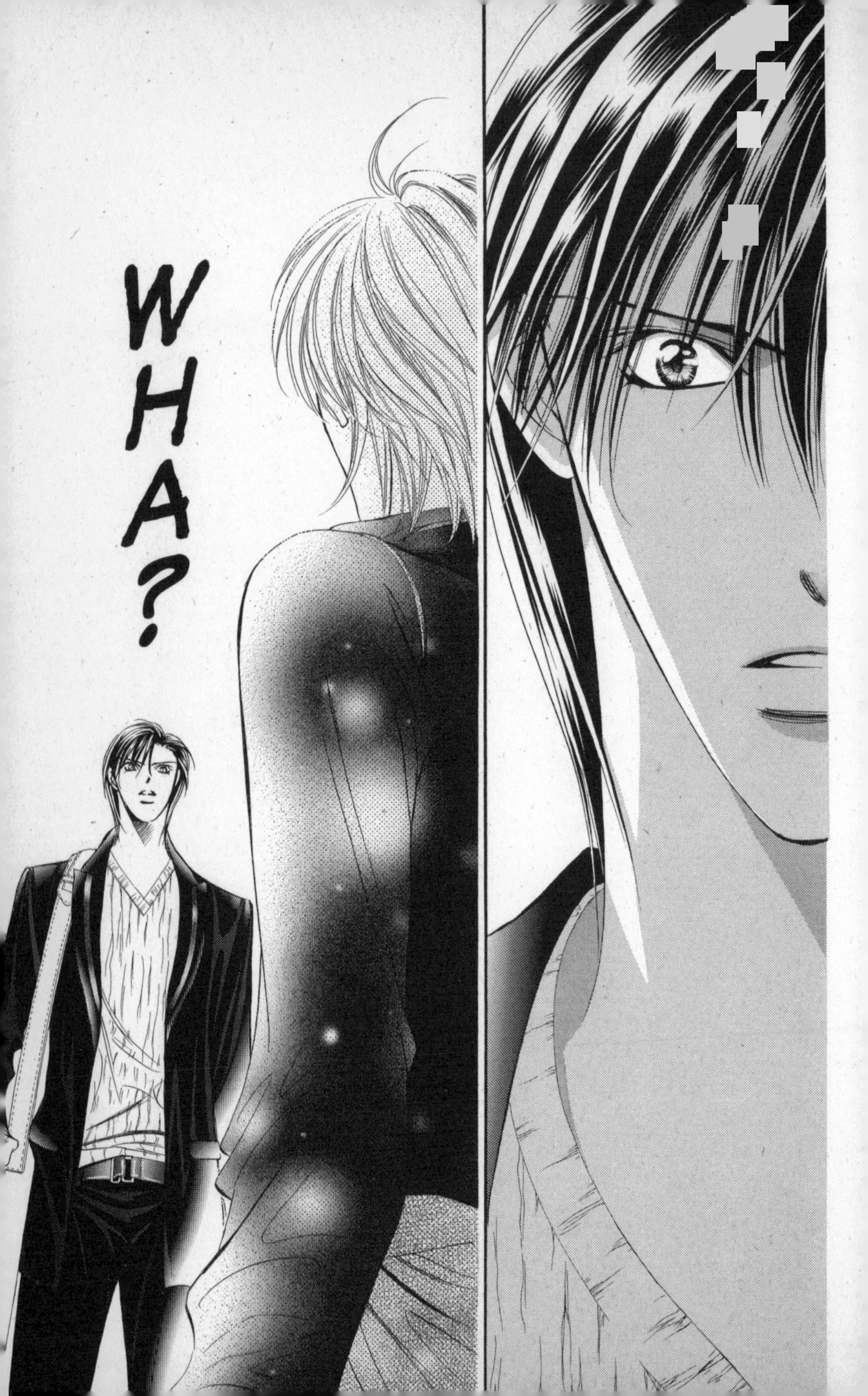
WHA?

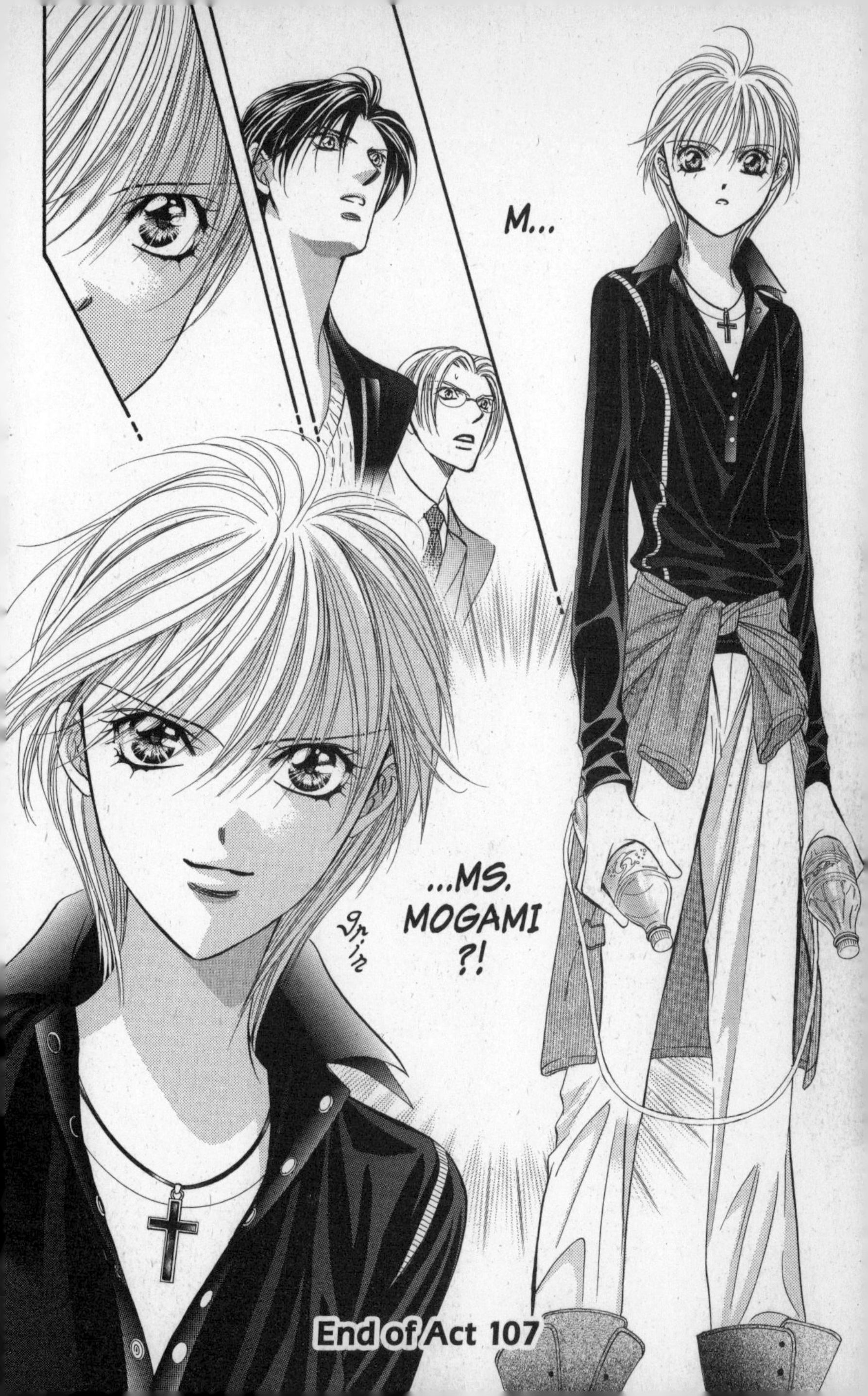
M...
...MS. MOGAMI ?!
grin
End of Act 107

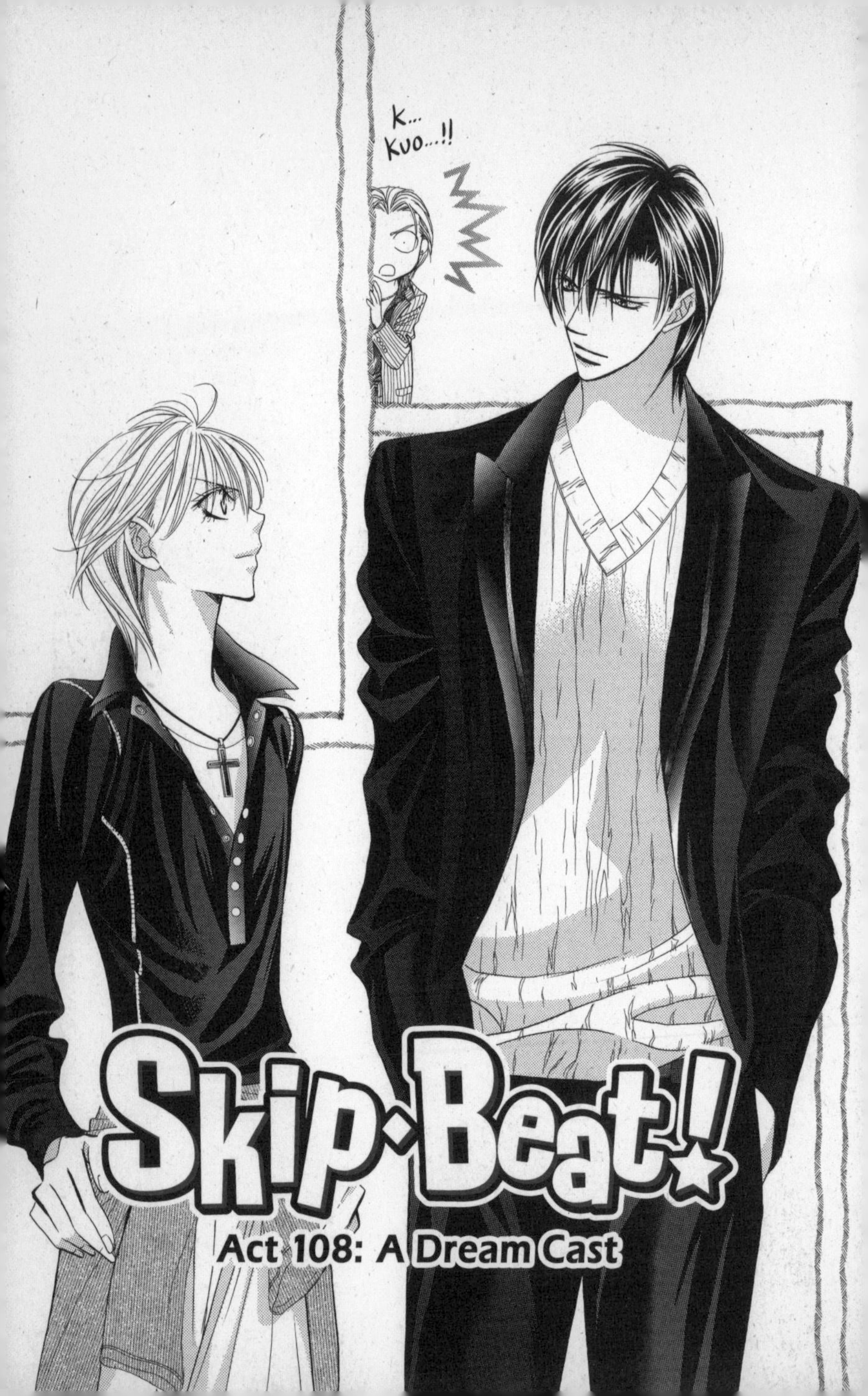
K...
KUO...!!
Skip·Beat!
Act 108: A Dream Cast

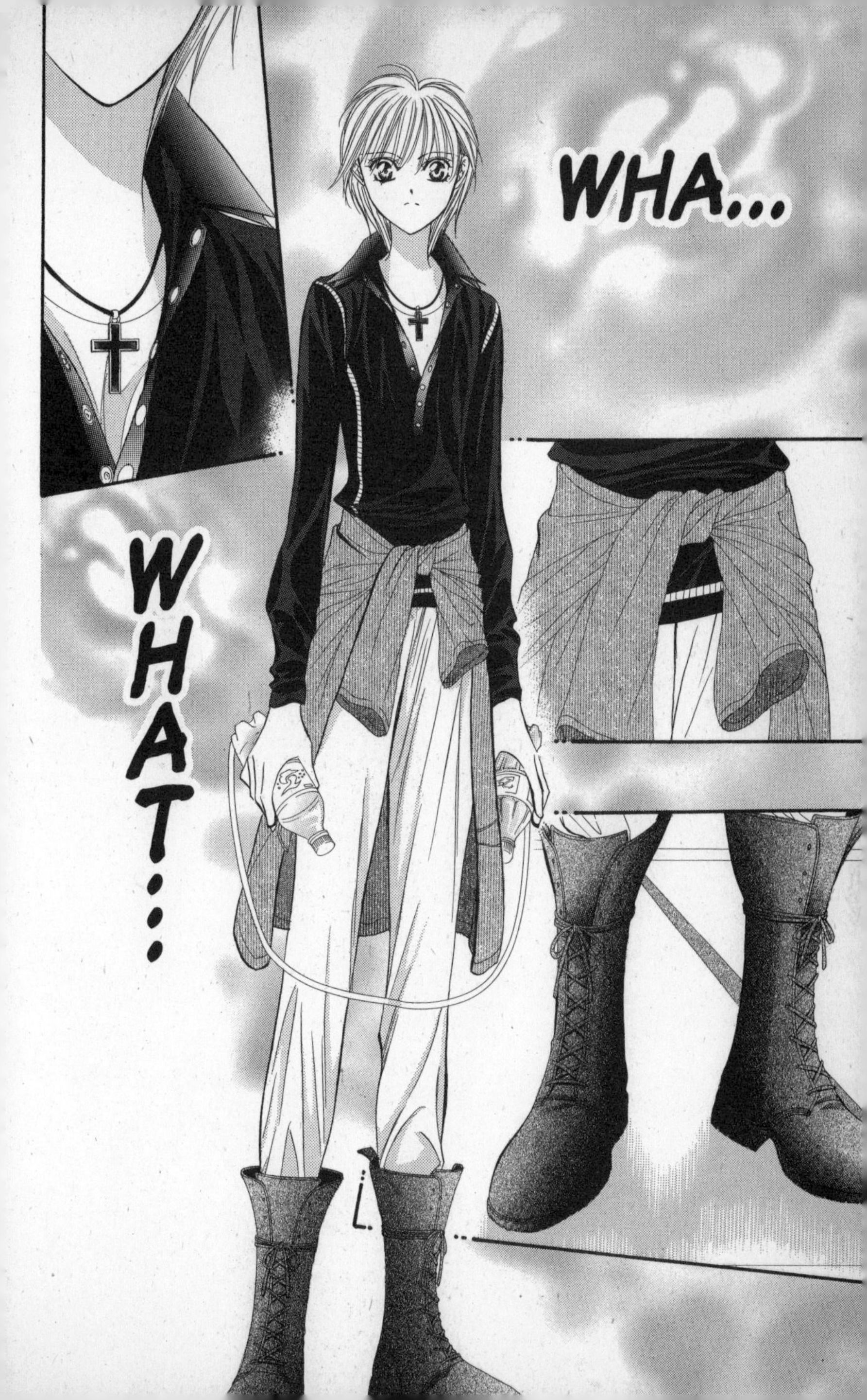
WHA...
WHAT...
L...

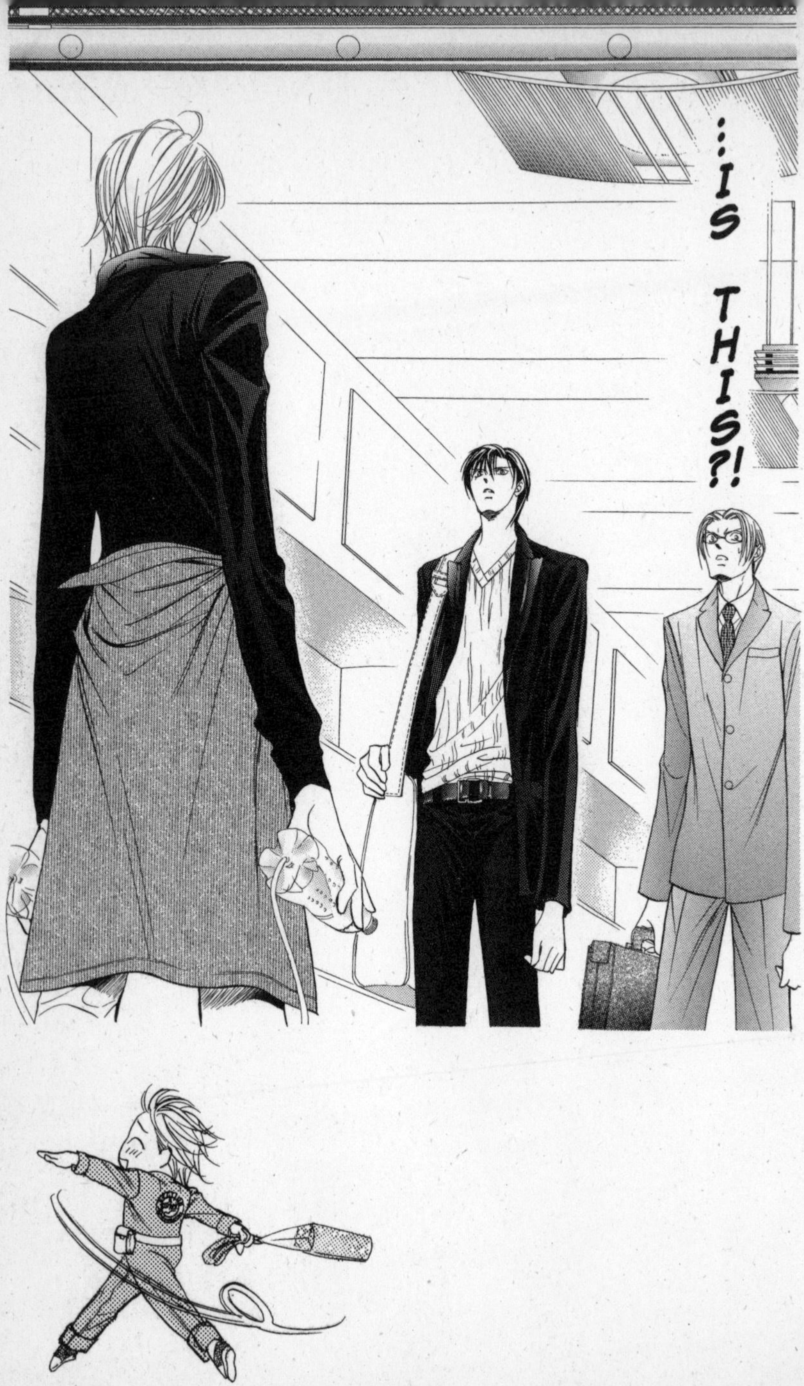
...IS THIS?!

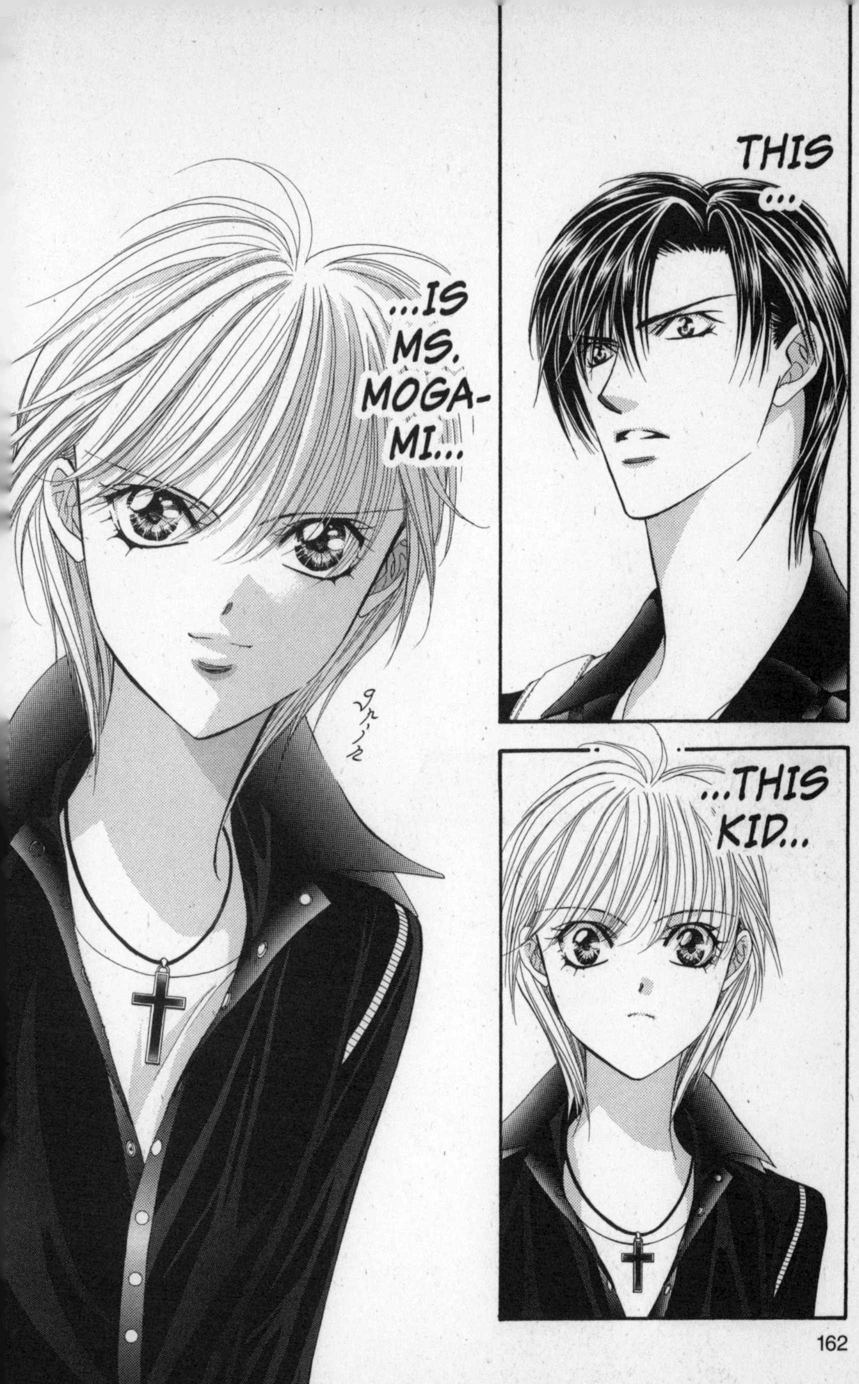
THIS...
...THIS KID...
...IS MS. MOGA-MI...

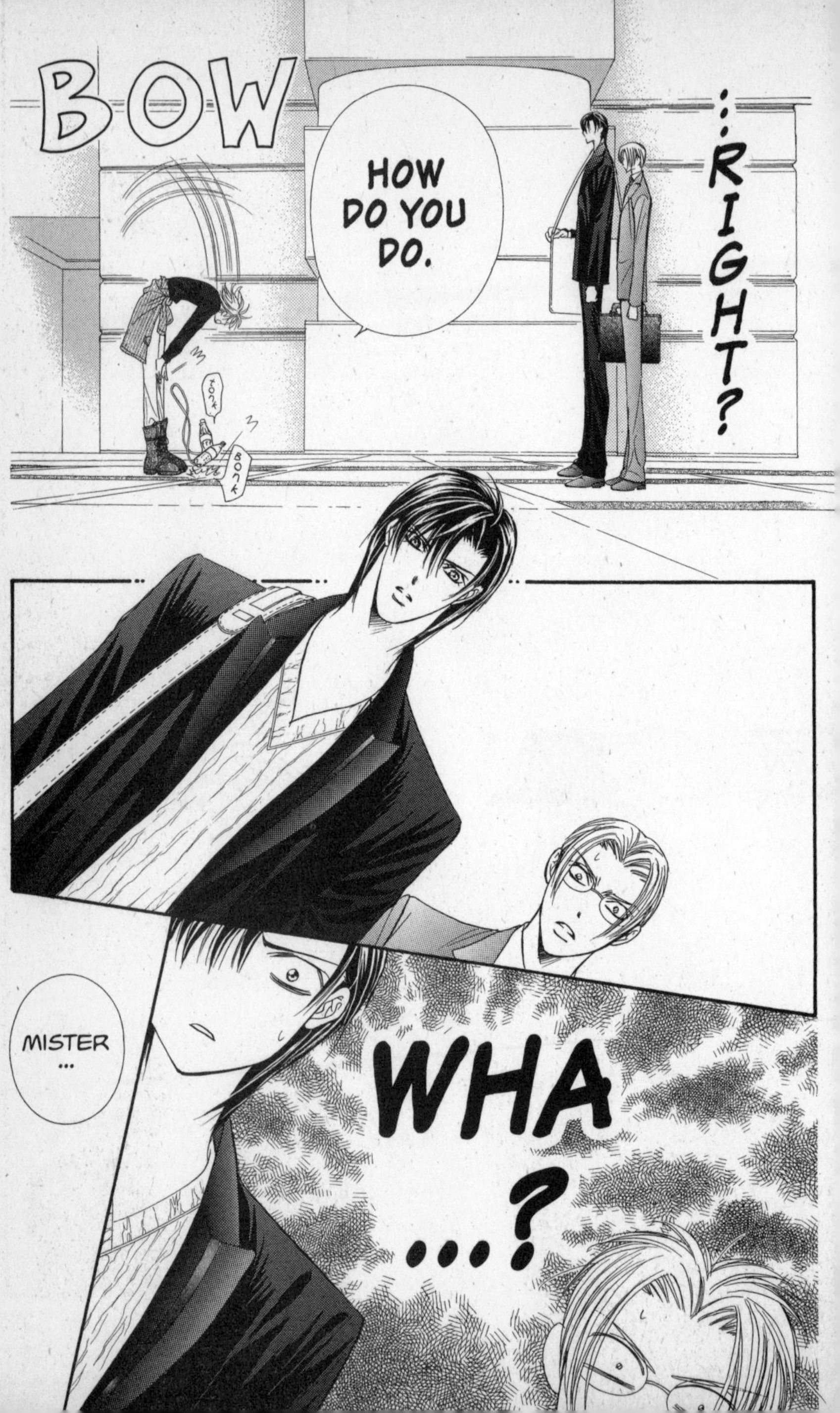
...RIGHT?
HOW DO YOU DO.
BOW
BONK
MISTER ...
WHA ...?

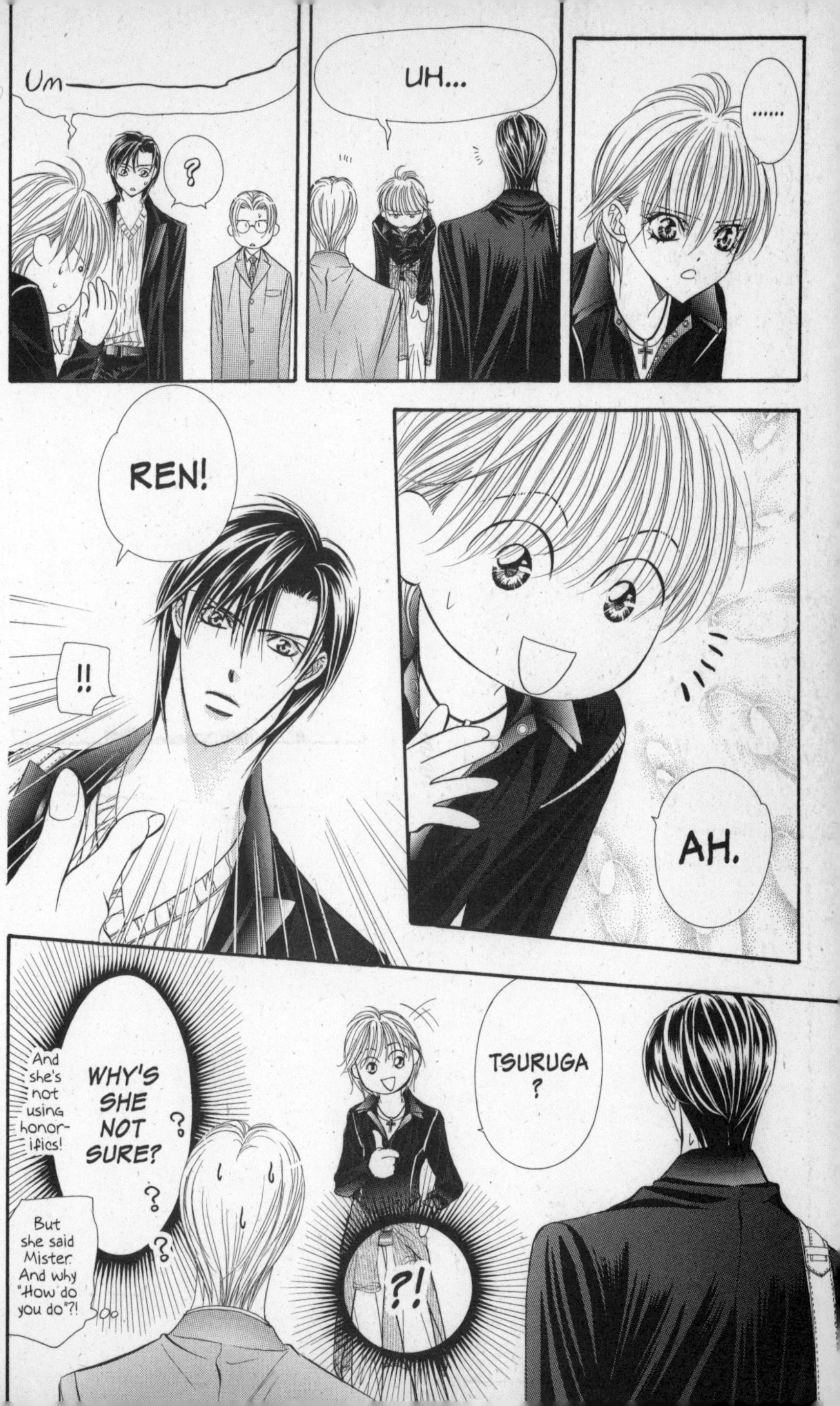
......
UH...
Um—
?
AH.
REN!
!!
TSURUGA ?
WHY'S SHE NOT SURE?
And she's not using honorifics!
But she said Mister. And why "How do you do"?!
?!

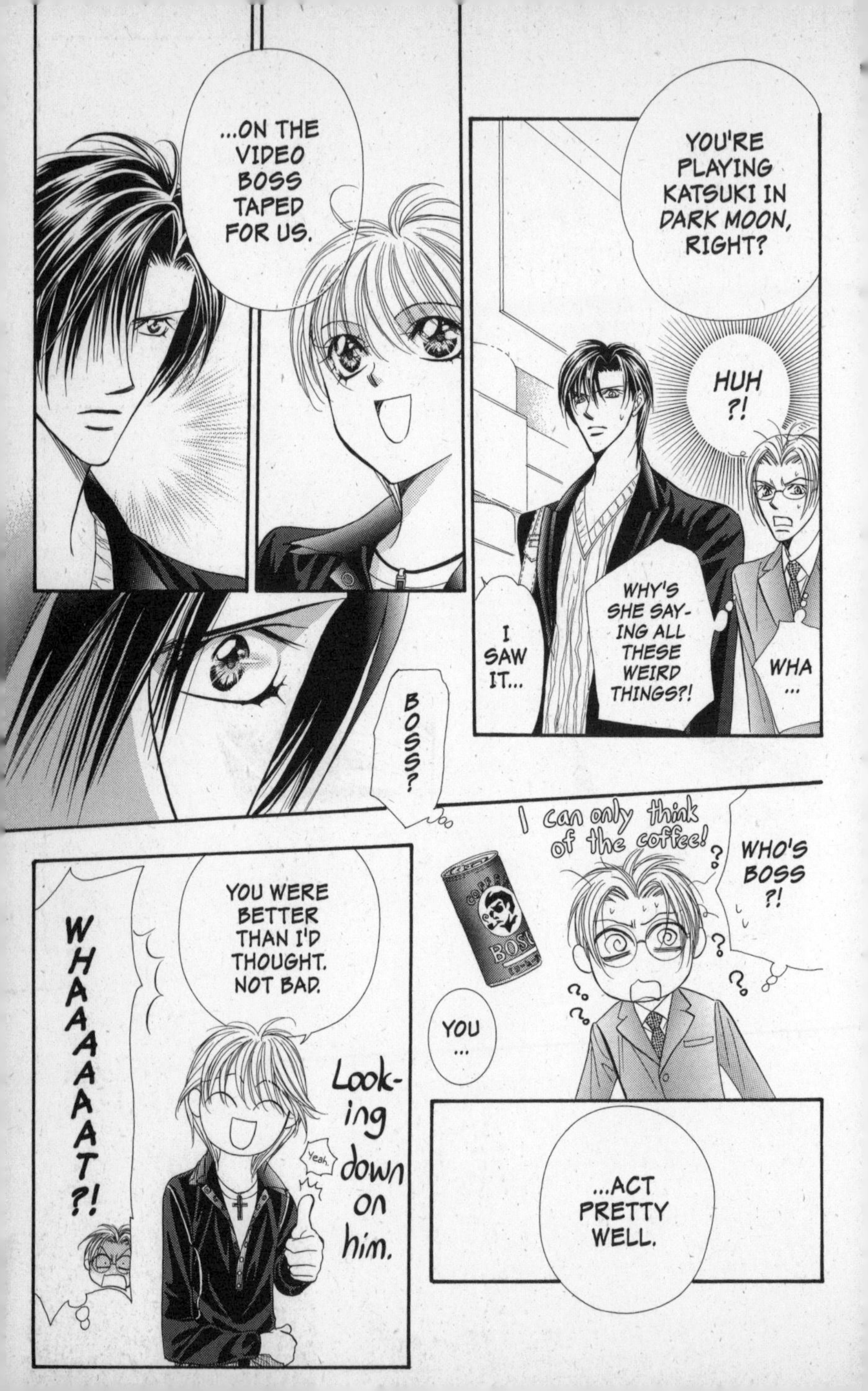
YOU'RE PLAYING KATSUKI IN DARK MOON, RIGHT?
HUH ?!
WHY'S SHE SAYING ALL THESE WEIRD THINGS?!
WHA ...
I SAW IT...
...ON THE VIDEO BOSS TAPED FOR US.
BOSS?
WHO'S BOSS ?!
I can only think of the coffee!
YOU ...
...ACT PRETTY WELL.
YOU WERE BETTER THAN I'D THOUGHT. NOT BAD.
Looking down on him.
Yeah.
WHAAAAAAAT?!

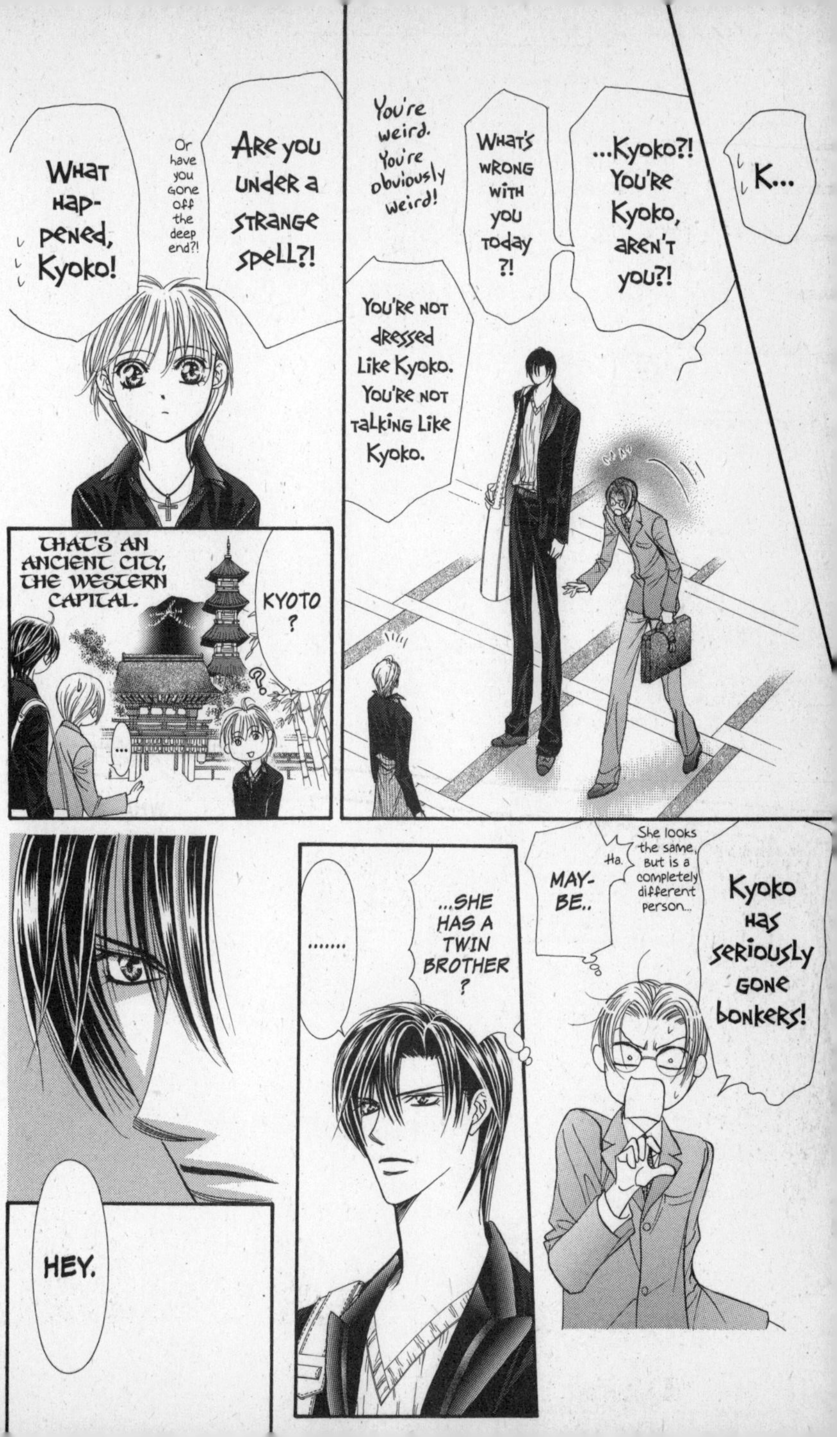
K...
...Kyoko?! You're Kyoko, aren't you?!
What's wrong with you today?!
You're weird. You're obviously weird!
You're not dressed like Kyoko. You're not talking like Kyoko.
Are you under a strange spell?!
Or have you gone off the deep end?!
What happened, Kyoko!
KYOTO?
THAT'S AN ANCIENT CITY, THE WESTERN CAPITAL.
...
Kyoko has seriously gone bonkers!
She looks the same, but is a completely different person...
Ha.
MAYBE..
...SHE HAS A TWIN BROTHER?
....
HEY.

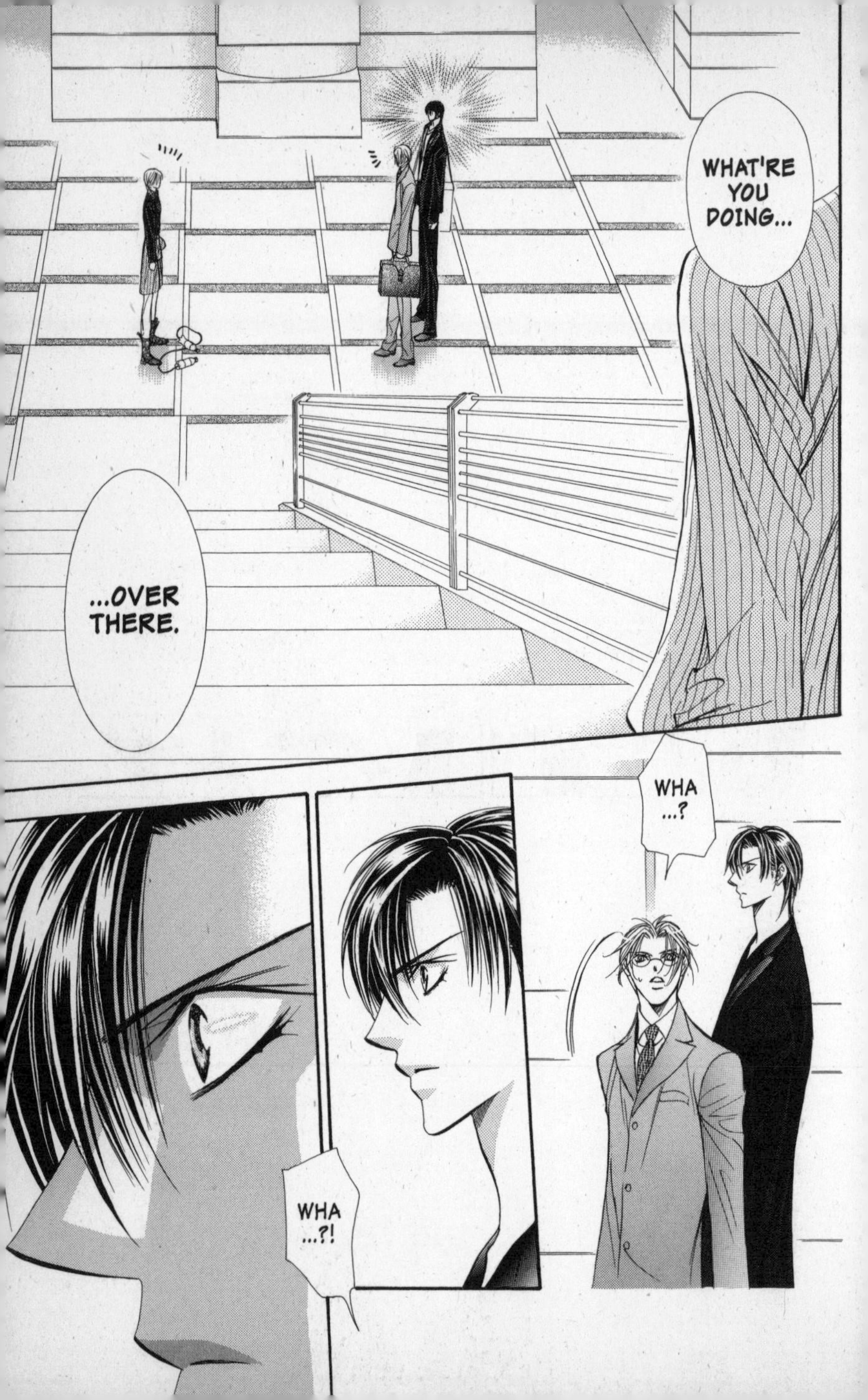
WHAT'RE YOU DOING...
...OVER THERE.
WHA ...?
WHA ...?!

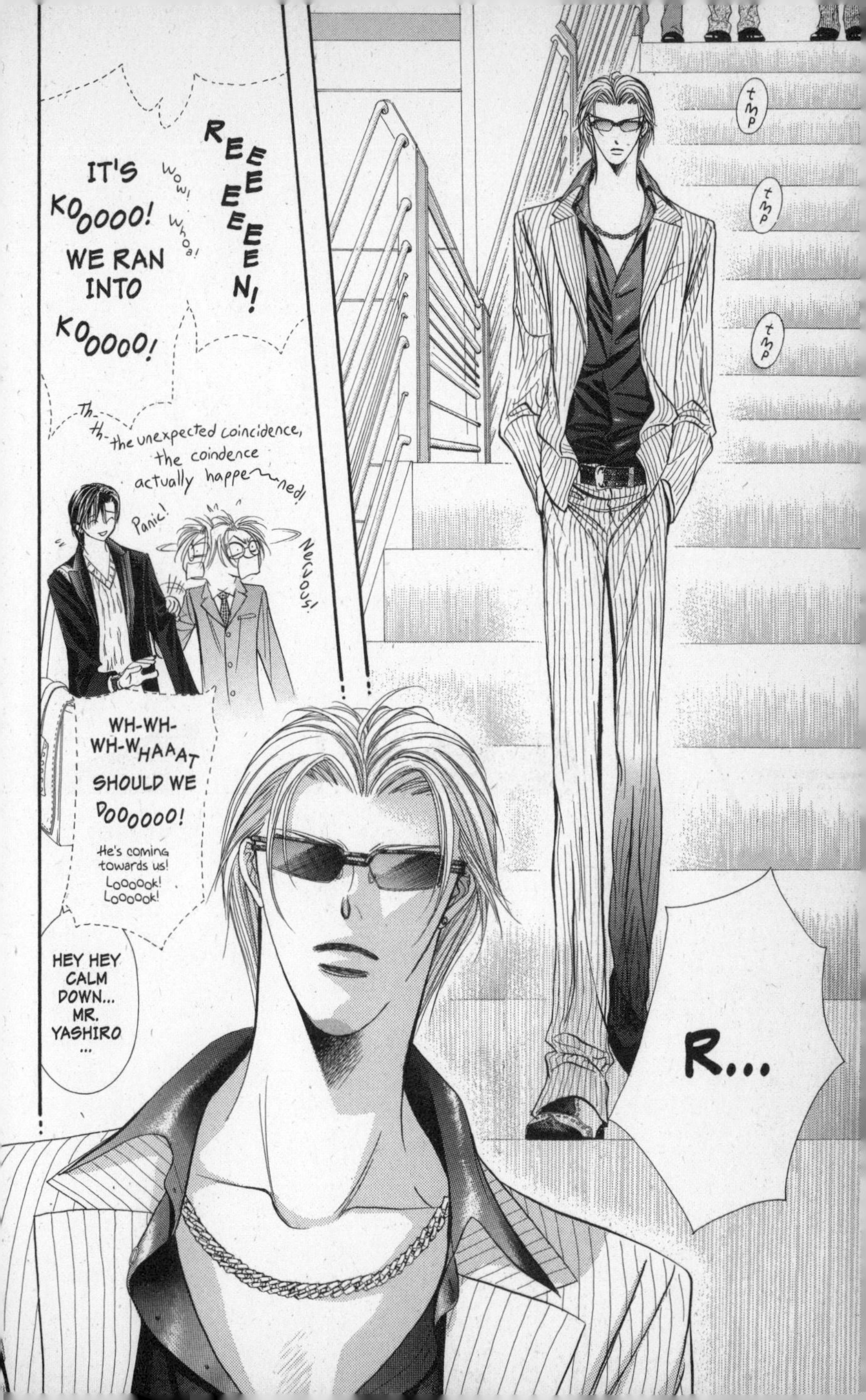
tmp
tmp
tmp
REEEEEEEN!
IT'S KOOOOO! WE RAN INTO KOOOOO!
Wow!
Whoa!
Th- th- the unexpected coincidence, the coindence actually happe~~ned!
Panic!
Nervous!
WH-WH-WH-WHAAAT SHOULD WE DOOOOOO!
He's coming towards us! Loooook! Loooook!
HEY HEY CALM DOWN... MR. YASHIRO ...
R...

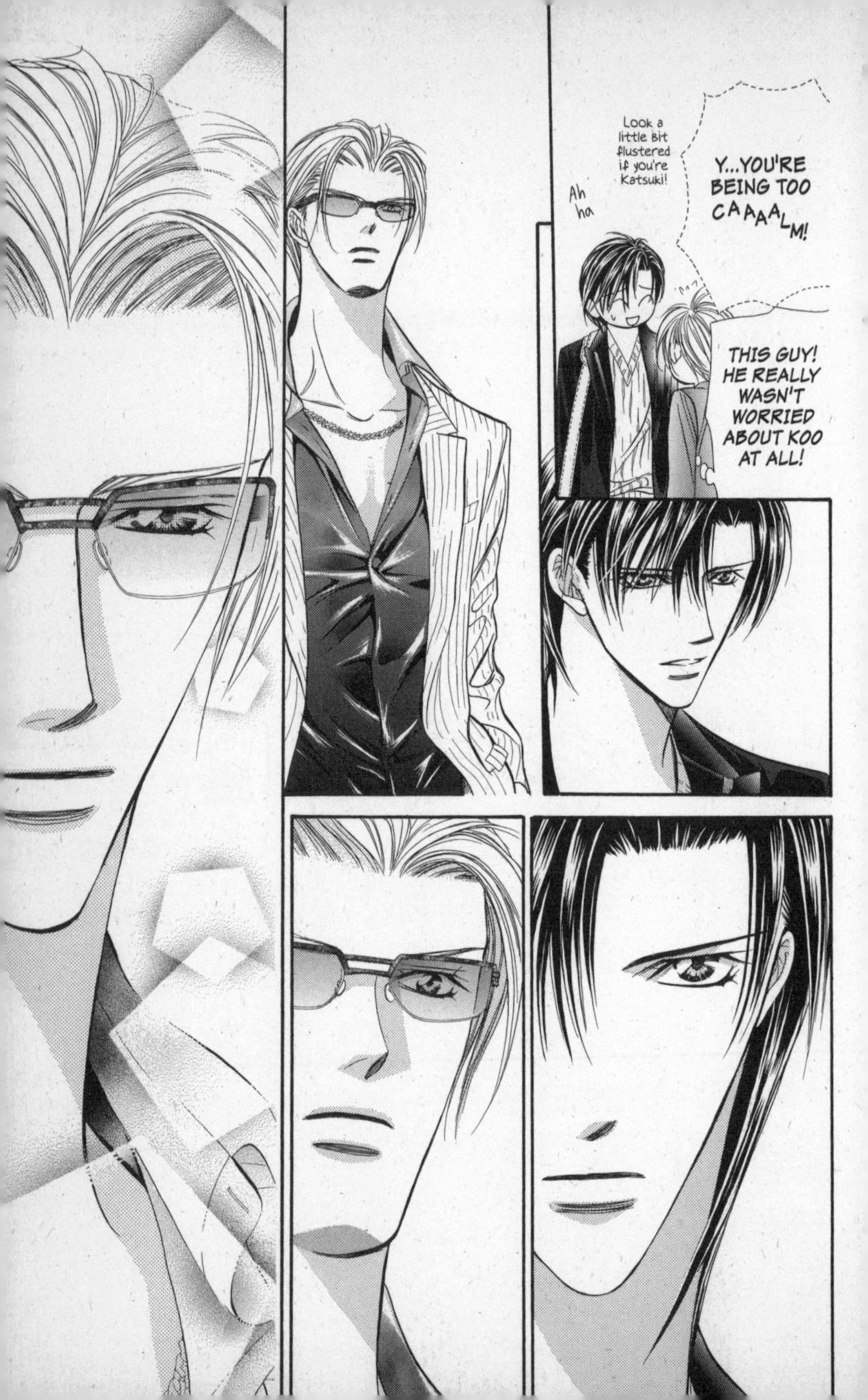
Y...YOU'RE BEING TOO CAAAALM!
Look a little bit flustered if you're Katsuki!
Ah ha
THIS GUY! HE REALLY WASN'T WORRIED ABOUT KOO AT ALL!

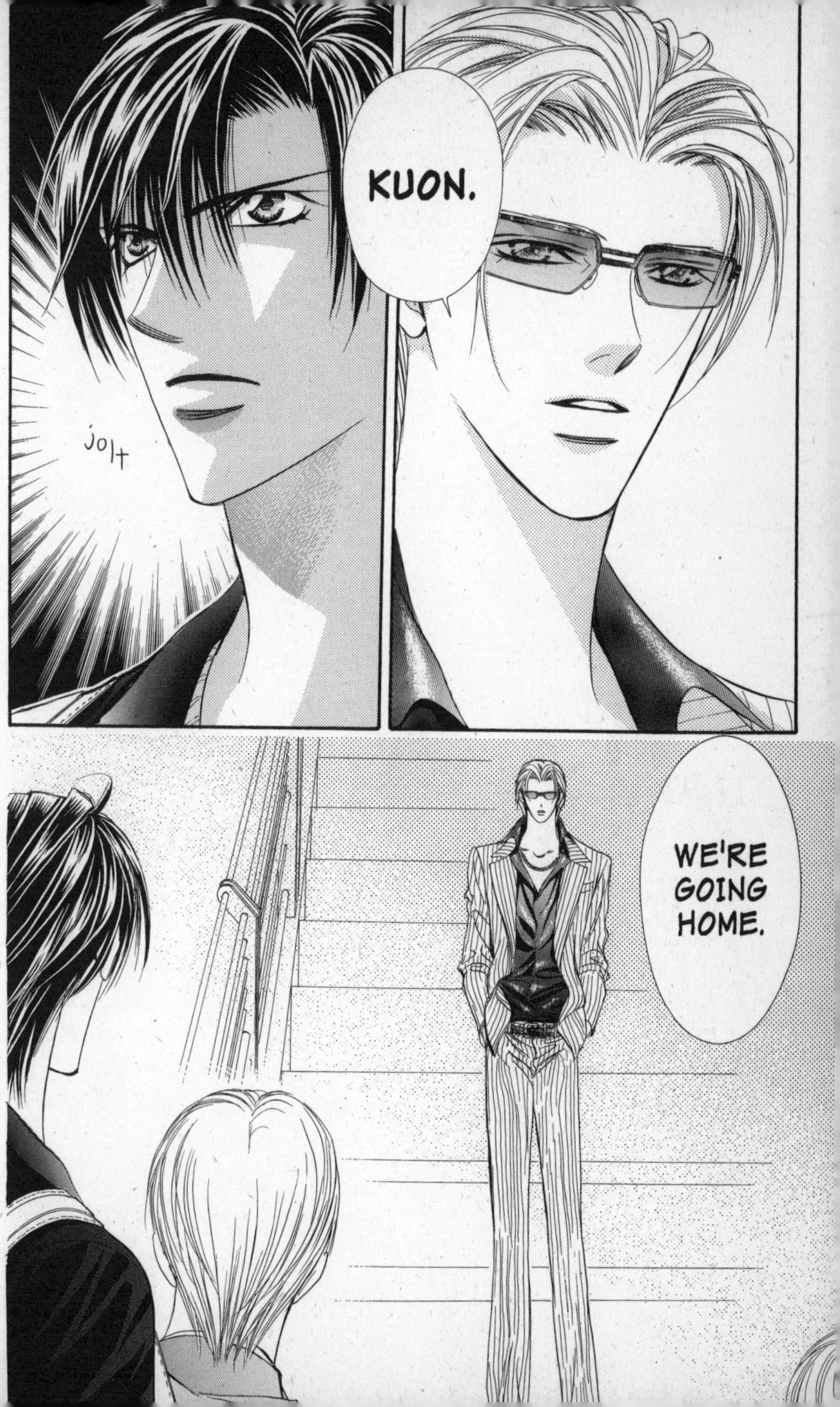
KUON.
jolt
WE'RE GOING HOME.

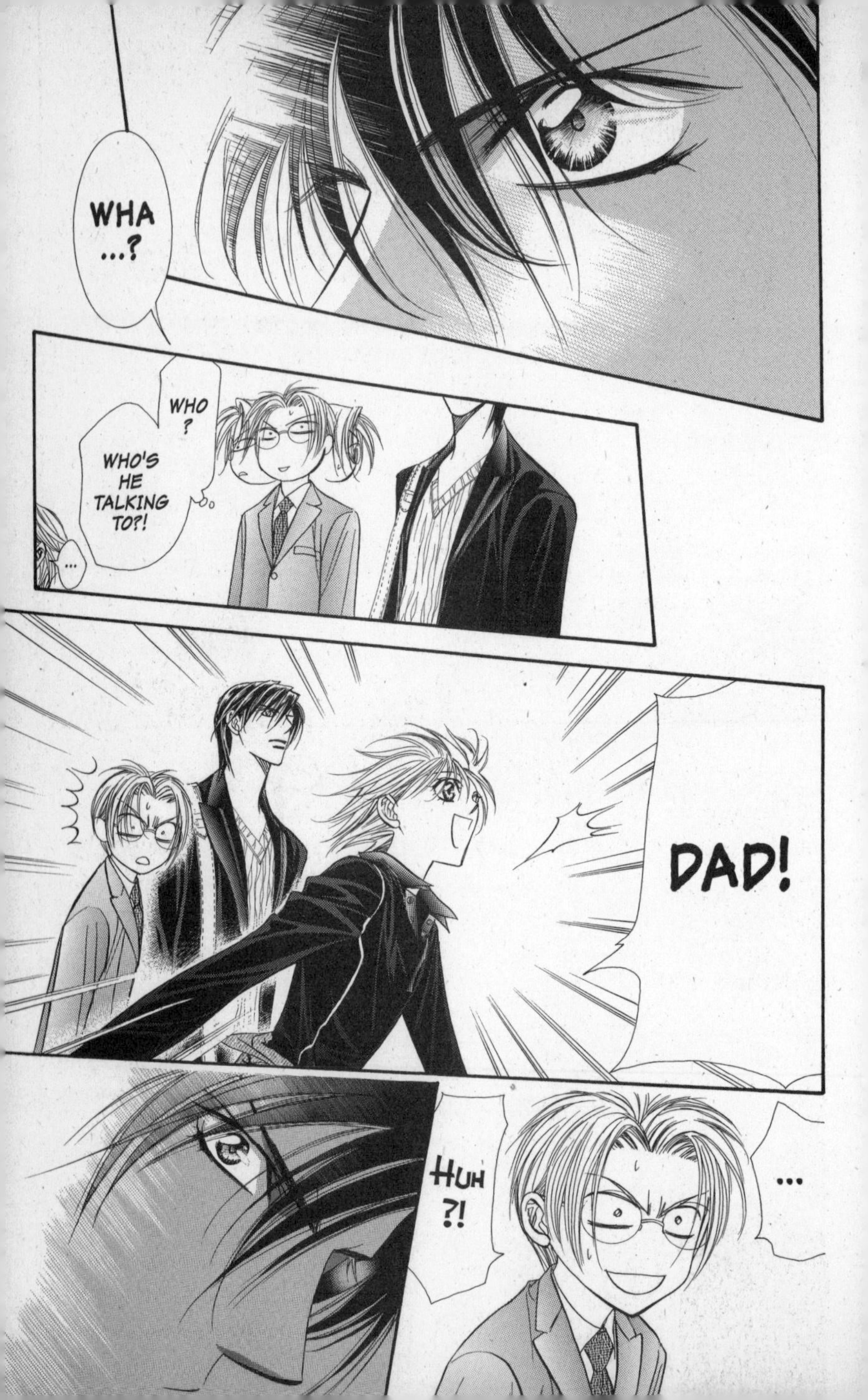
WHA ...?
WHO ?
WHO'S HE TALKING TO?!
...
DAD!
...
HUH ?!

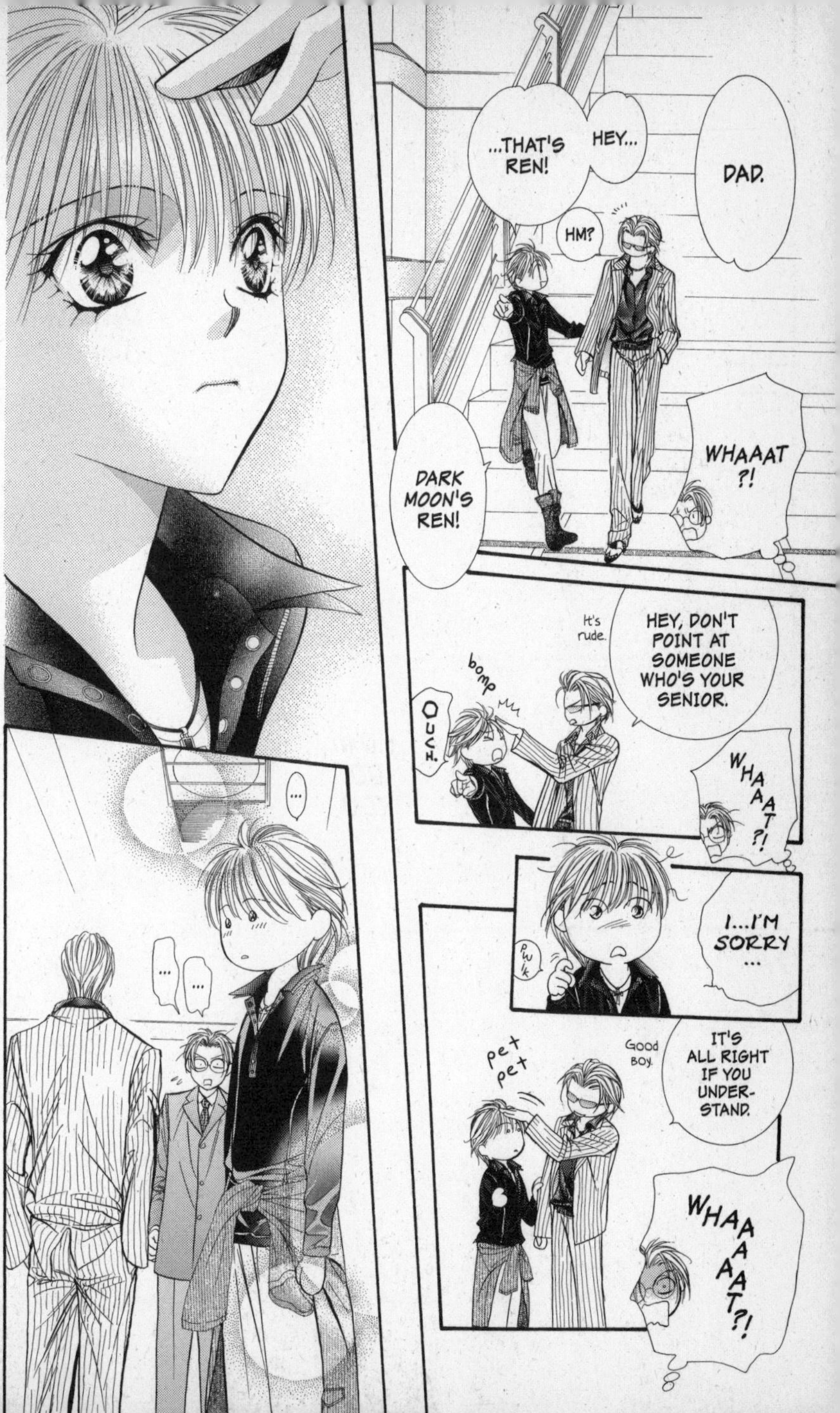
DAD.
HEY...
...THAT'S REN!
HM?
WHAAAT ?!
DARK MOON'S REN!
HEY, DON'T POINT AT SOMEONE WHO'S YOUR SENIOR.
It's rude.
bomp
OUCH.
WHAAAT ?!
I...I'M SORRY ...
pwik
IT'S ALL RIGHT IF YOU UNDER-STAND.
Good boy.
pet pet
WHAAAAAT?!
...
...
...

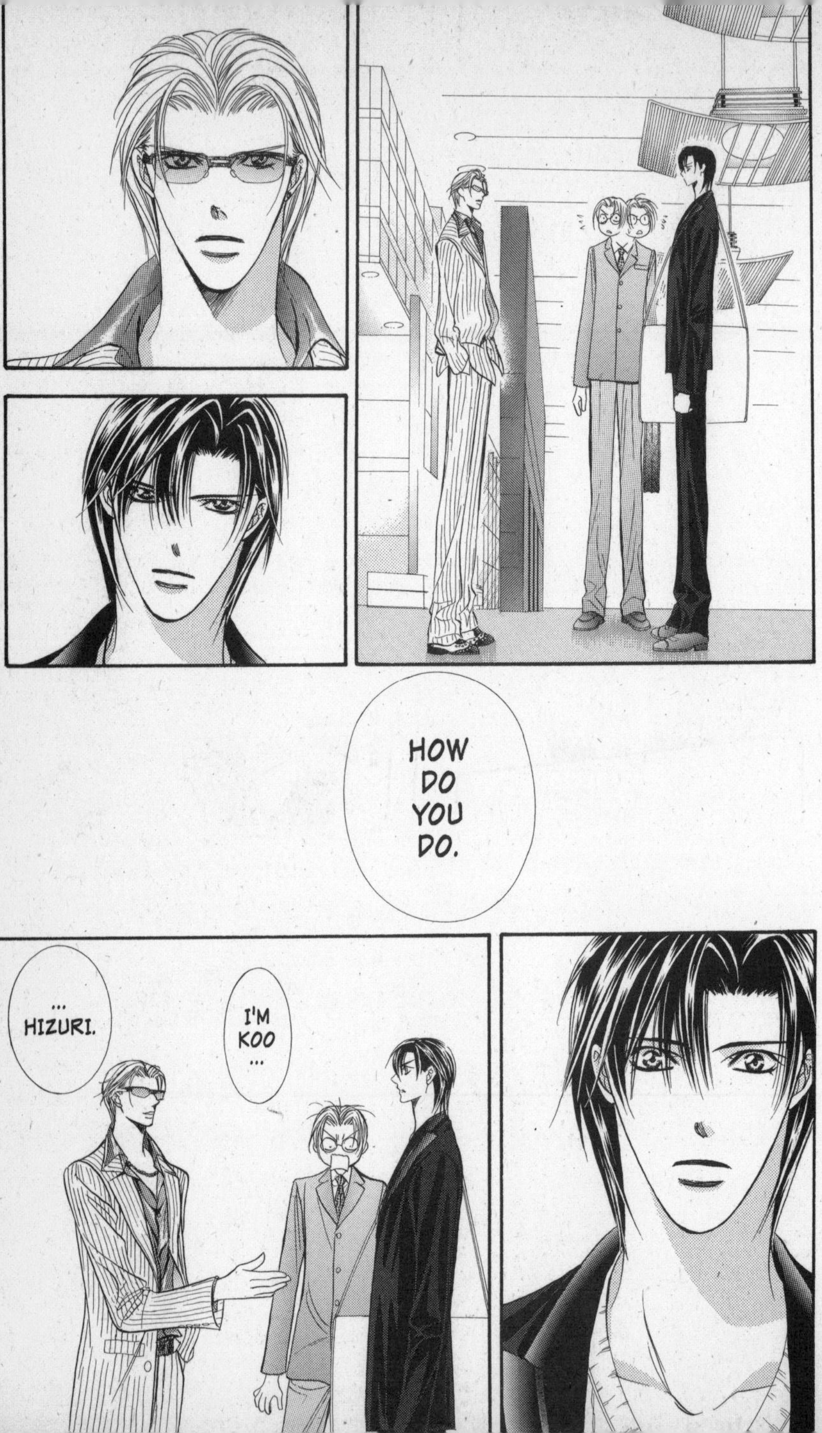
HOW DO YOU DO.
I'M KOO ...
... HIZURI.

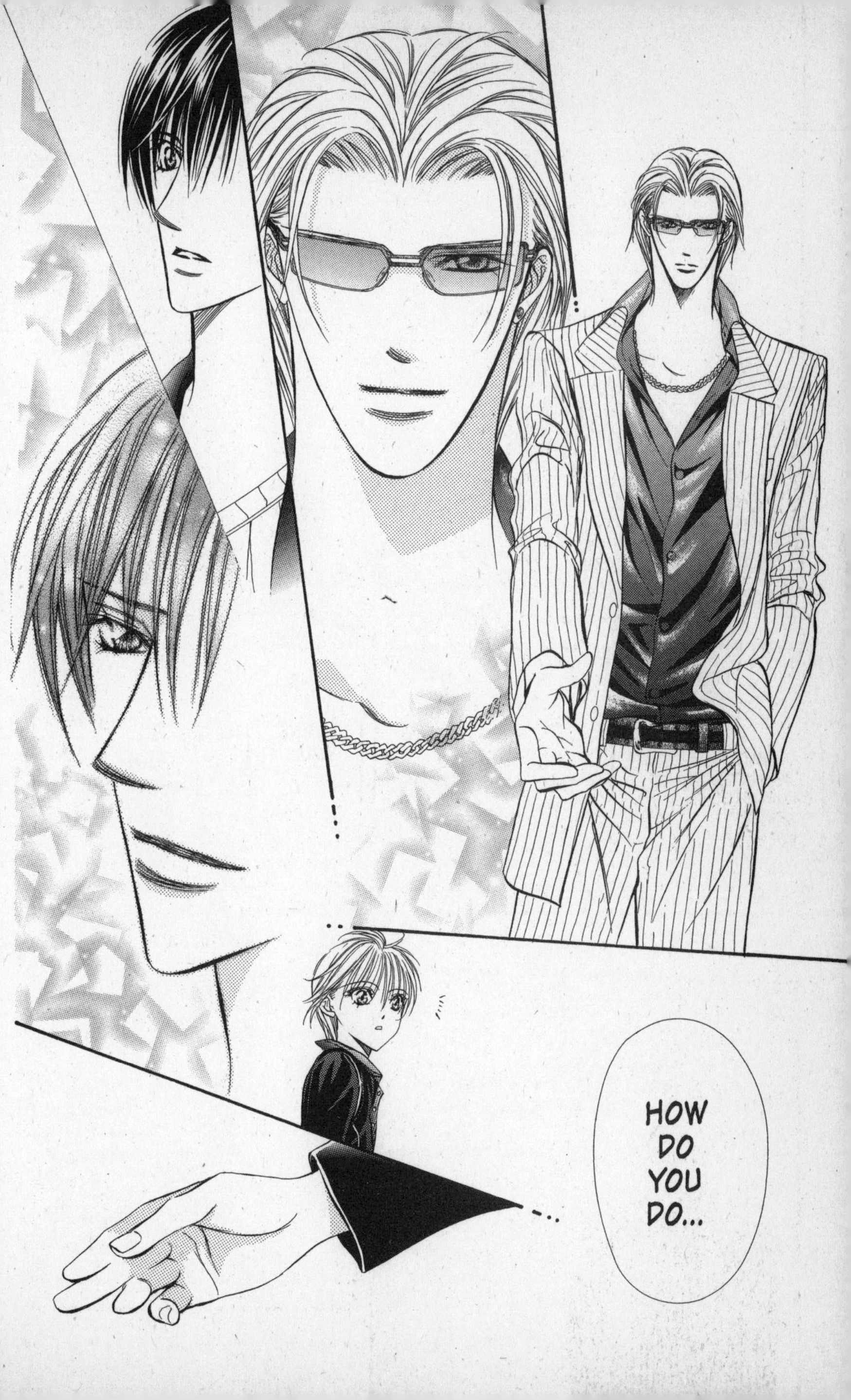
HOW DO YOU DO...

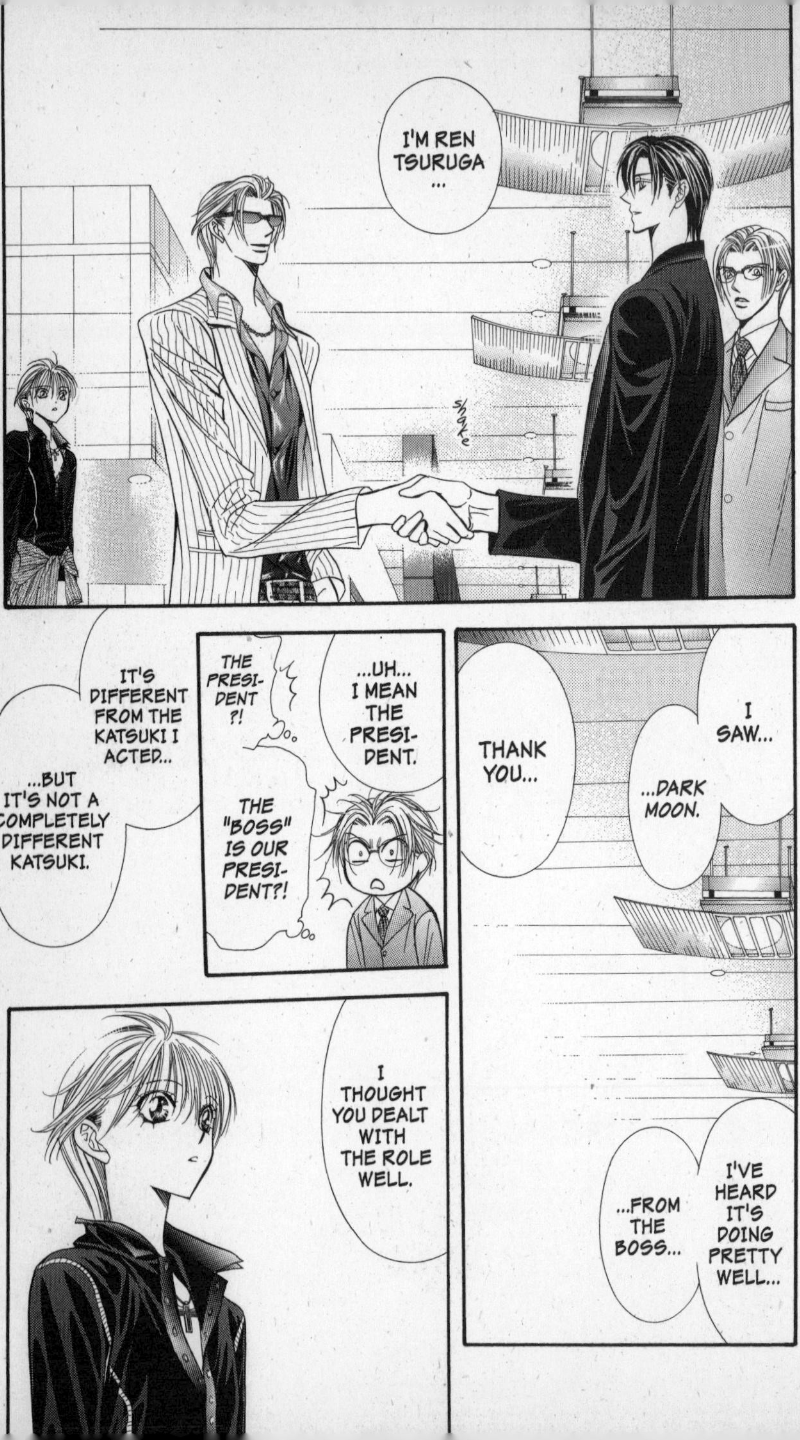
I'M REN TSURUGA ...
shake
I SAW...
...DARK MOON.
THANK YOU...
I'VE HEARD IT'S DOING PRETTY WELL...
...FROM THE BOSS...
...UH... I MEAN THE PRESIDENT.
THE PRESIDENT?!
THE "BOSS" IS OUR PRESIDENT?!
IT'S DIFFERENT FROM THE KATSUKI I ACTED...
...BUT IT'S NOT A COMPLETELY DIFFERENT KATSUKI.
I THOUGHT YOU DEALT WITH THE ROLE WELL.

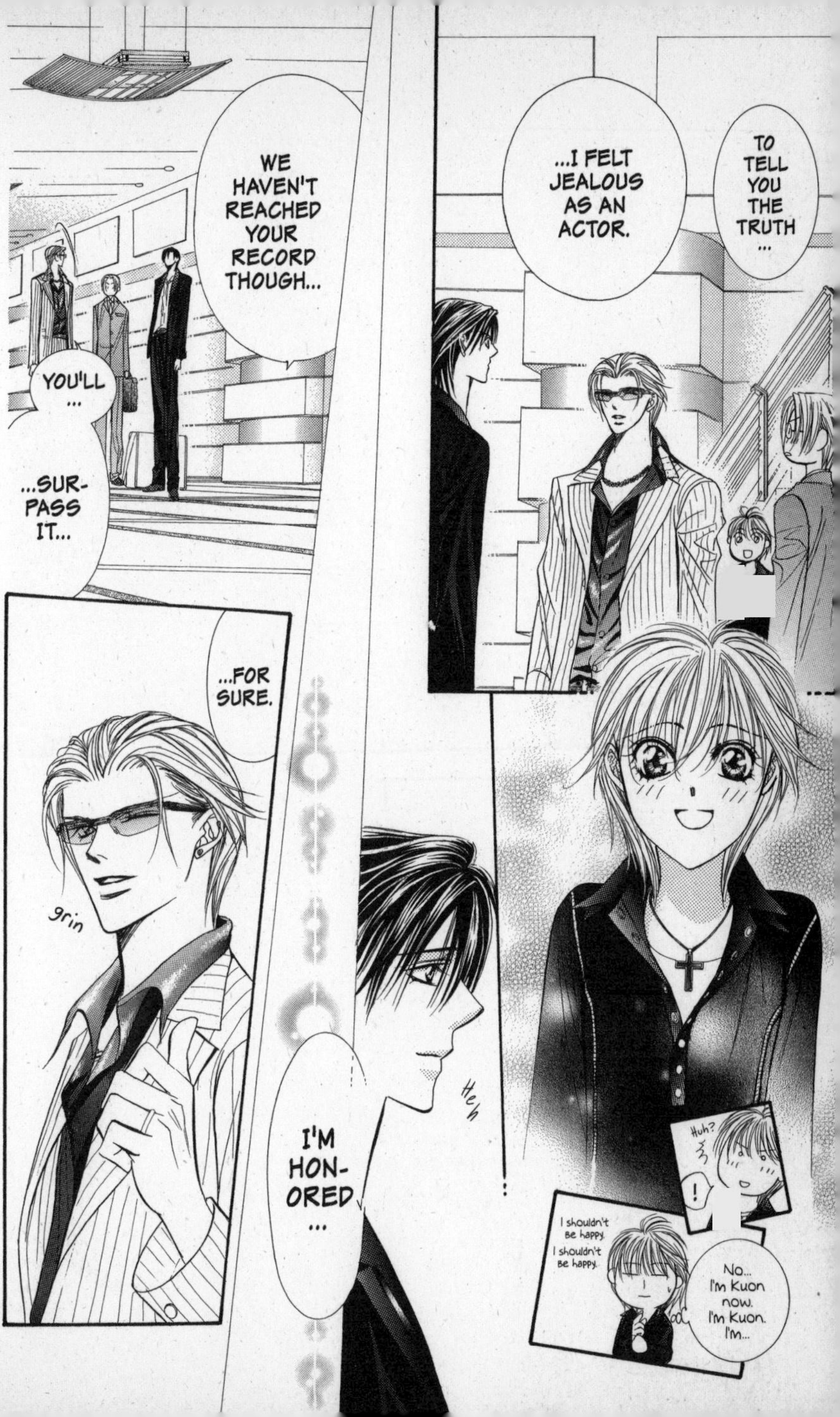
TO TELL YOU THE TRUTH...
...I FELT JEALOUS AS AN ACTOR.
WE HAVEN'T REACHED YOUR RECORD THOUGH...
YOU'LL...
...SUR-PASS IT...
...FOR SURE.
grin
Heh
I'M HON-ORED...
!
Huh?
!
No... I'm Kuon now. I'm Kuon. I'm...
I shouldn't be happy. I shouldn't be happy.

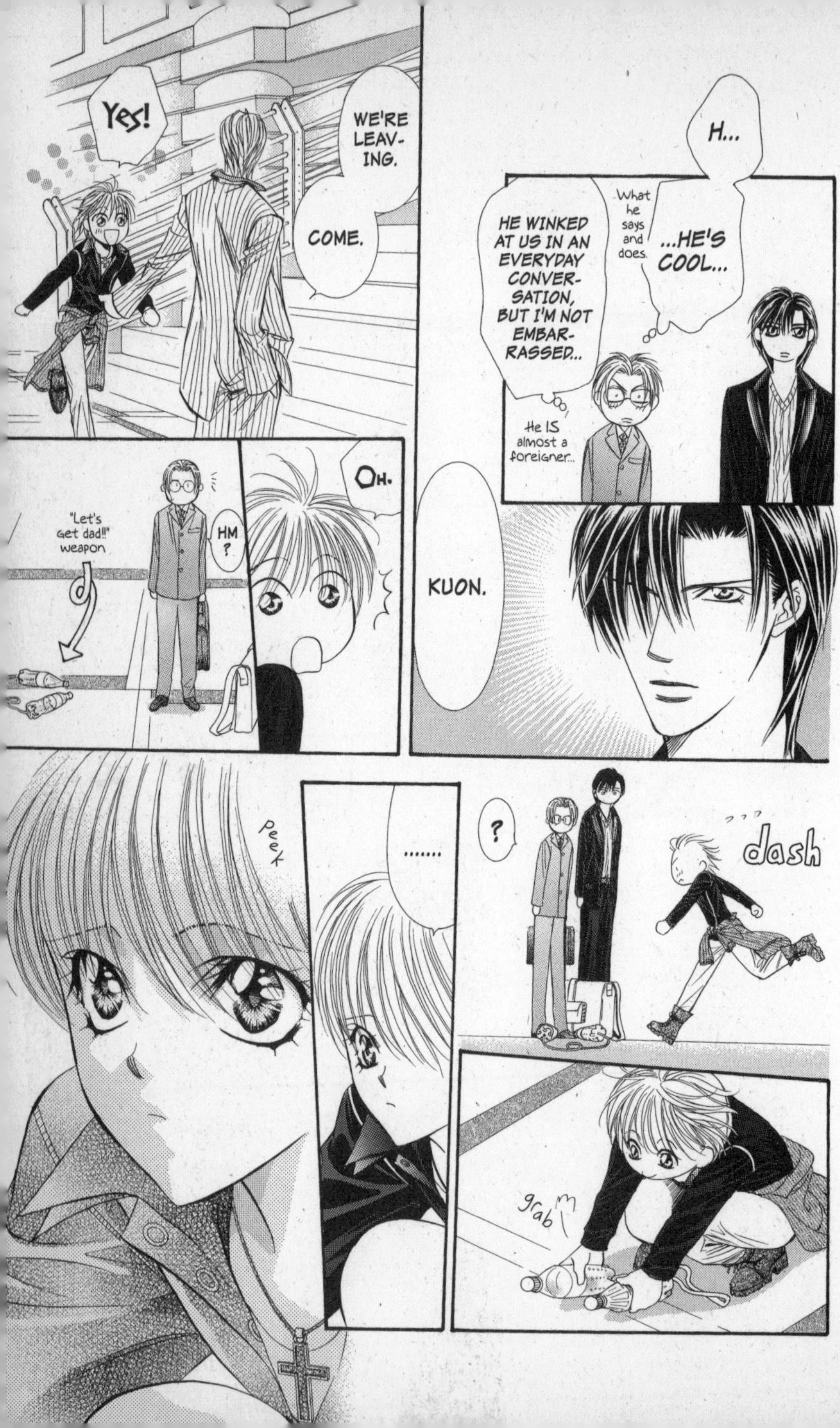

H...
What he says and does.
...HE'S COOL...
HE WINKED AT US IN AN EVERYDAY CONVERSATION, BUT I'M NOT EMBARRASSED...
He IS almost a foreigner...
KUON.
WE'RE LEAVING.
COME.
Yes!
OH.
HM?
"Let's Get dad!!" weapon
?
dash
grab
....
peek

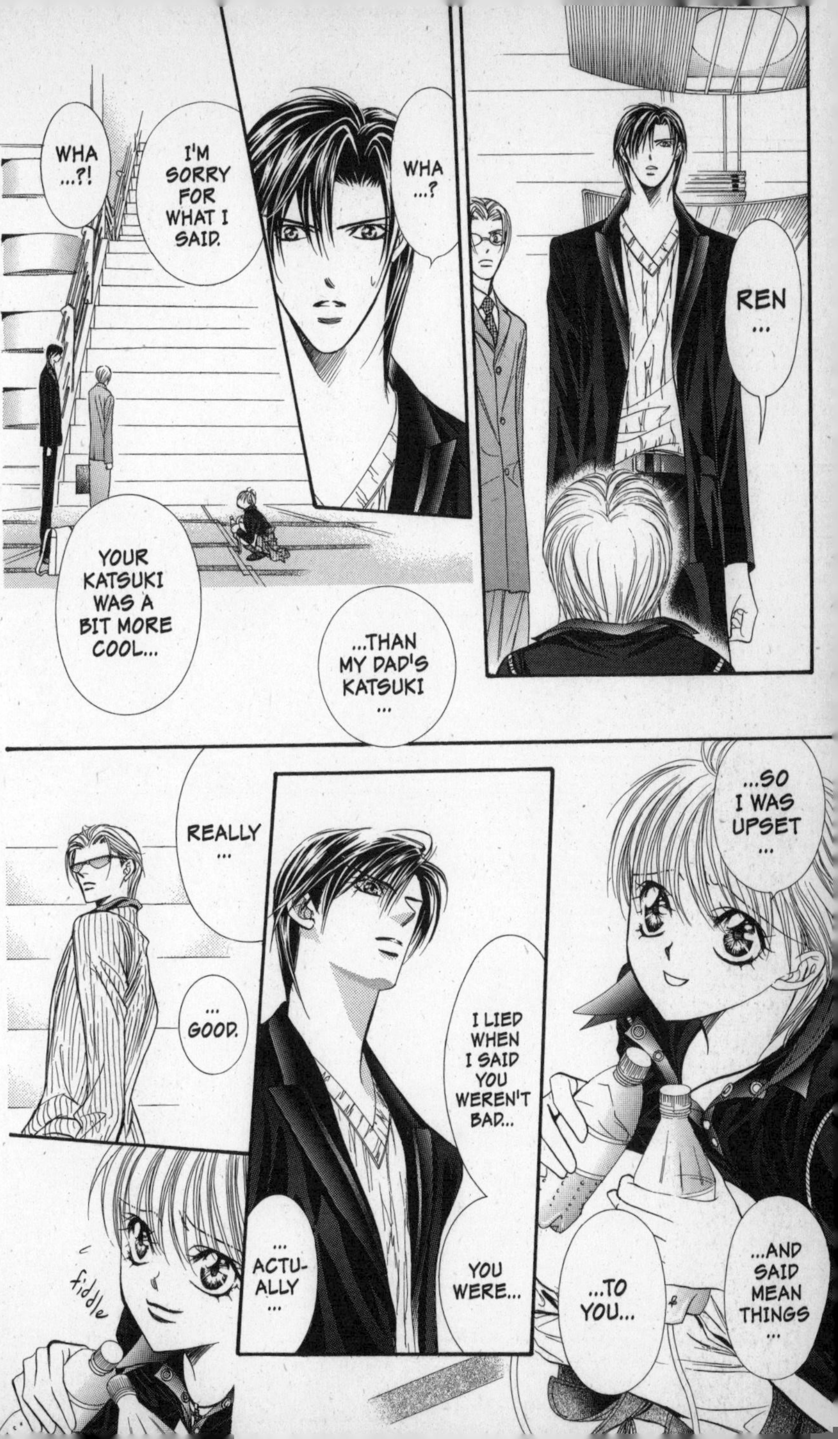
REN...
WHA...?
I'M SORRY FOR WHAT I SAID.
WHA...?!
YOUR KATSUKI WAS A BIT MORE COOL...
...THAN MY DAD'S KATSUKI...
...SO I WAS UPSET...
...AND SAID MEAN THINGS...
...TO YOU...
I LIED WHEN I SAID YOU WEREN'T BAD...
YOU WERE...
...ACTU-ALLY...
REALLY...
...GOOD.
fiddle

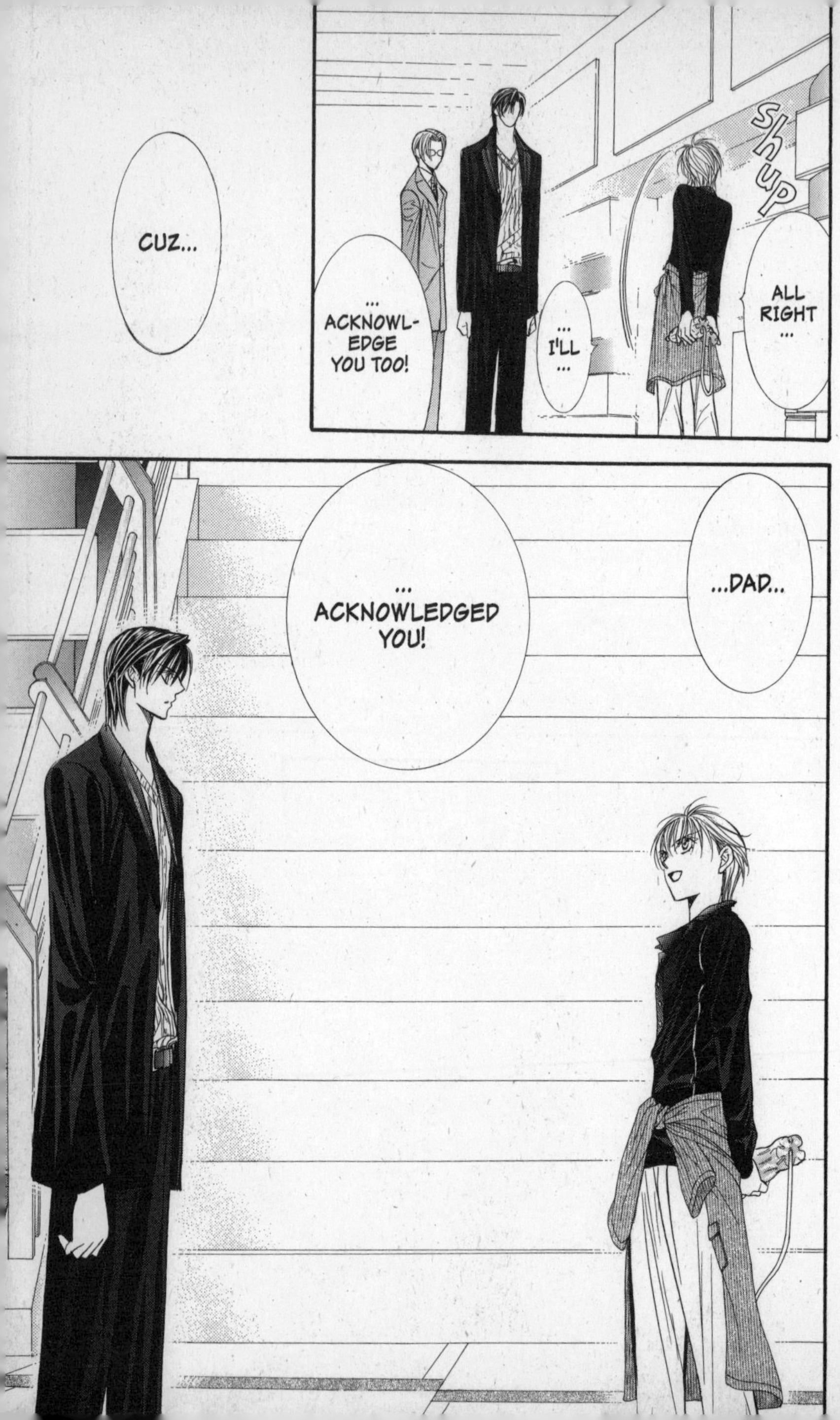
SHUP
ALL RIGHT...
...I'LL...
...ACKNOWL-EDGE YOU TOO!
CUZ...
...DAD...
...ACKNOWLEDGED YOU!

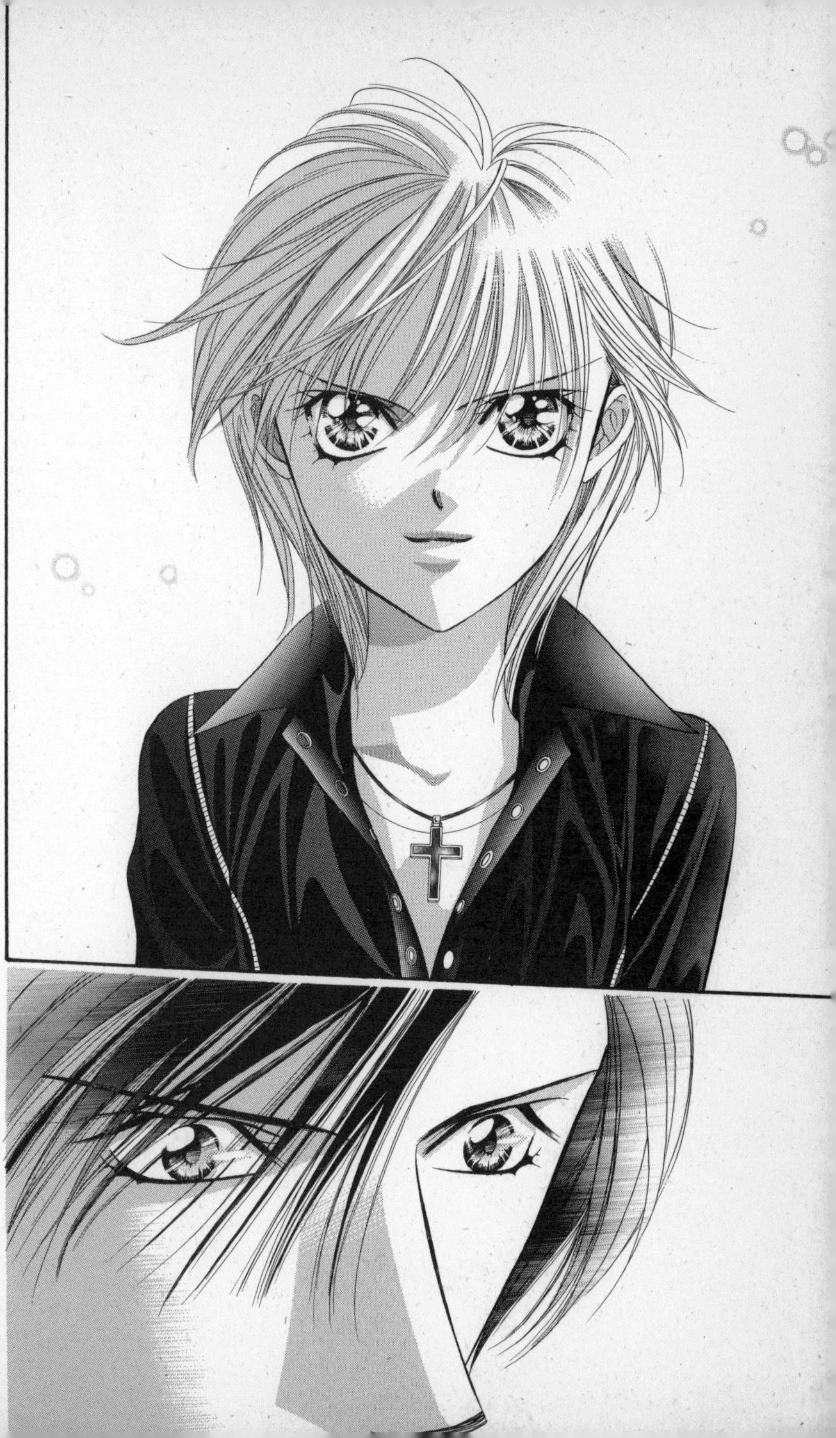

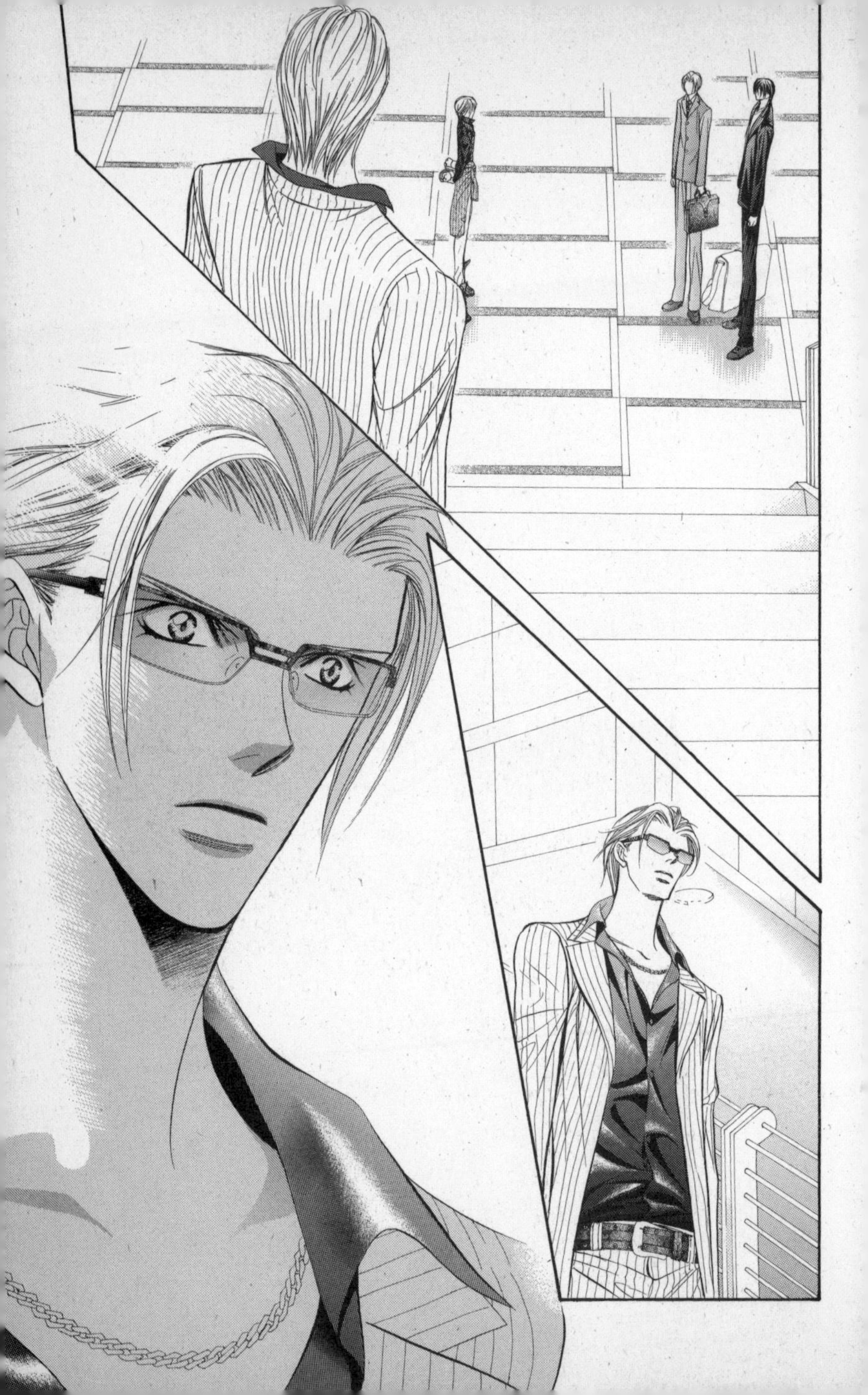

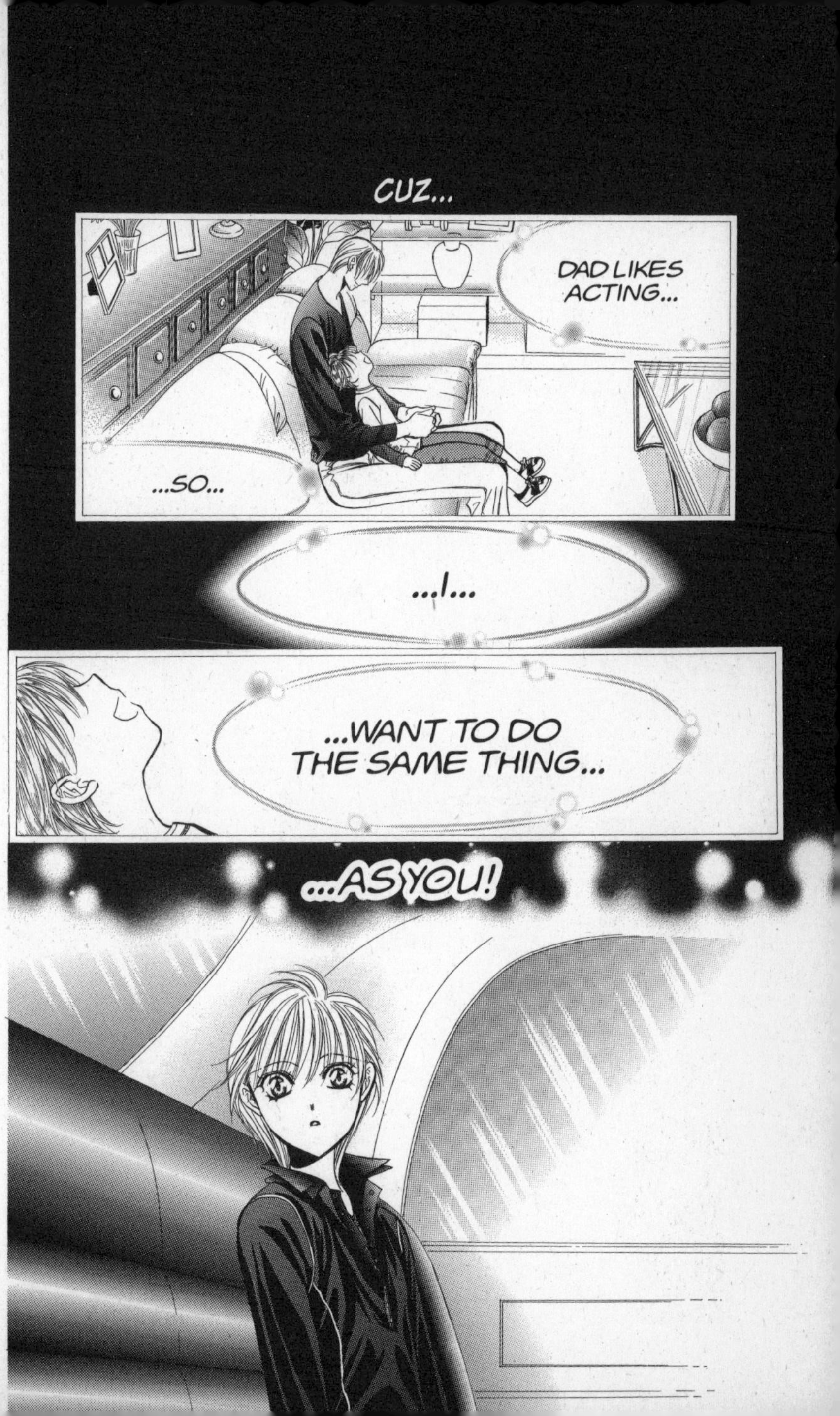
CUZ...
DAD LIKES ACTING...
...SO...
...I...
...WANT TO DO THE SAME THING...
...AS YOU!

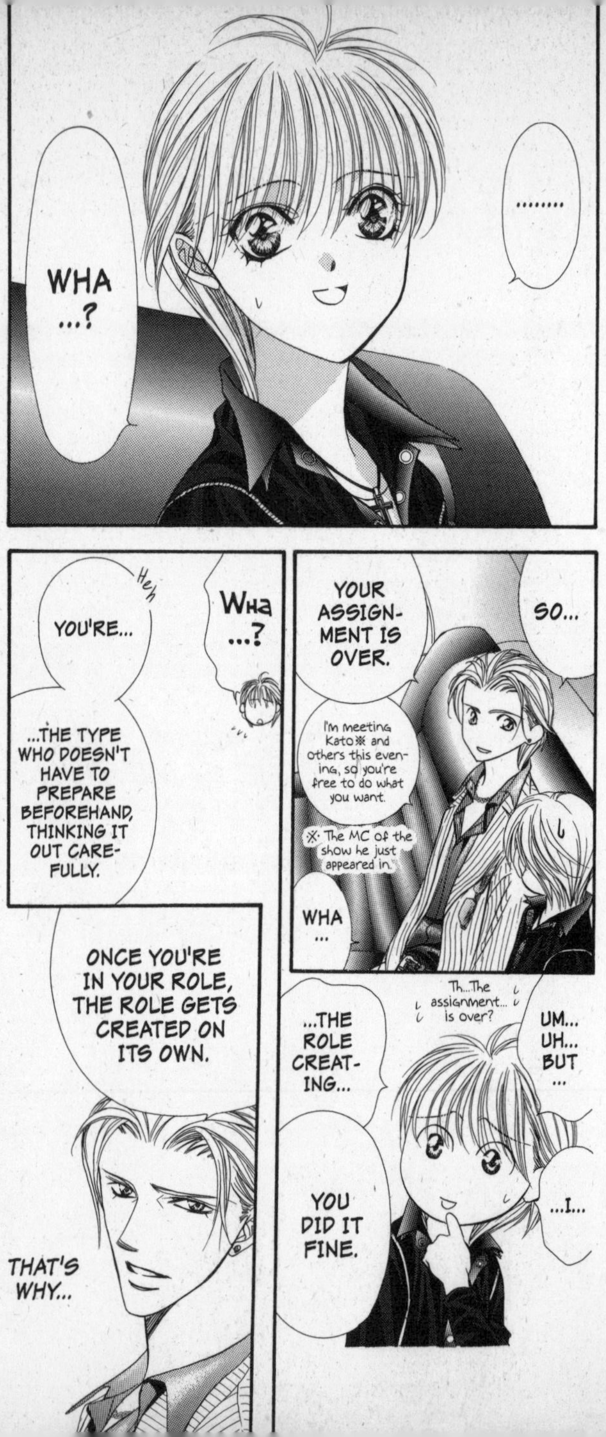
....
WHA ...?
SO...
YOUR ASSIGNMENT IS OVER.
I'm meeting Kato※ and others this evening, so you're free to do what you want.
※ The MC of the show he just appeared in.
WHA ...
WHA ...?
Heh
YOU'RE...
...THE TYPE WHO DOESN'T HAVE TO PREPARE BEFOREHAND, THINKING IT OUT CAREFULLY.
Th...The assignment... is over?
UM... UH... BUT ...
...I...
...THE ROLE CREATING...
YOU DID IT FINE.
ONCE YOU'RE IN YOUR ROLE, THE ROLE GETS CREATED ON ITS OWN.
THAT'S WHY...

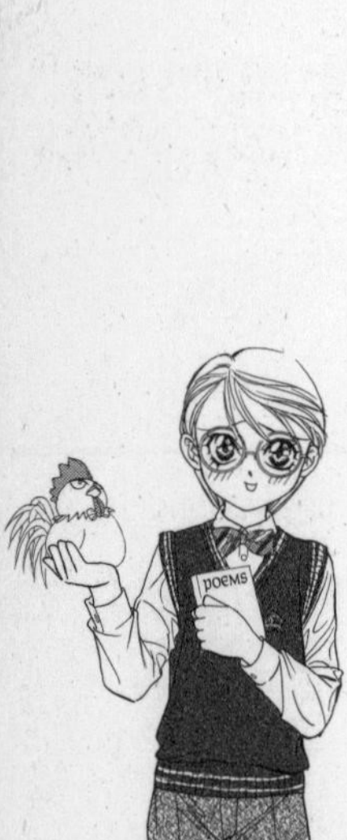
POEMS

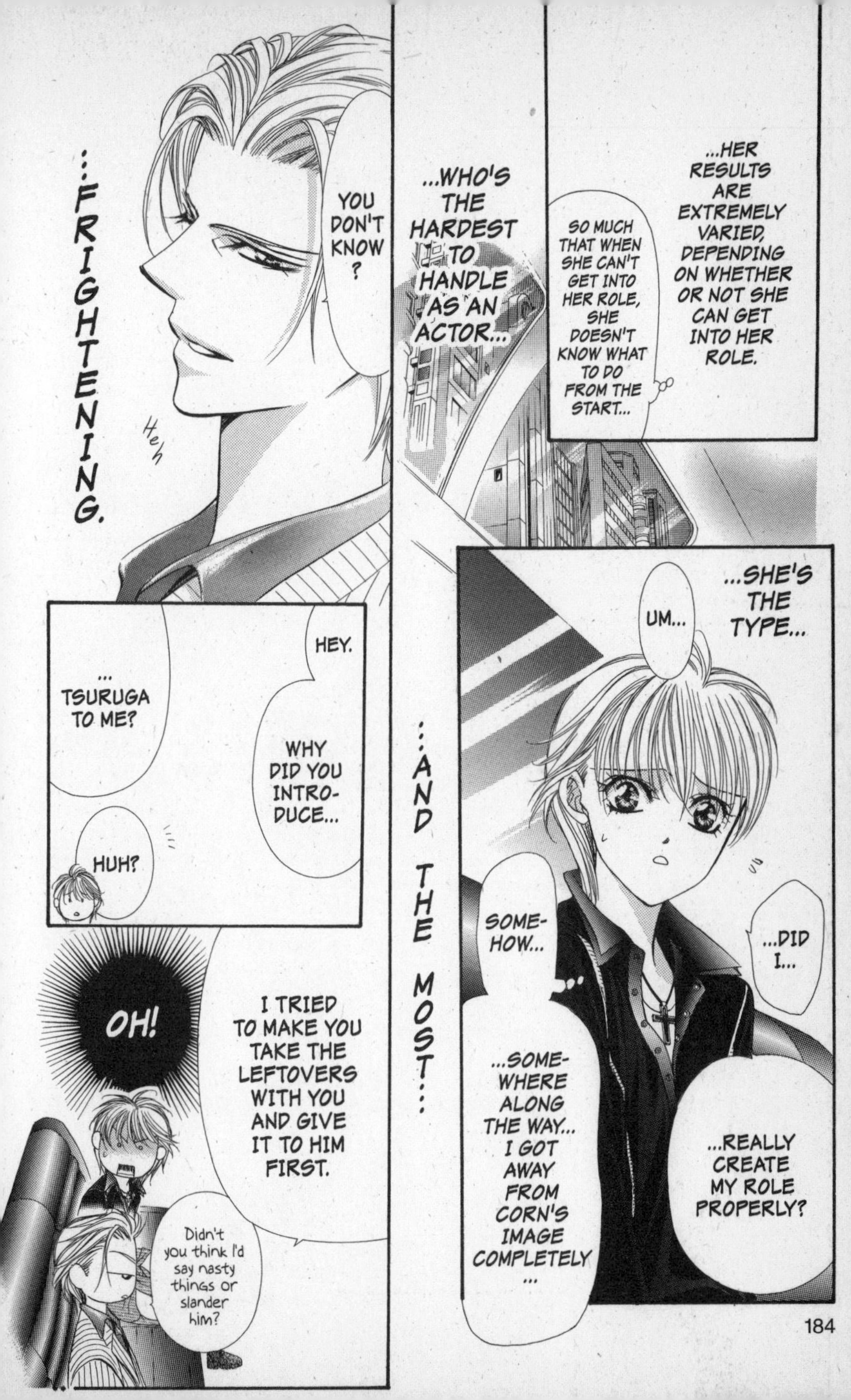
...HER RESULTS ARE EXTREMELY VARIED, DEPENDING ON WHETHER OR NOT SHE CAN GET INTO HER ROLE.
SO MUCH THAT WHEN SHE CAN'T GET INTO HER ROLE, SHE DOESN'T KNOW WHAT TO DO FROM THE START...
...WHO'S THE HARDEST TO HANDLE AS AN ACTOR...
...SHE'S THE TYPE...
UM...
...DID I...
...REALLY CREATE MY ROLE PROPERLY?
SOME-HOW...
...SOME-WHERE ALONG THE WAY... I GOT AWAY FROM CORN'S IMAGE COMPLETELY...
...AND THE MOST...
YOU DON'T KNOW?
...FRIGHTENING.
Heh
HEY.
WHY DID YOU INTRO-DUCE...
HUH?
... TSURUGA TO ME?
OH!
I TRIED TO MAKE YOU TAKE THE LEFTOVERS WITH YOU AND GIVE IT TO HIM FIRST.
Didn't you think I'd say nasty things or slander him?

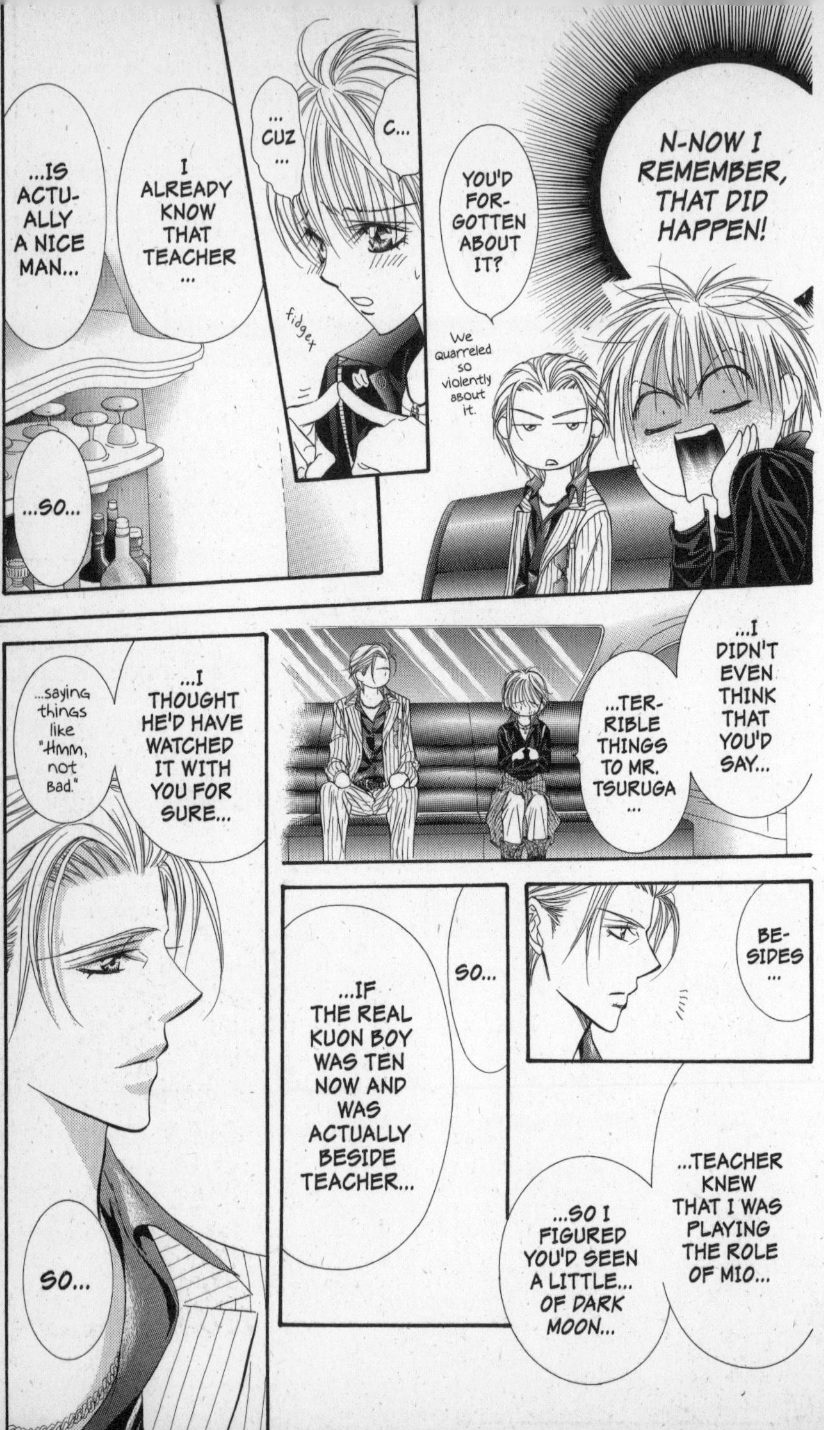
N-NOW I REMEMBER, THAT DID HAPPEN!
YOU'D FORGOTTEN ABOUT IT?
We quarreled so violently about it.
C...
...CUZ...
fidget
I ALREADY KNOW THAT TEACHER...
...IS ACTUALLY A NICE MAN...
...SO...
...I DIDN'T EVEN THINK THAT YOU'D SAY...
...TERRIBLE THINGS TO MR. TSURUGA...
BESIDES...
...TEACHER KNEW THAT I WAS PLAYING THE ROLE OF MIO...
...SO I FIGURED YOU'D SEEN A LITTLE... OF DARK MOON...
SO...
...IF THE REAL KUON BOY WAS TEN NOW AND WAS ACTUALLY BESIDE TEACHER...
...I THOUGHT HE'D HAVE WATCHED IT WITH YOU FOR SURE...
...saying things like "Hmm, not bad."
SO...

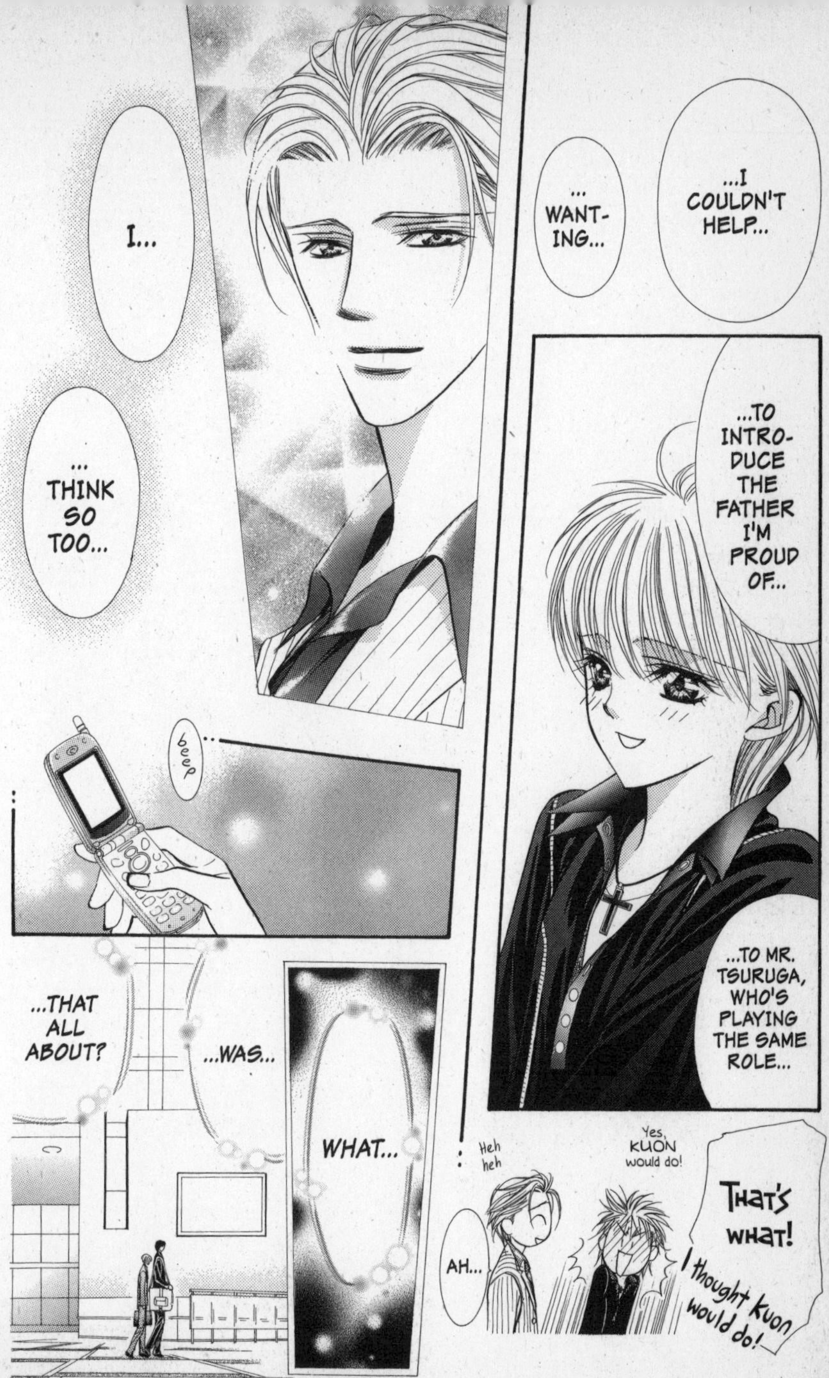
...I COULDN'T HELP...
...WANTING...
...TO INTRODUCE THE FATHER I'M PROUD OF...
...TO MR. TSURUGA, WHO'S PLAYING THE SAME ROLE...
I...
...THINK SO TOO...
beep
THAT's WHAT! I thought Kuon would do!
Yes, KUON would do!
Heh heh
AH...
WHAT...
...WAS...
...THAT ALL ABOUT?

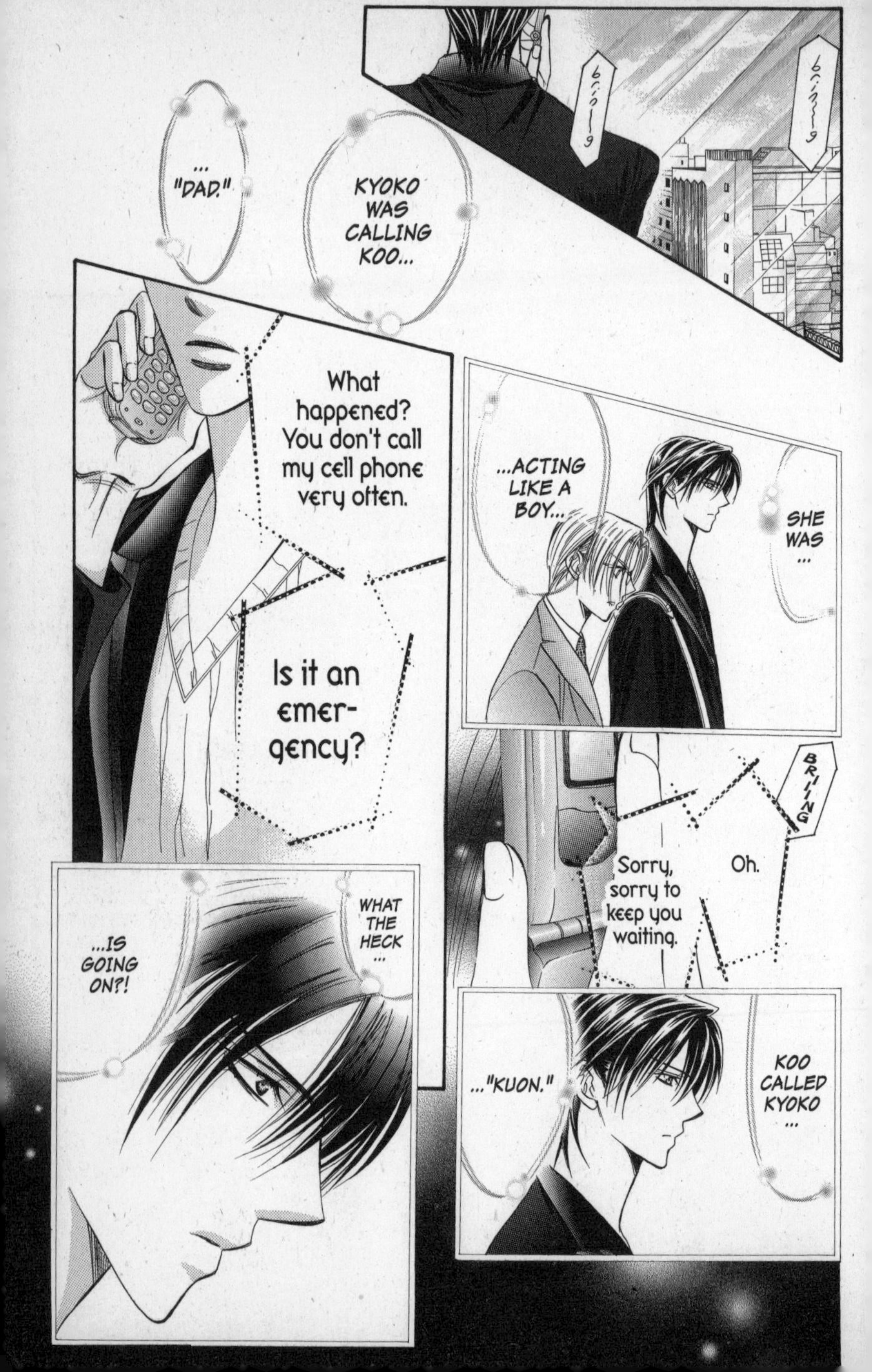

KYOKO WAS CALLING KOO...
... "DAD."
SHE WAS ...
...ACTING LIKE A BOY...
BRIING
Oh.
Sorry, sorry to keep you waiting.
KOO CALLED KYOKO ...
..."KUON."
What happened? You don't call my cell phone very often.
Is it an emergency?
WHAT THE HECK ...
...IS GOING ON?!

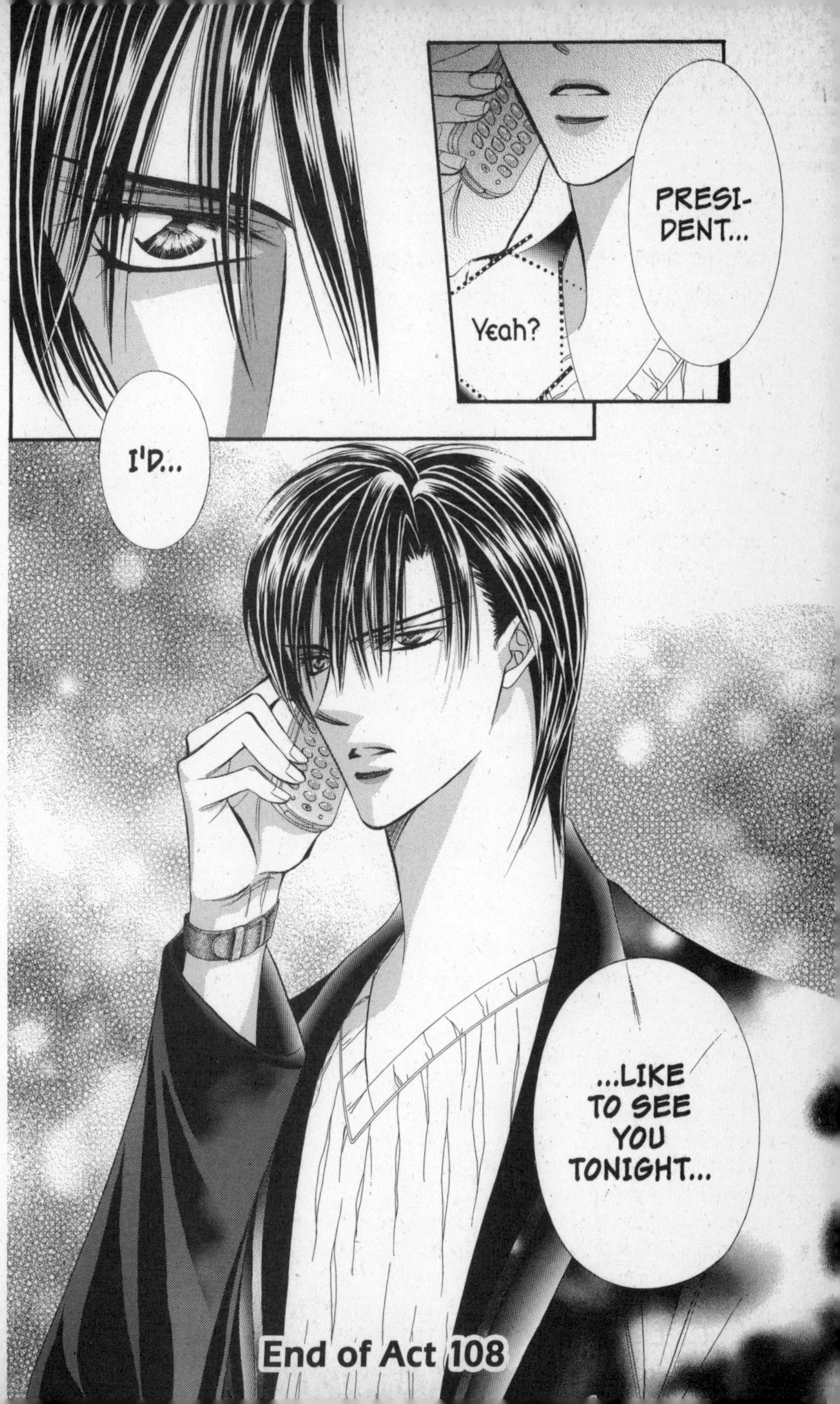
PRESI-
DENT...
Yeah?
I'D...
...LIKE TO SEE YOU TONIGHT...

End of Act 108

Skip·Beat! End Notes
Everyone knows how to be a fan, but sometimes cool things
from other cultures need a little help crossing the language barrier.

Page 20, panel 3: Slop
The original Japanese is *nekomanma* (literally "cat rice"), and usually refers
to miso soup on rice or fish flakes on rice. It is considered bad manners to
eat rice this way, and it is "commoner food," which is what probably offended
Koo. A second meaning is "food for the cat," and generally refers to putting
leftover fish on rice.

Page 45, panel 1: Furikake
Furikake is a seasoning mix you sprinkle on your rice. It comes in many
different flavors, but the base usually contains dried seaweed, bonito flakes
and salt.

Page 76, panel 2: Kuon (久遠)
The kanji can mean infinite time, distant past, distant future. The idea of
distance is key.

Page 82, panel 5: Kinpira
Ingredients braised or simmered in a broth of soy sauce and mirin (sweet
wine) or sugar. Root vegetables are the most common ingredients, such as
burdock root or carrots.

Page 82, panel 6: Nikujaga
Literally means "meat and potatoes," it is a Japanese version of beef stew
cooked in a sweetened soy sauce-based broth. Other ingredients can include
onions and carrots.

Page 115, panel 5: Suzume
Japanese for "swallow" (the bird).

Page 153, panel 2: Cha soba
Soba (buckwheat) noodles with green tea leaves or powder mixed into the
dough. They are often eaten cold, topped with shreds of nori seaweed, with
a bowl of lightly sweetened dipping sauce on the side. The sauce is often
accompanied by chopped green onions, grated daikon radish, and wasabi
paste that you mix in to taste.

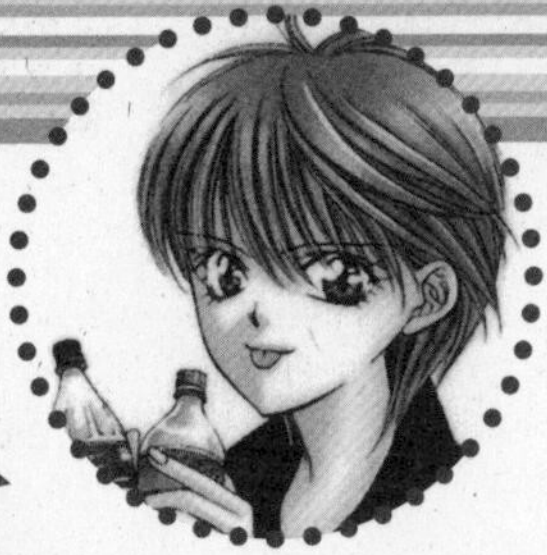

Yoshiki Nakamura is originally from Tokushima prefecture. She started drawing manga in elementary school, which eventually led to her 1993 debut of *Yume de Au yori Suteki* (Better than Seeing in a Dream) in *Hana to Yume* magazine. Her other works include the basketball series *Saint Love, MVP wa Yuzurenai* (Can't Give Up MVP), *Blue Wars* and *Tokyo Crazy Paradise*, a series about a female bodyguard in 2020 Tokyo.

SKIP·BEAT!
Vol. 18
Shojo Beat Edition

STORY AND ART BY YOSHIKI NAKAMURA

English Translation & Adaptation/Tomo Kimura
Touch-up Art & Lettering/Sabrina Heep
Cover Design/Izumi Evers
Design/Ronnie Casson
Editor/Pancha Diaz

Skip Beat! by Yoshiki Nakamura © Yoshiki Nakamura 2008.
All rights reserved. First published in Japan in 2008 by HAKUSENSHA, Inc., Tokyo.
English language translation rights arranged with HAKUSENSHA, Inc., Tokyo.

The stories, characters and incidents mentioned in this publication are entirely fictional.

No portion of this book may be reproduced or transmitted in any form or by any means without written
permission from the copyright holders.

Printed in Canada

Published by VIZ Media, LLC.
P.O. Box 77010
San Francisco, CA 94107

10 9 8 7 6 5 4 3 2
First printing, May 2009
Second printing, September 2011

www.viz.com

www.shojobeat.com

Tell us w... think about S... nga!

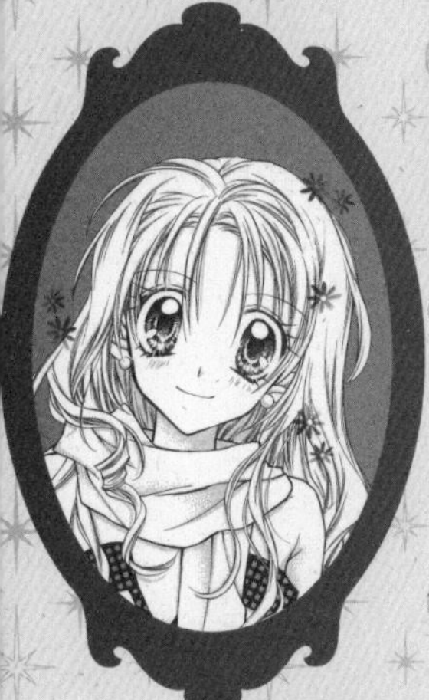

Our survey is now available online. Go to:

shojobeat.com/mangasurvey

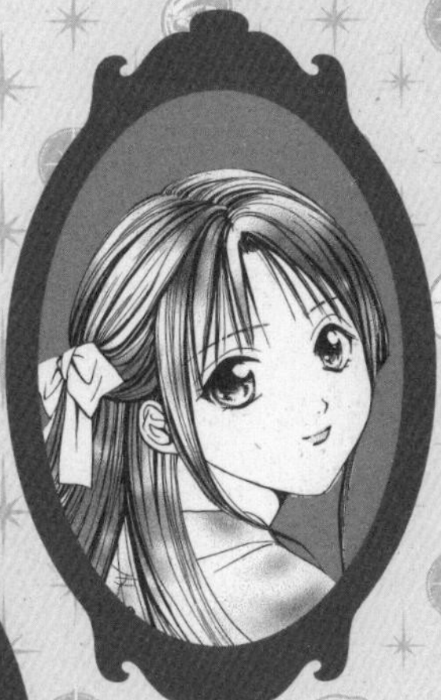

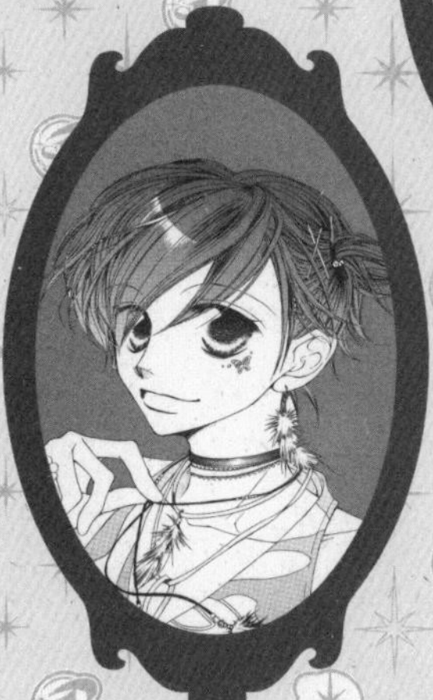

Help us make our product offerings better!

THE REAL DRAMA BEGINS IN...

Shojo Beat

viz media